UNDERSTANDIN

SARA RICH DORMAN

Understanding Zimbabwe

From Liberation to Authoritarianism

HURST & COMPANY, LONDON

First published in the United Kingdom in 2016 by
C. Hurst & Co. (Publishers) Ltd.,
41 Great Russell Street, London, WC1B 3PL
© Sara Rich Dorman, 2016
All rights reserved.
Printed in India

The right of Sara Rich Dorman to be identified as the author
of this publication is asserted by her in accordance with the
Copyright, Designs and Patents Act, 1988.

A Cataloguing-in-Publication data record for this book
is available from the British Library.

9781849045827 *hardback*
9781849045834 *paperback*

This book is printed using paper from registered sustainable
and managed sources.

www.hurstpublishers.com

CONTENTS

ACKNOWLEDGEMENTS

Many people have supported me through this project. Colleagues in Zimbabwe became friends, welcomed me back and shared their knowledge. Their tolerance, kindness and patience have been immense. Amongst many who are mentioned in the main text, David Chimhini, Barbara Chimhondo, Rachael C., Fischer Chiyanike, Mike Davies, Jonah Gokova, Sekai Holland, David Jamali, Niki Jazdowska, Bill Kinsey, Michael Laban, David Manenji, Simeon Mawanza, Regis Mtutu, Nicholas Mukaronda, Tawanda Mutasah, Ronald Mubaiwa, Deprose Muchena, Dumisani Ngwenya, Paul Themba Nyathi and Brian Raftopoulos all provided hospitality and friendship and helped me gain a better understanding.

I have been inspired and encouraged by colleagues, friends and students at Oxford, Edinburgh and further. Alex Beresford, Gareth James, Grasian Mkodzongi, Busani Mpofu, Enocent Msindo, Leila Sinclair-Bright, Miles Tendi and Takura Zhanghaza read portions of the text and provided crucial insights. My debts to them, and many others, are visible on every page. In particular, though, I'd like to thank Rita Abrahamson, Ailsa Henderson, Kate Meagher, Raufu Mustapha and Sam Spiegel for their encouragement when the going got tough. None of it would have been possible without Bill Dorman.

The book is dedicated to my parents, Nathan and Elizabeth Rich, and my parents-in-law, Marjorie and Philip Dorman, with thanks for their wholehearted support.

1

UNDERSTANDING ZIMBABWEAN POLITICS

Power is a cultural tool and the way people relate to it is crucial for the development of the imagination, the mind, the heart and the soul.[1]

Many accounts of 'African politics' omit Zimbabwe. Too different, too exceptional, too complicated—and that was before the post-2000 crisis. Zimbabwe has been described as a 'hard' state and as a failing state. It has held multi-party elections regularly since independence, and observers spoke of it 'democratizing' even as the government cracked down on dissent. It was seen as a model of racial reconciliation, only to be held up later as a hotbed of racial enmity. Its politics are often described as 'identity' politics, in which vertical cleavages define the dividing lines between social groups (ethnicity) more than horizontal ones (class, ideology).[2] But Zimbabwe also confounds facile accounts of ethnic politics, as we see how coalitions are shaped and formed, and the ways in which some individuals are able to move between groups. Simplistic accounts of political instrumentality prove inadequate. Understanding Zimbabwe's trajectory[3] requires drawing on a broader set of debates that incorporate the cultural and normative politics of citizenship, voice and nation-building, as well as the more obvious material drivers and power politics.

This book is therefore not just about Zimbabwe, but about how we study African politics. In 1980 when Robert Mugabe and his ZANU(PF)

1

party came to power after a bitter liberation war against the Rhodesian white settler regime, Zimbabwe's politics may have seemed exceptional. But in the years that followed, a process of politically driven nation- and state-building institutionalized ZANU(PF)'s control of the political sphere and monopoly on political representation in independent Zimbabwe. Transcending any narrow conception of spoils politics or clientelism, this project comprised a mix of discursive and material strategies, producing post-independence Zimbabwean political forms, norms and subjectivities.[4] It was not a totalitarian system, nor one in which the ruling party's imprimatur was stamped unilaterally on society, but a system formed through negotiation between competing, albeit unequal, interests, with moments of extreme brutality that brooked no resistance. Key to understanding this is thinking about how power was deployed, but also how we study the articulations of power in complex political settings. These elements help us to understand better not just Zimbabwe's politics, but also that of the rest of the continent, and perhaps beyond.

Analysing these processes enables us to understand how new nations emerged, state institutions took form, and society negotiated new identities and the reality of political power in the decades that followed independence. By examining the interactions of social groups—including churches, NGOs and political activists—from the liberation struggle through independence, we can begin to make sense of the complicated reality of contemporary Zimbabwe, not from an elite perspective, nor that of politics *par le bas*, but a politics of interaction and negotiation. We explore how these intermediary groups engage with the practice of politics, both contesting and contributing to the formation of the state and its people. Zimbabwe's politics are ultimately a battle over who speaks for the nation, and that battle is fought out in multiple spheres: control of political institutions, the media and civil society itself. It can seem easy to dismiss civil society as 'foreign-funded' or irrelevant to the lives of farmers and workers, but their ability to articulate alternative voices and challenge the regime's own myths makes them a crucial aspect of political life.

An empirically-rich account of the behaviour of social actors enables us to see how strategies of control and co-option were replicated and resisted across sectors, shaping expectations and behaviour. As in many other states, the politics of citizenship were central to debates and contestation, which means that we need to look beyond simplistic accounts of vote-buying or violence to understand the terms on which people were allowed to participate, and to identify themselves as Zimbabwean.

This book explores how Zimbabwe's politics were shaped by strategies, including discursive claims to foster national unity and delegitimize autonomous political action outside the ruling party, as well as the creation of an inclusive coalition providing a societal base for regime hegemony. Building this coalition entailed the 'demobilization' of ZANU(PF)'s original nationalist constituency which had backed it during the liberation war, and the 'inclusion' of new groups such as donors, white farmers and business interests. It also shows how legal practices and institution-building defused and constrained opportunities for contestation, even while the regime used the security forces to suppress those who challenged its political monopoly or who otherwise resisted incorporation. Paradoxically, the regime's seemingly fetishistic adherence to legal mechanisms also provided space for contestation, which in later years would prove remarkably effective.

None of this means that the nation being shaped was imaginary, artificial or illegitimate. Rather, it means that the nation, its shape and identity were contested, as were claims to representation and legitimacy within the state apparatus. In seeking regime durability and political gains, ideas and norms about citizenship took centre-stage in determining who could exercise power and in what ways. Even as the liberation war generation reluctantly exits the political stage, its influence continues to shape the interaction between citizens and state.

Although some accounts of Zimbabwean politics emphasize the personalized and coercive character of the political order since independence,[5] this book argues that Zimbabwe's enduring authoritarian rule should not be understood primarily in terms of greed and corruption, aptly termed the 'politics of the belly' by Bayart,[6] nor as the personalized and expedient use of the security apparatus.[7] The chapters that follow reveal a complex picture of how individuals and groups became bound up in the project of state- and nation-building, despite contesting or even rejecting aspects of it. If we are to make sense out of the surprising ability of the Mugabe regime to maintain itself in power even after the crisis of the 2000s, we need to understand the state, nation and political identities which it forged, and the nature of its control over those political institutions.

Regime power and stability can be thought of as drawing upon three sources or pillars: material benefits or interests; coercive force; and rhetoric or discourse.[8] None of these is sufficient on its own to maintain a hold on power over decades, but each is emphasized in different ways and at different times, producing particular norms and expectations of behaviour. While the unravelling of the nation-building project in the late 1990s correlates with increasingly patrimonial and erratic behaviour on the part of Mugabe and the ZANU(PF) hierarchy, it was not the inevitable expression of some latent African tendency to sultanism. Rather, the regime began to manifest internal contradictions, losing control of the strategically placed war veterans whose demands for compensation led to the financial exhaustion of the politics of inclusion. In turn, this contributed to the breakdown of the post-independence coalition, as manifest in the exclusion of previously incorporated groups, such as the white farmers who were subsequently despoiled. The collapse of this coalition—combined with the growing articulation of dissident voices within ZANU(PF) and Zimbabwean civil society more generally—set the stage for opposition to mobilize and mount a critique of ZANU(PF)'s exclusivist notion of nation-building. By virtue of their control over the security apparatus and willingness to deploy a politics of predation and terror, Mugabe and ZANU(PF) managed to see off their opponents, the Movement for Democratic Change (MDC). However, coercion alone cannot provide a sustainable replacement for the nation-building project which was previously the basis of their rule. And so we see also the rebuilding and persistence of institutions and practices which the MDC was never fully able to challenge, enabling ZANU to re-establish itself as the power in the land thirty years after independence.

The political conflicts that emerged in 2000 are very much the result of the flawed nation-building project initiated in 1980, but shaped by the years before that too. The nationalist emphasis on 'unity', which creates a de facto single party, is characterized by attempts to paper over conflicts and societal divides. But the regime's narrow and self-serving nation-building has failed to bring the desired benefits of liberation. The negotiated transition itself constrained and shaped the political opportunity structures of the post-liberation regime, both legally and normatively, driving pressures for demobilization and depoliticization.

These issues of nation-, state- and party-building are not exclusive to Zimbabwe, and much of the argument that follows has relevance to the study of other African states; but until 2000 Zimbabwe was often portrayed as a peaceful and stable state, in which nation-building had been relatively unproblematic. The period after 2000 is therefore sometimes interpreted as unexpectedly violent, or the 1980s and 1990s are seen as an improbable interregnum, after which Zimbabwe reverted to more 'typical' African politics. Instead, I argue that we must explore this apparent paradox. Taking my cue from Chris Allen's iconic article 'Understanding African Politics', I seek an account which allows us to understand processes of change, rather than simply categorize or label.[9] The 'peaceful' years and the 'violent' periods have continuities as well as ruptures, and both are significant parts of this story. The centrifugal forces that contributed to 'spoils' politics in the 2000s are intimately linked to the early patterns of organizing and 'doing' politics, as well as the institutions of the post-colonial 'gatekeeper' state, which attempted to centralize and control society.[10]

Through an examination of the changing politics of social groups which engage with the state on multiple levels, we can interrogate the changes in the exercise of power, and the similarities in strategies for containing autonomous challenges across the decades. Many strategies and discourses that drew attention in the international media after 2000 had earlier manifestations that were less controversial—the willingness of both Zimbabweans and outside observers to turn a blind eye to human rights violations early on signals the importance of changing expectations and norms. The evidence presented suggests that there are continuities of strategy that stretch from the early post-independence period (or even earlier) through to the 'crisis' period after 2000.[11] But, more importantly, we see that the strategies of societal control and rhetorical defence adopted in and after 2000 had profound resonances with earlier discourses and tropes. These resonances meant that claims and policies, like urban clearances or anti-Western rhetoric which seemed purely instrumental to outside viewers, often made sense or contained meaning for those socialized into Zimbabwe's cultural politics, even as they were also contested by counter-hegemonic forces. An integrated analysis of both periods reveals how Zimbabwe's failed nation-building in the 1980s and 1990s led to the delayed crisis of 2000, but also how it shaped the way that crisis played out and was understood. These two periods are intimately related and mutually constituted in each other. For that reason, we shall examine how the regime draws on the provision of material interests; the use of coercive force; and the power of discourse to maintain itself in power in the post-independence years. This next section briefly sets out why previous attempts to describe Zimbabwean politics have proved inadequate to the task, before elaborating a framework that builds on interpretative approaches and methodologies, and outlining the structure of the following chapters.

Approaches to Zimbabwean politics: the need to explain change

Attempts to explain and understand Zimbabwe's politics have mirrored trends in the discipline in both their strengths and their weaknesses. The dominant approaches reflect the discipline's mainstream—political economy, institutionalism and democratization—and respond to contemporaneous concerns and debates. I suggest that they have proved unsatisfactory in explaining the changes and continuities in the relationship between state and society in Zimbabwe, because they were trying to answer particular questions and focused on discrete aspects of state power, rather than investigating interconnections between material, coercive and discursive aspects of power as developed by the regime. Nor do they examine similar patterns of governance which extend across rural and urban governance, state engagement with different societal groups, and the shaping and politicizing of state institutions.

Coming to statehood in 1980, it is unsurprising that Zimbabwe's politics were studied through a typically Cold War-driven matrix: with institutionalists on one side and a diverse group of Marxists on the other. The dominant political economy approach within Zimbabwe and left-leaning academe focused on policy-making and emphasized the role of ideological and class-based factors in driving policy decisions.[12] This approach also emphasized the international factors—the negotiated settlement of Lancaster House, international capital and geo-political considerations—

that constrained decision-making in independent Zimbabwe, rather than the internal legacies of either the settler state or the liberation war.[13] This approach was particularly influential in the 1980s, when Zimbabwe's precarious position in the front lines against South Africa and the Cold War intensified the ideological rhetoric of the state, and academic fellow-travellers often failed to look beyond the rhetoric and consider the implementation of policies.

In the 1990s, political economy approaches became more sensitive to the distinction between ideological discourse and actual policy-making, and began to challenge the internal influences as much as the external. In a massive tome, Bond argues that Zimbabwe's economic policy since 1980 has been predominantly capitalist, covered up with socialist rhetoric.[14] Indeed, much of the ideological 'gloss' of ZANU slipped away with the end of the Cold War—with the party 'debating socialism', introducing economic liberalization and encouraging the development of indigenous capitalists.[15] The conspicuous accumulation of many ministers and party officials and increasing accusations of corruption within the state further damaged any pretensions to 'socialist' development. Although many continued to see the state as captured by international financial institutions, Hevina Dashwood's perceptive account argues that economic policy changes reflected the embourgeoisement, and concomitant ideological shift, of the ruling class in Zimbabwe.[16] These accounts are important sources of explanation of the increasingly predatory nature of the regime, and the emerging economic crisis of the 1990s.

Disdaining these preoccupations with ideology, but still concerned with decision-making and policy-making in the 1980s, American-trained political scientists tended instead to focus on studying the institutions of the new state. Jonathan Moyo assessed the state's accomplishments in education, health, agriculture, land reform and the economy, and its success in bringing 'stability...during the first decade of transition'.[17] Herbst, like Moyo, focused primarily on the state's 'distributive' role in education, health, agriculture and the economy.[18] Moyo and Herbst describe a state that attempts to meet the needs of constituents: a state driven more by societal pressures than by asserting control over various constituencies. Their emphasis on empirical analysis, in contrast to the sometimes more programmatic ideologists, is welcome. However, this 'institutionalist' approach presumes a neutral administrative state, assessed solely on the basis of its material accomplishments, and ignores the role of the party or fractions within the party in assuming and retaining power, much less any account of the regime's legitimating framework. They ignore the regime's use of state power to shore up its support, and therefore these theories prove particularly weak in explaining the emergent tensions of the 1990s. Given Moyo's role as a key manipulator of cultural politics after 2000, his blindness to it in these early studies is baffling.

With the end of the Cold War, Zimbabwean politics, as elsewhere on the continent, came to be talked about in terms of 'civil society' and 'democratization'. Generally optimistic, authors from a range of ideological perspectives emphasized the role of organizations like NGOs and churches in challenging the state and pressing for political and economic reform.[19] While they were correct to identify civic actors as taking on new and important roles, the theorization of these groups too often presumed a liberal separation of society and state in which groups aspired to hold the state to account and press for change.[20] As the subsequent chapters will show, this interpretation was driven as much by a desire to see change, and an ahistorical romanticization of civic actors, as by conditions on the ground. This led to unrealistic prognostications of the likelihood of transition to a more democratic form of rule. Instead, Zimbabwean NGOs and other groups were constitutive players in the political hegemony of party and state, where legitimacy was derived from the liberation war and contributions to post-independence development.[21] This positionality made them unwilling to challenge the state in some instances, and shaped the way they did it in others, as is explored in the subsequent chapters.

But equally problematic has been the tendency since 2000 of commentators emphasizing the politics of disorder and patrimonialism, and the state's use of violence. Although this reading originated with a small group of authors, with little grounding in the country, it has proven influential,[22] alongside a fascination with the personality of Mugabe.[23] These more pessimistic accounts tend to read the current situation back into the past, and identify the coercive nature of the regime as constitutive, failing to provide an interpretative account that accords with the empirical record, or people's lived experience.

Studying continuities as well as change requires us to be anchored firmly in empirical observation and historically grounded analysis, with an eye for nuance and ambiguity. Michael Bratton's significant *Power Politics in Zimbabwe*[24] situates the 2008–12 power-sharing government against not only the wider African experience of power-sharing, but also the political settlements literature. This enables him to examine the colonial and post-colonial political settlements as precursors for the flawed agreement of 2008. His state-focused study eschews 'big man' politics to pay particularly close attention to the civil-military coalition and how it deployed power in Zimbabwe. By contrast, my key entry point in this study is the organized social groups, such as NGOs, trade unions and churches, and their interactions with political power over many decades. This approach has much in common with other research that was being undertaken in the late 1990s and early 2000s, such as Erin McCandless's remarkable study of Zimbabwe's war veterans and the National Constitutional Assembly, and Adrienne LeBas's insightful comparative study of the emergence of opposition parties as an effective political force.[25] But it seeks to situate that period of crisis in a broader time frame, through taking seriously not just the discursive but also the institutional impact of the nationalist struggle and the liberation war in shaping politics in Zimbabwe. This demands that we balance the study of material networks by also paying attention to the ideological, discursive and cultural manifestations of politics in the post-colonial state.[26]

The importance of the liberation war on state formation has been examined by anthropologists,[27] historians[28] and literary critics,[29] but has rarely been systematically incorporated into political analysis, although an exciting new generation of scholars is increasingly taking ZANU's 'intellectual project' as their main focus.[30] Perhaps even less well understood is the impact of nationalist organizational imperatives, distinct from the tensions of war. If we move beyond paying lip-service to history, we can integrate the power of people's experiences into our analysis of political science in Africa. Norma Kriger's important study of the politics of war veterans accomplishes this.[31] She interrogates the apparent contradiction between the legitimation claimed by politicians on the basis of their status as liberation war veterans, and the veterans' claims that they were marginalized and under-rewarded for their wartime sacrifices. Kriger's answer to this puzzle emphasizes the importance of rhetorical and symbolic politics in Zimbabwe. But in doing so, she does not ignore the importance of material politics and coercion in framing power and contestation in post-1980 Zimbabwe, which have been central to much of her other work.

Other fields of research in Zimbabwe also provide remarkable insights into Zimbabwe's trajectory and how to study it. A gender lens immediately brings issues of power to the fore, as well as highlighting discrepancies between discourse and practice.[32] These constructivist accounts enable us to identify clear winners and losers in the post-independence dispensation and how certain groups are relegated from the front lines of power politics. But no topic has stimulated more writing about Zimbabwe than land. Bringing together diverse disciplinary approaches including the historical, anthropological and economic, the so-called 'land question' provides unparalleled insights into the complex factors that shape power and decision-making, but also into the ways in which academics have studied it. Literature on land has been crucial for identifying the remarkable tenacity of colonial technical practices, often glossed as technocracy, which shaped post-independent land reform until, and perhaps past, 2000.[33] It also highlighted the government's concern with 'productive' use of land and focus on export crops over access to land as poverty alleviation or restitution of ancestral lands. These reveal the distance between elite policy-making and bottom-up demands, but also how embedded certain norms and expectations became in the post-colonial state. Grounded analysis by scholars such as Jocelyn Alexander and JoAnn McGregor show how histories of contestation and struggles over local authority shaped these dynamics. The richness of this literature sets a particularly high standard for studies of more generalized Zimbabwean politics.

Influenced by these projects, as well as Christine Sylvester's election studies[34] and Brian Raftopoulos's insightful analysis of nationalism,[35] which link together the discursive and ideational projects with the empirical practice of politics, this book seeks to build on these approaches to examine the relationship between state and society in Zimbabwe. It argues that politics in Zimbabwe has been about contestation over control of the nation and the state, and hence about claims to legitimate exercise of political power in a post-colonial state. In this way, it overlaps with anthropological interest in the state, citizenship and politicized ethnicity.[36] But in order to interrogate these ideas, it focuses on three politically mundane questions: firstly, how the post-1980 government used the mechanisms of state institutions to build its hegemony over the society; secondly, how societal groups respond to their political environment; and thirdly, how the regime resists challenges to its hegemony through laying claim to the nation, thus setting the stage for the violent confrontations since 2000, and through its attempts to rebuild hegemony after 2008.

The plan of the book

Our study of Zimbabwean politics begins in Chapter 2 with an examination of nationalist politics, and the legacy of the liberation war on guerrillas, civilians and their relationships. This period is shown to be characterized by ambiguity and contestation between competing political groups and their civilian supporters. Despite these years of mobilization and violence, after 1980 Zimbabwe is characterized by societal quiescence and demobilization: the politics of inclusion. Chapter 3 therefore explores how the construction of consent integrated social groups into the ruling nationalist coalition between 1980 and 1987. This potentially disparate coalition of workers, business, churches and peasants, among others, was based on alliances dependent to differing extents on coinciding interests, ideological commitment and the threat—and actuality—of the use of force. The rhetoric of inclusion closes out alternative social and political space, rendering projects outside the ruling party's sphere nearly unthinkable and profoundly unimplementable. But such inclusionary politics depend upon the regime making material and social resources available to alliance members. As Chapter 4 explores, when these resources are reduced, either because of competing ideologies or fiscal exhaustion, the coalition's stability is threatened and coercion is used against a broader set of social groups, as between 1987 and 1997.

Exclusionary politics reflect a diminution in the ideological or cultural elements of power, as well as the material. This leaves coercive force on its own, in a much weaker position than when justified by rhetoric or resource distribution. Chapter 5 shows how the mobilization and privileging of certain members of the coalition weakens the regime's hold over others. It also opens spaces for alternative accounts of nationalism or other ideologies to flourish. This resulted in a dramatic polarization of society between 1997 and 2000, as social groups formed networks and an electorally successful political party. In Chapter 6, we see that after 2000 exclusion was no longer unthinkable because the ever-increasing ranks of the excluded developed their own justificatory rhetoric and resources, but continued to be challenged by the regime's hold on state institutions and its appeal for some social groups. Competition for control of the state is based on competing ideologies and interests, which manifest themselves in electoral and physical conflict after the 2000 election. Chapter 7 examines how the regime re-established itself after the economic and political crises of the 2000s, remobilized key supporters, and redefined the terms of political contestation and the institutional basis for continued rule. Chapter 8 then returns to the over-arching themes of nationalism, demobilization and post-liberation politics in the independent state, situating the period of crisis in a broader time frame, through taking seriously the discursive and institutional legacies of the nationalist struggle and the liberation war in shaping politics in Zimbabwe.

Scope and limitations

This book presents a picture of contemporary Zimbabwean politics that is grounded in historical and anthropological material, as well as political science. It attempts to balance and integrate the study of the discourses and practices of the Zimbabwean state through an examination of the social groups which the state attempts to dominate and control. It focuses primarily on domestic rather than international politics to explain the Mugabe regime's longevity, although the two interact in complex and important ways. Rather than focus on one sector alone, such as trade unions or NGOs, it draws parallels across sectors, identifying similarity and accounting for difference. Within chapters then, the discussion is not chronological but thematic, analysing and comparing the different discourses which have dominated Zimbabwean politics since 1980, with the policies elaborated and implemented, and explanations of how they are experienced on the ground. The discussion focuses particularly on how this construction of hegemony by the ZANU(PF) regime has affected counter-hegemonic struggles.

In doing so, it engages with 'society' in an unapologetically broadbrush manner, eschewing detailed local or rural studies (with all their specificities and complexities) for a more comprehensive account of particular 'interest groups', particularly churches, NGOs, unions and students, and how they negotiate these discourses. Especially in the early years of independence, neither the state nor the regime was seen as something distant or external, because these elites move within and are absorbed into much the same intellectual, cultural and social milieu as the politicians and civil servants with whom they interact. This is why dyadic understandings of state-society relations which posit an inevitable antagonism between them fail to explain transitional politics successfully.[37] Focusing just on the social groups, without analysing the ways in which their environment is shaped by the state, would only tell half the story.

Elections provide a further example of formal political interaction. They prove to be a key forum in which societal groups, mobilized as election observers, challenge the neutrality of the state and question the actions of regime elites. Elections are also significant, not so much for their results, but because they reveal the ways in which the regime uses its legislative and bureaucratic control to maintain itself in power. They are a key aspect of state-society interaction because they enable us to study in more depth the ways in which societal contestation of the regime's power evolves.

But this focus on formal politics means that the study does not capture the experiences of the grass roots, the marginalized or the subalterns in the depth they deserve. Instead, the middle strata, which mediate between the subaltern and the power structure, are the main focus and formal sources—newspapers, public meetings and interviews—are the main sources used, drawn from my research and work trips to Zimbabwe between 1991 and 2012. Even when I have been present at events, I have tended to cite newspaper accounts, and where possible to triangulate sources against each other, in order to avoid inconsistencies. I hope that the extensive footnotes will also serve to guide readers to the rich primary and secondary sources on Zimbabwe.

Neither do I consider the politics of land in isolation. Land is analysed as a key element in the state's development agenda, and as a particularly significant zone for interest group politics. I have tried to give added weight to those areas which have not received much public examination, or where existing narratives are confusing or conflicting, while referring readers to easily accessible secondary material where it is available. Excellent published studies exist of the politics of labour and land, as well as much unpublished material on students, churches, urban development and the media. I have relied heavily on these and attempted to weave together an analytic narrative that brings out similarities and differences between a number of spheres of state and societal interaction, in order that we can begin to make sense of the path Zimbabwe has taken since independence.

As I wrote, I was struck by the depth of existing narratives, not just from Zimbabwe's political analysts, but by musicians, poets, novelists and playwrights. In particular, I have drawn excerpts from Chenjerai Hove's collection of contemplative essays, *Palaver Finish*; I encourage readers to read more than just the excerpts that grace the pages that follow.[38]

This manuscript has taken shape over some very bleak years. I hope that this text contributes to our understanding of the complexity of Zimbabwe's recent history, and enables Zimbabweans and friends of Zimbabwe to reflect on where they have come from, and perhaps, in the process, to make the path ahead a little clearer.

2

THE POLITICS OF LIBERATION (1965–1980)

...the liberation war was a reshaping of our destiny. Our stars became different. Our stories, our history held new potential. We could re-create them, to tell ourselves our own truth, our own lies, like everyone else.[1]

Nationalism was not an episode or a fleeting phase in Africa, but a deep reconceptualization of power relations, that is, of politics. As in other former colonies, nationalist politicians were poised to dominate the post-colonial political scene ideologically and symbolically, because, as Kaviraj pointedly reminds us:

> Nationalism, making colonialism responsible for everything wrong with colonial society, was making an insidious preparation for its own title to dominate all domains with unquestioned legitimacy ... it spoke for everyone.[2]

This was particularly true in those nationalist movements that transformed themselves into armed movements and fought bitter wars of liberation. The politics of post-liberation societies are shaped by the experience of warfare, by the transformation of relations between guerrillas and civilians, and by the organization and power relations within the movement. In Zimbabwe, as in other African states which underwent negotiated transitions rather than victories through 'the barrel of the gun', the pressures on nationalist movements generated

15

forms of coalition-building that translated into demobilized and quiescent political cultures after independence.[3] The limited form of pluralism which typifies these political systems helps explain the particularity
of the durable authoritarian—but not totalitarian—rule that follows.

Although the main focus of this book is on the post-independence
period, many of the relationships examined took shape during the liberation war. We can best make sense of the potency of claims to 'represent the nation' that resonated in the 1990s and 2000s by examining
their genesis in the 1960s and 1970s. This chapter examines the legacies of that period, as they emerged within the political movements and
society. As we shall see, nationalist movements generate particular
kinds of discourses and norms of political behaviour. It is these norms
which valorize unity and challenge democratic movements outside the
liberation movement, which shape political understandings and expectations in the post-independence period, enabling and legitimizing the
Mugabe regime's dominance. Nevertheless, the historical evidence
shows that movements did not always conform to these expectations,
being instead heterogeneous and complex, which is also reflected in
the post-independence period.

Political scientists studying Zimbabwe are lucky in that much
nuanced and excellent historical analysis is available, but all too often
the history of the liberation struggle becomes simply a required narrative backdrop, rather than a constitutive part of the analytical framework. A significant exception to this was Masipula Sithole's writings on
schisms within the nationalist movement. More recently, Scarnecchia's
work has analysed the evolution of 'sell-out politics' to provide a significant analytical purchase on the mode of nationalist organizing, while
Sabelo Ndlovu-Gatsheni's detailed exploration of the nationalist project has provided a crucial intellectual framework for thinking about
such issues.[4]

This chapter likewise attempts to move beyond a simple narrative
or political chronology. It examines the motivations and experiences of
the nationalists; relations within and between the nationalist movements; and relations between the nationalist movements and the civilian populations during the 1960s and 1970s. In considering the implication of these power relations for post-independence politics, we see
that despite much overt and covert support for the liberation move-

ments, experiences during the war were ambiguous and often contra-dictory. This challenges the myths and simplistic narratives which have come to dominate 'official' histories of the war, in which 'whites' are positioned against 'blacks'. [5] We also see that there was no single nation-alist ideology, but rather that the nationalism of liberation was com-posed of many strands which competed for dominance, sometimes violently. The nationalist movement that took control in 1980 was not internally coherent, nor did it draw its adherents from a cohesive group, nor were the wartime experiences of its supporters homoge-nous. These factors contribute greatly to shaping the possible political configurations after independence. At the same time, the myth and demand for unity reveals the homogenizing, authoritarian tendencies that generate the post-independence expectations of depoliticization, demobilization and delegitimization of groups not firmly linked to the nationalist movement, which itself takes on the mantle of the sole rep-resentative of the independent nation.

This chapter starts by setting out the social terrain of the mid-colo-nial period, when the nationalist parties emerged, and the divisions within and between them. It argues that the juxtaposition of diverse ideological and personal divisions of these groups, alongside great pres-sure for 'unity', is crucial for understanding the dynamics of nationalist coalition-building that extend into the post-colonial period. The chap-ter then explores the mobilization of support and the complex rela-tionship between key supporter groups—rural peasants, urban dwell-ers of all races, labour and church organizations—and the nationalist movements, as well as intersectional complexities of gender and race. In particular it highlights the often under-appreciated tensions of urban residential growth during the liberation war. The chapter concludes by situating the Zimbabwean case against the broader backdrop of nation-alist politics in Africa, setting the stage for the societal demobilization and limited pluralism of the independence era.

Politics by other means

The groups that we talk of as 'nationalist' movements emerged as rep-resentatives of an ethnically, linguistically and socially heterogeneous population. The Rhodesian settler state drew political boundaries around ethnic groups including the Zezuru, Karanga, Manyika, Ndau and KoreKore—which we now collectively call 'Shona'—inhabiting the north and east plateaus of the country, with the 'Ndebele' bringing together groups including Kalanga, Rozwi, Venda, Sotho and Tonga in the southern and western lowlands. In some accounts the Shona are thought of as the descendants of empires that traded with the Chinese and Portuguese, and who constructed the great stone enclosures that stretch across the territory. Likewise, the Ndebele are most closely identified with the great dispersal northward of the Zulu kingdom from what is now South Africa. But the reality was much more complex, with historical and archaeological research increasingly emphasizing the diversity of those groups. Gerry Mazarire's attempt to 'fragment' these 'meta-narratives' reminds us that the 'Shona' only came to be identified by that label in the late nineteenth century, and most peoples who took on that name lived in smaller units, albeit not in isolation.[6] The constant 'movement of peoples, goods and ideas' and 'multitude of different self-identifications' are also at the heart of Msindo's painstaking research which challenges the notion of 'the Ndebele' by emphasizing how diverse groups were brought together through extended processes of conflict and accommodation.[7]

These ethnically and linguistically heterogeneous groups also experienced colonialism, and indeed the liberation war, in different ways, depending on factors including their proximity to mines and farms, which generated demands for labour and land, often leading to forced labour and removals, as well as incomers from neighbouring colonies.[8] Ranger and Maxwell's work also shows how the beliefs and background of missionaries affected their relationships within local communities.[9] The experience of and response to these transformations also depended on gender and standing within kinship systems, such that some experienced colonialism as a dramatic loss of status, while for others it brought new alternatives and opportunities.[10]

Political associations before the 1950s thus tended to be divided by class, location and interests, but mass nationalist political parties brought together the black-led trade union, church and welfare organizations,[11] as well as elite-based, inter-racial associations that dominated the associational sphere in the 1930s and 1940s.[12] In 1957, two civic organizations—the Bulawayo branch of the Southern Rhodesian

Native Congress and the Harare-based Youth League—organized the Southern Rhodesia African National Congress (SRANC), and began the era of nationalist mass politics.[13]

Given their divergent origins, it should be unsurprising that nationalist party politics in the 1960s and 1970s were marked by successive struggles and schisms over leadership and the direction of the movement. As Masipula Sithole reminded us in his classic work: '... infights within and between liberation organizations ... are a fact of political life'.[14] Pressure from the Rhodesian security state, which regularly banned party structures and imprisoned leaders, contributed to these divides, but does not wholly explain them. The ANC, banned in 1959, was replaced by the National Democratic Party (NDP), itself banned only nine months after its formation. Late in 1961 the Zimbabwe African People's Union (ZAPU) was formed, taking up the mantle of the NDP and SRANC. The founding of the Zimbabwe African National Union (ZANU) in 1963 is commonly interpreted as a generational and ideological schism in reaction to Joshua Nkomo's leadership of these organizations.[15] But Msindo's careful analysis challenges this interpretation, as well as suggestions that the split reflected 'tribalism', proposing instead that the divide is best understood as an elite split over leadership and unmet expectations.[16] Other divisions emerged, however, as the two parties competed against each other for leadership of the movement and external recognition. While the most visible, and perhaps most lasting, divisions that developed were ethnic,[17] partisan interpretations have also stressed their differences in ideology, strategy, recruitment and organization. The emergence of inter-party violence should also not be downplayed. By most accounts, these divisions became more salient, especially for their on-the-ground supporters, as ZANU, based in Mozambique, sent guerrillas into the predominantly Shona-speaking areas accessible from the eastern border. Based mainly in Zambia, ZAPU's fighters operated largely in Matabeleland and the Midlands. In addition, ZAPU aligned itself ideologically with South Africa's ANC and the Soviet Union; ZANU with China and the PAC. While some have emphasized the impact of these alliances on the parties' own ideological frameworks, both were also riven by internal ideological schisms: the Nhari rebellion in ZANLA (ZANU's military wing) the 11 March movement in ZIPRA, ZAPU's armed wing.[18]

19

These ideological divides were intertwined with tensions generated by the experience of the armed struggle: fighting with inadequate weapons, unequal privileges for leaders and subalterns, critiques of certain leaders and their lifestyles. In addition, women soldiers' experiences in the camps were unequal, and often exploitative.[19] The significance of ethnic divisions within ZANU remains contested, but many believe that tensions between intra-Shona ethnic groups played a role in the assassination of Herbert Chitepo.[20]

Insecurity, ideology and personal rivalries made it difficult for these movements to accept internal contestation, and the rhetoric of unity was deployed to delegitimize subaltern voices within the movements, as well as those who threatened the power balance. As Tim Scarnecchia shows, calling people 'sell-outs' (*mutengesi* or *umthengisi*) emerged as early as the 1950s as a form of censure or criticism that is central to the nationalist movement's political culture.[21] At the same time, external pressure also generated unsuccessful attempts to unify the nationalist movements, most notably FROLIZI (the Front for the Liberation of Zimbabwe) in the early 1970s and ZIPA (Zimbabwe People's Army) in 1975.[22]

A third group of parties and leaders also sought allegiance from the black Rhodesian populace. One of these, ZANU Ndonga (also known as ZANU Sithole and ZANU Mwenje, *inter alia*), was the result of a further split within ZANU. In 1975, Robert Mugabe took control of the party and was eventually recognized as its leader even by the important figures of Machel and Nyerere. Ndabaningi Sithole, the Methodist minister who had been chosen as leader of ZANU after the break with Nkomo, refused to acknowledge the shift in power, and continued to assert himself as leader. In contrast, another group, the United African National Council or UANC, began life as a political organization uniting the various strands of the liberation movements in order to engage with the British government in the early 1970s, led by another clergyman, the Methodist Bishop Muzorewa. This gave the previously apolitical Muzorewa substantial legitimacy as a political spokesman.[23] Yet as Muzorewa subsequently negotiated with the Smith regime, supporters of the armed struggle backed away from his leadership.

Both Muzorewa and Sithole accepted the March 1978 'internal settlement', and joined with Chief Chirau to head a transitional government and then to contest elections in 1979. Muzorewa and Sithole also controlled 'auxiliary' forces, which were under the authority of the Rhodesian Special Branch, but functioned in many cases like private, albeit party-based, armies. These auxiliaries, who numbered about 10,000 in 1979,[24] included former guerrillas who had deserted from ZIPRA or ZANLA, while others were sent directly from the parties for training in Gadaffi's Libya and Amin's Uganda.[25] Luise White's research into Rhodesian army papers archived in Bristol suggests that the army intended them to control rural areas in the absence of the security forces, despite some doubts about their efficacy.[26] During the 1979 election, however, they were a much more political force, accused of intimidation and violence towards voters—forcing them to vote, as well as influencing their votes.[27]

This diversity within the nationalist movement, reflecting antagonisms and personal conflict, contributed to the diverse lived experiences of elite and subaltern nationalists, and their civilian supporters. Yet, the need to create a single national history has downplayed the complex motivations and multifarious trajectories of this period.

Problematizing peasant support

Support from social groups was important for all these political movements, whose legitimacy and effectiveness were often predicated on visible public support. Yet, as the sections above suggest, they often competed for this support. Questions of how and why support was generated and maintained help explain both the course of the liberation struggle and the structure of power in independent Zimbabwe.

Because the liberation struggle was mainly based in the rural areas, academic debates have focused on the experiences of peasant communities. In particular, questions have been raised about the extent to which guerrilla leaders utilized existing grievances within peasant communities to mobilize them, and the extent to which coercion was used to draw out material support. Ranger, in his landmark *Peasant Consciousness and Guerrilla War*, proposed a model of nationalism in which peasants were mobilized to support guerrillas because of concerns about land use and agricultural production, areas in which the Rhodesian state had intervened to the detriment of small-scale producers.[28] Kriger challenged this influential account by documenting guerrillas' use of coercive force against 'sell-outs' (*vatengaesi*) in order to gain peasant acquiescence.[29] Her account also emphasized the ways in which local power struggles were played out against the backdrop of the liberation war; women and youth used their relations with guerrillas to enhance their status vis-à-vis local elites. In intersecting discussions looking mainly at north-eastern Zimbabwe, Lan emphasized the role of spirit mediums in mediating between guerrillas and peasants,[30] while Maxwell calls for further differentiation between different mediums and different guerrilla units, emphasizing the importance of local-level historical experiences in determining reactions.[31] In Matabeleland, Alexander, McGregor and Ranger argue that ZIPRA was able to build on traditions of support for the NDP and ZAPU to a much greater extent than in other rural areas, where party organization had been curtailed.[32] These differences in the context of guerrilla-peasant relations depended on their earlier historical experiences, as well as their proximity to security forces and accessibility to guerrillas, and their different groupings within local areas divided by age, gender and access to land. Gender should not be taken to mean simply women's experiences. Mike Kesby argues convincingly that both the Rhodesian state and the guerrillas undermined 'what it was to be a man' to a greater degree than they destabilized women's roles and identities.[33] The war changed social relations profoundly, but in ways that were neither monolithic nor consistent. Even where sympathies lay naturally with the guerrillas, the relationship was not always straightforward or easy. Peasants' experiences of violence and hardship during the struggle shaped their attitudes towards the guerrillas, and subsequently the post-independence government, although 'official' histories often seek to play this down.

Untangling urban dynamics

Much less is known about relations between urban residents, especially black workers, and the nationalist parties during the period of armed struggle. Workers were the main participants in the early nationalist movement, but unions *per se* were relatively little involved after 1965, partly because the struggle had moved to the countryside. Perhaps because of the early urban base of the nationalist movements,

Rhodesian labour legislation was constructed to prevent union linkages with nationalist parties.[34] Although worker militancy is often considered to have reached a peak with the general strike of 1948,[35] strikes continued into the 1950s, and unionists were leading members of the newly formed nationalist parties. Raftopoulos speaks also of the 'increasing subordination' of trade union activities to nationalist politics during this period.[36] Ranger notes that there were strong demands for societal groups at this time to unify themselves under the banner of the nationalist movement:

> the first Congress movement in the late 1930s and 1940s was a more or less powerless federal grouping of much more potent and virtually autonomous association; the rhetoric of unity failed to overcome effective pluralism. But this was regularly lamented in the black press as a grave failure; the idea of a sphere outside the political process in which issues of religious belief, domesticity, education, gender, sport, work etc etc were resolved came more and more under attack. By the late 1950s with the emergence of mass nationalism it had come to be accepted that the nationalist movement must now dominate all these other spheres.[37]

But the factionalism of nationalist politics also afflicted their supporters in the trades unions: 'by 1965 … there were serious divisions in the trade union movement, and they were part of the broader divisions in the nationalist movement'.[38] Trade union history has thus been an important angle in deconstructing the myths of 'nationalist unity', reflecting and revealing the contestation and complexity inherent in these movements.

After the 1965 Unilateral Declaration of Independence (UDI), workers were also increasingly constrained by legislation which limited their ability to organize or represent workers, much less to lead political movements.[39] Although the version of this period's history supported by the Zimbabwe Congress of Trade Unions (ZCTU) speaks of politicized trade unionists often being detained by the Rhodesian authorities because they were seen as 'dangerous', it is not possible to get a sense of the strength of this movement within urban areas or amongst workers.[40] Schiphorst is much more sceptical, suggesting that party or ideological divisions were less significant than divides based around personalities and accusations of corrupt practices.[41] Tim Scarnecchia's study of the 1950s and 1960s gives a clear sense of the tensions and difficulties of urban life, highlighting the violence that accompanied political factionalization.[42] By the time of the internal settlement, certain unions and umbrella organizations were perceived to be linked to ZANU, ZAPU, UANC and ZANU Ndonga because of their leaders' affiliations. Despite these linkages, it remains difficult to assess to what extent workers actually identified with particular parties or leaders. We know very little about miners and farm-workers during this period or the experiences of migrant workers from outside Rhodesia. John Pape's account of domestic workers from ZANU-infiltrated rural areas taking goods and money to the guerrillas provides fascinating hints as to urban experiences of war and party affiliation, but is based on a handful of interviews.[43] The urban civilian experience of the 1970s remains almost entirely unexplored.

Despite this, we know that the Rhodesian state's attempts to limit the presence of blacks in cities has had a profound impact on norms of citizenship and identity in the post-colonial period. As in other settler states, the Rhodesians used mechanisms of 'influx control' which limited the presence of those not working in the formal sector, and provided housing for single men, not for families.[44] But as the war intensified in the 1970s, more and more people fled from the rural areas to the cities. In addition, increasing numbers of men seeking jobs and young unmarried women were sent to urban areas by their parents, to avoid the dangers of both the guerrillas and the security services; and married women took their children and joined their husbands in town. This growth in the urban population, and increasing levels of unemployment, contributed to the development of squatter settlements around Harare, and changed the gender and racial composition of the cities.[45]

Ennie Chipembere argues that the UDI government 'went out of their way' to deal with the urban influx: they took over the construction of low-income housing, and developed new partnerships with private industry, financial institutions and mortgage lenders. In addition to the new townships which were developed, in 1972 the presence of 'lodgers' in high-density townships was legalized. New housing designs were developed, which facilitated the presence of lodgers by adding extra rooms, often with separate outside entrances.[46] Diana Patel also suggested that between 1976 and 1980 'the government adopted a more tolerant policy towards squatters'.[47] Until this time, squatter settlements around Harare were demolished, and in only one case were alternative arrangements made to shelter those who were displaced. But in 1977, the municipal and national governments cooperated to relocate squatters and provide them with land on which they could build, in what would become Chitungwiza. And in 1979, faced with overcrowding in 'African' areas, and shanty towns emerging on vacant land and in the urban periphery, 'transit camps' were authorized within the city, on which temporary shelters were erected.[48]

A careful reading of contemporary sources on Harare further challenges the notion of the controlled, regulated colonial city. By the early 1970s, public transport for urban commuters was overstretched, with buses regularly carrying passenger numbers well above their official occupancy. 'Pirate' taxis emerged to absorb some of this demand: at least a thousand passengers were travelling from Highfield into town daily in illegal and poorly maintained vehicles carrying an average of ten passengers per trip.[49] Urban agriculture also grew dramatically from the late 1960s onwards. Mazambani's research shows a 67 per cent annual increase in 'illegal' cultivated areas from 1965 to 1980.[50] All of this put together suggests that black Rhodesians had made the cities their own, and claimed them as living and work spaces, challenging both the Rhodesian state's hostility and the liberation war's rhetoric of land and peasants. Yet these urban experiences of the war years are missing from the historical record.

We also know little about the impact that urban lived experiences had on political affiliation, although there has long been a presumption that urban blacks did not support the guerrillas. Voting records do not distinguish between occupational groups, nor the cruder indices of rural and urban voters. In the 1979 election, Bishop Muzorewa's UANC won 78 per cent of the vote in Mashonaland East, a constituency which included Harare. Yet, this apparent support faded dramatically once independence arrived, and ZANU won 80 per cent in the same province. Little research has been done on the apparent support for Muzorewa in 1979, and its disappearance in 1980. In the rural areas, there was substantial documentation of intimidation of voters by both Muzorewa and Sithole's auxiliaries. Muzorewa also drew heavily on spirit mediums for legitimation, bringing them to the platform of his rallies.[51] Nevertheless, it is probable that many urban voters did support Muzorewa. Thomas Turino tells of asking a middle-class friend about support for Muzorewa in the 1970s, and his friend replying 'Tom, back then we were *all* for Muzorewa.'[52] People may have voted for Muzorewa in the hope that he could stop the war, as his campaign promised, and because of lingering legitimacy garnered as spokesman for the liberation movements. After his election, however, the war grew more intense. In 1980, both urban and rural voters supported Mugabe, because he really could, and did, stop the war.[53] But a suspicion lingered that they were not 'true' supporters, that by living in the city they too had been *vatengaesi* (sell-outs).

The smaller, urban-based communities of 'coloured' or mixed race and Asian Zimbabweans also faced accusations of not fully supporting the liberation struggle. Some members of the coloured community had been active in the inter-racial associations of the 1950s, while Asians had supported 'self-help and improvement schemes' run by black nationalists.[54] A few coloured activists maintained links with the nationalist parties into the 1960s, especially ZAPU, which was more sympathetic to their interests.[55] Young members of the Bulawayo Asian community were similarly involved in ZAPU, with three activists being imprisoned at Gonakudzingwa.[56] By the late 1970s, there were coloured politicians on the executives of ZAPU, UANC and ZANU Ndonga. The rural character of the war in the 1970s precluded much involvement by either the coloured or Asian communities, although some did raise money for detained nationalists and provided support for urban guerrilla activities. A few members of the younger, more radicalized generation even fought in the guerrilla armies. Many others were conscripted into the Rhodesian army, or fled the country to avoid conscription.[57] Others, perhaps threatened by the 'Africanist' rhetoric of the nationalists, maintained support for the UDI government.[58] Muzondidya emphasizes their economic vulnerability, which contributed to concern for their uncertain future in a majority-ruled Zimbabwe.

White settlers and missionaries: not singing from the same hymn sheet

As mass nationalism intensified among the black population, the white settlers' politics also radicalized, with the election of the Rhodesian Front (RF) in 1962 leading to Ian Smith's infamous Unilateral

Declaration of Independence (UDI) from Britain in 1965. UDI led nationalists to embrace the armed struggle, and in doing so militarized white Rhodesia as well.[59] It is dangerous to generalize about the experiences of white Rhodesians, or to see them as a homogenous community. Despite Rhodesia's perceived need for more white inhabitants, Italian, Greek and Jewish settlers were seen as undesirable immigrants, as were Afrikaners.[60] Josiah Brownell and Alois Mlambo's work also emphasizes the transitory nature of white Rhodesians—few remaining within the country for long. Political attitudes differ across age groups and are difficult to assess. Election results show that the Rhodesian Front faced little threat at the polls between 1965 and 1980, but the propaganda machine left little space for alternative views. Angela Davies quotes an interview with a farmer who served in the army during UDI, and stayed in Zimbabwe after 1980:

> …I think we were totally brainwashed into believing we were right and the world was behind us and that we were going to win… I never changed my mind, right up to the elections. We were told well you know, if you get the farm workers to vote the way you want them to, the elections will be walked. But it was a total turn about. It was actually…I was shocked… [*real astonishment and bitterness in his voice*] I was totally brainwashed. Anyway…I knew we had been fooled…[61]

Despite the experiences of such young men, and the existence of a strong nationalist discourse celebrating all things Rhodesian, the myth-making machine was probably never completely hegemonic.[62] Luise White's work on conscription shows high levels of disaffection with the war within the white community, as young men resisted and evaded their national service commitments, despite familial pressure for them to fight.[63] Once the internal settlement was signed in 1978, many whites seemed to accept the inevitability of black rule, although emigration also reached record levels. In January 1979, 84 per cent voted in favour of the new constitution, which brought about the 1979 internal settlement elections based on a universal franchise.[64] One of the hallmarks of the subsequent election was the 'enthusiasm' with which many white employers drove workers and servants to the polls, complying vigorously with the government's determination to 'get the vote out'.[65]

An obvious social division existed between farmers and urban residents, although this was not absolute. White urban councillors in local government remained overwhelmingly non-partisan, running successfully as independents against RF candidates. But Angus Selby argues that at least four presidents of the farmers' union were explicitly anti-RF, and that much of the membership was similarly amenable to reform.[66] The supporters of the several white opposition parties tended to be pragmatists; Hancock suggests that they were often recent immigrants linked to business interests, who saw that the segregationist policies made development unsustainable. 'It was impossible,' said one industrialist, 'to build a great urban population out of bachelors and prostitutes.'[67] Although this group was often derisorily referred to as the 'left' in Rhodesia, they were for the most part economically right-wing and critical of the Rhodesian Front's tendencies towards protectionism.

In addition to this somewhat muddled group of pragmatists, an even smaller group of white radicals emerged, the most prominent of whom were linked to missionary work.[68] While the Protestant churches were distinctly ambiguous about involvement in nationalist politics, Catholic priests and nuns became more radicalized as the war deepened.[69] The Catholic Church's position was further reflected in the formation of the Catholic Commission for Justice and Peace (CCJP) in 1972. The first objectives of the CCJP were to research and educate the public on questions of sectoral injustice, for example amongst mineworkers, domestic workers and land distribution. The intensification of the war in 1972–3 brought the CCJP to the more confrontational task of investigating and documenting the human rights abuses of the security forces. The CCJP denounced the internal settlement as a non-solution to the problems of Rhodesia, and was active in the negotiations and diplomatic efforts throughout 1978 and 1979 that led to the Lancaster House peace agreement and independence.[70]

Despite the sacrifices of a few brave souls, church and NGO politics in the 1960s and 1970s were segmented by tensions of race, class and ideology. As the above discussion suggests, relations between the 'mission' churches and the nationalist movement were ambiguous. Many of the early members of nationalist movements had been ordained pastors, and the congresses of church and mission bodies provided an important early forum for the pursuit of social and political equality.[71] Later, the 1960s and 1970s also saw the formation of several church-related bodies in response to the intensifying racial politics of the post-UDI Smith government. The Christian Council was founded in response to a division within the Protestant Christian Conference over the 'hanging bill', which became the Law and Order (Maintenance) Act (LOMA).[72] The Council's mandate was ostensibly to work with youth in African townships and to support Christian values in home and family life. However, the intensification of political activity leading to the UDI in 1965 meant that the Council became an important support for the families of detained nationalists.[73] This action brought them under fire from the Rhodesian Front government. The introduction of the Welfare Organisations Act would have prevented the Christian Council from visiting political detainees in prisons and camps.[74] Despite creating a new organization, Christian Care, to take over these tasks, the Christian Council did not keep away from politics; it continued to demand immediate independence, and campaigned against UDI.[75] Bishop Skelton noted that statements issued under the aegis of the Council were few and far between, because it was felt that 'the more we spoke the less we should be listened to'.[76] As he recognized, these pronouncements had little effect on government policy and offended many white churchgoers; instead, they built up confidence among black members in the leadership of the churches.

As the liberation war progressed, the Anglican Church showed itself more responsive to white Rhodesian society and became less militant.[77] Individual members of the Anglican hierarchy were especially noted for their close ties to the Smith government.[78] These conservative Rhodesian Anglicans were influential in restraining the Christian Council. Their influence was counterbalanced, however, by the World Council of Churches' Programme to Combat Racism (PCR) which supported the guerrilla movements. However, the continuing presence of Methodist Bishop Muzorewa within the Council was complicated when he became Prime Minister of 'Zimbabwe-Rhodesia' in 1978. The liberation movements refused to recognize the validity of this settlement, and continued their struggle until the Lancaster House agreement in 1979. The Council, presumably influenced by Muzorewa, supported the internal settlement, although this was subsequently underplayed in its official history.[79]

Conclusion: the shape of nationalist politics

Ambiguity stalks all aspects of politics in the years leading up to 1980. With the exception of a few hagiographic and quasi-official accounts of 'the struggle',[80] Zimbabwean historiography has quite properly emphasized the non-monolithic nature of the liberation struggle and of nationalism itself. As far back as 1970, Ranger ended his study of African politics 1898–1930 with the hope that his book suggested 'the complexity out of which nationalist politics have arisen'.[81] And in the post-colonial period Phimister suggested that the very nature of the 'revolution' that brought the Mugabe regime into power was 'profoundly ambiguous', bringing further contradictions in its wake.[82] Not that there should ever have been any ambiguity about the importance of majority rule, the abolition of discriminatory legislation and the remedying of socio-economic inequalities. However, for all that the political battles required a pretence of unity,[83] the reality was much more complex.

In thinking about post-colonial politics, these ambiguities must be foregrounded. As Christine Sylvester argued, divisions between radicals and reformers in ZANU, as well as between liberals and 'nationalists' within the Rhodesian state and within the peasant communities, all contribute to explaining the lack of a ready-made integrative hegemonic discourse on which the new state could easily draw.[84]

However, we should not think that Zimbabwean nationalist politics differed greatly from nationalist politics elsewhere on the continent. Studies of nationalism in both East and West Africa were among the first to problematize the myth-making tendencies of post-colonial states. Zolberg, for instance, emphasized the ways in which the early 'one-party states' were in fact based on coalitions of interests, which attempted to incorporate, not exclude, potential opponents.[85] These one-party states were indeed *partis unifiés* rather than *partis uniques*.[86] It is perhaps most useful to think of nationalist politics as fundamentally the politics of coalition-building, i.e. incorporative or inclusive rather than exclusive, although the composition of the coalition may change over time.[87] At the same time, when groups did not accommodate themselves to the politics of inclusion, they were violently excluded—

as alleged 'sell-outs' discovered during the liberation war, and the denizens of Matabeleland would learn in the 1980s.

Further, we can suggest that this nationalist coalition-building manifests itself post-independence as *limited* pluralism in a pattern typical of authoritarian states, where demobilization is a strategy for balancing conflicting interests within the coalition: 'Effective mobilisation, particularly through a single party and its mass organisations, would be perceived as a threat by the other components of the limited pluralism, typically, the army, the bureaucracy, the churches or interest groups.'[88] Or as Mamdani put it, nationalism depended upon the 'delegitimation of all contemporary democratic struggles as detracting from national unity'.[89]

The post-independence demobilization that such patterns of behaviour encouraged and the subsequent societal quiescence are the key to understanding the nature of the state in East and Central Africa, the success and durability of authoritarian regimes which shaped these states, and their problematic transitions to multi-party rule. Those few societal forces which were not included or incorporated within the nationalist project—especially opposition political parties—were delegitimized and excluded from participating within the political sphere. This pattern, and expectations of behaviour, persists throughout Zimbabwe's post-1980 political trajectory.

3

THE POLITICS OF INCLUSION (1980–1987)

There was so much goodwill among the citizenry [just after independence] that you could have asked all working people to donate a week's pay to a national cause and they would have gladly done it. There was so much national energy and such vision that if it had been properly mobilised we would have travelled a long way as a nation.[1]

Following its overwhelming victory in the 1980 election, Mugabe's ZANU government set about welding together the disparate elements of the nationalist movement, attempting to develop hegemony over the new nation. In order to understand this period, we must examine the 'complementary, contradictory, reciprocal, and symbiotic aspects of the complex relationship between nationalism, democracy and development'.[2]

For much of the 1980s, the ZANU government was able to capitalize ideologically on its successes in the liberation war and its substantial victory in the independence elections to build a network of informal alliances with its former supporters and enemies. This coalition was broader than that which had fought the liberation war—incorporating such disparate elements as white farmers, former Rhodesian politicians and Western donors. The demands of these groups were carefully balanced against those of the historic nationalist coalition, which was demobilized or selectively integrated into the state apparatus.

The politics of inclusion typified ZANU's approach to nation- and party-building, but coercion was not absent. The external South African threat and Cold War tensions, coupled with the strength of the inherited Rhodesian security state, made for the continuation of a strong militaristic tendency. Repressive legislation from the Rhodesian era was maintained in place, along with an extended state of emergency.[3] Less important political individuals and groups were harassed and marginalized from power. Significant challengers to ZANU's authority, like ZAPU and its civilian supporters, were summarily crushed and incorporated by force. Yet coercion was but one strand of the power relationship which relied on and contributed to the party's control of institutions and ideological hegemony. The regime's control over the media, army and other state institutions gave it impunity over the massacre of civilians in Matabeleland, domestically and internationally.

ZANU's success in demobilizing the victorious nationalist movement might at first glance seem surprising, but this depoliticization and discouragement of organized or visible lobbying reproduces the nationalist pattern of organizing,[4] which itself was reinforced by the electoral victory. Indirect and informal means of working through and within existing power structures were instead valorized in the name of unity, development and nationalism. For much of the 1980s, these nation-building metaphors and policies shaped societal demobilization as groups took the government at its word and contributed to the development of the new nation. Rhetoric of participation and decentralization concealed the continuation of Rhodesian-era top-down decision-making patterns. Tangible and real progress on the extension of services to rural areas and the deracialization of education, healthcare and the civil service were seen as evidence of the regime's commitment to development. The few groups with access to funds independently of the state, like churches and unions, were firmly and thoroughly incorporated into the new regime. Like other nationalist governments in Africa, faced with governing newly independent societies, ZANU developed corporatist strategies to absorb and contain demands.[5] Of course, most organizations had already been brought underneath the nationalist umbrella during the nationalist movement and liberation struggle.[6] Those organizations such as unions which had remained formally outside the nationalist network were brought inside through structural reforms, while others such as churches and NGOs retained formal independence but continued to be symbolically and

rhetorically united with the government. As this suggests, demobilization cannot be understood as a simplistic top-down process. In the
years after 1980, many organizations and activists who had supported
the liberation movement were keen to work with the state to build a
new country. Thus they distanced themselves from overt political
involvement, other than through ZANU, and dedicated themselves to
development work with the best of intentions.

It is also worth bearing in mind that many state actions against
potential or fragmentary social movements that challenged demobilization were *ad hoc* or incomplete.[7] The regime rarely seemed to plan
what, with hindsight, resembles a strategy of control. The actions of
individual state or party representatives were frequently quashed by
the courts, and policies were ignored by those tasked with implementing them. Incremental battles won against the state, in which government policies were rejected by parliament or, more frequently, condemned as unconstitutional by the courts, meant that the government's
agenda was implemented piecemeal. In other cases, policies proposed
in the 1980s—such as national service—were simply never followed
through until much later, as we shall see in subsequent chapters. It
would be a mistake to see these strategies as monolithic or univocal,
but the overlapping and reinforcing practices across sectors and audiences generates a particular set of norms and imaginaries which shaped
the way that Zimbabweans understood how to 'do politics'.

This chapter first explores the way in which unity, development and
nationalism became the dominant and interlocking themes of public
discourse, rather than 'liberation'. Focusing on the deployment of these
discursive tropes enables us to see how ZANU was aided in their programme of nation-building by the external and internal legitimacy
provided by its electoral mandate, which supplied it with willing
accomplices, even—perhaps especially—amongst those sectors that
had not supported its aims during the war. Demands for political unity
justified attacks not just on ZAPU but also on the civilians of
Matabeleland, while in the name of 'development' land reform focused
more on productivity and export markets than poverty alleviation. We
also see how symbolic capital was deployed in renaming streets and
monuments within a less than radical cultural policy. At the same time,
the regime's new legislative and security powers, based upon the

oppressive laws of the Rhodesian state, allowed it to regulate widely and provided a political-military framework through which to dominate and demobilize society. As Norbert Tengende argued, 'Nation-building ... became an instrument of domination and control ... marked by the marginalization of popular participation.'[8]

The second half of the chapter moves the focus from discourse to practice in analysing how these discursive strategies contributed to the demobilization of society from 1980 until 1987. The state that was inherited from Rhodesia was bureaucratically robust, with remarkably effective reach and broadcast. The chapter shows how the new regime used those state institutions to impose policies which regulated and demobilized NGOs, urban dwellers, academics, unions, churches, the media and opposition parties in ways that were similar and reinforcing across sectors. This focus enables us to see how societal demobilization came to characterize this period through the shifting register of discourse, while still ensuring the continued dominance of the nationalist movement. Taken together, the two halves of the chapter show how ZANU's strategies were driven by both the carrot and the stick and imposed through both violent and rhetorical means, constraining and shaping both the discursive sphere of the polity and the ways in which Zimbabweans organized and engaged with politics.

'Reconciliation, unity and development': framing political engagement

On the eve of independence, Mugabe 'enjoin[ed] the whole ... nation to march in perfect unison'.[9] This gesture was widely seen as a pragmatic acceptance of existing forces in the country and the region, as well as the international climate,[10] yet the emphasis on unity concealed and excused authoritarian policies, the abuse of coercive institutions, and violations of human rights and freedoms. This strategy was aimed at including whites and non-ZANU-supporting blacks, whether they wanted to be or not, while power bases outside the ruling party were delegitimized and destroyed. Karekwaivanene similarly highlights the 'central legitimating claim' of the new government's 'promise to bring about development and modernisation'.[11] As this suggests, in Zimbabwe the liberation struggle was for some years sublimated discursively, while 'development' took centre stage. This is in marked contrast to Namibia, which Henning Melber describes as having a 'struggle mentality' as 'national gospel'; or Eritrea, where the 'bitter struggle' still dominates national discourse.[12] Although there are many similarities in patterns of memorialization, leadership and political domination, in Zimbabwe the theme of 'struggle' was only one discursive thread in the 1980s, which was intertwined with broader themes. We can think of 'the struggle' and 'liberation' as an underlying theme that shaped and conditioned what 'unity' meant and how 'development' was understood, but which only emerges into its own at times of intense pressure. ZANU's leaders were aware that 'liberation' contained within itself the potential for deeply divisive factional politics. The emphasis on unity was thus pragmatic in a state riven not just by unequal development, but also by explicit policies of divide and rule practised by the Smith regime and its predecessors,[13] and the schisms that had emerged in exile and in the bush. And so a major part of policy was to dominate the available political space, squeezing out competing voices which could lay claim to the nationalist discourse or otherwise appeal to the voting population. Nation-building was narrowly conceptualized 'from a party political perspective'.[14] Yet it also framed and perpetuated a set of political strategies and norms of citizenship. Most crucially, attempts to sideline ZAPU in the early eighties had 'far reaching implications for certain newly-emergent yet basic political realities: for nation-building, for state-made ethnic polarisation, for the concentration of power within the state and indeed for the very critique of what state power could or should be'.[15] The policies and state actions, captured here under the rubric of nation-building, were to shape a generation's ideas about citizenship: what it meant to be Zimbabwean, who could speak for and represent the nation; but also conceptions of the state, and the role of the state in regulating identities and behaviour.

Deracialization proved both the most straightforward and the most difficult, part of the 'reconciliation and unity' package to implement. Some segregatory and discriminatory policies had already been removed under the internal settlement. Many formerly white neighbourhoods already had black residents by 1980, and they gained more rapidly, as whites left the country.[16] The civil service and the lower levels of industry and commerce—secretarial and shop-floor assistants, for example—were rapidly 'indigenized', especially because these jobs had been held by lower-class whites, who were the most likely to have left before or at independence.[17] At more senior levels of the government—especially in the security forces and intelligence—there was remarkable continuity between Smith's personnel and those retained in the first years of independence.[18]

The introduction of a minimum wage in May 1980 also benefited workers in many sectors. In the mining sector minimum wage increases led to 76 per cent average increases in earnings during 1980–3, although once inflation was taken into account this gain was in real terms only 18 per cent.[19] Industry, banking and other sectors of the economy remained white-controlled at the top levels with the implicit connivance of the state, aiming to avoid the 'white flight' which had typified Mozambique's decolonization. Because of this, it is in economic policy-making that the continued influence of whites remained most visible. Indeed, students of interest group behaviour argued that in the 1980s the strongest interest groups in Zimbabwe were those identified as 'white', such as commercial farmers and industrialists.[20] This was due in part to their organizational and research strengths, as well as their strategic economic importance. Ministerial dominance in decision-making is said to have increased the strength of white interest groups, who became 'much stronger outside Parliament than ever the [Conservative Alliance of Zimbabwe (CAZ), a successor to the RF] would have been inside'.[21] While a few whites held ministerial positions, and others remained as opposition senators and MPs (some as independents, others with the CAZ), most retreated from formal politics and concentrated on their businesses and social lives.[22] Social divides between whites and blacks remained clear-cut, especially at churches, sporting events and restaurants. These were unsubtly signposted in public discourse: 'The *Herald*, the *Chronicle* and the *Sunday Mail* [refer] to almost every black person as "Comrade" and almost every white person as Mr, Mrs., Ms or Dr...'[23]

The constitutional requirements of Lancaster House also prevented the government from acquiring land, other than through willing-seller agreements. The resultant stability of tenure did much to reassure farmers and investors of the regime's willingness to support white endeavours. The presence of Denis Norman in Cabinet as Minister of Agriculture between 1980 and 1985 further reassured white farmers.[24]

This meant that farmers, white farmers in particular, became significant stakeholders in the ZANU(PF) coalition, both politically and economically. Many became active party members, and were often seen alongside ministers and party elites at rural events. But, as we shall see in the next chapter, this policy created long-term contradictions as pent-up land hunger amongst the poor became a potent mobilizing force for and against the Mugabe regime throughout the 1990s.

Unity was not just about relations between blacks and whites, but also about relations between the ruling party and its opposition. As Christine Sylvester reminds us, each manifestation of the claim to 'unity' by the ruling party 'can be deconstructed to bring disunities into the spotlight'.[25] In the post-independence period, the never-realized unity of the nationalist struggle became mythologized: 'in unity we fought for independence and in unity we must now strive to consolidate it,' President Canaan Banana claimed in early 1981.[26]

This theme of unity was then elaborated in terms of party unity, supposedly an ideological demand for a form of rule appropriate to African society, but in reality a demand for control by ZANU(PF). In 1980, ZAPU was given four seats in cabinet, with Nkomo initially holding the position of Home Affairs Minister, but being downgraded to Minister without Portfolio early in 1981. In 1982 Nkomo and three other ZAPU ministers were removed from the cabinet when the army claimed to have 'discovered' substantial arms caches on properties owned by ZAPU. Seven former ZIPRAs, including senior cadres Lookout Masuku and Dumiso Dabengwa, were detained and put on trial for treason. Although six of the defendants were found to be innocent, they were immediately re-detained under emergency regulations by the Home Affairs Minister; two were released in 1984 and the others not until 1986. Nkomo fled into exile in 1983, alleging threats on his life, but he returned the next year, in order to keep his seat in parliament. In 1984, the remaining ZAPU ministers were shuffled out of cabinet, leaving only a deputy minister, Jane Ngwenya, who later joined ZANU. Many other MPs and party officials were arrested, detained and assaulted during these years. Karekwaivenane also reminds us that ZANU used similar tactics against its own internal malcontents, when nine ZANU provincial officials were detained and tortured in 1983, for refusing to acquiesce to the removal of Patrick Kombayi as Mayor of Gweru.[27]

The rhetoric of the time reflected and justified these actions. The relationship between citizens, party and state was described by one deputy minister as being like the Holy Trinity: 'the people are God the Father; the Government is God the Son; and ZANU(PF) is the Holy Spirit'.[28] The proposed—although never accomplished—implementation of a one-party state further extended this thinking: 'We are one state, with one society and one nation, one party, and one leader.'[29] As Eddison Zvogbo, ZANU's publicity secretary, claimed in late 1981: 'ZANU is aiming at a situation where there is no separation between party and state … we are convinced … that before the middle or end of next year, we will have so re-organized the party that it will be impossible for any other party to operate on the ground.'[30]

The use of violent force to control and remove threats to ZANU was further justified through reference to destabilization attempts by South Africa.[31] The Matabeleland security organs, which included the Central Intelligence Organisation (CIO), the army and various police units, were deployed against any civilians who were seen to be 'anti-unity, anti-government and disloyal to the state'.[32] The CCJP's conservative account identified a minimum of 3,000 dead and 'disappeared' civilians, with thousands more known to have been beaten, detained, raped and tortured during nearly seven years of violent intimidation.[33] More recently, an estimate of at least 20,000 victims has come to be widely accepted.[34] The imposition of curfews and restrictions on movement, which prevented the distribution of food aid during drought years, increased the suffering of rural people. Much of this violence was attributed to the infamous North Korean-trained Five Brigade, a predominantly Shona force, trained, armed and equipped separately from the rest of the army.[35] Five Brigade's motto, 'Gukurahundi', became synonymous with the Matabeleland crisis itself. Peasants in Matabeleland explained to Dick Werbner that Gukurahundi, literally translated as the first heavy spring rains, represented the 'sweeping away of rubbish' and said that they were the rubbish that the Shona wished to clear away.[36] International condemnation of these events was muted. Zimbabwe's success in the economic and developmental field seemed to protect against public censure, in ways that are reminiscent of post-genocide Rwanda.

The leaders of other opposition parties, with their less significant followings, experienced less brutal, but not dissimilar, tactics. Bishop

Muzorewa, who remained head of the UANC, was detained for ten months in 1983–4 on charges which stretched from conspiring with his 'intimate friends in the leadership of the South African government'[37] to 'making derogatory remarks about the government of Zimbabwe'[38] to funding 'former ZIPRA dissidents' and conspiring with Israel, Zaire and Uganda.[39] Ndabaningi Sithole, whose ZANU Ndonga retained support in the Ndau areas of Manicaland, remained out of the country in self-imposed exile for most of the 1980s.

The violent conflict in Matabeleland between 1981 and 1987 was part of ZANU(PF)'s determination to assert its dominance over the whole country. This derived both from the divisions of the liberation war and also from the under-resourced and under-organized demobilization of ZIPRA and ZANLA. Exacerbated by the 'negotiated' nature of the settlement, the demobilization exercise was conflict-prone from the start, with guerrillas and leaders disagreeing over access to stockpiles of arms, and skirmishes breaking out around designated Assembly Points.[40] While the government media contributed to claims that there was an 'organized pattern' to outbreaks of violence, Jocelyn Alexander argues that it was violence within the newly created Zimbabwe National Army (ZNA) that led many ex-ZIPRA combatants to desert—these were the men subsequently labelled dissidents.[41] While there seems to be little basis for the government's claim that dissidents adhered to a political agenda, the regime's claims were 'congenial with its *own distinctive interests* in consolidating state power and entrenching ZANU hegemony in the political system'.[42] The government's rhetoric against the so-called dissidents is redolent of unity as both a historical good and as necessary for future development. Mugabe said:

> If you show divisionist attitudes the enemy will come among us and will destroy us. Our forefathers fought together during the first Chimurenga war and it is our duty to be united as well. ... Dissidents still have shallow mentality, because they are encouraging tribalism in the country. Zimbabwe was not liberated for any one tribe and it is pertinent that she remains united.[43]

Ironically, but perhaps not surprisingly, the experiences of these years, intended to subordinate ZAPU and sublimate regional identities, instead deepened and strengthened Ndebele ethnic identity. Björn Lindgren argued appositely that 'the enactment of Ndebele identity in

41

the 1990s and early 2000s is largely the *result* of the ZANU-PF government's national politics... Ndebele-speakers...have been excluded from taking part in the construction of the independent nation-state they once fought to bring into being.'[44]

Following this conflict, negotiations between the parties did lead to ZAPU being dismantled as an independent party and incorporated into ZANU in 1987. The agreement known as the Unity Accord created a 'new' party named ZANU(PF). The 'PF' stood for the Patriotic Front, under whose banner ZANU and ZAPU had negotiated the Lancaster House accord. Despite the rhetoric of partnership and unity, the terms of the agreement symbolized by the loss of ZAPU's name reflected ZANU triumphalism.[45] This, and the installation of Mugabe as Executive President, set the stage for the de facto one-party rule which characterized the political system between 1987 and 2000.

At the same time as they were laying the groundwork for political control, the regime also undertook a more gradual—and predominantly symbolic—nation-building programme. Typified by the omnipresent 'official portrait' of the president, this development tended to reflect 'presidentialism' rather than nationalism, especially after the establishment of the executive presidency. In a moment of grand political theatre, Patrick Kombayi escorted the members of the Gweru City Council from their council meeting to remove a picture of Ian Smith from an office wall and replace it with one of Mugabe.[46] In at least one case, a Dutch national's defacing of the official portrait was punished by his extended detention without charge, followed by deportation.[47] However, the father of the nation motif was not pushed to the extent seen in Zaire or Kenya.[48] Nor did the attribution of divine qualities or status to the political leader extend as far as in Malawi,[49] although the occasional reference appeared in public discourse, such as when novice MP Tony Gara used his maiden speech in parliament to announce that 'this country and its people should thank God almighty for giving us His only other son, by the name of Robert Gabriel Mugabe'.[50]

Nationalist and liberation war iconography also came to have a visible presence in Zimbabwe, from the change of the country's name to that of towns and streets between 1982 and 1990.[51] Just as the streets of Salisbury had elevated the heroes of the pioneer column, their new names are mostly those of dead ZANU heroes of the liberation war, although the Tredgold Building in Bulawayo retained its name, in honour of the Chief Justice, Sir Robert Tredgold, who resigned in protest against the implementation of the Law and Order (Maintenance) Act in 1960.[52] No living Zimbabweans were honoured, with the notable exception of Mugabe, whose name was given to roads throughout the country in 1990.[53] Memorials to whites killed during the liberation war were removed,[54] but memorialization remained subdued, rarely at the forefront of the agenda.

The school curriculum proposed for the new nation was said to be designed to emphasize 'national unity, patriotism, civics and local history',[55] although curriculum reform was the weakest aspect of the government's programme in education until after the Unity Accord.[56] The Minister for Education and Culture also called for the creation of a 'national dress',[57] reinvigorating the cultural nationalist debates of the early 1960s, but this too was more talk than action, and never came into being.

Turino describes the Ministry of Education and Culture's investment in the creation of the National Dance Company, through which Zimbabwe would 'present and represent itself as a unique and yet "modern" nation'.[58] Musicians, especially those who had been active in supporting the nationalist movement in the 1970s, also continued to play important roles in the cultural promotion of a new national identity: '… in 1980, the nationalist government was determined to control and direct the content of popular songs towards praising the leaders for … winning the war' although more established singers had more 'free space [in which to] sing songs that both celebrated independence and also questioned certain state policies'.[59] Like other sectors, artistic contributions coincided with and reinforced official mythologizing, while also providing a limited alternative perspective.

The state also abolished Rhodesian holidays and created the new Zimbabwean Independence Day, as well as Heroes' Day (and in 1998 Unity Day to celebrate the 1987 signing of the Unity Accord). The mass celebration of these public holidays, in Rufaro Stadium or the newer National Stadium, became controversial and increasingly unpopular with the younger generation. Welshman Ncube dates the decline in turnout to such events from 1988, and suspects that the Unity Accord made these celebrations less politically salient.[60] Increasingly, workers travelled to their rural homes, or remained in the high-density areas, instead of turning out for the formal celebratory speeches.

Heroes' Acre monuments were designated at the national, provincial and district level, as places to commemorate the dead of the liberation war. The National Heroes' Acre in Harare is an imposing monument built by North Koreans. Despite its nationalist credentials it is designed to honour the few, not the many—as only selected 'national' heroes are buried there. It is also—for 'security reasons'—not accessible without a special permit issued by the Ministry of Information, and one is escorted around the premises by military personnel. This makes it a formal site, more often visited by tourists than by Zimbabweans from the surrounding townships, except during state funerals.

More controversial have been the politics of choosing heroes, determining who should be buried in the National Heroes' Acre. This, in Norma Kriger's words, 'exposed the gap between the political rhetoric of equity, participation, and unity on the one hand, and the realities of an enormous disparity between … leaders and masses' on the other.[61] Politicized decision-making came into question as early as 1982, during the construction of the National Heroes' Acre, when ZAPU MPs asked for clarification in parliament of the criteria for selection.[62] In practice, heroes have been chosen by the ZANU(PF) politburo, not by the nation or its parliament.[63] Provincial and District Heroes' Acres are under-resourced, and often little more than dusty burial sites. Werbner contrasts the top-down hierarchical establishment of national, provincial and district heroes' acres with 'popular counter memorialism' in Matabeleland. Ex-soldiers of ZIPRA (ZAPU's armed wing) erected shrines to fallen comrades in unofficial sites in rural areas, 'sacralizing their own traces of national sacrifice on the landscape of Zimbabwe … [denying] the regime the legitimacy of unquestioned national symbolism'.[64]

Attempts to nationalize museums and monuments were also less than successful, falling into conflicts over whether archaeology should serve local interests, the interests of the wider nation, or be aimed at revenue-creating international tourism.[65] While nationalist historians and politicians attempted to claim the Great Zimbabwe ruins as a secular landmark—especially potent as the derivation of the new name of the state and the source of symbolic imagery—local chiefs and spirit mediums continue to contest their authority.[66] Similarly, at the prototype 'Culture House' in Murehwa, which was intended to include local people in the preservation of local culture, conflict arose between the intentions of the policy-makers, the local community and a Christian administrator who banned the practices of spirit mediums and traditional healers.[67] Although many Zimbabweans have a general knowledge of and pride in their heritage, museum policies were less than inclusive and remained predominantly oriented towards the tourist trade.

Nation-building was thus disjointed and often superficial, but for the most part it was not discordant, with the important exception of those excluded from the increasingly 'Shona' and 'ZANU' state. By contrast, 'Development' proved a less problematic motivating force for government ideology—encapsulating all that had been denied by the Rhodesian regime. In this, Zimbabwe was fervently encouraged by a wide range of donors, aid agencies and international supporters. At the same time, however, people were able to measure the changes in their day-to-day lives and assess for themselves how well the new regime was meeting their expectations. In her useful discussion of how developmentalism sustains authoritarian rule through legitimization and societal demobilization, Crystal suggests that developmentalism is an ideology of 'indefinitely deferred gratification' against which states cannot easily be held accountable.[68] But the Zimbabwean state's emphasis on its achievements vis-à-vis the Rhodesian state did enable comparison. Development therefore needs to be understood as both a material good and a rhetorical form, an ideal with which to motivate, but also be a material gauge against which the government's record was judged.

Aimed primarily, but by no means exclusively, at the rural population, the government implemented a policy of 'national development' focusing on reconstruction after the war years and the deracialization of service provision.[69] In particular, emphasis was put on deracializing education and health service provision, implementing a minimum wage and extending agricultural buying points in former tribal trustlands. Between 1979 and 1989, the numbers of students in primary and secondary education expanded by 332 per cent.[70] Better access to health clinics and the deracialization of hospitals also lowered infant mortality rates. Child mortality in 1980 had been at 100–150 per 1,000 births, but by 1989 had fallen to 46 per 1,000. Expanded immunization covered 80 per cent of the population and decreased the incidences of communicable diseases.[71] Although the greatest increase in spending on healthcare occurred between 1980 and 1982, expenditure levels were maintained throughout the 1980s.[72]

Questions have been raised about the neutrality of the 'developmental' state both in terms of regional equity and in terms of social groups. Certain areas of the country—namely Matabeleland, the Zambezi valley and Chipinge—are generally thought to have received less in the way of post-independence reconstruction and improved services. Bulawayo, the centre of industry in Rhodesia, declined in prominence vis-à-vis Harare. Matabeleland and Chipinge consistently elected opposition MPs through the 1980s, while the Zambezi valley is the home of the minority Tonga ethnic group. At the same time, other regions—notably including Mugabe's home area of Zvimba—began to be seen as receiving excess largesse. Nonetheless, data collected in the late 1990s does not entirely reflect these perceptions, revealing widespread poverty in both the apparently wealthier commercial farming areas of Mashonaland and the peripheral districts in Manicaland and Matabeleland.[73]

The perception that '*chefs*' were benefiting at the expense of the '*povo*' began to circulate by the mid-1980s. The first significant post-independence scandal involved the falsification of claims made by transport firms contracted to distribute drought relief. Along with contractors and civil servants, a cabinet minister, Kumbirai Kangai, was implicated in this scandal, but neither convicted nor forced to resign.[74]

In the 1980s, the government did invest seriously in social welfare and agricultural sectors and reached some of its developmental goals, especially in the rural areas. Rural agricultural services were also extended into communal farming areas, providing small farmers with access to agricultural extension workers, marketing depots and inputs. High producer prices also contributed to a much-lauded agricultural boom in both food and export crop production.[75]

But rural development was not a simple matter of service provision, or even resource extraction. The state's 'high modernist' approach[76] carried with it a set of practices, policies and assumptions about the ordering of rural lives and livelihoods. In the years after independence, small groups of rural Zimbabweans settled themselves on commercial farms abandoned during the war or at the instantiation of majority rule, and began to farm. While some were grudgingly allowed to stay on the land they had occupied and others were incorporated into resettlement schemes, still others were forcefully removed.[77] As is discussed below, resettlement was designed to create modern farming zones and life-styles, rather than replicating the apparently 'unplanned' communal areas. Meanwhile, other policies continued from the colonial era shaped daily life in communal areas: pressure to build villages with houses in straight lines, to conform to land-use restrictions on cropping, grazing and tree-planting, and to adopt the use of 'improved' grains.[78] Premised on perceived 'backwardness' on the part of the peasants, these policies elevated technology, or technocracy, above consultation, and generated authoritarian tendencies in the quest for development.[79]

Land resettlement was always key to overall developmental goals, but it became a prime example of how institutional, ideological and social constraints prevented a radical redistribution of wealth and power, while reinforcing state dominance in production and livelihood. Land reform in Zimbabwe was not designed to provide restitution to those who had lost land, nor was it redistributive. It followed a particular developmental logic—of ensuring productivity for domestic and foreign markets, rather than poverty alleviation. For the most part, it was not the land-poor masses who were prioritized for resettlement, but skilled farmers with expertise in modern farming techniques. The one exception to this was in the cooperative farming schemes, the members of which tended to be ex-combatants who had little experience in farming or management. Thus, in the early 1980s 52,000 families were resettled on about a quarter of what had been commercial-sector land (much of it land which had been abandoned during the war). The scheme stalled after this, constrained by the relative unavailability of land on the market and high land prices, as well as pressure from donors and the World Bank after 1983 to reduce expenditure.[80]

Assessments of the resettlement programme have by no means all been negative. Kinsey's research suggests that resettlement schemes did meet the goals of decreasing poverty and increasing social welfare.[81] An ODA assessment of the household resettlement schemes in 1988 was broadly positive, but the cooperative schemes were unpopular and unsuccessful.[82] By the late 1980s, the resettlement programme was becoming tainted as it gradually became known that '*chefs*', including cabinet ministers, had acquired commercial farms, while population pressure in communal areas continued to grow.[83] Among those who were resettled, insufficient technical support was provided. Bureaucratic control also made the schemes less than popular with families, as farmers were not given security of tenure, their access to land in communal areas was removed, and the head of household was not allowed to pursue wage labour, but had to farm full-time: 'settlers were expected to sever all social and cultural ties with their past lives'.[84] The government's over-ambitious target of 162,000 households probably contributed to the perception that land reform was a failure, even while agricultural policies more broadly were seen as successful in boosting food and export crop output.[85] Land reform thus reinforced the state presence in rural areas, without accomplishing either symbolic restitution, or alleviating overcrowding in communal lands.

Societal demobilization: limiting pluralism in the interests of development

While the nation-building and development schemes described above took place, the regime was also conducting campaigns against those groups which might potentially comprise an opposition, often using the legislative and administrative tools of the Rhodesian state.[86] The rhetoric of unity was the theme which drove this demobilization. Unity, meaning unity with the government, was demanded of apparently non-political social groupings such as schools, churches, businessmen, unions and the sexes in a series of ministerial speeches in the early 1980s. Secondary school teachers were adumbrated to 'create unity between their students regardless of colour' by the Minister of Education.[87] The Minister of Community Development and Women's Affairs urged 'unity of sexes for progress'.[88] A breakthrough was heralded in the 'battle for unity of all businessmen'.[89] Workers and their unions were told repeatedly to 'unite or be disowned'.[90] At the same time, leaders within these groups themselves claimed legitimacy on the basis of unity. The Zimbabwe Congress of Trade Unions (ZCTU) claimed that 'unity among rival unions in each industry' was its main task.[91] A prominent commercial farmer said in a newspaper report entitled 'unity vital': 'We cannot stand apart as a separate community. If there is no future for the country as a whole, there is no future for us. If we are to prosper, we must do it alongside other Zimbabweans.'[92] It is this ethos which permeated the regime's engagement with its erstwhile opponents, as much as with its supporters. As we shall see below, the regime set out to ensure that all these groups—organized and unorganized—cooperated within the state's framework of developmentalism.

Demobilizing soldiers

The first major challenge for the new state was the integration of the three fighting forces into the new Zimbabwe National Army (ZNA) and the reintegration of demobilized ex-combatants back into society. As mentioned in the earlier discussion of the Gukurahundi, the integration of ex-ZIPRA forces rapidly became politicized and broke down into violence that lasted until the government's amnesty in 1987.

Ex-combatants who did demobilize and sought training or the means to invest in farming also faced steep hurdles. Demobilization payments were often exhausted in supporting re-housing and education for family members.[93] NGOs like the Zimbabwe Project, Danhiko and the Mafela Trust emerged to work specifically with ex-combatants in supporting producer cooperatives and training. Although formal data are lacking, oral reports seem to indicate that most ex-combatants gained little to recompense their sacrifices post-independence. Many, indeed, felt rejected or abandoned by both their party leadership and by society in general.[94] Norma Kriger's study of war veterans argues that they consistently made claims for 'preferential access to state resources' based on their 'allegedly superior contribution to the liberation struggle'.[95] They wanted not only 'symbolic recognition' but also 'commensurate material benefits' which were not forthcoming until much later.[96]

Although the party used veterans in 'labour committees' to negotiate with private sector employers, this practice diminished after the state gained control of labour relations through the creation of the ZCTU. Kriger suggests that after the early 1980s veterans became less useful to the state;[97] we might also read this as a realization by the state that a mobilized group of ex-combatants would prove difficult to control. Only after the signing of the Unity Accord at the end of 1987 were veterans finally permitted to create the Zimbabwe National

49

Liberation War Veterans Association (ZNLWVA), firmly under the control of the party and the patronage of the president.[98]

NGOs: reoriented

Independent NGOs which had existed before independence were allowed to continue their activities, but came under intense scrutiny to ensure that they adhered to the new political agenda. For the most part, previously welfarist or political organizations turned to development, following the government's lead in reconstruction and deracialization. In general, local and international NGOs were accepted contributors to the development process, in contrast to countries which had become independent earlier when state-led development was *de rigueur*, such as Tanzania or Malawi, or Eritrea ten years later. In keeping with the government's socialist ethos, cooperatives were prominent on the government's agenda, but the government made it clear that as long as NGOs complemented the government's development efforts, they would be left alone.

An early Minister of Social Welfare advocated: 'NGOs must keep in step with government. ... It's completely counter-productive to contradict government thinking.'[99] Reflecting on this period, former President Banana noted: 'many NGOs ... accepted our prescriptions [of socialism]—should I say, joined us ... we became partners in development.'[100] In general, groups which had been active during the liberation war found themselves suddenly working not against the government but with it. This brought certain adjustments. Because many organizations now had links with the state, Paul Themba Nyathi—who had supported ZAPU in exile—said, 'we laid down our advocacy'.[101] As Raftopoulos has noted, 'their accommodating role stemmed from a perspective of shared goals and a belief in having emerged from a common tradition of struggle'.[102] This relationship was more complicated for those groups which did not clearly have a liberation war pedigree, and who came under internal and external pressure to prove their loyalty to the new regime's developmentalist agenda.

We can see this clearly in the etiology of the organization which became NANGO—Zimbabwe's NGO umbrella. The Southern Rhodesian National Council of Social Services (NCSS), at that time predominantly white-run, renamed itself Voluntary Organisations in Community Enterprise (VOICE) in 1981, asked the new president to be its patron and, in keeping with the new rhetoric, proposed to move from supporting welfare projects towards self-help and development.[103] At the same time, they appointed Zebediah Gamanya, a minor nationalist politician and ex-combatant, as National Director.[104]

Organizations which did not make such a public effort to reorient themselves in line with the state's agenda were more likely to encounter difficulties. One such NGO was the Family Planning Association of Rhodesia. Family planning had been a sensitive point during the liberation war, with ZANU directing both rhetoric and violence against the family planning infrastructure, shutting down its operation in most rural areas. Upon coming to power, ZANU first banned Depo-Provera, the most common contraceptive under the Rhodesians, and then following a 'war of words' which saw the resignation of the Family Planning Association's white senior staff, turned the association into an official government agency, overseen by the Department of Health.[105]

The Self-Help Development (SHD) NGO, founded in 1963 by a white Catholic missionary and two white laymen, faced similar challenges. The group supported the establishment of savings clubs among small-scale farmers. By the time of independence, there were approximately 200 clubs with 4,000 members, organized under the name Savings Development Movement (SDM). Soon after independence, the movement was targeted by the Department of Cooperatives, which threatened to absorb the movement into the government system and seize their assets because they were running cooperatives outside its remit.[106] Michael Bratton's nuanced study suggests that it was the very success of the organization that prompted this intervention.[107] The founding members argued that they had not been aware of the risks associated with calling the clubs co-ops. The ministry accused the treasurer, Peter Arnold, of financial mismanagement, an allegation that was not substantiated by auditors' reports. Arnold took the ministry to court, and won his court action.[108] However, faced with the forced appropriation of their buildings and organization, they followed government advice and removed the (white) founding members and replaced them with black members 'to cool it down' and changed its name 'as a way of trying to escape from this problem'.[109] By 1995, the movement had an MP on its board of directors and the relations with the government were considered much improved, as the organization worked extensively with Agritex and the Department of Cooperatives. Raftopoulos and Lacoste further note that this good relationship developed after the 1987 Unity Accord, and emphasize that conflict between a ZAPU supporter on the original board and the government contributed to the tension during the Matabeleland Conflict.[110]

As this suggests, while NGOs working in areas like Mashonaland and Manicaland found it easy to deracialize their staff, reinvent themselves as development organizations and embrace the new agenda with enthusiasm, this was not so easy for groups working in Matabeleland. In the early 1980s, the Catholic Commission for Justice and Peace (CCJP) began receiving reports from church members and priests on the grounds of human rights abuses against civilians being perpetrated by the security forces. The CCJP's attempts to document and publicize the abuses were rebuffed and denied by the state.[111] The CCJP Director, Nick Ndebele, and the Chairman, Mike Auret, were arrested in 1986, although they were eventually freed through the direct intervention of Prime Minister Mugabe.[112] The CCJP's reputation helped guarantee their release, but it led to an immediate cooling of the formerly close relationship between the Catholic Church and the governing party.[113]

Similarly, the Matabeleland branch of Christian Care experienced friction with the government during the period of unrest in Matabeleland, because government officials suspected that if NGOs were not being targeted by ZAPU 'dissidents', then they must be collaborators. Nevertheless, Christian Care, among others, reckoned it benefited from the linkages with the government during the liberation war: 'when in trouble [the government] will call upon us to assist them'.[114] Strikingly, the Organization of Rural Associations for Progress (ORAP) described itself as having answered '... the open but sincere invitation to all those who wanted Zimbabwe to succeed to come forwards and collaborate with the Government in its development efforts',[115] but like other NGOs, they found that curfews and banning of meetings made it difficult to carry out programmes. Because ORAP worked only in Matabeleland and the Ndebele-speaking areas of the Midlands, it was perceived as being a tribal organization.[116] Yet after the 1987 Unity Accord, ORAP was 'rehabilitated': Sithembiso

Nyoni, the founder and director of ORAP, was elected to parliament in 1990 as a ZANU(PF) MP and later became a junior minister, although disagreement remained within the organization about their proximity to the ruling party.[117]

The Zimbabwe Project (ZimPro) had been formed in the UK in 1978 by exiles and deportees from Smith's Rhodesia, to raise awareness of and raise money in support of refugees in camps. In 1981, ZimPro relocated to Zimbabwe and started working with ex-combatants: 'Zimbabwe Project Trust was transformed from a channel for emergency humanitarian aid to a service and development agency that complemented the government's efforts for growth and development.'[118] The director was Judith Todd (daughter of the former liberal Prime Minister Garfield Todd), who had supported the liberation struggle for many years. As the decade progressed, ZimPro widened its client base and worked with Community Based Organizations (CBOs) from all backgrounds, reflecting that the ex-combatants themselves did not exist apart from the rest of society: 'over the years the role of the organization was redefined, sometimes not very consciously, by developments within Zimbabwe'.[119] Like the Savings Development Movement, the Zimbabwe Project also endured opposition because of its leadership's ties to ZAPU and its work with ex-combatants, but 'after a lot of advocacy work and lobbying, it ... improved'.[120]

Although, as this suggests, NGOs with links to opposition parties were required to 'prove' their loyalty, the 1980s were relatively free of conflict between NGOs and the state. The examples given above reflect the experiences of only a handful of the hundreds of NGOs working in the field of development, which, for the most part, worked with ministries and local government, as well as with donors and international organizations. During this period, even externally funded NGOs were firmly incorporated within the ZANU(PF) regime, working through and with the party and state officials to accomplish their goals. NGOs were vulnerable to co-option because of their roots in the liberation war and their commitment to the government's agenda of development. As I have argued elsewhere at more length, material and organizational factors also reinforced NGOs' inclination to work cooperatively within the state's framework.[121]

Rural demobilization

Given the legacies of the liberation war, the peasant population might have been expected to be a militant, mobilized force, influencing government agendas in the post-independence years. Instead, they were reduced to apparently passive supporters of ZANU(PF). Peasant farmers benefited as their production of marketable crops improved, from policies that provided access to credit, marketing boards and extension services. Generally high producer prices benefited those with a marketable surplus and access to buyers.

Village committees, which were established in semi-liberated areas before the war and in others afterwards, are often portrayed as being systems of participatory local democracy with the potential both to liberate the peasants from the 'traditional' rule of chiefs and headmen and to provide local governance for the nation.[122] However, the rhetoric of decentralization and participation did not, in practice, enable peasant priorities to be achieved. Maxwell and Alexander both document peasants initially confronting the new state and demanding resources, but gradually recognizing the intransigence of the bureaucracy.[123] Kriger suggests that the village committees permitted a 'conservative' revolution of elders who recouped power temporarily lost to guerrillas and the young (*mujibas* and *chimbwidos*) during the war.[124]

Rural government reforms may have been intended to empower rural residents and provide for democratic participation in decision-making. Rural local government reforms were brought in through prime ministerial directives in 1984 and 1985, which created District Councils in former communal areas, in turn subdivided into Village Development Committees (VIDCOs) and Ward Development Committees (WADCOs). Helmsing argues that District Councils were 'the only fully democratic local government structures'.[125] In practice, however, these forums became channels to implement directives from above and inform lower-level officials of policy decisions. These local institutions had neither the resources nor the expertise to develop policy.[126] And as Makumbe discovered a decade or so later, this under-resourcing led to disenchantment and disillusionment amongst those intended to participate in the process.[127] Although party membership was required for participation in such institutions, the party itself 'had been "demobilized"'.[128] These reforms also contributed to the sidelining of traditional authorities. Between 1981 and 1984, chiefs lost their legal authority to allocate land in communal areas, to adjudicate in disputes, and to provide representation in government, although their salaries were maintained.[129] In practice, however, traditional authorities retained many of their roles, because VIDCOS were 'widely viewed by rural communities as an illegitimate structure with no credibility, nor any real power and resources to implement its role'.[130] The state's one attempt at radical restructuring was a failure, and it failed because of the tension between the 'demobilized' form of governance and the need for mobilized cadres on the ground, if transformation was to be successful.

Despite their apparent 'modernizing' approach, the local government reforms of 1984 and 1985 maintained separate modes of administration for the communal areas and commercial farm areas, and so perpetuated a dual system of governance. In 1988, the Rural District Council Act was promulgated, with a proposed aim of unifying the predominantly black District Councils and the predominantly white Rural Councils. However, even under these reforms, finally implemented in 1993, farm-workers and mine-workers remained disenfranchised. These reforms maintained divisions at the ward level, between communal, commercial, urban and resettlement wards. In communal and resettlement wards, all adult residents were entitled to vote. In urban and commercial wards, only rent-paying residents or owners of immovable property were entitled to participate.[131] This meant that farm-workers did not participate in local elections until 1998.[132] In theory, farm-workers might have been represented through appointed 'special interest councillors', but this does not appear to have happened on any wide scale.[133]

As this suggests, despite farm-workers making up an estimated 10–20 per cent of the population, they were un-integrated into the new political dispensation. Zimbabwe's farm-workers are descended from migrant labourers from Malawi and Mozambique who emigrated under the aegis of state-sponsored recruitment in the 1940s and 1950s.[134] In addition to their 'foreign' origins, farm-workers had, on the whole, not been active supporters of the nationalist movement, being 'caught between two sides' especially during the war years. They might therefore have been suspect, but instead the ZANU distributed what were thought to be citizenship cards and encouraged them to vote in national elections. ZANU also established local committees among farm-workers, but those whom Blair Rutherford interviewed said that this trailed off after the 1985 election.[135] Farm-workers and peasants then, despite forming the rural backbone of the economy and the party, had little influence over local or national policy-making. Instead, they became recipients of top-down developmental approaches, mediated through overlapping state and party structures.

Urban demobilization

Urban residents of Zimbabwe, less mobilized during the 1960s and 1970s, were something of an 'unknown' quantity for the new leaders of the state, who suspected urbanites of not being wholehearted supporters of the struggle. Urban areas, especially the downtown economic and political cores, were to a certain extent visible markers of deracialization and the new political order. But these urban areas, and the urban lived experience, changed remarkably little in the years immediately after independence, as the post-independence order sought to maintain modern, orderly spaces.

In cities like Harare, former 'white' suburbs were renamed 'low-density neighbourhoods' and middle-class black, Asian and coloured families moved into them—a process that had actually begun in the late 1970s, and even earlier in Bulawayo.[136] Urban high-density neighbourhoods expanded, but slowly. Few new suburbs were developed. Harare's urban housing backlog, 56,000 units in 1981, had grown to 64,000 in 1982. It appears that in Harare housing production *decreased* in the post-independence period.[137] Bulawayo's waiting list for housing was 4,054 in 1980, but had grown to 13,779 in 1982.[138] Gweru's growth rate of 4.9 per cent between 1982 and 1990 resulted in a municipal housing waiting list of 14,000 households at the end of the decade.[139] Although government plans in the early 1980s proposed to build 115,000 units across the country, by 1985 only 13,500 were complete.[140] Housing developments instead took the form of aided self-help, in which serviced sites were made available and owners expected to build to particular standards, with housing plans approved by the municipality.[141] But the costs of building materials and the high standards expected were beyond the resources of the poor households intended to benefit from these schemes.[142] This meant that poor households were increasingly unable to house themselves, and resorted to 'lodging' in crowded conditions.

Squatter areas which had been tacitly tolerated in the dying years of the Rhodesian regime were 'cleaned up'—processes which showed little respect for their desperate inhabitants. Those who could not afford to live properly in urban areas were expected to return to 'backward' rural spaces. Potts and Mutambirwa report that in 1984 there were eight squatter settlements in Harare, but that forty-two others had been 'cleared'.[143] Chirambahuyo, a community near Chitungwiza established by squatters relocated in the late 1970s, was demolished soon after independence. Patel reports that although they were offered ultra-low-cost houses in Chitungwiza, most could not afford them. Some resettled themselves in another squatter area, which was itself demolished in 1982. She quotes the Minister of Housing's 'disappointment' that so few of the residents wanted to return to rural areas.[144] Similar attempts were made to return people living at the Mbare Msika 'transit camp' to their rural homes, but most were eventually rehoused in former hostels in Mbare, while others were moved 'further away from the road, out of sight'.[145] In 1989, homeless people sleeping outside Harare's railway station were evicted and many of their belongings destroyed. They relocated to a piece of land in Eastlea, outside the city centre. By 1990, when that 'village' was destroyed, there were between eighty and 150 adults.[146]

The one exception to this policy in Harare was Epworth, originally mission-owned land, for which an upgrading programme was designed.[147] Other forms of informal housing emerged instead. In 1981, it had already been noted that 'tenants' or 'lodgers' in privately-owned homes and those rented from the council had 'increased rapidly' since independence.[148] Many of these lodgers lived in rooms or shacks (*zvihwendi*) added as extensions to existing houses, some with planning permission, others without. In 1987, 9,000 illegal structures were reported within Harare's high-density suburbs.[149] In 1991, Potts and Mutambirwa suggested that these were 'often' targeted for demolition;[150] but more recently, Potts notes that 'full-scale demolition … did not proceed'.[151] Epworth was very much an exception rather than the rule.

Urban agriculture on public land was perceived as the 'ruralization' of the urban areas; colonial era bans on the practice were kept on the books. Surveys in the 1980s tell us that about 10 per cent of urban households cultivated land outside their own gardens, although this is likely to be an under-estimate.[152] In the early 1980s, urban councils turned 'a blind eye' to the practice, but this changed under influence from the central state.[153] In 1982, Maurice Nyagumbo, Minister of Mines and ZANU(PF) national secretary, told party members:

> If people want to go into large scale farming, they must apply to Government for proper resettlement... Zimbabweans must know that urban areas and farming areas are different. They must not do as they please. They must follow regulations and adhere to them. City Councils must act now and stop this.[154]

From 1985 onwards, Harare city council officials, accompanied by the police, slashed maize and vegetables growing on council land. Although some areas were demarcated for cultivation and were allocated to cooperatives, many crops were slashed, even in areas where cultivation had been permitted pre-independence, leading to confrontation between residents and council officials during periods of economic hardship and drought.[155] Colonial assumptions that residential areas were not appropriate sites for small industry—car repairs, welding and carpentry—were also maintained through 'an impressive array of legal stipulations that were meant to control the conversion of homes into workplaces'.[156]

Attempts were also made to keep the central business districts 'modern' and 'clean'. In a remarkable continuity with the colonial discourses, only those with 'legitimate' (i.e. formal) business were supposed to be found in the city. 'Authorized' markets, opened in the late 1970s, were the only places where vegetables could be sold;[157] informal markets, hawkers and the informal selling of food were banned.[158] Pirate taxis, which carried multiple passengers from townships into town, were licensed at the end of 1982, providing a level of regulation and control over a burgeoning informal sector. This was justified as an 'emergency' response to a temporary public transportation crisis, and indeed the taxis themselves were called 'Emergency Taxis', or more commonly ETs.[159]

As mentioned above, squatters were targeted for removal, often over-ambitiously.[160] In 1983's infamous 'Operation Clean-up', police arrested over 6,000 women in urban areas on the pretext of removing prostitutes from the streets. The women arrested included the elderly, schoolgirls and women with babies, who were arrested while they waited for buses or walked home from work; some were taken out of theatres and their own homes. In Gweru and Harare, they were taken first to prisons; in Mutare, to a football stadium; and then from all over the country, they were taken to the Zambezi Valley, where some were kept for weeks. On release, they were told to go to their rural homes.[161] A similar operation took place in 1986, dumping women in the Zambezi Valley at Mushumbi Pools—'cleaning up' the city in preparation for the Non-Aligned Summit.[162]

Urban residents were as much subject to technocratic, top-down developmentalism, it seems, as their rural siblings. And indeed, while in rural areas the implementation of governmental directives was only ever partial, in the face of resistance and accommodation, in urban areas the availability of riot police and the visibility of informal practices on the landscape made them more vulnerable to authoritarian and intolerant state practices.

Intellectuals and students

Less vulnerable than most urban residents, the intelligentsia and students were also seen as potentially disloyal, as many were suspected of having supported Muzorewa's UANC.[163] However, the state became a prime facilitator of upward mobility, with 'academics and intellectuals who otherwise might be leading social critics ... being appointed as ambassadors and directors of parastatals'.[164] Many others were absorbed into the civil service. Such a relationship did not engender 'fully critical and engaging debates surrounding the emerging character of the state and ruling party'.[165]

In 1982, the Zimbabwe Institute for Development Studies (ZIDS) was launched by Ibbo Mandaza, then the Deputy Secretary in the Ministry of Manpower, Planning and Development, to provide training and education for civil servants. The Institute was designed to 'unite all the ministries to serve not only the short-term goals of the government but also the long-term ambitions of the people'.[166] At its inauguration, the board of directors included nine cabinet ministers. An observer reporting for the *Guardian* newspaper emphasized that the institute had been planned during the liberation war and that:

> It is not a part of the University of Zimbabwe but it is an integral part of the government... The deliberate decision not to bring ZIDS within the framework of the university had its roots in the regime's disenchantment with academia as ... less than enthusiastic about national liberation.[167]

Writing from within ZIDS six years later, Raftopoulos suggests that the state's ambivalence towards researchers led the latter to be 'hesitant and at times even subservient. ... Uncomfortable information is not always conducive to job security, promotion prospect, and organizational consensus.'[168] The ambiguous role of intellectuals in the post-colonial state was also reflected in the writing of intellectuals outside the formal remit of the state. The relationship was burdened by the history of conflicts between the younger intellectuals and 'old guard nationalists' during the liberation war. Others were seen as having only been peripherally involved in the war, which could be equally damning.[169] Reflecting back on this period some decades later, President Mugabe said: 'It was not easy to get black intellectuals to swap their cosy professions for the rough life of struggle. We had many of them, particularly lawyers, for whom education and training had meant keeping within the straitjacket of the oppressive and racist Rhodesian political system.'[170] In general, however, post-colonial researchers tended to support the government's socialist inclination, and were relatively uncritical. As David Moore noted in a review of significant post-independence political studies, 'the major lack in this "political economy" is a study of politics'.[171]

Despite this, in the mid-1980s, with the creation of an active African Association of Political Science (AAPS) Zimbabwe chapter and the development of the Southern African Political and Economic Series (SAPES) Trust 'think tank', public debates began to be pursued within a generally left-leaning academic sphere. Mandaza and others were active in these circles, which became significant fora for the one-party state debate at the end of the 1980s, when intellectuals, journalists and activists came together in a relatively united front to combat the ruling party's agenda. Nevertheless, in 1990, Morgan Tsvangirai criticized 'so-called progressive intellectuals who have the habit of lecturing workers and peasants through journals published from their mansions in low density suburbs', suggesting that this alliance remained an uneasy one.[172]

In the 1980s, youths were 'demobilized' and left mainly to their own devices, except when the ZANU(PF) Youth League was called upon to mobilize votes during elections. Despite repeated claims that a national service programme would be implemented to provide a framework for continued youth mobilization, no such scheme was implemented until after the 2000 elections. Higher education students, however, as incipient members of the intelligentsia and bureaucracy, were the subjects of rather more attention from the state. After independence, the renamed University of Zimbabwe was 'reoriented' and 'harnessed to the national development objectives of the newly elected government'.[173] Angela Cheater points out that when the university was originally established, its founders sought a Royal Charter to protect the institution, in the context of colonial racism, from political control: 'after independence … however, many people, (including some within the university) believed that the threat of government intervention had passed'.[174] The 1982 University of Zimbabwe Act increased government control, in ways unforeseen at the time. In particular, the state president, then a ceremonial officer, was made chancellor of the university and given extensive powers. The shift from a ceremonial to an executive presidency in 1987 gave this action a new significance.

A close relationship also existed between students and the state/ ruling party nexus in the early 1980s. Although some students did not want to be associated with the party Youth Brigade, which they perceived as uneducated, the Students' Representative Council (SRC) leadership was linked into ZANU(PF) networks: until 1986, the candidates for SRC president were formally vetted by the party structures on campus. Like their lecturers, students also saw the public service as their best career option, and most graduates were assured jobs: 'the SRC afforded the opportunity to establish "radical credentials" which could secure a job in government'.[175] In 1981, students turned out in support of the government's fight against dissidents: '… the students shouted slogans against the leader of ZAPU, Dr Joshua Nkomo, and encouraged the government to embark on a national service programme "to prepare them to defend the country"'.[176] Although some students did become involved in the one-party state debates after the Unity Accord, for the most part their leadership was happily ensconced within ZANU(PF).

Workers and labour

Workers, on the other hand, despite their links to the nationalist parties of the 1950s, were rapidly identified as a problem for the post-independence state. Almost immediately after independence, workers initiated a series of small strikes—perhaps inspired by the experience of freedom and the existence of an apparently less authoritarian regime. In 1980–1 there were 150 strikes in all sectors in Zimbabwe and over 300,000 production days were lost.[177] Workers were castigated by the new regime for not having used strikes as political mechanisms against the Rhodesian era—and these new strikes were portrayed as illegitimate tools of a 'labour aristocracy' which refused to wait patiently with peasants and veterans for the fruits of liberation.[178] Workers who remained in the cities were thought not to have supported the nationalist movement which now formed the government. The affiliation of some union leaders to internal settlement parties further alienated them from the new government.

Unions were also deeply fragmented and very weak, as a result of Rhodesian legislation. In attempting to incorporate the labour movement more firmly within its sphere, ZANU took advantage of this weakness. They seized control of the fragmented trade unions, creating the Zimbabwe Congress of Trade Unions (ZCTU) and stacking it with ZANU-affiliated members and staff.[179] Accusations of supporting opposition parties were used to silence opponents: 'most of the problems of rivalry which the ZCTU is facing are caused by supporters of minority parties bent on introducing their politics of disunity into the ZCTU'.[180] Where more than one union existed within an industry, unions were pressurized to unite and then join the new ZCTU.[181]

The ZCTU and ZANU(PF) relationship was so close for much of the 1980s that they shared offices,[182] and through the introduction of the minimum wage policy, which reduced income disparity and mitigated worker militancy—and gave the ZCTU little negotiating power—the government turned the party into a supra-union and established the workers as a client group.[183]

Gradually between 1980 and 1985, the ZCTU began to distance itself somewhat from the party, criticizing government policies for being anti-worker. The Labour Relations Act of 1986, in particular, was condemned for giving the Minister of Labour 'draconian powers'.[184] By 1987, it was claimed that the ZCTU was functioning as a labour relations 'watchdog'.[185]

Churches

Like unions and NGOs, initial relations between the post-independence state and church denominations depended overwhelmingly on the stance which they had adopted during the liberation war.[186] With few exceptions, the church hierarchies moved quickly to link themselves to the state's developmentalist ambitions, in both discourse and practice.[187] Indeed, many of the churches and church organizations, with their origins in the struggle for independence, were only too keen to accommodate themselves with the state. At the same time, those churches implicated in support for the UANC internal settlement, such as the Methodists, were attempting to (re)gain favour with the government. The President, Revd Canaan Banana (a Methodist), and the Prime Minister, Robert Mugabe (a Catholic), strongly encouraged them to do so. In addresses made to the heads of denominations, the President and Prime Minister both called for unity between the churches and state, with the churches urged to cooperate in 'developing' the newly independent Zimbabwe.[188] The Catholic Church was widely reported to support the government's policies.[189] In a letter to the *Herald* written in her personal capacity, A. K. H. Weinrich, a sociologist and Catholic sister, appealed 'to all church leaders to give their full support to, and participate actively in, all the efforts made by the Government to raise the dignity of the human person'.[190] President Banana, in a much publicized press conference in 1982, said that while some churches had 'joined with the government in promoting unity in the nation, there were still a few who were asking for the resuscitation of the political past'.[191]

After this warning for churches not to 'continue associating with the enemy', the Roman Catholic, Anglican and Methodist churches all 'affirmed their support for the Government's policy of reconciliation'

UNDERSTANDING ZIMBABWE

and said that 'their churches stood firmly behind the Government's intentions to rebuild the country and pledged their continuing support for non-racialism'.[192]

The Catholic bishops, perhaps in response to these appeals for unity, reasserted control over the Catholic Commission for Justice and Peace (CCJP) in 1981, through constitutional changes that limited the commission's autonomy from the Bishops' Conference. In particular, the reforms required the CCJP to obtain the permission of two bishops for all public statements.[193] In addition, the bishops were opposed to the continuing directorship of John Stewart, the acting director. Stewart suggests that this was because he was potentially outspoken and not easy to control, but it may also have been because he was white.[194]

The churches' perceived antagonism to socialism was potentially an issue of contention. Prime Minister Mugabe explicitly exhorted the churches to 'help create socialism ... the Church should find no objection to socialist philosophy because Christian teaching could not be reconciled to the "avaricious" nature of capitalism'.[195] Similarly, the Minister of Lands said that 'the church should change its old role as a colonial, capitalist institution' and should instead 'help build a socialist Zimbabwe'.[196] Deputy Prime Minister Muzenda called on preachers to use the pulpit to 'counter the untruths, prejudices, crude stories and myths about Zimbabwean socialism'.[197] Although rhetoric during the liberation war had suggested that some churches were anti-socialist, after independence the Catholic Church rebuffed this notion. Roman Catholic Archbishop Chakaipa called for church organizations to 'promote the government's socialist policies'.[198] Anglican Bishop Hatendi, on the other hand, was more equivocal: 'we are not being asked to preach socialism, as the Government interprets it, from the pulpit. I am bitterly opposed to scientific socialism ... which is atheistic'.[199] However, elsewhere he indicated his support for a Christian Socialist Movement in Zimbabwe.[200]

The state took a particular interest in the Zimbabwe Council of Churches (ZCC), as the largest ecumenical grouping of churches. In November 1981, President Banana criticized the ZCC in the national press for taking a 'wait and see' attitude towards the government.[201] He claimed to have heard this from the World Council of Churches (WCC), which was withholding funding because of the 'unco-opera-

64

tive attitude of the Christian Council towards the Government's policy of reconciliation and reconstruction'.[202] The continuing involvement of Bishop Muzorewa with the ZCC, and the Ndau ethnicity of the General Secretary which associated him with Ndabaningi Sithole's ZANU Ndonga, apparently led the state to see the ZCC as a political irritant.[203] These developments led the ZCC to replace its General Secretary, in the hope of restoring relations with both the state and the WCC.[204]

The independent churches were castigated and sidelined for being 'traditional' and 'anti-development'. The Apostolic Faith and Jehovah's Witness communities, known for their reluctance to immunize children and accept other Western treatments, were portrayed as sites of disorder and disease, and forced to accept 'bio-medicine'.[205] Gradually, they too were targeted for integration into the developmental state.[206]

Probably the most significant post-independence division between church and state came as the state sent troops into Matabeleland, allegedly to quell 'dissident' activity instigated by ZAPU, which retained political strength in the area, and South Africa. As detailed above, the CCJP's cautious attempts to document and publicize the abuses being perpetrated by the security forces were rebuffed and denied by the state.[207] This incident captures well the ambiguous position of the churches—deriving some protection from the state, but unable, or unwilling, to challenge its moral authority for fear of weakening their position.

Media and politics

The media were seen as a key element in the nation-building project. The Minister of Information, Nathan Shamuyarira, stated that the government deplored all censorship, and emphasized various roles for the media, 'to be a channel of constructive information and dialogue between the Government and the people … [to] be a mirror of all burning issues in society … to be a vehicle for education … to provide wholesome entertainment … [and to] mobilise our people for the national effort to self-defence and self-reliance'.[208] But Richard Saunders's study of the media in the 1980s captures how the media moved from being a 'civic appendage of the ruling white fraction' into an equally dominated and controlled arm of ZANU.[209] Both the bureaucracy of the Ministry of Information and the media it controlled were repoliticized, as vacant posts were filled by party members and former 'bush-broadcasters'—veterans of the Voice of Zimbabwe which broadcast from Maputo during the liberation war.

The creation of the Mass Media Trust was intended to nationalize the media, which had previously been dominated by white Rhodesian and South African financial interests, 'in the interests of development and unity'.[210] But this masked party-political control over the print media, accomplished through behind-the-scenes ministerial contact with editors and publishers, and firings—or promotion—of editors who challenged government policy.[211] Foreign media representatives faced more explicit sanctions. In 1986, the *Times* (UK)'s correspondent Jan Raath was reportedly declared a prohibited immigrant and was expelled.[212] Peter Godwin, then with the *Sunday Times*, claims that he was warned of his impending detention after publishing reports of the Matabeleland atrocities in 1984.[213] These reports, primarily in British newspapers, were greeted by the Mugabe regime as 'orchestrated propaganda'.[214] The local print media carefully maintained the government line, of South African destabilization in Matabeleland, and made no mention of the government-led atrocities.

In addition to the state-controlled radio, TV and newspapers, however, local independent print media flourished in the 1980s. The *Financial Gazette*, a tabloid-sized business weekly, underwent substantial growth, as well as shifts in ownership and readership. At independence the *Financial Gazette* had a print run of 4,000 copies, while at the end of decade it had increased to 20,000. Readership shifted from an estimated 20 per cent black readership at independence to 80–85 per cent in 1990.[215] The *Financial Gazette* provided a key forum for the one-party state debate. In 1989, Geoff Nyarota, who had been removed from the editorship of the Bulawayo *Chronicle* for revealing the Willowgate scandal, was appointed editor.[216] When the state attempted to discredit the *Financial Gazette*, accusing it of maintaining 'Rhodesian' links, its publisher, Modus, was bought out by black businessmen.[217] The monthly magazines—*Moto*, *Parade*—and their more didactic partners—*SAPEM*, *Read On* and *Social Change*—also contributed to the deracializing of the media because they reached a primarily black readership, but only *Parade* could boast a wide circulation. Despite some diversity within the sector, the government-owned media retained their dominant position, controlling the airwaves and much of what was published in Zimbabwe.

Throughout these years, government control over the media enabled ZANU(PF) to create and then maintain its dominance within both local and national elections in the 1980s. This position was aided by legislation, state funding, violence and election rigging. Both major parties benefited from pre-independence legacies—ZAPU benefited from the continuity of older party structures in Matabeleland, while ZANU gained seats primarily within its former operational areas of Mashonaland.[218] But ZANU's control of the state and media enabled it to push its message throughout the country with little challenge. Christine Sylvester emphasizes the way in which the party continued to mouth socialist rhetoric in the 1985 election, while actual campaign speeches emphasized instead the dominance of the party:

> Less than 11% of the pro-ZANU(PF) comments … propagated Marxist myths of class empowerment. Instead, nearly 33% advocated that oligarchic power should be vested in ZANU(PF), because it is the only vehicle for achieving national unity, for rooting out colonialism, and for establishing a government which is not composed of personalist leaders …[219]

On the national level, ZANU(PF) consistently controlled parliament during the 1980s, but opposition parties were significant. At independence, in addition to the 20 seats reserved for whites which were all held by the Rhodesian Front, the UANC took 3 seats and ZAPU held 20, mainly in Matabeleland and the Midlands. In 1985, ZANU Ndonga took 1 seat, while ZAPU was reduced to 15; 20 seats were again reserved for white voters. The Conservative Alliance of Zimbabwe replaced the Rhodesian Front, and kept 15 seats, with 4 going to the Independent Zimbabwe Group, and 1 to an independent. While the transitional elections were alleged to have irregularities and intimidation from guerrillas and UANC auxiliaries,[220] they were generally thought to reflect the majority opinion. The 1985 elections revealed a more concerted adoption of state-led coercive mechanisms by the incumbent regime.

In addition to the endemic state violence in Matabeleland, the election period was marked by pre- and post-election violence. Although the actual polling days were relatively peaceful, the days before and after the election were not. In 1984 ZAPU and UANC offices in Kwekwe and Gweru were attacked and ransacked.[221] ZAPU was then banned from holding rallies in the Midlands and Mashonaland West.[222] Senior members of both ZANU and ZAPU died under mysterious circumstances, with the deaths and funerals often sparking further rioting and violence. Nkomo's attempts to hold rallies were repeatedly met by hordes of ZANU youths throwing stones, and sometimes bullets. In February 1985, five UANC supporters were reported to have been murdered in Hwange after addressing a rally in Bulawayo.[223] Violence erupted after the election as well, with ZANU supporters in urban areas harassing, beating up and destroying houses of hundreds of opposition party supporters.[224]

Abortive discussions on party unification had occurred throughout the 1980s, but as discussed above, in 1987 the Unity Accord incorporated ZAPU into ZANU to 'eliminate the thorniest source of opposition to [ZANU]'.[225] Following the Unity Accord, three former ZAPU MPs were brought back into the cabinet. Nkomo was appointed vice president in 1988, a position he held until his death in 1999.

Although local-level politics have been little studied, it is clear that they were at least as politicized, if not more so, than at the national level. In local elections after the war, low-level ZANU(PF) officials prevented non-members from being appointed to temporary district commissions and from contesting the first district elections. In Mutoko, the commission was forced to stop holding meetings because 'it had been appointed by a white district commissioner and it was not a monolithic ZANU(PF) commission', while in Wedza it was demanded that non-ZANU(PF) commissioners be removed.[226] In Chimanimani, new policies were introduced 'through the party structures'.[227] Current confusion about distinctions between party and government developed out of processes such as these in rural areas, where not only were the institutions of 'councils' discredited by their associations with the former Rhodesian regime, but also the incoming regime was indistinguishable from the party. This confusion could only have been exacerbated by the appointment of ex-combatants, especially those who were political commissars within ZANU as 'Local Government Promotion Officers',[228] thus permanently blurring the lines between party and state in rural areas.

Makumbe's focus group research suggests that, especially in rural areas, respondents were aware of the need to organize within the party, but also that even where they attempted to mobilize and identify needs, most decisions were taken without considering their input. As he argues, the 'winner' of local government reform has been 'the ruling ZANU/PF party, central government ... and selected or favoured regions in the country'.[229] At all levels of government, then, ZANU dominated decision-making and was able to use governmental structures to extend its purview and control. Nevertheless, we shall see in the following chapter that some of the most significant early challenges to the ZANU(PF) regime occurred in local councils.

Conclusion

This first decade of independent politics marks Zimbabwe out as a 'post-liberation' state of a particular kind. It is not like Rwanda, Ethiopia or Eritrea where armed soldiers literally marched into the capital and took control. Rather, Zimbabwe's transition, like that of South Africa and Namibia, was the product of a negotiated ceasefire and transition to majority rule. This has a number of implications. Firstly, the new regime does not have a clean slate. Not only do institutions remain with their histories and practices, which are powerful constraints in and of themselves. But the negotiated transition also demanded compromises and balancing of interests. To those who had demonized Mugabe and ZANU, the ease with which they seemed to adapt to this style of governance may have been surprising. But as we have seen in the previous chapter, inclusive coalitions were the norm and practice of nationalist politics, if only to prevent the emergence of rival power bases. And so we see coalitions expanding and widening to include new interest groups. At the same time, the very real threat of South African destabilization gave weight to the forcible exclusion of others, enabling the regime to draw a curtain over its excesses and violations. The regime ensured that no forces would emerge with either interest or capacity 'to set about reshaping the nation's arsenal of repressive powers and structures'.[230]

What is striking about this period is how easily the discourse of liberation was sublimated. The regime didn't disown the discourse, and it did not disappear entirely; but it was not the dominant discourse, nor did it infuse policy-making. For liberation to have remained as the guiding motif would have required a level of mobilization which the regime could not afford, outside Matabeleland. And it would have proven much more difficult to disarm ideologically the forces that had been arrayed against it—whether white Rhodesians, Asians, 'coloureds', those who had supported the internal settlement, or those who sought to create alternative power bases within ZANU. Instead, these groups were given scope to work 'with' the new regime, implicating them in its project, while repressive legislation and other institutions were maintained. Marked by enthusiasm for the new state to begin with, their fervour was increasingly damaged by state-led violence in Matabeleland and overshadowed by destabilization in Mozambique and the continuing threat of apartheid South Africa. At the same time, legalism—a paradoxical hallmark of Rhodesian state control—also came to typify the new regime. Demobilization as a technique for authoritarian rule proved a sleek, surprisingly efficient way of maintaining control.

The risk that continued mobilization might have given rise to debates about 'whose liberation', and the thrashing out of those difficult divides within and between the liberation movements was averted. Instead, the constraints of negotiated transition, coupled with the exigencies of the later stages of the Cold War, enabled the depoliticization of discourses. Development proved a welcome distraction from liberation.

4

THE POLITICS OF DURABILITY (1987–1997)

One thing ... that Zimbabweans will never lack is slogans.[1]

The Unity Accord signed in 1987 rather unexpectedly changed the dynamic of politics in Zimbabwe, providing something of a puzzle to political scientists. Despite having absorbed its main political rival through the Accord, the Mugabe regime experiences more rather than less contestation in light of damaging allegations of corruption and new forces of political opposition. Major policy changes were forced on the regime, obliging it to turn its back on both socialism and the one-party state. Gradually, economic weaknesses impeded the effectiveness of the mantra of 'unity, development and nationalism' that had hitherto been markedly successful in garnering support. Yet, the regime endures. While many accounts of this period depicted it as a period of political and economic liberalization, even speaking of democratization,[2] suggesting that the 1990s were a period of change, it is the Mugabe regime's durability, despite the deepening political and economic crisis as the decade wears on, that needs to be explained. Policies mimicking liberalization weaken societal groups and limit their influence in the public sphere, rather than contributing to democratization. These years set the stage for the emergence of Zimbabwe's first counter-hegemonic movement, the National Constitutional Assembly, and the first effective opposition party, the Movement for Democratic Change, but also explain much of their incipient weaknesses and vulnerabilities. We see how the 'limited pluralism' typical of negotiated transitions shapes the relationship between regime and society, constrains the articulation of counter-hegemonic aspirations, and limits the mobilization of alternative norms and practices of citizenship.

The chapter starts by examining how economic challenges led strategies and rhetorics of 'nation-building' to become more extreme and exclusive between 1987 and 1997, just as the franchise was extended to all urban residents, transforming the electoral dynamics. A more critical public perception of President Mugabe and of the party elites emerged as reportage of corruption scandals became commonplace. The increase in availability—and aggressiveness—of the independent media was significant, especially in urban areas, as structural adjustment and liberalization programmes were adopted, and economic weakness impeded the government's ability to distribute goods and services, diminishing politicians' claims to be 'bringers of development' and generating new challenges for citizens. The chapter then moves to focus on how state institutions generated new legislative controls even as the earlier mechanisms which co-opted individuals and organizations become less effective. Elections and the judiciary are explored in some detail, as they form key parts of this story and set the stage for contestation in the following years. The expansion of coercive mechanisms is also charted, through a new security apparatus and militarization of existing bodies. However, these responses are not fully orchestrated or pre-planned; often they appear *ad hoc* and reactive. The final section of the chapter explores how apparent 'liberalization' was used as a strategy of divide and rule to weaken and fragment societal groups such as trade unions, academics, students and NGOs. Focusing on elections, opposition parties and the changing reactions of unions, churches, students and NGOs, the chapter explores their tentative moves to build coalitions and lobby publicly. This process was notable for its ambiguity and uncertainty, as attempts to build good relations with the state continued to exist side by side with strengthening non-governmental initiatives and networking. We see that new discourses and debates emerged, but their proponents struggled to navigate and mobilize against the prevailing political consensus. Against many expectations, the regime endured, but faced increasing internal contradictions and external pressures.

Economic development and growing unrest

The years after 1987 were typified by heightened, although mostly peaceful, contestation between the regime and society, although this dynamic was itself contested inside both groups and did not follow a consistently upward pattern. A combination of economic and political factors contributed to the weakening of the regime's development agenda and apparent integrity, thus challenging the effectiveness of the nation-building rhetoric, and providing openings for alternative perspectives and critiques. The economic policies of the 1980s sparked the Willowgate corruption scandal, seriously denting the regime's reputation for probity, while in the 1990s attempts to reform the controlled economy of the 1980s led to further scandals, which were picked up on by the nascent opposition, and catalysed protests and strikes.

The 'socialist' economy of the 1980s had succeeded in bringing many social welfare benefits to Zimbabweans, and a growth rate of 4 per cent per year during 1986–90, but the economy was not without its internal weaknesses.[3] Shortages of foreign exchange, an overvalued currency, and concomitant shortages of paper, cement and passenger vehicles were experienced. Such burdens may have disproportionately affected the urban elite, but the impact of cement shortages, for instance, was felt both in rural areas where people were attempting to build dams and in the home construction industry in poor urban areas. The transportation crisis was particularly disruptive for urban workers, many of whom spent up to six hours a day commuting.[4] In response to these tensions and to external pressure from international financial institutions about debt levels, in 1990 ZANU(PF) reversed its public stand and the government implemented a structural adjustment programme known as ESAP (Economic Structural Adjustment Programme), modelled on similar liberalization and stabilization plans implemented elsewhere. This led to an increase in imported goods, while weakening local industrial producers, and to the removal of subsidies and price controls. ESAP was generally seen as starting with the 'liberalizing' budget announced in 1991, although in practice much economic policy before 1990 had already reflected fairly classical macro-economics, masked in a protectionist rhetoric.[5] The changes in Zimbabwe's development policy were not simply the result of external constraints on government expenditure; shifting domestic political constituencies and agendas also influenced these changes. Dashwood argues convincingly that not only were peasants and the working class increasingly marginalized in policy discourses, but 'progressive' voices within ZANU(PF) were subdued.[6] She attributes this to the changing configuration of class forces within ZANU(PF), which led to a changing set of priorities within government: 'The embourgeoisement of the ruling élite explains the failure to combine [market-based reforms] with measures that would protect the welfare of the poor.'[7] This does not mean that the government backtracked entirely from its developmentalist origins. Rural crises, such as droughts, were responded to with food aid, but Dashwood suggests that this approach represented an *ad hoc*, reactive response to crises, rather than a coherent welfarist strategy.[8] Economic policy was increasingly driven by the needs of the elite.

Throughout the 1990s, the development agenda, still adhered to rhetorically, was constrained by the implementation of ESAP, declining living conditions and the impact of AIDS. Adjustment redistributed some economic burdens, helping urban commuters through the deregulation of the transport sector which briefly improved availability of transport. However, increased fares soon came to dominate household budgets. Rising unemployment and increased costs of living affected interlinked urban and rural households.[9] Access to imported building materials eased shortages for large construction firms, but did little to help small contractors and self-builders on limited budgets.[10] De-industrialization caused by the opening up of import markets resulted in massive urban job losses, particularly for skilled workers, and reduced the manufacturing sector's contribution to the economy.[11]

The education and health systems, key aspects of the 1980s' developmentalism, suffered in the 1990s. Many of the earlier gains began to be negated. The implementation of structural adjustment led to declining performance in education and health indicators. In particular, the introduction of user fees in education and health led to lower take-up levels.[12] The breakdown of the rural infrastructure was particularly noted in shortages of nurses and doctors to run community hospitals and clinics. Educational facilities were equally under stress, with teacher shortages, as well as a shortage of schools and boarding facilities in rural areas.[13]

The health sector was further devastated by the AIDS pandemic. The Zimbabwe government had recognized the seriousness of the AIDS crisis early on, and was one of the first countries to screen donated blood in 1985. From 1986, the Ministry of Health had an AIDS advisory committee and initiated a major AIDS awareness campaign in 1987, which was extended into the 1990s.[14] However, HIV prevalence in women attending ante-natal clinics in Harare increased from 10 per cent in 1989 to 36 per cent in 1994. By 1999 an estimated 1.5 million Zimbabweans were believed to be infected, 1.4 million of whom were adults aged between 15 and 49 years, representing an estimated 25 per cent of the most economically active age cohort.[15] High infection rates among teachers, doctors and nurses further affected the provision of healthcare and education, while the prevalence of the disease among the general population overstrained the healthcare system. Life became increasingly difficult for most Zimbabweans, as average incomes declined and the cost of living increased, while families were struggling to deal with new burdens of care for the sick.

Claims to be both 'liberators' and bringers of 'development' were further threatened as evidence of large-scale corruption surfaced. The Willowgate scandal of the late 1980s implicated several senior ministers in the re-selling of cars and trucks assembled at the Willowvale plant, at much higher prices than they had paid. Ministers had been granted preferential access to vehicles, because of the shortage of internally assembled cars and limits on imports. This scandal led several ministers to resign, and one to commit suicide.[16] It also stimulated the first public protests by workers and students to criticize government policy. Scandals in the 1990s revolved around the allocation of tenders to ZANU-connected businesspeople, in particular President Mugabe's nephew, Leo Mugabe.[17] Cabinet overturned a tender board decision and awarded the contract for the building of a new Harare airport to the highest rather than lowest bidder.[18] A cabinet secretary also intervened during the introduction of cellphone networks, overturning another tender board decision, although the High Court later nullified the decision.[19]

Other scandals revealed looting of government funds. The so-called VIP housing scheme involved illegal—and massive—loans to senior government officials, from a fund designated to support low-income housing.[20] Senior government and party officials were similarly implicated in looting funds intended for the assistance of veterans who had been injured or disabled during the liberation war. The Chidyausiku Commission investigated and confirmed that 'prominent persons' had created a 'fast-track' scheme for compensation, that claims had been falsified and that officials responsible for the fund had received substantial kick-backs for the processing of claims.[21] In particular, the Commission noted that Dr Chenjerai 'Hitler' Hunzwi, the president of the War Veterans Association, had falsified claims of examination, submitted false claims on behalf of his family, and attempted to disguise his signature so as to hide his involvement.[22] These scandals, widely reported in the media and discussed at every level of society, contributed to a new scepticism concerning the '*chefs*' in power, not helped by the increasingly challenging living conditions experienced by many.

Urban living conditions, in particular, declined throughout the 1990s, and urban residents began to make their criticism of economic policies public. By the end of the decade, it was clear that government policies would fail to meet their target, set in 1985, of housing for all by the year 2000. In 1991 it was estimated that there was a deficit of 70,000 dwellings in Harare. This figure is probably derived from the housing waiting list, which by 1994 had increased to 92,251 households.[23] In Bulawayo the waiting list was 38,900 in 1991.[24] Even small rural 'growth-points' faced housing shortages.[25] For the country as a whole it was estimated that up to 1.5 million people were without adequate housing in 1994.[26]

Although the minister responsible for housing claimed that the roots of the crisis were to be found in the spiralling costs of land and building, it is not clear that this is an accurate assessment.[27] Evidence gathered by a number of experts suggests that the problem was in fact neither a shortage of land, nor a simple shortage of financial support. Carole Rakodi argues convincingly that there was no land shortage in Harare. Rather the shortage was in the availability of technical support, such as surveyors, to make the land available for building. She also argues that it was not that too little money was allocated to housing by the state, but that the funds allocated were insufficient because the large plot sizes made servicing them expensive. In addition, the standards required made house-building too expensive for the poorest— for whom they were supposed to be aimed; although housing by-laws were revised in 1992, permitting the use of sun-dried and soil cement bricks, as well as prefabricated panels in housing construction.[28] The poorest also found it difficult to access financing. All studies seem to concur that even the most basic housing schemes, originally aimed at the poor, have benefited those with incomes higher than intended, leaving the poorest as lodgers in overcrowded areas. The government's desire not to build sub-standard housing paradoxically left many without any housing of their own.

In response to the need for affordable housing, and their own declining incomes, home-owners increasingly turned to renting out rooms or backyard shacks to lodgers.[29] Unable to spread out onto vacant land, Harare's townships 'densified' or accommodated more and more individuals within their limited space. For house-owners, the rents derived from lodgers were an increasingly important source of income, and this appeared to be grudgingly tolerated by councils, who issued permits for some of these conversions and outbuildings, and turned a blind eye to others in both high- and low-density areas.

But, as in the 1980s, reactions to visible urban poverty also continued to include 'clear-ups' and the removal of squatters, estimated at 110,000 people in and around Harare in 1994.[30] Throughout the 1990s, street children and the urban destitute were targeted for removal to holding camps, training centres and former refugee camps.[31] In the best known case, squatters were moved to the peri-urban Porta farm in 1991 from Mbare, Epworth and nineteen other settlements before Queen Elizabeth's attendance at the 1991 CHOGM meeting.[32] Rakodi reprints a notice dated May 1991, stating that 'the City of Harare will soon destroy all squatter camps', emphasizing the potential danger to public health of the 'mushrooming' of squatter settlements, creating a 'powder keg'.[33] In 1992, a new set of regulations on squatters was gazetted, with particular emphasis on urban and peri-urban land, which established national and provincial level 'squatter control committees'.[34] In 1993, an estimated 20,000 individuals were moved off Churu Farm, on which Revd Ndabaningi Sithole had allowed them to settle despite the area not being zoned for residential use. An evictee reported being told to 'go where I came from', meaning 'back to the rural areas'.[35] Most simply settled on the roadside near the farm, having no money for transport or alternative accommodation. Despite several court orders acknowledging the illegality of these evictions and granting the reinstatement of the families, the police refused to allow them to return until the end of December.[36] Some of these 8,000 families eventually 'settled' at Porta Farm. Those who had put their names on court applications were not allowed to move to Porta Farm, but grudgingly allowed to stay at Churu Farm until October 1994, when they were moved to the former refugee camps, near the Mozambican border.[37] Dzivaresekwa extension and Hatcliffe extension, originally intended as high-density suburbs, joined Porta Farm as official 'holding camps' or 'transit camps' for removed squatters. Justified as 'temporary' solutions, the holding camps met none of the minimum standards for housing in Zimbabwe.[38]

But in a dramatic, albeit unannounced, policy shift, tolerance of the informal economy seemed to increase as the decade went on. While such measures are often seen as 'coping strategies' on the part of the urban poor, from a political perspective they also serve as an indirect form of 'distribution'. Even if the government was increasingly unwilling or unable to distribute welfarist goods, it could still prevent household living standards decreasing too much by permitting access to informal sources of social goods, such as housing, transport and food. After the drought of 1991–2 the Harare municipal council relaxed controls on urban agriculture, and by the late 1990s maize-slashing had ceased, despite concern about the pollution of Harare's water sources among environmental NGOs.[39] The introduction of commuter omnibuses signalled the partial deregulation of public transport. Limited resources to expand the government-owned ZUPCO fleet of buses, and the difficulties of importing spare parts, had contributed to the transport crisis. These multiple-passenger vehicles, known as Kombis, began to be imported in 1994 and greatly improved travel into and out of cities, replacing the 'pirate' (unlicensed) Emergency Taxis that had proliferated as pressure grew on the transport system.[40] Despite this, by 1999 the *Herald* was reporting that the Kombis were now 'overwhelmed' by the city's population, and that the '80s transport blues' had resurfaced.[41]

Regulations on informal trade were also relaxed in the early 1990s, and the numbers of hawkers and vendors increased.[42] Kamete reports that the spread of small-scale industrial workshops within low-income residential areas was tacitly accepted in the early 1990s: 'there is no single report of a major crackdown on illegal land and building use'.[43] Indeed, in 1994, a policy change emanated from central government which partly lifted restrictions on industrial activities.[44] Kamete suggests that the motives behind this shift were political. Designed to 'empower the hitherto disadvantaged minority' and provide an 'enabling environment for emergent businesspeople',[45] the policy change was clearly influenced by the 'indigenization' lobby.

Tevera and Chimhowu's study of backyard shacks (*zviwhendi* or *tangwenas*) is doubtless correct to make a similar link between the apparent tolerance for informalization and 'the need to maintain a rapidly eroding political power base and to soften the impact of political hardships'.[46] This logic becomes more evident when we realize that the municipal franchise was first extended to all urban residents, not just ratepayers, at this time. This delayed reform of the Rhodesian 'qualified franchise'—often overlooked in studies of Zimbabwe's political transition—generated a more diverse group of voters, while the creation of executive mayors to run the cities made urban politics 'more of a zero-sum game', in the words of a white former councillor.[47] Until this point, although rural residents had been enfranchised at both the local and the national level, only urban residents who were property-owners (and who likewise tended to be male) could vote in local elections.

This dramatic shift in the urban political landscape—the final extension of the franchise—expanded the numbers of urban voters and changed their racial, gender and socio-economic profile. It also opened up scope for the emergence of 'residents' associations' where once there had only been 'ratepayers' associations' concerned more for their property values and with little interest in the concerns of the poor and disenfranchised. Although the franchise extension was probably intended to help ZANU(PF) maintain control of urban elections in low-density areas, it occurred just as the high-density urban areas became fertile territory for opposition mobilization.[48] The ruling party's dirty tricks played on Margaret Dongo in the 1995 parliamentary election and on Priscilla Misihairambwi and Fidelis Mhashu in municipal elections, not to mention Margaret Dongo's victory in Harare South, which are discussed in more detail below; all suggest that urban discontent was being channelled into political manifestations as well as into informal income generation. At the same time, residents' associations in both high- and low-density areas became more active; in 1999 they organized themselves into the Combined Harare Residents' Association,[49] and began a sustained lobbying campaign against the Harare Municipality, which was increasingly unable to provide basic services to residents.

Even before these political organizations emerged, spontaneous demonstrations and strikes had begun to occur in urban areas. The increase in protests, strikes and stay-aways that gradually spread throughout the previously quiescent workforce during the 1990s was probably the most politically sensitive result of the decreased expenditure and weakened economy. When bread prices doubled in 1993, followed by the removal of maize subsidies, consumers fought back with the first food riots in independent Zimbabwe, a dramatic repudiation of the regime's developmental claims. In March riots erupted when maize meal importation was disrupted and shortages were encountered. Armed riot police accompanied trucks distributing supplies of maize meal. In September bread riots broke out in Harare and Bulawayo.[50] Consumers then boycotted bread and maize. In one bakery, sales dropped overnight from 6,000 dozen loaves to 200 dozen, when the price of a loaf of bread increased from ZWD1.63 to ZWD2.20. Similarly, when the wholesale price of maize was raised by 55 per cent, consumers began buying their meal in the rural areas and grinding it at hammer-mills, in the home industries centres and backyards of high-density urban areas.[51] Later, rent demonstrations erupted in Zvishavane and other regional centres.[52]

A major civil service strike in August and September 1996, spearheaded by nurses and doctors, appeared to be resolved when civil service employees were awarded a 20 per cent rise.[53] But nurses and junior doctors in Harare resumed the strike in October, in protest against delays in contractual negotiations to confirm the increment.[54] The dismissal of the striking workers and the prosecution of the strike leaders caused the strike to spread to Bulawayo and other regional hospitals.[55] In November the Zimbabwe Congress of Trade Unions (ZCTU) called for a two-day general strike in support of the medical profession, although it was not widely heeded.[56] The strike eventually petered out, with most personnel being reinstated, although fifty-eight strike leaders who were not re-hired were still claiming unlawful dismissal five years later.[57]

A further wave of strikes in all sectors of the economy in 1997 articulated widespread popular discontent. In July 1997, a series of apparently unrelated strikes occurred with bank employees, railway workers, petrol attendants, telecommunications workers and security guards all striking concurrently over demands for wage increments, citing the increasing cost of living.[58] A two-day general strike, called by the ZCTU in December 1997 in protest at electricity and fuel price increases, erupted into violence.[59] And in January 1998, food riots occurred in urban areas across Zimbabwe, starting in Harare's high-density suburbs, but spreading to neighbouring towns and as far south as Beitbridge on the South African border.[60]

But it was not only the 'disloyal' urban elements that were spurred to protest by the economic and political challenges of the 1990s. A much more politically salient group—the fighters of the liberation war—were also mobilized, to rather more political effect. The Zimbabwe National Liberation War Veterans Association (ZNLWVA) had been formed in 1990 in response to the existence of impoverished war veterans 'whose plight was not only an embarrassment to the government, but who had also become ... potential recruits to [the opposition Zimbabwe Unity Movement] ZUM'.[61] Indeed, while the ZNLWVA was affiliated to the ruling party, and led by party loyalists, it contained the potential to deliver a radical critique to the government's post-colonial achievements.

The ZNLWVA negotiated with government over the content and implementation of three pieces of legislation designed to ameliorate their position: the War Veterans Administration Bill (1991), the War Veterans Act (1992) and the War Victims Compensation Act (1993).[62] These were intended to provide compensation for injuries received in the war, as well as support to war veterans' families. In 1996, the MP and ex-combatant Margaret Dongo brought to the attention of parliament the looting of the War Victims Compensation Fund by senior party and government officials. The Chidyausiku Commission, mandated to investigate, suspended payments to veterans, leading to a series of riots and protests in June–August 1997.

The continued saliency of the liberation war to national mythology was particularly evident. Few, if any, issues compelled the same level of passion and eloquence during parliamentary debates. The war veterans were the only social group able to protest and demonstrate with impunity. In 1997, war veterans not only held regular protests without being tear-gassed and dispersed or charged, but occupied and looted the ZANU(PF) party headquarters, took over a courtroom (chasing out judges and court officials), disrupted Heroes' Day celebrations across the country and successfully demanded meetings with senior party officials and President Mugabe.[63] Ministers holding meetings in Harare were forced to flee; in Bulawayo, veterans threatened to beat up Home Affairs Minister Dumiso Dabengwa; in Lupane, John Nkomo, Minister of Local Government, Rural and Urban Development, ran away from the fury of ex-fighters; elsewhere ministers were faced with verbal abuse and were shouted down.[64] Unlike in later demonstrations, these were 'authentic' war veterans, resembling nothing so much as a Brechtian staging of the *Beggar's Opera*: disabled, elderly and poor veterans took over the streets of Harare, dancing and singing in front of the president's residence—publicly shaming him and drawing attention to their neglect. For a few days, Harare seemed a very different place. Both the temerity of the war veterans and the impunity which the state accorded them spoke volumes about their symbolic importance in the national power structures, even if in reality they had been neglected and ignored.[65]

The government rapidly conceded to their demands. Erin McCandless's interview with a high-ranking ZNWLVA official captures the power dynamics of the time:

> At first the government took it very lightly and attempted to silence us but we became very forceful; as a strategy we functioned with our old ideology that we were our own liberators even if this involved confrontation with our very own leaders. This is the reason why there were those demonstrations by war vets that you probably saw on television or read in the papers. The military was consulted and they agreed that nothing had been done for us. We then got what we wanted and all the legalities followed after. The statutory instrument authorising such payments came well after we had been paid. One thing quite apparent then as now is that it was only the president who was in full support of all this; others were resistant citing all sorts of economic theories in protest.[66]

The government's decision in October 1997 to award lump sum 'payouts' to war veterans, to be paid through a proposed 5 per cent levy on salaries, was rejected by both parliament and ZANU(PF).[67]

Taxpayers and MPs were appalled that these concessions were granted parliamentary approval,[68] and the government was forced to back down on the levy, but not the 'payout'. Irene Zindi MP, an ex-combatant herself, accused the government of 'playing with fire' and suggested that the leadership should 'tighten their own belts' first before expecting sacrifices from the masses.[69] However, the concessions made to them strongly reintegrated the war veterans into the party and state security apparatus, as we shall see in more detail in Chapters 5 and 6.

Developing discourses: the re-emergence of land, race and unity

In retrospect, we can see the events in the mid-1990s as re-establishing the use of strikes as political manifestations, bridging the gap between economic discontent and public political expression. Throughout these years, the rhetorical aspect of nation-building had continued, but the discourse was increasingly discredited and the reality judged inadequate. Public discontent and rejection of formal nation-building efforts became visible in different ways over the decade. One indication of this was the declining attendance at public celebrations of the politically significant holidays—Heroes' Day and Independence Day—throughout the decade.[70] With the creation of an 'executive presidency' after the Unity Accord, criticism of presidentialism and of President Mugabe himself became public, with questions asked and jokes made about the need for the heavily armed outriders of his motorcade, his fortified residence and extensive travel.[71] The rhetoric of reconciliation, described in Chapter 3, was maintained, but its practice became increasingly problematic, as the continuing economic dominance of white-owned businesses became less acceptable in the no-longer new nation. Demands were made for control of more of the economy to be shifted into the hands of black investors and producers. Powerful interest groups took shape in the form of the Indigenous Businessmen's Development Centre (IBDC) in 1990 and the Affirmative Action Group (AAG) in 1994, and other associated groupings demanding access to capital, markets and technology. In the 1980s, ZANU(PF) had shunned the promotion of indigenous business in part because it was problematic for the purportedly socialist party-state nexus, but also because a black bourgeoisie might present an alternative power struc-

ture in 'civil society'. However, the economic reform programme and
pressure from international organizations and donors gave greater
legitimacy to demands for indigenization. The emergence of the ZUM
as an opposition party, able to 'mobilise frustrated and ambitious members of the Black Middle class',[72] highlighted the potential challenges
to ZANU. The ZUM, which contested the 1990 election, was rapidly
eliminated as a political force and some of its constituency lured back
into ZANU(PF), as is discussed further below. Gradually, the regime
moved away from a stance in which whites were left alone to pursue
their business interests, into one in which the advancement of black
business became integral to advancing the interests of ZANU(PF).

The IBDC and the AAG were thus tolerated because of the growing
overlap between them and ZANU(PF) in both membership and interests. Tor Skålnes interpreted the formation of black business organizations (in implicit opposition to the white-dominated business groups)
as reflecting the failure of the government policy of 'one sector, one
organization'.[73] However, it may have been more akin to a 'divide and
rule' tactic, ensuring that the black businessmen stayed within the
ZANU(PF) coalition. Raftopoulos suggests that the strategy of these
groups was to 'subordinate themselves to the ruling party, seek political patronage and to pursue their objectives as an integral part of ruling
party politics'.[74] The establishment of groups like the IBDC and the
AAG, not to mention ZUM, may have reflected a failure of government
policy, but one which they quickly acted to remedy, by re-incorporat-
ing these disgruntled groups.

Racial scapegoating, which was given much attention in the international press in the late 1990s and 2000s, becomes apparent in public
discourse from at least 1993 onwards, as the Mugabe regime picked up
on themes of racial discord when it needed to distract attention from
economic problems or land shortages. Faced with food riots, labour
strikes over economic policy and general discontent, Mugabe and various ministers accused whites of fomenting unrest and economic instability.[75] Because of the nature of the liberation struggle, discourses of
race, development and opportunity frequently overlap. Joshua
Nkomo's clash with Bulawayo city council in 1993 over indigenization
is often quoted, both because he explicitly invoked 'struggle metaphors' and criticized white and Asian businesses: 'he harangued coun-

cillors in Ndebele, though some were white, saying that he had spent 11 years in jail, claiming that it was illogical for Zimbabweans to have to pay for development in their own country'.[76]

We can also see the beginnings of an anti-foreigner and anti-NGO discourse, as race begins to be a strategically effective tool against NGOs and political parties, who were accused of being funded by international whites and supported by local whites. Labelling whites, foreigners and city-dwellers as 'foreign' was an attempt to limit the legitimacy of such groups—with their foreign funding and predominantly urban support—to speak on national issues.[77] These tendencies intensify after 1997, but the discourse has already appeared in the years before this, as the economic conditions become more difficult with the introduction of structural adjustment, and the cracks in the 1980s nation-building strategy begin to be revealed.

At official functions, however, the rhetoric of unity continues to be exercised. Party officials were warned against regionalizing or tribalizing ZANU(PF) and told that development would only come through unity: 'Without unity there is no peace, without peace there is no development. … Indeed, this unity we are celebrating now is the key to the future development of this country.'[78] These were not so subtle reminders to political entrepreneurs that splits within the party or initiatives to form new parties would not be tolerated. Resistance to the regime's agenda would be met by exclusion from the benefits of development, that is, of state largesse. Thus 'development' was neatly linked to 'unity'—meaning a lack of opposition. The 1990 ZANU(PF) election manifesto had set out 'The Imperative of National Unity' and this rhetoric continued through the decade.[79] In 1995 and 1999, faced with personalized schisms and regional factionalism within ZANU, the president called almost desperately for the cessation of intra-party divisions which threatened the party's stability.[80] This message was also spread to those outside the party. During the 1995 election, government minister Kumbirai Kangai warned the people of Chipinge, whose MP was ZANU Ndonga leader Ndabaningi Sithole, 'that there will be no development in their area if they continue to vote for opposition parties'. Kangai said, 'People in Chipinge should unite. If you do not unite … there will be no development.'[81] Other Manicaland and Matabeleland constituencies, perceived as sources of dissent, were given similar warnings.[82] This tone is also found in Mugabe's threat that 'we may go back and remove the clothes of reconciliation';[83] and the ominous warning of Colonel Dube, of the Zimbabwe Defence Industries, that 'peace is vital for development and the main ingredient for peace is unity'.[84] More concretely, election monitors reported that access to drought relief and seed packs was linked to voting ZANU(PF) by party officials and traditional leaders during the 1995 election.[85]

This discourse of 'unity' might seem to be an overworked idea, increasingly devoid of meaning, but it continued to resonate within society well beyond ZANU(PF) claims to dominance. Even the weak opposition parties of the 1990s, who might have been expected to resist and resent this discourse of unity, used it themselves. The slogan of the United Parties (so called because they brought together the remnants of earlier parties) was 'Unity is Power', and their manifesto declared their intention to form a 'united, stable and strong' opposition, with the capacity to be a basis for an alternative government.[86] Similarly, the Zimbabwe Union of Democrats, led by Margaret Dongo, took the famous balancing rocks as a party symbol because they symbolized 'unity, stability and political balance'.[87] To some extent, this may have been simply an attempt to counter criticism that opposition parties, and independent candidates, were threats to Zimbabwe's stability which only ZANU(PF) could maintain. The creation of a new national holiday, 'Unity Day', to celebrate the 1987 signing of the Unity Accord between ZANU and ZAPU, was doubtless intended to remind voters of the dangers of opposition. However, the opposition's use of the same language also suggests that ZANU(PF)'s discourses did resonate with Zimbabweans, still recuperating from the independence war, and aware of the potential damage that could be inflicted on regions which strayed. Discursive threats to those who challenged 'unity' were not empty of meaning.

However, at the same time as they were threatening to deprive unruly areas of 'development', the economic constraints of crisis and the austerity of structural adjustment meant that the regime actually had less capacity to bring development in the form of schools, clinics and infrastructure. At this point, we begin to see the ruling party returning to the rhetoric of the independence struggle, as the rhetoric of land became a political trump card for the ruling party, and a substitute for actual progress. During the 1990 election, promises of land were revived—by the party, not by land-hungry peasants; as Alexander notes, 'the government's promises of resettlement depended to a great degree on its perception of its political vulnerability'.[88] The Lancaster House constitutional restraints on land reform had ended in 1990. As expected, the government then brought in a constitutional amendment that enabled expropriation of land, followed by the 1992 Land Acquisition Act. Yet, the implementation of land reform under these new laws was typified by bureaucratic bungling. Little progress was made. Out of the seventy commercial farms designated for acquisition and resettlement in 1993, thirty-three were later excluded. Then in 1997 the government proposed a new list of 1,471 farms to acquire. In March 1998, in the face of widespread donor criticism, it agreed that the list was problematic and that 'no productive land would be nationalised, that white farmers would be fully compensated, and that reforms would be carried out within the government's limited money and administrative capacity'.[89] Inaccuracies on the list and its failure to accord with previous criteria led analysts to suggest that it had been politically motivated.[90] Little resettlement occurred, but the rhetoric remained important. With this intensification of the land issue, the discourse changed from reconciliation back towards racial inequalities, with Mugabe calling white farmers 'a greedy bunch of racist usurpers'.[91] The nation-building project of the 1980s was beginning to reveal its inadequacies, as the papered-over cracks emerged from behind the rhetoric.

Competition and control: state institutions

At the same time as its discursive dominance was threatened by on-the-ground reality and spending constraints, the state continued to have control over a wide range of bureaucratic and governmental institutions. Despite an apparent opening in political space after the Unity Accord and the decision not to pursue a *de jure* one-party state, the 1990s were marked by the introduction of a series of distinctly illiberal laws designed to control the university, NGOs, trade unions and political parties. This section explores the ways in which the various branches of government contributed to the creation and implementation of these laws, setting the stage for their contestation by societal groups.

Despite the Unity Accord, contestation of elections did not lapse after 1987. Indeed, the 1990 and 1995 elections were hotly contested, as is discussed later in the chapter, yet they were firmly under the control of the state electoral institutions. Although irregularities were much discussed with reference to elections in June 2000 and after, much of the institutional framework was put in place in the 1990s, revealing a number of ways in which elections were made unfair for opposition parties. Elections were organized by the Registrar General, Tobaiwa Mudede, and the Elections Directorate, as well as the Election Supervisory Commission (ESC). The Registrar General and the Directorate supervised the Delimitation Commission and the voter registration process, while the ESC observed and reported on the process. One of the key roles of the Registrar General was to maintain the voters' roll. The voter registration exercise in 1990 was a dubious procedure, and just before the elections the Registrar General announced that all Zimbabwean citizens would be allowed to vote upon presentation of proof of citizenship and residence.[92] Although his office did produce a voters' roll, it was only made available late in the nomination period, impeding candidates' attempts to find registered voters who could nominate them. The 1995 election revealed more irregularities in the polling process. Margaret Dongo's court challenge over the election fought in Harare South revealed that in addition to irregularities in the voters' roll, the government also stuffed the ballot boxes, such that there were over 1,000 more ballots counted than had been issued to voters.[93]

In both 1990 and 1995, questions were raised about the impartiality of the Delimitation Commission. In 1990 last-minute 'corrections' were issued which moved the high-density area of Mkoba from Gweru Central to the predominantly rural Gweru South, giving Muzenda an edge over Kombayi. As Moyo pointed out, 'the general public was left with the impression that President Mugabe had used the commission to protect his Vice-President, Simon Muzenda, who appeared to be heading for certain defeat'.[94] Similarly, Harare North (contested in the 1995, 2000 and 2005 elections by Trudy Stevenson for successive opposition parties) was mainly a low-density suburb but included Hatcliffe number 1, a high-density area, and Hatcliffe extension, a holding camp for squatters. Bulawayo South, a mainly low-density constituency, also had the high-density suburb of Nketa added to it in 1995. The ESC, which might have been expected to oversee this process, was widely considered underfinanced and understaffed.[95] Criticisms have also been made about the president's control of appointments to the ESC.[96] Makumbe and Compagnon speak particularly bitterly about the ESC's failure to support Margaret Dongo's complaints in 1995.[97] Irregularities led to the election being widely condemned as 'free but unfair'.[98]

Political interference was also visible in less oblique ways. During the 1996 Harare municipal elections, ZANU(PF) attacks on independent candidates included the assault on Fidelis Mhashu, who was attacked and beaten by ZANU(PF) supporters at a rally attended by four MPs, including cabinet minister Witness Mangwende. Despite Mhashu being badly beaten, the police, who were present at the time of the attack, did not press any charges.[99] Priscilla Misihairabwi's attempts to stand for election in the Avenues ward of Harare were also subject to explicit political meddling, as it was shown that officials had taken action to block her nomination after consulting ZANU(PF) representatives. Judge Korsah, who presided over Misihairabwi's appeal to the Supreme Court, implicitly acknowledged party political interference, saying, 'The facts are screaming out from the page; why did the judge below [in the High Court] not declare it? What is the motive for his resistance?'[100] The unspoken fact, as all in the courtroom were aware, was that the High Court judge was a ZANU(PF) appointee.

These election challenges were significant because until that time there had been no substantiated allegations that ZANU(PF) was rigging elections, although intimidation was frequently alleged. While monitoring organizations noted structural irregularities, such as the ruling party's access to funds, vehicles and the media, they rarely suggested that voting had been manipulated in or at the polls. However, in 1995 the independent candidates repeatedly showed how the manipulation of electoral rolls was accomplished by the ruling party using the official electoral machinery. As we shall see in Chapter 6, this intensified during subsequent elections.

Other governmental institutions also reveal much about the politics of the 1990s. Despite being overshadowed by the policy-making role of the party and the executive, parliament was a significant forum for political debate in the 1990s, primarily because it provided an arena for MPs to publicize issues of concern to them. In the early 1990s, MPs, including members of the ruling party, were frequently much more critical of policies than journalists or academics. Issues of particular interest to them and their constituents, such as the treatment of war veterans, led to much debate.[101] Although there were only a handful of opposition MPs, outspoken members of ZANU(PF) frequently harangued their colleagues for allowing themselves to be 'steamrollered' rather than turning up for debates and scrutinizing legislation.[102] A few left-leaning MPs also encouraged NGOs and others to criticize economic policy, and supported their interest in parliamentary scrutiny.

In 1991 parliamentarians made their opposition to the executive known on such disparate issues as the reintroduction of school fees and the establishment of a sports commission. In the case of school fees, back-bench MPs criticized Fay Chung, the Education Minister, for having failed to consult them.[103] In the case of the oddly controversial Sports Bill, MPs slowed the progress of the bill through parliament and vigorously challenged the minister's impartiality.[104] In 1992, parliamentarians twice blocked a vote on salaries for provincial governors, calling instead for the unpopular appointed posts to be abolished. However, they were eventually bullied into supporting the budgetary allocations on the premise that the governorships were constitutionally guaranteed positions. In reality, the debate was less about loyalty to the constitution than loyalty to the executive. The president was recorded as saying, 'True, let them [MPs] make all the noise. Don't forget we are ruling. Otherwise they will be saying government has no power.'[105] The motion was eventually passed unanimously.[106]

In 1997, MPs challenged government over a number of particularly sensitive cases, including the tender and loans for the building of a new Harare airport, about which more below.[107] Later that year, as the government attempted to amend nineteen acts through the passage of one bill, MPs questioned the method and decisions of the executive.[108] In response to this, MPs were chastised in parliament by the Minister of Justice, who suggested that any difficulties should be worked out in caucus, not in the public forum of parliament. In response, Moses Mvenge, MP for Mutare Central, argued that membership of ZANU(PF) did not mean that MPs had to support every government policy.[109] In

1997, the issue of corruption within the administration regarding the War Victims Compensation Fund also led MPs—for the first time since independence—to support and pass a private member's bill sponsored by Margaret Dongo, the lone independent MP.[110]

A parliamentary reform process in the late 1990s also made a number of significant changes, the most visible of which was the move away from white wigs and black robes, and the relaxation of the visitors' dress code.[111] The parliamentary reform committee, led by Speaker Cyril Ndebele, held hearings across the country in 1997, in an attempt to make parliament more effective.[112] Their most substantive contribution, however, was the creation of portfolio committees to oversee government ministries and departments.

Yet, despite these expressions of autonomy, the executive retained control. As Ncube notes, 'quite often the ruling party's Parliamentarians are sufficiently objective to oppose particular legislative proposals during debate and yet when the Government insists on enactment of the objectionable provisions … the parliamentarians vote in favour of the provisions they [have] spoken against'.[113] This was certainly the case in the ratification of the tender for the new international airport terminal, which involved loans said to be worth ZWD 1.2 billion to Air Harbour Technologies (AHT), a company represented locally by the president's nephew Leo Mugabe, although the tender board had ranked AHT fourth because it had neither the financial resources nor the technological know-how of other tenderers. Cabinet overturned the Tender Board's recommendation, causing the withdrawal of ZWD 1 billion in foreign donor support. After making it clear that they, and the public, were unhappy with this tendering, MPs were faced with a three-line whip, which would have forced their resignations from the party if they had defied it.[114] On an even more sensitive note, the ZANU(PF) MP Dzikimai Mavhaire brought a motion to the house calling for constitutional reform and recommending term limits on the presidency, famously going so far as to say, 'The President must go'; he was suspended from the party, although the Speaker Cyril Ndebele enforced the right of parliamentary immunity and protected him from further attack.[115]

The courts also provided a strong check against executive and legislative challenges to the constitution.[116] However, the judicial checks and balances were effective only at its topmost levels, and even then only partially. Magistrates were not only poorly paid and overworked, but also subject to pressures from the executive.[117] Despite this, court judgements were an important component in the success of the independent candidates' challenges to electoral procedures. In 1997, the courts also ruled as unconstitutional the Private Voluntary Organisations (PVO) Act and the Political Parties (Finance) Act. However, despite the profound impact of these decisions going against the government and in some cases also ZANU(PF), it was not a crusading bench. In several cases, including a ruling on the regulation of NGOs, which is discussed in more detail at the end of this chapter, the Supreme Court 'decided not to decide', rendering a more limited judgement than might be considered necessary in order to 'uphold the constitution'.[118] Several of its landmark decisions were subsequently overturned by constitutional amendments.[119]

Not always finding existing state institutions responsive, the regime turned to re-incorporate and strengthen the position of traditional authorities. Already in the late 1980s, the government had begun to take an interest in chiefs, leading to a high-profile meeting between Joshua Nkomo and chiefs in 1992, and culminating in an even more significant meeting between Mugabe and the chiefs.[120] Later that decade, the Traditional Leaders Act (TLA) was passed which granted the chiefs substantial governmental and administrative roles, including land allocation and tax collection.[121] In a move that would become more important than was at first obvious, the 1998 Act also gave chiefs authority over resettlement areas, which had previously been technocratic strongholds with 'modern' governance structures. Alexander suggests that the reforms were in part 'simply intended to strengthen state capacity, but the measures also marked an important ideological shift away from the democratizing and modernizing efforts of the early years on independence'.[122] But as lines between state and party became blurred, these reforms also strengthened the link between party and chiefs, giving the party more purchase in rural areas.

Competition and control: societal response

The state institutions which the regime needed to use to build its hegemony were themselves weak and factionalized. The society which these institutions were designed to dominate was also not uniformly opposed to or in support of the political forces. As a result, the period between 1987 and 1997 was characterized by ambiguity on the part of society, which contributed to the regime's durability. In a few cases, societal groups came together in unified action, but at most times they remained divided or apolitical, thus rendering the outspoken few more isolated and vulnerable. Ironically the 1987 Unity Accord *had* increased public discourse. Activists, especially those of Ndebele origin who had felt unable to speak in the early and mid-1980s because they would have been labelled 'opponents' or 'traitors', felt more able to be critical of the state after the Unity Accord.[123] This section, by discussing opposition parties, elections, the media, labour, churches, NGOs and students, will show how these tendencies interacted and resulted in the regime maintaining itself in power.

The most dramatic shift during this period was that the regime's intention to create a one-party state after the Unity Accord was blocked by the emergence of a new opposition party, and unprecedented expression of public disapproval of the ruling party. In the wake of the Willowgate car resale and the creation of the powerful new executive presidency, the potential one-party state was seized upon and criticized by students, academics and the churches, who found common ground for the first time on this issue.[124] Debate on this issue not only took place within the meetings of political scientists, or the pages of independent magazines, but penetrated even into the official media.[125] While ZANU(PF) seemed to continue to favour a one-party system, in September 1990 the party's Central Committee took the unexpected decision not to legislate for a one-party state.[126] This was most likely an internal revolt motivated by the fear that a one-party state would preclude the 'exit' option for ZANU(PF) radicals, rather than by any real commitment to multi-party politics.

ZANU(PF) faced significant opposition in the 1990 election, albeit mainly in urban areas, from the Zimbabwe Unity Movement (ZUM), which had been formed by the former ZANU MP Edgar Tekere in 1989 as an explicit attack on the proposal to create a one-party state.[127] Violence was prevalent in this election. Patrick Kombayi, another prominent ex-ZANU member who was contesting the Gweru Central constituency for ZUM, was shot and other supporters were beaten. In a sign that this violence was condoned at the highest levels, Mugabe pardoned the two men convicted of Kombayi's assault.

As discussed above, both ZANU(PF) and ZUM capitalized upon the dominant discourse of unity, operating, as Sylvester puts it, 'in and against the ambiguities of the situation'.[128] ZUM's insistence on its own commitment to unity was doubtless reinforced by the parallel emergence of a more exclusionary discourse, which targeted ZUM for its alliance with the white-dominated Conservative Alliance of Zimbabwe (CAZ).[129] Mugabe accused ZUM of being a puppet organization of former Rhodesian Front leader Ian Smith,[130] and alleged that Tekere was plotting a coup that included the assassination of all the ZANU(PF) leadership.[131] It was also contended that ZUM was being backed by South African interests, and had connections with the Mozambican RENAMO, the implication being that ZUM supported or was supported by Zimbabwe's external enemies.[132] The predominantly white Commercial Farmers Union (CFU) and the Confederation of Zimbabwe Industries (CZI) were quick to distance themselves from ZUM.[133] The election was won by ZANU(PF), which garnered 117 seats and 81 per cent of the popular vote. ZUM won only two seats in the parliamentary election but 18 per cent of the overall vote and 30 per cent of the urban vote.[134] These quite dramatic results, despite concerns over the accuracy of the voters' roll and constituency gerrymandering,[135] were seen by contemporary observers as indicators of the re-emergence of a competitive party system in the 1990s, but this optimism was unwarranted, as ZUM subsequently fragmented. One splinter regrouped as the Democratic Party,[136] while other fragments of ZUM moved into the Forum Party in 1993, which was expected to provide a strong challenge to ZANU(PF) in the 1995 elections, but which was also weakened due to factional divisions. Forum did contest municipal elections, and challenged the outcomes in the courts with mixed success—winning nullifications in Masvingo, Bulawayo and Harare, but not in Gweru.[137]

The 1995 elections were preceded by the arrest and trial of Ndabaningi Sithole, leader of ZANU Ndonga, for treason. Widely seen as politically motivated, the accusations were interpreted as a warning to other would-be presidential contenders.[138] Convicted and sentenced to one year in jail, Sithole denied allegations that he plotted to assassinate

President Mugabe and organized military training outside the country for his recruits.[139] The designation of Sithole's Churu Farm for acquisition also appeared to be influenced by political pressure.[140]

The main opposition party in the 1995 election was the United Parties (UP), which combined Muzorewa's UANC with Forum, ZUM and ZANU Ndonga as an electoral front. The UP made little impact in the 1995 election, not helped by their call for a boycott late in the campaign, on the basis that the regulations had created an unfair contest.[141] After the election, the UP contested the validity of the Electoral Act and the Political Parties (Finance) Act in the Supreme Court, winning a partial, but not unsubstantial, victory in 1997—when the Political Parties (Finance) Act was declared unconstitutional.[142]

The 1995 election, however, was more noted for the emergence of Margaret Dongo as an opposition force. Dongo, an ex-combatant, ex-Central Intelligence Organisation (CIO) agent and the ZANU(PF) MP for Harare South, was not re-selected as the ruling party candidate in 1995. Along with a small group of other de-selected candidates she decided to run as 'ZANU (PF) Independents'. When Dongo lost the election, she contested the result; it was overturned in court and she convincingly won the re-run election, setting a precedent by challenging ZANU(PF) hegemony, and revealing its clumsy attempt at ballot stuffing.[143] Dongo built on her success by developing an informal grouping of opposition candidates in 1996 to challenge ZANU(PF) in the municipal elections. This began a crucial process of consistently and thoroughly fighting elections, not just complaining about unfair playing fields or calling for boycotts.[144] The candidates who ran under the banner of Independent Candidates—later the Zimbabwe Union of Democrats (ZUD)—rapidly became expert both at exposing fraudulent registrations and encouraging their supporters to register to vote. Margaret Dongo and her Independent Candidates group won prominence through the twin measures of court challenges and campaigning primarily in restricted areas—municipal wards and mayorality contests. Following on from the UP and Forum, the Independent Candidates used the judicial system to great effect.

Priscilla Misihairabwi, an NGO activist who sought to contest the urban council elections as an Independent Candidate, compiled such a convincing dossier of fraudulent voter registrations in Harare's Avenues district (including vacant lots with hundreds of registered voters) that ZANU(PF) sought to force her out—with the Registrar General, Tobaiwa Mudede, declaring her candidacy invalid. Misihairabwi took her case all the way to the Supreme Court, which ratified her right to contest the election.[145] Similarly, Fidelis Mhashu, a former ZANU(PF) municipal councillor who contested the Chitungwiza mayoral election as an independent candidate after failing to get selected as the official ZANU(PF) candidate, convinced the High Court that the Chitungwiza electoral roll—comprised of lists of home-owners rather than residents or voters—'was so defective that it cannot be said that the electoral process was itself not flawed'.[146] Neither of these two battles was ultimately successful because the elections were not re-run, yet they revealed the lengths to which ZANU(PF) would go in order to maintain control of the electoral process. However, two members of the Independent Candidates did win municipal council seats in the high-density suburbs of Mbare and Sunningdale.

Elections in the 1990s thus did not provide for any large-scale transformation of elective government, but they did reveal widespread discontent with the ruling party in urban areas, and the regime's use of repressive mechanisms to suppress the expression of these sentiments. In addition, the incremental court victories won by these small parties and independents set important precedents for future campaigns, as well as drawing significant media attention to the candidates and the possibility of defeating ZANU(PF).

Although the media did provide detailed coverage of the court cases during the 1990s, it too reflected the muddled nature of this period of Zimbabwean politics. State control remained visible on television and in the state-controlled newspapers, where presidential or ministerial activities regularly held the spotlight, and opposition party campaigns received little coverage (unlike the court cases). Newsreaders and their editors continued to check with the Minister of Information before broadcasting items that might reflect badly on the government. Although pre-publication censorship rarely occurred within the official press, 'the government hardly ever had to use all the resources at its disposal ... [e]ditors were conscious that the government could have them demoted, fired or transferred'.[147] Radio 3, which broadcast in English and played Western music, was perceived as less subject to control; but the ousting of disc jockey Gerry Jackson, after she broke a news blackout during the December 1997 strike, revealed that insubordination was not tolerated there either.[148]

In the early 1990s, the monthly magazines *Parade* and *Horizon*, which had been key independent sources of information, 'shifted their editorial content away from critical political features towards light entertainment and sports. Politics and investigative journalism it appears, no longer sell magazines in a congested, restricted market.'[149] However, other technologies continued to make alternative viewpoints available. Satellite television boomed with the increasing accessibility of satellite dishes, which, while they are obviously owned only by the elite, are often watched by individuals in businesses, hotels and private homes.

In the early 1990s, the publishers of the *Financial Gazette* had attempted to launch a second weekly, the *Sunday Gazette*, and a daily entitled the *Daily Gazette*, but neither paper lasted more than a few months. However, following the launch of the weekly *Zimbabwe Independent* in 1995, and the Sunday *Zimbabwe Standard* in 1997, there was a vital and lively alternative press. All three weeklies suffered from being perceived as 'white' and 'elite' papers because they were originally owned and published by local white-owned companies, and because they were quite expensive compared to the *Herald*. It was rare to see papers other than the *Herald* being read on the streets, or by non-white-collar workers.

Reaching a much broader audience, popular musicians also began to articulate concerns with economic and political conditions. Vambe argues that in the late 1980s and early 1990s musicians were 'concerned with deconstructing official truths about the process of nation-building'.[150] This seems relatively clear in the music of Thomas Mapfumo, who raised concerns about political leadership in the late 1980s, yet his music retained ambiguities. Younger singers were more constrained by their producers and the state-controlled media, but even they articulated the desperation induced by poverty.[151] The increasing popularity of gospel music, for example, has been linked to socio-economic difficulties, although this may not always be explicit. Banning Eyre cites a well-known musician saying, 'I … just write my songs about our life … how we are living and how we are surviving?'[152] But as Chitando argues, this can itself be political:

although most gospel musicians in Zimbabwe would expressly distance themselves from [politics] … they capture the popular discourse that centres on themes of decline, hopelessness, corruption and hardships … effectively questioning the competence of the rulers of the day.[153]

These popular discourses were also reflected in the upsurge of labour activism that affected many sectors of the working public by the end of the 1990s. However, it would be wrong to see the 1990s as a straightforward period of 'activism'; these years marked both high and low points of labour activism. The culmination of the ZCTU's transformation from 'lap dog' to 'watch dog' is attributed by Schiphorst to the election of Morgan Tsvangirai as Secretary General in 1988. Until then, management of the ZCTU had continued to be disorganized and susceptible to allegations of corruption.[154] After Tsvangirai's election, Schiphorst asserts that the ZCTU was 'no longer an organization that was led by one man … strategies, tactics and direction that the ZCTU adopted … were all the result of deliberations and decisions of the general council … this made the ZCTU a stronger organization'.[155]

In August 1988, the ZCTU retracted its previous calls for representation within ZANU(PF), claiming to be politically neutral vis-à-vis existing parties, and in April 1990 it formally supported a multi-party system.[156] May Day 1990 demonstrated this change in the ZCTU approach, as workers demonstrated against the one-party state and in support of the right to strike.[157] In September, the ZCTU also withdrew its long-standing request for corporate representation within parliament.[158]

In reaction to the ZCTU's increasing independence, in the 1990s the government attempted to weaken the unions. In direct contradiction to its earlier emphasis on 'unity' between workers, attempts were made to re-fragment the movement. Tengende illustrates how efforts were made, starting in 1991, to weaken the railways union by creating an unlawful 'splinter union'.[159] Both Tengende and Nordlund suggest that this was part of a larger process, preparing the way for the removal of the 'one-industry-one-union' policy, in which the ZCTU's opposition was portrayed as rejecting pluralism and freedom of association.[160]

And indeed, in 1992 the government introduced legislation to amend the Labour Relations Act which revoked the policy of 'one-industry-one-union' and thereby weakened the ZCTU. The Bill was presented to parliament before the ZCTU knew the draft was in existence.[161] Somewhat reluctantly, the ZCTU leadership organized a protest march on 13 June, which went ahead despite the lack of police permission, as required under the Rhodesian-era Law and Order (Maintenance) Act (LOMA).[162] Police presence was heavy, and the arrest of six protesters in Harare led to the 1994 striking down of the LOMA as unconstitutional, an unintentional outcome of the march, but one which was to have a profound impact on the ability of protesters to assemble in future.[163] Despite the ZCTU's opposition, the new labour regulations were rapidly implemented.

This was the final hostile encounter between labour and the state for some time. As the ZCTU's members encountered the increasing difficulties of structural adjustment, the labour movement 'adopted a different tone … a conciliatory approach. … It now presented itself as an advisor to Government.'[164] Gradually, the ZCTU moved towards cooperation on structural adjustment policy, social security and tripartite bargaining.[165] After the previous confrontation between unions and state, by 1995 there was a relatively less conflictual relationship, based more on give-and-take bargaining.[166]

However, as discussed above, between 1996 and 2000 a series of disruptive strikes began in both the public and the private sectors. The ZCTU changed its strategy again and began calling national strikes or stay-aways in response to particular policy decisions—starting with the call for workers to stay out in support of striking doctors and nurses in 1996, and the increasingly effective protests against the war veterans' levy in December 1997, and food and fuel tax increases in March 1998.

These successes were not without retribution. After the protest against the war veterans' levy, Morgan Tsvangirai was attacked and beaten. The day after the national strike in March 1998, the ZCTU's Bulawayo regional office was set on fire.[167] The government's labelling of the ZCTU as an 'opposition party … playing politics' after the series of strikes in 1998 was also a clear warning that they were raising the stakes in a battle for control.[168] Throughout 1997 and 1998, the government attempted to make the calling of strikes over political issues illegal.[169] Here we can see the emergence of the more divisive and exclusionary tactics that would dominate the years to follow.

However, the unions were by no means operating on their own. In the late 1980s the student movement had been the most visible face of protest in Zimbabwe—images of students leading protest marches and their running battles with the riot police and tear gas were common long before any other groups found such behaviour acceptable. Student activism was sparked in 1987 by the election of 'activist' Students Representative Councils (SRCs) in 1987 and 1988 and their subsequent concern with issues of student welfare, such as accommodation, transport and finance. Attempts to negotiate with the university administration became problematic, and the riot police aggressively dispersed student demonstrators. In September 1998 student demands moved further into the political sphere, with the anti-corruption protests linked to the Willowgate scandal, which led to further conflict between students and police when the police refused to give permission for the students to march into town. In reaction to this and subsequent unrest, the government withdrew the loans and grants of all fifteen SRC members in January 1989. In September 1989, attempts to organize a 'commemoration' of the previous year's demonstrations led to the arrest of SRC members and students. ZCTU Secretary General Morgan Tsvangirai's support for the detained students in the form of a press release led to his own arrest for issuing subversive material.[170] These anti-corruption protests merged into the one-party state debate, with students taking a prominent position in opposition to the proposed constitutional change, and aligning themselves with labour and civic groups. At SRC-convened meetings, the students voted overwhelmingly against the one-party state on the basis of both events in Eastern Europe and lessons from one-party states elsewhere in Africa.[171] The government's response was to close the university and send the students home.[172]

In October 1990, the government rushed the University Amendment Act through parliament in a week. The act increased the role of the Minister of Education in the administration of the university, strengthened the Vice Chancellor's powers and reduced the academic freedom of staff and students.[173] This led to two years of often violent protest on the part of the students. The state's main levers of control over the students were expulsion and the withdrawal of grants.[174] Conditions of study also became more difficult for students. With the price increases that accompanied economic liberalization, student grants had less buying power, and their families were less able to help them out financially.

The university was also affected by a 'brain drain' as it was no longer so attractive to either local or ex-patriate staff. Students were increasingly taught in large classes, with few resources. To some extent, then, protests about student welfare issues were also critical of government economic policy: 'students linked their own demands with broader national political and economic issues'.[175] But students rapidly became seen as focusing on their own rather parochial concerns about food, accommodation and 'payouts' rather than broader societal issues.[176] Through the later 1990s, cycles of student protests—usually about their living conditions—were predictably followed by tear gas attacks by riot police, periodic closure of the university, and the expulsion of successive generations of SRC leaders.[177]

In this period, students seemed unable, or unwilling, to merge their protests into any larger projects. The portrayal of students as pampered hooligans in the state media further alienated them from possible allies. Alliances might have been formed with the national youth cohort or with workers. The regime's continued socialist rhetoric effectively disarmed any critique from the left, which students and workers might have pursued jointly.[178] Similarly, the mobilization of the ZANU(PF) Youth League to demonstrate against the university students was doubtless designed to prevent any potential alliance between the two groups.[179]

It is also intriguing that although the formation of universities outside Harare was first broached in the 1980s, it was only after 1990 that this became possible, with the passing of the National Council for Higher Education Act.[180] The National University of Science and Technology opened in 1991, the Methodist Church-run Africa University in Mutare in 1992, and the Seventh Day Adventist Solusi University in 1994.[181] This proliferation of higher education institutions is most often interpreted as the 'liberalization' of the education sector, but it also reflects a 'divide and rule' strategy paralleling the move away from a 'one-industry-one-union' labour policy. If groups such as students and workers could not be controlled through corporatist mechanisms, then encouraging internal divisions proved to be a more successful way of weakening them.

Groups like churches, however, were inherently divided, and difficult for the state to control. Unsurprisingly, then, relations between the churches and the regime proved contradictory and fluid. In the late

1980s, the church, like the students and labour movements, involved itself in the one-party state debate, with the Catholic magazine *Moto* a key site of debate. The Zimbabwe Council of Churches (ZCC) organized a day of fasting against the one party-state.[182] The Catholic bishops issued a pastoral letter which argued against constitutional changes that might curtail peaceful ways of changing the government, while the Catholic Commission for Justice and Peace (CCJP) spoke explicitly against 'the formation of a *de jure* one party state in Zimbabwe'.[183] The CCJP later claimed that the one-party state debate was one place where it had concretely affected government policy.[184]

After this, and for most of the 1990s, the Anglican and Catholic hierarchies remained entwined with the ZANU state. The Anglicans were particularly active. Along with the Pentecostal movement, they linked themselves fervently to Mugabe's crusade against gay people in Zimbabwe.[185] The Catholic Church also retained its close links with the Mugabe family—two of the president's sisters worked at Silveira House, the Catholic development institution, and in 1996 Bishop Mutume married President Mugabe to his much younger secretary, despite widespread public condemnation.[186] In 1997, the CCJP/LRF (Legal Resources Foundation) report on the Matabeleland atrocities was published in South Africa. Although this report had been compiled under the auspices of the Catholic Bishops' Conference, the bishops refused to make the report public in Zimbabwe without the acquiescence of President Mugabe.[187] The power struggle between CCJP staff and members—most of whom wanted to be more publicly outspoken—and the bishops—who were inclined to take up issues with the president privately—weakened the organization, and led to the resignation of the much respected National Director, Mike Auret.[188] Nevertheless, the church-NGOs associated with the mainstream Protestant and Catholic Churches became increasingly important players in policy advocacy and voter education as the decade went on, as is discussed in more detail below.

The Pentecostal and Apostolic Churches, which had been somewhat sidelined during the 1980s, also became more significant players in the political sphere in the 1990s. Maxwell has suggested that in the early 1990s hierarchies of the evangelical churches courted the president's approval (and vice versa), rather than seeking to distance themselves from secular authority.[189] These groups were targeted for inclusion in the ZANU(PF) political project as elections became more and more contested. During the 1995 election, Mugabe, a Catholic, was noted raising his hands above his head in the distinctive Pentecostal form of prayer at a prayer breakfast.[190] A year later, during the Chitungwiza mayoral election, when the ruling party was unsure of its ability to beat the independent candidate, Mhashu, they called on the support of the normally apolitical *Vapostori* or apostolic faith congregations. At the close of the voter registration exercise, a church leader claimed that at least 3,000 members had registered in the hope that ZANU(PF) would provide them with land on which to worship.[191] At a meeting with 2,000 members of the *Vapostori*, Zionist and Pentecostal Churches in Chitungwiza, ZANU(PF) leaders used both religious rhetoric ('Mugabe could not take you across the river [Jordan], so he gave you a Moses called Jiri [the ZANU-PF mayoral candidate] to take you across the river') and pragmatism: 'if Mhashu [the independent candidate] were elected mayor he would not be able to present the grievances of Chitungwiza's residents to the government effectively because he would be like "paraffin in the sea" which could not mix well with water. "In his absence, no councillor would represent him because all the councillors are ZANU(PF)."'[192] While the state was not shy of demanding the obedience and participation of the churches in the development process, it stopped short of legislating explicit controls on them, drawing on rhetorics of shared values and Christian imagery to engage them instead.[193]

Of all the societal groups discussed in this chapter, NGOs probably experienced the most change and growth in the 1990s, as the development sector, with which they were intimately involved, was itself transformed. These changes were reflected in a gradually evolving relationship between NGOs and the state; the cases below reveal the ways in which these changing relationships played out, in the economically straitened and politically charged atmosphere of the 1990s. After the signing of the Unity Accord in 1987, it had seemed easier for NGOs to function, as they were less likely to be accused of supporting ZAPU and constituting a divisive influence on national unity. At the same time, international funding was beginning to move away from states and towards NGOs; in response, new groups emerged to deal with new sets of issues. Environmental NGOs proliferated, as did organizations working with street children and on women's issues.[194] These three areas are particularly indicative of the changing relations between NGOs and the state during this period.

At the start of the 1990s, the existence of street children was seen as an affront to the government's development agenda. Three distinct tactics were used by the state in responding to NGO and donor interest in the issue. In one case, an organization that wanted to make videos and publicize the plight of street children was prevented from forming when the government deported the American volunteer who had started the project, and harassed the Zimbabweans who were working with him.[195] At the same time, however, two local NGOs—Streets Ahead and the Harare Street Children's Organisation—started up with little difficulty, although the latter's close links with the prominent ZANU(PF) mayor of Harare may have facilitated matters. In 1995 a further strategy was implemented, in which the government attempted to take advantage of donor funding for NGOs working with the urban poor. The state established and funded the National Organisation for the Development of the Disadvantaged (with the unpromising acronym NODED), described in parliament as a 'government NGO' to remove street children and destitute families from the streets of urban areas and relocate them to the refugee camps on the eastern borders, from which Mozambicans had recently been repatriated.[196] In other words, in the area of street children, the government moved from preventing organizations from forming, to tolerating their existence, to trying to set one up for themselves.

The proliferation of women's organizations in the 1980s and 1990s was also met by relatively unsubtle attempts to bring them into a submissive relationship with the state. From at least 1986, the government attempted to introduce legislation to create a National Women's Council that would regulate women's organizations, arguing that existing NGOs were failing to support rural women. NGOs, however, interpreted this as being 'swamped by the [ZANU(PF)] Women's League'. The proposal was effectively stalled until the 1990s, when NGOs argued that the proposal was out of keeping with post-Cold War trends towards deregulation and liberalization.[197] Although the sector is very diverse, women's NGOs established post-independence have tended to be policy-oriented, with an emphasis on changing laws to enhance women's social, political and legal status.

The Women's Action Group (WAG), for instance, was founded in reaction to the 1983 'Operation Clean-up' in which 6,000 women were arrested. A group of middle-class women, mainly foreigners and whites working in the NGO sector, met with the intention of researching the incident and lobbying parliament, and thereby created what became the Women's Action Group (WAG).[198] The process cata-lysed further meetings with women, and advocacy around other issues of concern to women including access to birth control. At this stage, WAG's campaigning efforts were quite high-profile. Although they failed to meet with then Prime Minister Mugabe over the women's continuing detention without trial, they did have a sympathetic hear-ing from the Minister for Women's Affairs.[199] When they later pro-tested to then President Banana over discrepancies in sentences passed on women convicted of infanticide (which the press referred to emo-tively as baby-dumping) compared to male murderers, twenty-three women were given presidential pardons and freed from prison.[200] Nevertheless, the attitude of the government to WAG's intervention is clear in an anecdote reported by a former women's ministry official that 'a directive was issued to staff at the ministry [that] WAG must be discredited and destroyed'.[201]

In 1986, WAG became a donor-funded rather than a voluntary orga-nization, with paid workers.[202] By 1998, it had a full-time staff of four-teen, plus six field workers. All but two of the original volunteers had moved away, died or left the organization. When I interviewed the direc-tor (who was also the wife of a cabinet minister), she emphasized:

> When we have our members meeting, I always call for a government official to attend, to show we are not doing anything wrong. I always emphasize that as NGOs we complement the government. Strategies are important ... lobbying depends on the issue we are dealing with, what level you should act on ... there are situations where confrontation doesn't help. If people agree to sit down with you then you can get some-where ... you may seem to be weaker but you can make mileage that way, try not to make enemies. ... If you are allowed to sit at the right table, that is where you can have influence.[203]

Although this attitude had been common earlier in the decade,[204] the director was making these statements at a time of polarization between

NGOs and the state. Considering WAG's radical origins, some of those involved in WAG felt that the organization was 'moving from critical engagement to co-option ... they want to bring everyone into ZANU'.[205]

But it was a less radical women's NGO than WAG which felt the full force of the government's institutional power. In November 1995, the newly-passed Private Voluntary Organizations (PVO) Act was used to remove the executive members of the Association of Women's Clubs (AWC), a grass-roots NGO with over 40,000 members. The Act was an amended and revised version of the Rhodesian-era Welfare Organisations Act (1967), which gave the minister responsible for NGOs the power to suspend members of executive committees, simply by issuing a 'gazette' or notification of the suspension.[206] The AWC was a well-established organization, with an eminent pedigree. Originally founded in 1938 by Helen Mangwende, the wife of Chief Mangwende, to 'uplift the lives of her fellow women', the AWC had experienced administrative and financial difficulties in the 1980s as membership had declined in the later years of the liberation war.[207] The first post-independence chair of the AWC, Mrs Betty Mtero, appointed in 1982, was also at that time employed in the Ministry of Women's Affairs and Community Development.[208] She then became the National Director of AWC, but was dismissed in 1992 for financial mismanagement.

In the 1990s the AWC had begun to revive, under the leadership of Sekai Holland and the promise of substantial donor funding.[209] Holland was the daughter of the first black editor of a newspaper, M. M. Hove, later a Rhodesian MP and ambassador to Nigeria for the Federation of Nyasaland and the Rhodesias. A student overseas in the 1960s, Holland represented ZANU in Australasia, South East Asia and the Far East in the 1970s, although she left the party in the aftermath of Herbert Chitepo's assassination.[210] However, in 1995, the government suspended the Executive Committee of the AWC, using the provisions of the new Act.[211] A caretaker administration was installed, which was later replaced with a committee of women alleged to be 'loyal' representatives of ZANU(PF)'s Women's League. The former chair and director, Mrs Mtero, was reappointed, which led to suspicions that the attack on the AWC was little more than her orchestrated revenge.[212] The suspended executive members applied to the Supreme Court in May 1996, asking the court to rule on the constitutionality of the act.[213] In February 1997, the judges found unanimously that their right to a fair hearing had been obstructed, and hence that part of the act was indeed unconstitutional.[214]

The regime's reaction to the formation of the Matabeleland Zambezi Water Project (MZWP) further highlights the political sensitivities of NGO interventions around the development agenda. The MZWP was formed by a group of mainly white businesspeople in Matabeleland to promote the idea of a pipeline to bring water to the drought-stricken areas of Matabeleland from the Zambezi River. Despite its narrow origins, this group galvanized public support from all sectors of Bulawayo society, with donations coming from schoolchildren, factory workers, the city council and local businesses. In a high-profile public-ity stunt, Arnold Payne, a 'coloured' former ZAPU member, carried a barrel of water from Victoria Falls to Bulawayo.[215] By 1994, the MZWP had collected a total of ZWD 8 million. Despite having Dumiso Dabengwa, then Deputy Minister of Home Affairs, as chair, the scheme was viewed with some suspicion by the ruling party. This sort of high-visibility lobbying was uncommon, and seemed to make ruling party officials uncomfortable. In 1994, a 'new' NGO called the Matabeleland Zambezi Water Project Trust was launched, which had representation from the MZWP, the Bulawayo City Council, the Matabeleland Chamber of Industry, the Chamber of Commerce, the Matabeleland Action Group (a group of ZANU(PF) politicians), ZANU-PF Bulawayo, ZANU-PF Matabeleland North, ZANU-PF Matabeleland South, the Commercial Farmers Union, the Zimbabwe Farmers Union and the government. In effect, the project had been absorbed into ZANU. While the government had not been hostile to the MZWP and seemed to have accepted the involvement of an NGO in the policy-making process, it required that it be less confrontational.[216] Gwebu argues that the MZWP demonstrated the limited 'extent to which community participation could influence central government policy';[217] unfortu-nately, it also illustrated the government's unwillingness to permit autonomous movements with a popular base.

More difficult for the regime to control was the growing move towards policy advocacy on the part of long-standing and respected NGOs, which had previously focused on service provision and devel-opment projects. For example, in 1993 the Zimbabwe Council of

Churches created a Justice, Peace and Reconciliation (JPR) desk, to deal with issues of economic justice and civic education.[218] The ZCC also claims credit for having lobbied the Electoral Supervisory Commission to permit NGOs and Churches to monitor the 1995 parliamentary election.[219] That led to the creation of a Church-NGO coalition which organized workshops and meetings throughout the country, bringing local church members and community activists together to talk about civic issues.[220] This shift towards advocacy made the ZANU(PF) regime increasingly suspicious that NGOs were no longer cooperating with its development agenda.[221]

However, relations between NGOs and the state were obscured by the incompetence that characterized the NGO 'umbrella body', leaving NGOs disorganized and poorly supported. In 1990, faced with economic difficulties serious enough to prevent the payment of staff salaries, the original director of VOICE was dismissed for mismanagement, and VOICE was renamed.[222] The new National Association of NGOs (NANGO) was intended to be more decentralized and to represent a broader coalition of groups, reflecting the newer NGOs and their concerns with social and economic issues and human rights; however, its constitution and format remained much the same.[223] NANGO, like VOICE, also continued to receive an operating grant from the Department of Social Welfare.

Through the 1990s, NANGO continued to experience financial and administrative problems which were exacerbated, rather than solved, by decentralization into regional offices. For most of this period, around 500–800 NGOs were registered with the Department of Social Welfare (as required by law), but at most only 140–300 of those were members of NANGO, and even fewer paid their membership dues.[224] The impending financial and administrative crisis climaxed in 1996. Like its predecessor VOICE, NANGO had lost the capacity to pay its staff, who left for jobs elsewhere in the sector. While no monies were misappropriated, they had been spent improperly. Administrative funding had ended in 1994, but activities had carried on, using programme funds to finance NANGO's day-to-day administration and salaries. NANGO was unable to report to donors on the expenditure of their funds, and donors refused to continue support.[225] This led to a debt-load of at least ZWD 1.5 million (USD 150,000). Attempts to reverse the decline failed, including a detailed external evaluation and two workshops involving staff and membership.[226] The entire northern region committee resigned, despite comprising powerful Harare-based NGOs.[227] Also, at this critical time, NANGO was given notice by its landlord Lonrho, who had for many years subsidized their rental of a prime piece of real estate along Samora Machel Avenue, which housed the increasingly dilapidated head offices.

NANGO's economic and administrative weakness meant that at a crucial juncture it was incapable of effectively representing the interests of NGOs towards the state. In January 1995 the then acting director (subsequently director) of the Department of Social Welfare had informed NANGO that the ministry was in the process of revising the law on NGOs.[228] However, both NANGO and most NGOs insist that the details of the amendment only came to the attention of NGOs after its second reading in parliament on 7 February 1995 led to a report in the daily newspaper.[229] NANGO failed to organize NGOs or to lobby the Social Welfare Department on their behalf. Its main contribution seems to have been a letter to the Minister of Public Services and Social Welfare pointing out that the proposed name change from 'Welfare Organizations' to 'Private Voluntary Organizations' (PVOs) was 'rather alien to Zimbabwe'.[230] A second submission, written after a meeting of concerned NGOs and addressed to the Director of the Social Welfare Department, detailed a few other minor concerns.[231] NANGO had abrogated its responsibility to represent the interests of NGOs vis-à-vis the state.

However, even as NANGO's ability to network with NGOs weakened, advocacy-oriented NGOs began forming coalitions with other civil society groups, like churches and unions, a crucial step for Zimbabwean politics. Spearheaded by the established church-NGOs such as the ZCC and CCJP, they were also joined by newer, smaller organizations like Ecumenical Support Services, run by an ecumenical and inter-racial group of lay Christians,[232] and ZimRights, a human rights organization founded in 1992 by a high-profile group of professionals and activists including Chenjerai Hove, Morgan Tsvangirai and Garfield Todd.[233] One such coalition was the Campaign for the Repeal of the PVO Act. As discussed above, NANGO had failed to take seriously the new act to regulate NGOs. In doing so, it was not out of touch with its membership. In mid-1995, when Revd Kuchera of the Zimbabwe Council of Churches was asked what his organization was doing about the new act, he said, 'I am not really very worried about it ... the basic welfare operations will remain the same ... so I am not going to spend my time and my energy trying to look at the dots and the full-stops ... what difference does it make?'[234] However, some NGOs were concerned about the potential for ministerial abuse. ZimRights publicized concerns about the act at the 1995 Zimbabwe International Book Fair,[235] and other Harare-based NGOs also voiced concern that the 'Act goes beyond the legitimacy of the Government to oversee the work of NGOs ... the Act has every room to cater for abuse, corruption and even threatening the independence of NGO work'.[236]

Finally, in June 1996, seven months after the act was used to 'gazette' the leadership of the AWC and remove it from power, and eighteen months after the introduction of the act, ZimRights organized a workshop on NGO Activism, 'instigated by the failure of NGOs to unite in opposition to the PVO Act';[237] it was followed by a second meeting in September 1996. Out of these workshops came the Steering Group of the Campaign for the Repeal of PVO Act,[238] which was composed of staff members from five Harare-based NGOs.[239]

The PVO campaign was handicapped by the limited networking of NGOs in Zimbabwe and the reluctance of the mainstream press to print articles on the PVO Act. Faced with this lack of awareness, the campaign decided to 'conscientize' NGOs first and then 'go public'. Many NGOs did not know about the gazetting of the AWC, and had little knowledge of or interest in the new act. The campaign prepared fact sheets[240] and a briefing paper which suggested that 'serious and constructive dialogue between the Government of Zimbabwe and leaders within the NGO community from across the country is long overdue. ... Otherwise the conflicts and antagonisms will continue to *the detriment of development*.'[241] A petition was also launched in October 1996 which argued that:

> civil society has always and continues to *make valuable contributions to the development of this nation* and that Government has on numerous occasions committed itself to promoting good governance, democracy and the rule of law. The Private Voluntary Organisations Act runs contrary to these commitments. We the undersigned are therefore determined to have the

Private Voluntary Organisations Act repealed. We demand a democratic environment free of the threatened government interference *for meaningful NGO participation in Zimbabwe*. We call upon the Minister to institute an open and serious discussion with NGOs so as to involve them in the drafting of acceptable NGO legislation.[242]

All of these steps—calling for an act to be repealed, launching a coalition 'outside' NANGO, and asking for signatures on a petition— were unprecedented. As the italicized text above makes clear, the campaign was careful to phrase its complaints in 'developmental discourse', as it was still stepping on many toes. The campaign was seen as trespassing on NANGO's space, since NANGO remained the government-endorsed umbrella organization for NGOs. Some were sceptical of the campaign's motives, which were perceived to be working behind NANGO's back: 'We've never had any such thing in this country, we have been working so well with government'.[243] Concern was expressed that forming a coalition outside NANGO risked creating divisions within the sector. The suggestion that there was no reason that all NGOs must be united, decrying the Zimbabwean 'fetish for unity,' was met with incredulity and concern.[244]

The government's discourse also took into account that the lead NGOs within the campaign were not necessarily representative of the NGO community in Zimbabwe as a whole, but were instead a Harare-based elite, concerned with issues less 'grounded' than those of more developmentally oriented, rural or small-town NGOs. Soon after the Supreme Court ruled the new act unconstitutional, the Director of Social Welfare argued that the act was intended to recognize the shift of NGOs from charity work towards development, that '*the soul of the new Act places emphasis on development*'.[245] Although not directly attacking this pronouncement, a campaign representative said: 'It is essentially *the right to development* of our entire society that is at stake. ... This is why people should not be unnecessarily confrontational. ...We need to come up with a process that will continue the discourse of government and civil society.'[246] At a subsequent meeting the director insisted, 'we want to see NGOs operating with us as partners. NGOs are doing a very good job in this country, and we want to facilitate that ... we want to see NGOs being complementary to Government activities.'[247] Even as the campaign sought to mobilize NGOs, there was also a similarity of discourse, and a recognition that too abrupt a break with conventional modes of operating was risky.

While the Social Welfare Ministry seemed to try to avoid confrontation, the security and intelligence branches of the government were also taking an interest in these 'activist' groups. The AWC women and the PVO campaign received threats in the wake of the Supreme Court ruling.[248] CIO paid visits to coalition member NGOs. In addition, NGOs were warned that their registration with the Social Welfare ministry must be in order, or else they would be closed down.

The state's stonewalling or non-decision-making tactics—aided and abetted by the divisions within the NGO community—were effective in keeping the campaign at arm's length. Nevertheless, the campaign stirred up NGOs in Zimbabwe and became a model for further lobbying and advocacy. The campaign's depiction of NGOs as development actors, deserving of input into state policies, made a mockery of the state's own discourse of facilitating development, while also seeking to legitimize its own interventions.

Conclusion

Between 1987 and 1997, the ideas and practices on which the regime based its legitimacy were challenged both by the failures of economic policy and the evidence of enrichment and privileges that accumulated around the '*chefs*' and their families. It was also a period when the number and range of societal organizations exploded: no longer did most organizations trace their origins and painful histories to the liberation war; instead, NGOs, professional groups, interest groups, new universities and Churches established themselves on an increasingly diverse landscape.

With the introduction of economic liberalization came hardship for some, but also a remarkable expansion in the middle classes and elites. The politics of inclusion reached out to incorporate more firmly the black business and middle classes, affirming their capitalist ventures. War veterans were granted permission to form an interest group, in an attempt to keep them under party control, but they emerged as a potent political force in 1997. The rhetoric of land resurfaced before the 1995 elections and again in 1997, but there was little actual land redistribution.

THE POLITICS OF DURABILITY (1987–1997)

In the period after the Unity Accord, public debate did emerge to challenge the government's commitment to socialist development. The revelation of corruption amongst the ranks of ministers was particularly damaging. Groups formally outside the party—academics, lawyers and students—debated the value of the party's demand for a *de jure* one-party state. Yet, in a *coup de grâce*, the regime internalized even this debate and resolved it within the party, taking away the incipient opposition's strongest card and retaining control of political debate. For much of this decade, attempts by NGOs to mobilize or articulate alternative policy positions were stymied by a deeply internalized reluctance to criticize government, or move outside the regime's framing discourses of unity and development. Strategic use of government institutions and law-making, along with a discourse of liberalization, weakened unions, students and academics as interest groups. Development as a discourse had the paradoxical effect of both raising the profile and presence of development and NGOs, and limiting their ability, and often their interest, to act critically.

This combination of strategic policy responses, rhetoric and the selective distribution of benefits ensured that the regime endured. Yet, this can only be seen to have been an uneasy balancing act, typified by *ad hoc* reactions, not a carefully thought out plan. As a result, this equilibrium was fragile and easily disrupted.

5

THE POLITICS OF POLARIZATION (1998–2000)

You must choose, are you with the nation or the state?[1]

Between 1998 and 2000, politics in Zimbabwe were dramatically transformed in tone and form. In contrast to the ambiguity of previous years, relations between state and society became deeply polarized. This chapter tracks these changes, looking in particular at how the National Constitutional Assembly (NCA) brought together a broad range of societal organizations to shape some profound political outcomes by the end of the decade. NGOs, unions and churches catalysed a very public debate which was seized upon by citizens across the country to articulate critiques of the political and economic environment. This period is notable also for the extensive use of popular culture and the media to articulate the regime's position, and for the limited use of coercion. The deliberations and strategizing that took place around the constitution provide a lens through which to identify significant shifts in state-society discourse.

The chapter starts by examining the economic conditions in the late 1990s, which provide the context for much of the ensuing debate. It then delineates the changing alignments and increasing polarization between state and society, in a dramatic contrast to the previous decade. It traces the origins of the National Constitutional Assembly, and the unease with which it was met by some NGOs and churches. The ways in which this debate is framed and advanced fundamentally challenge the post-independence record of the Mugabe government, its development agenda and its liberation credentials. The focus of the chapter then turns to the regime's reaction: both institutionally, in the form of the Constitutional Commission; and rhetorically, as it first intensified the nationalist rhetoric of previous decades and then labelled those who chose to work with the NCA as illegitimate interlocutors, disloyal to the state and the legacy of liberation. Ultimately, the question is about who can represent and speak for the nation. Are those without liberation war pedigrees legitimate interlocutors? And what is the proper relationship between NGOs, churches and trade unions and formal political institutions? Activists and voters alike were forced to choose between aligning themselves with the regime, or with the NCA and the new opposition; there was no room left for ambiguity. The strikingly public process undertaken by the government's Constitutional Commission and the referendum it called in early 2000 created a new, popular and remarkably transparent platform on which these crucial transformations unfolded.

In an important article, Adrienne LeBas argues that polarization occurred because of the selective, short-term decisions taken by the political parties. Her sophisticated analysis links the processes of polarization that occurred across the late 1990s and early 2000s, as the new opposition party, the Movement for Democratic Change, emerged.[2] While her account is convincing in unpacking the implications of these transitions for political parties, the account given below focuses on the origins of polarized politics in the interaction of the NCA and the Constitutional Commission up until the 2000 referendum. In isolating this political moment, we can see the unexpected way in which the constitutional debate caught people's imagination and dragged ZANU into an entirely unintended public process of deliberation about the political foundations of the state. Not only was the debate itself unanticipated, but, as we shall see, the ability of civil society to set the terms of discussion was unprecedented.

Economic conditions and labour unrest

By the end of 1997 a series of incidents, including the crisis over the claims of the war veterans, Zimbabwe's entry into the Congo war and the weakening economy, had sent reverberations across the political sphere. The regime's basis of legitimacy was called into question as veterans of the liberation war camped outside the president's official residence and stormed the ZANU(PF) headquarters, in reaction to Margaret Dongo's revelation in parliament that a fund set up to compensate war veterans injured during the liberation war scandal had been looted by high-level ZANU(PF) functionaries.[3] As detailed in the previous chapter, these embarrassing disclosures led Mugabe to commit funds to war veterans' pensions in November 1997. This fiscally imprudent gesture led the Zimbabwe dollar to collapse from 12:1USD to 24:1USD in 1998.[4] While import and investment sectors of Zimbabwe's economy had benefited under the Economic Structural Adjustment Programme (ESAP), the dollar's collapse meant that conditions worsened for all but a very few.

These economic pressures, typified by the fuel shortages of 1999–2000, plus the continuing issues of unemployment, declining health and education standards, catalysed an unprecedented and public critique of the Mugabe regime. In 1999, even the *Herald* commented that the failing urban transport system was back to pre-structural adjustment conditions, with many workers cycling and walking to their jobs.[5] Although the failures of economic policy were mainly blamed on ESAP, the *Herald* further noted that workers were on average ten times poorer in 1999 than in 1990.[6]

In protest at tax increases, the Zimbabwe Congress of Trade Unions (ZCTU) successfully called for a 'stay-away' in December 1997, which they estimated was supported by 3.5 million workers.[7] While this estimate may have been optimistic, the stay-away was the first widely observed national protest at government policy since independence. In January 1998 food riots erupted throughout Chitungwiza and Harare's high-density areas,[8] followed by a two-day stay-away called by the ZCTU in March.[9] The government's first reaction to these 'stay-aways' was to ban all demonstrations[10] and then to send in the army.[11] After the December stay-away, Morgan Tsvangirai was attacked in the Harare ZCTU offices; and after the March stay-away, the ZCTU offices in Bulawayo were destroyed by fire.[12] Further protests occurred in November and December 1998, in reaction to increased fuel prices and the decision to send the Zimbabwe army to the Congo in support of Kabila's government.[13]

These protests were concentrated in urban areas, where residents were suffering from declining services and difficult living conditions. Housing shortages in urban areas, always a problem, intensified at the end of the decade. The government's 1985 goal of 'Housing for all by the year 2000' had become a joke. By 1999, there was a backlog of 1 million units of housing (670,000 of these in Harare), with only 200,000 housing units/serviced stands having been created in the intervening period.[14] Municipal facilities, including refuse collection, sewage disposal, water supplies and roadworks, were under stress, with city councils increasingly unable to provide basic services. The Harare Council called upon residents to 'hold meetings among themselves to discourage refuse dumping'.[15] Municipalities also suffered as the central government failed to pay bills, leaving them 'cash-strapped'.[16] The decline of socio-economic standards appears also to have sparked the increasing militancy of rate-payers associations in most towns.[17] But concern was by no means limited to 'activists' or potential opposition supporters. In March 1999, MP Sabina Mugabe, the president's sister, used her reply to the President's Address to detail the problems of access to water in her constituency, Zvimba, and to call for more dams to be constructed. But then she went on to discuss the urban water system: 'I have never seen a situation whereby a person uses someone else's yard as a toilet, but the city of Harare has done it ... how can we have health for all by the year 2000 ... with squatters at Manyame river as well as the companies that are dumping their waste into the river?'[18]

Parliamentarians representing rural constituencies used their position to articulate growing grievances about the declining capacity of the developmental state. Questions from some backbenchers continued to ask ministers when electrification, telephone exchanges, post offices, clinics and secondary schools would come to their constituencies. But others extended their critique more deeply. One MP appealed to the house:

> Mr Speaker, I have emerged from groups of people who feel abandoned and sometimes betrayed. The task given to me by Vungu Constituency is to cry out aloud make this House aware of the plight our people find themselves in. The eighteen years of independence have seen our constituency sink to the lowest ebb ever because of the decline in the quality of services in the social sector.

He went on to detail concerns about education, veterinary services, resettlement and access to water. On health, he noted:

> Although many clinics have either been built or upgraded, this has been in terms of structures only. Many-a-time there is neither the staff nor the medicine/drugs to be used to cure the sick. It is in this light that the so-called free services in rural clinics have lost meaning to those who seek the services.

Calling for an urgent debate during the doctors' strike in October 1999, Mr Chigwedere moved a motion which began: 'Parliament deplores the near collapse of the country's health delivery system'. He went on to speak in some detail of the strengths and weakness of the medical system, in particular health delivery in rural areas:

> What has gone wrong if our budget aimed at providing health facilities to the entire nation? We have failed to do that. ... Look at the irony, where hospitals have been provided: no nurses, no drugs. For example, Hauna Hospital in Honde Valley; it is an excellent institution that has no doctor and hardly any nurses, and to crown it all, no drugs.[19]

Public protest was less visible in rural areas, but in these years we do see a resurgence of land occupations and farm-workers joining the bandwagon of strikes. Notably in 1997 and 1998, land occupations again became visible in the media, and public discourse rose as squatters began to occupy land on a large scale.[20] These incidents were alleged to have been at the instigation of ZANU(PF) officials—as some of them overlapped with the 1998 Donors' Conference and were thought to be a 'demonstration' of the need for land.[21] However, Rachel Knight's interview research with Svovse villagers in the months after the first invasions describe a somewhat more nuanced process:

> communal villagers from Svovse ... travelled together to a neighbouring commercial farm owned by a white farmer. The villagers did not attempt to seize the farm for their own use, but instead established a makeshift temporary settlement from which they demanded that they be taken and resettled immediately onto nearby fertile fields slated for redistribution to communal farmers under the government's land redistribution program.[22]

The peasants understood their actions as 'demonstrations', confirming their support for government policies, but also revealing its failures:

> the idea was started with the President when he said that we are going to take the land. We wanted to show our support. That was the first idea to

organise people—to show the feelings of the people. We had lots of comrades here. They came up to this house and after talking about how the
government was not actually speeding up the programme [we thought]
what should we do? Then we thought that maybe, maybe the best way was
to show that we also needed land, that it was not only the President who
was saying that the people should have land.[23]

While the demonstrations were politically oriented, and orchestrated by the local Development Committee, inevitably a ZANU(PF)
body, they were also driven by land hunger:

> One woman explained '... the whole Svovse area—all the women and the
> grandmothers and a few boys and grandfathers—we met and talked about
> how this past year—1997—we had hunger and we didn't want the same
> thing to happen again. And we know of the neighbouring farms—some of
> those farmers have five farms and they are not fully using them—so we
> thought of going and talking to the farmer to get a small piece of his farm.
> Because in this area we cannot plough—we only shift rocks and plant
> around the boulders. We are tired. Our crops die even if it is raining
> because we are growing crops on stones. We went to invade the farms
> because we are hungry. We know that some of these farms are where our
> ancestors are buried but that is not the reason we invaded. It was our
> hunger and the congestion up here in the rocks.'

The Svovse demonstrations sparked off other similar protests, some
led by politicians and others more spontaneous. As African Rights points
out, there were also several cases of squatters targeting senior party officials who themselves owned farms.[24] This suggests that land hunger was
a potent force, especially when combined with years of unmet promises
from government officials. Protests reinforced government rhetoric, but
at the same time revealed the very real failures of policy.

These unprecedented protests must be contextualized against the
emergence of major political scandals. Three of these—the VIP housing
scheme, the war veterans and the airport tender—had hit the headlines
in 1997. As the decade continued, the list of scandals unearthed by the
increasingly vigilant media and discussed in parliament increased. In
1999, the Social Dimensions of Adjustment Fund, designed to shield
the poorest of the poor from the impact of structural adjustment, was
reported to have been 'looted'.[25] Monies allocated to government
agencies such as the District Development Fund (DDF) were used to
buy cars for officials instead of for digging boreholes; and agricultural

equipment was used to develop the farms of senior officials.[26] Allegations also surfaced that bribery was widespread within the Attorney General's office.[27]

The Harare city council was disbanded after charges of corruption and fraud were laid against the mayor and senior officials.[28] At the same time, senior ministers were implicated in corruption scandals within two significant parastatals: the National Oil Company of Zimbabwe (NOCZIM) and the Grain Marketing Board (GMB).[29] Ministers were reported to have benefited from clandestine fuel deals, which cost NOCZIM an estimated ZWD 1 billion.[30] The consequent debts resulted in the fuel crisis of 2000–2001. Kumbirai Kangai, a long-serving cabinet minister, was alleged to have siphoned ZWD 228.4 million from the GMB while Minister of Lands and Agriculture.[31]

In 1999, parliamentary reports also revealed political interference and corruption within the University of Zimbabwe and the Zimbabwe Broadcasting Corporation (ZBC). In presenting and responding to these reports, the MPs spoke openly about the abuse of power, conflicts between civil servants and ministers, and between ministers and backbenchers. But their concerns were also with the failure of the ZBC to provide adequate programming to the entire nation, such that many Zimbabweans were listening to radio and watching television from neighbouring countries: 'If you want to seriously consider that Zimbabwe is an independent country, you want to see and hear it announcing its policies through its own broadcasts, but this is nowhere to be seen.'[32] They were also concerned about the implications of incompetence and corruption for the nation, and for ZANU(PF). Irene Zindi, for example, emphasized:

> This is public funds, we are doing this [broadcasting] for the nation, the trust has been bestowed upon us ... that trust we as leaders are abusing ... for as long as we continue to do this, I am afraid we are getting to the doomsday of ZANU(PF) ... we are seen to be a leadership of just looking at how I should line my pocket.[33]

Forced to respond to this barrage of criticism from within and outside the party, the president established an anti-corruption commission in the lead-up to the 2000 election.[34] But other political crises also marked this period. In August 1998, the Zimbabwean government sent soldiers to support Laurent Kabila's government in the Democratic Republic of the Congo (DRC), which was being militarily challenged by internal rebels allied with Rwanda and Uganda. The motives for this intervention remain somewhat murky, but probably include two main factors. First, Mugabe's concern to present himself as the leader of the Southern Africa Development Community (SADC), whose charter obliges members to assist each other in the case of foreign invasion. Second, the Zimbabwean government had an interest in preserving Kabila in power because of substantial outstanding loans, which the rebel forces would doubtless not repay.[35]

As Zimbabwe's commitment to the Congo war was extended and expanded, economic interests—especially investments made by army officials—came to dominate explanations of Zimbabwe's involvement. Increasing emotional costs to the families of soldiers, and financial costs to the Treasury thought to be worth USD 3 million a month, led to questions being asked about how the army supported its Congo activities.[36] It was alleged that soldiers were being paid bonuses directly from some DRC companies, and more significantly, that concessions and joint ventures had been set up to facilitate the expansion of Zimbabwe's investment, benefiting companies controlled by high-ranking military officers and ZANU officials.[37] A UN Security Council report suggests that '[a]mong all of its allies, Zimbabwean companies and some decision-makers have benefited most from this scheme', which they refer to as 'incentives for assistance'.[38] The World Bank's suspension of a much-needed USD 140 million loan in October 1999, and aid cancellations by bilateral donors, after a leaked government memo revealed the extent of government expenditure in the Congo, further contributed to economic strain.[39] Unsurprisingly, many Zimbabweans viewed these developments as further evidence that the developmental priorities of the state had shifted away from poverty reduction and towards providing investment opportunities to the elite.

During these same years, media and communication technology within Zimbabwe expanded greatly, with urban consumers able to access cellphones, email and independent radio, television and more newspapers than ever before; but at the same time, government attacks on such media intensified. In 1999, the independent editors were accused of being used by 'hostile forces in the UK, South Africa and the United States to plot the downfall of President Mugabe's government.'[40]

A turning point for the media was the South African publication of the CCJP/LRF report on human rights abuses in Matabeleland in the weekly *Mail and Guardian*.[41] Not only was the *Mail and Guardian* widely available in Zimbabwe, but the local independent media immediately carried the story and followed it up.[42] In response, the government acknowledged the human rights abuses perpetrated by government forces and, for the first time, made commitments to compensation.[43]

In response to the increasing willingness of the independent media to publish stories critical of the government, the state seemed to change tactics radically vis-à-vis the media in 1999. After the *Standard* published a story written by Ray Choto alleging that an attempted army coup had been foiled, its editor Mark Chavunduka was detained illegally by the army for seven days.[44] After the courts ordered his release, the army handed him over to the police. Having evaded the army, Choto turned himself in to the police but was, with Chavunduka, handed over to military officials who tortured them for 36 hours.[45] Clive Wilson, their managing editor, was also detained by the police, after holding a press conference at which the journalists alleged torture. Ibbo Mandaza and Grace Kwinjeh from the *Mirror*, another weekly launched in 1998, were arrested on 8 February 1999 and charged in connection with an article published in October, also concerning the war in the Congo.[46] Kwinjeh's story alleged that the family of a Zimbabwe man serving in the Congo had received not his body, but only his head. Like Choto and Chavunduka, she and Mandaza were charged with publishing false information which is 'likely to cause fear, alarm or despondency among the public',[47] although charges against them were eventually dropped.[48] The political unpopularity of the war in the Congo was blamed for the government's harsh reaction. Mark Chavunduka said, 'if things had been normal, I think they would just have laughed it off'.[49] The government was also clearly concerned about ensuring the loyalty of the army, as the torture of the reporters was aimed solely at uncovering their sources.[50] The contest between the government and the independent media was intensified with the establishment and rapid popularity of the *Daily News* in 1999.[51]

In the same period, the government also began to exercise more control over the state-run media, which had previously been subject to self-censorship rather than outright control. In 1997, it was revealed that a

'D notice' had been issued to all ZBC sub-editors the previous year to the effect that: 'All stories on Margaret Dongo, Councillor Lawrence Mudehwe [the independent Mayor of Mutare], and Strive Masiyiwa … should be referred to the chief subs for radio news before being used in our bulletins.'[52] A ZBC radio personality was fired after she permitted callers to her 'open-line' programme to criticize police violence against protesters during the 1997 anti-tax demonstrations; and another similar programme was abruptly cancelled in December 1998.[53]

ZBC was at the same time experiencing financial and political crisis. In 1999, a parliamentary committee reported that 'successive Ministers of Information, Posts and Telecommunications have contributed immensely towards the instability at the corporation in that they seem to enjoy intervening directly in the day to day running of the organization … leading to chaos'. Ministers were accused of hiring and firing boards of directors 'at the slightest disagreement' and of showing 'vested interest' and intervening 'illegally' in ZBC affairs.[54] This vulnerability to political interference rendered the media available for manipulation and distortion as debates polarized. ZBC in particular was ripe for the role it was to play as the key purveyor of pro-regime discourses.

The National Constitutional Assembly

Starting in May 1997, staff members at the Zimbabwe Council of Churches (ZCC) called a series of meetings for NGOs, Churches and unions to consider the Constitution. This group became the nucleus of the National Constitutional Assembly (NCA). The initiative started with two staff members of the Justice, Peace and Reconciliation (JPR) office, Tawanda Mutasah and Deprose Muchena, who were both 'veterans' of student politics as well as the NGO coalitions discussed in Chapter 4. Initial funding for the period June 1997–June 1998 was provided by the German social democratic NGO, Friedrich Ebert Stiftung (FES).[55] Their budget was later supplemented with funding from Oxfam, HIVOS, the Friedrich Naumann Foundation, and the embassies of Denmark, the Netherlands, Canada, Australia and Sweden.[56]

The provisional taskforce was headed by Morgan Tsvangirai representing the ZCTU. A steering committee was chosen, which included both representatives of particular constituencies, including the

Churches, human rights NGOs, labour, women's groups and youth groups, and individuals acting in the role of 'consultants', primarily lawyers and academics.[57] Masipula Sithole, emphasizing the democratic and representative nature of the NCA, has also stressed the attention paid to ethnic balance within its leadership.[58] Labour-oriented academics, on the other hand, describe the NCA as a middle-class alliance because trade union participation was 'not extensive'.[59] Munyaradzi Gwisai claimed that 'the popular ZCTU leader Morgan Tsvangirai was put at its head in order to hoodwink the masses that such a body represented them'.[60] While membership was dominated by NGO and Church members and staff, veteran unionists were present and effective participants in discussion from the start.[61]

Unlike the NGO coalitions described in the previous chapter, the NCA was a large and disparate group of over a hundred NGOs, community associations and trade unions, as well as an indeterminate number of individual members.[62] With NGOs operating in Zimbabwe estimated to be in the thousands, the thirty to forty NGOs that joined the NCA cannot be considered representative of the wider sector, but they did include many high-profile organizations with legitimacy and influence within Zimbabwe. In addition to its large taskforce of nineteen members, the NCA also created an advisory committee of ten members, and legal, disciplinary, media and information, finance and management, gender and youth committees chaired by taskforce members, all of which had six to eight members. It also had a much larger budget and a permanent secretariat. So, the group of people working together in the 'coalition' was much broader and much more numerous. Importantly, many of the key leaders were 'veterans' of previous NGO coalitions.

The NCA capitalized on both the latent critique of the government and the newly expanded independent media. Despite the sense of crisis rapidly emerging in 1997, public criticism of government policies had remained until then the domain of a few activists. But using the framework of the constitution, which was described by NCA members as a 'non-political' way of talking about the exercise of politics, the NCA rapidly gained momentum. The NCA was premised on a critique of the constitution, which emphasized the multiple amendments made to the Lancaster House constitution by the ZANU(PF) government. Many of these amendments were perceived as 'panel-beating', designed to constitutionalize laws which the Supreme Court had ruled unconstitutional.[63] This meant that the issues discussed by the NCA inevitably touched on many of the key political issues of the past decades, in a political environment which was much more volatile than at any previous point after independence. Starting with this issue of the amendments, Morgan Tsvangirai highlighted the lack of 'public scrutiny and accountability' in the legislating of those amendments and linked them to 'abuse of power ... personality cults, and lack of transparency in our governance'.[64] As Masipula Sithole sagely observed, the NCA was formed more in reaction to the creation of the executive presidency in 1987 (Amendment 7), rather than the Lancaster House constitution.[65] So, just by bringing up the issue of the constitution and encouraging public participation, the NCA catalysed and regularized a debate which until then had had no formal place in the public domain.

The ZCC's presence as organizer was particularly valuable in legitimating the process. Some participants wanted the NCA to be a freestanding body, autonomous from the ZCC, but were told in response that 'we need an umbrella ... the church is always considered impartial. If we have ZCC as our umbrella no one will say we are being political.'[66] Even an outspoken human rights activist suggested that '[t]here is risk of a boycott or attack if not under ZCC ... the ZCC umbrella is strategically a good one'.[67] NCA members were therefore strategic about their organizing: aware that the coalition might well come to the attention of the intelligence agencies, they were determined to make it appear non-partisan to potential members.

From 1998 the NCA developed materials and trained facilitators to provide grass-roots 'conscientization' using 'participatory civic education' techniques. In its series of pamphlets entitled 'Debating the Constitution', the NCA addressed issues using simple English and cartoon sketches, designed to be used in workshops by facilitators. The booklets addressed the issues of citizenship, the constitution, finance, principles of democracy, declaration of rights, the executive, parliament and the judiciary. These cartoons effectively combined realistic situations with humour and the occasional didactic message. By the end of 1999, 576 facilitators across the country were trained to hold district-level meetings, using these booklets to elicit feedback from participants.[68] In its newspaper adverts, the NCA similarly used graphics effectively to bring up sensitive issues. One advert depicted a combat boot, 'the executive', crushing parliament. Readers were asked, 'What should the powers of parliament be?' Similarly, another advert showed the familiar image of bystanders being forced off the road by the presidential motorcade and the readers were asked, 'What should the powers of the Executive be?'

Yet these booklets and their intended users were not ready until 1999, and during 1998 the NCA carried out a more typical NGO agenda of urban-based meetings.[69] Much effort and many resources went into the urban-based thematic discussions of land, business, youth and women's issues, which attracted wide participation, including at least one cabinet minister. Although it was clear that some within the NCA coalition retained concerns about the 'political' nature of their agenda, the NCA was also involved in protests against the Public Order and Security Act, which was intended to replace the Rhodesian-era Law and Order (Maintenance) Act, sections of which had been declared unconstitutional. Similarly, in October 1998, the NCA organized a protest march against the Zimbabwean intervention in the DRC. But NCA members became increasingly uncomfortable with this move from 'educating' people about the constitution towards advocacy on issues concerned with government policy. On the eve of the march, the moderator of the NCA, Methodist Bishop Peter Nemapare, who was also Vice President of the ZCC, issued a press release stating that the ZCC would not participate in the march. This enabled police to claim that the march had been cancelled by its organizers, and to use tear gas to disperse those who had gathered.[70] Informed sources within the NCA and ZCC believed that Nemapare was pressurized by President Mugabe, to whom he was closely aligned, to call off the march.[71] This was the first public schism between the 'activists' and the NCA coalition members who sought to retain their connections with the regime.

The Constitutional Commission

Concerned by the NCA's increasingly critical tone and its growing dominance of public debate, the government launched its own constitutional commission (sometimes referred to as the Constitutional Review

Commission, or the CC) in March 1999.[72] While there had been suggestions that the NCA process might feed into the government's proposed
commission, and talks were held between the two groups, there was no
agreement guaranteeing the commission freedom from presidential
interference, and the two reviews proceeded in parallel.[73]

Unlike the NCA, the CC has emphasized not the amendments to the
constitution, but the problematic nature of the Lancaster House constitution, written by a small elite group in the UK. The CC's goal was
thus often described as a 'home-grown' constitution. Minister Eddison
Zvobgo said, 'we are not amending the Lancaster House constitution
but moulding it in our own image as you cannot have a nation which
breathes the historical experiences of another nation'.[74] Aware of the
need for transparency, the CC went far beyond any previous commission in Zimbabwe in using paid advertisements and press releases to
outline exactly how it would function because 'the whole world is
watching'.[75] The CC launched its consultation by printing a document
entitled 'Constitutional issues and questions' which ran as a multi-page
submission in the main papers.[76] It raised a series of themes accompanied by questions, such as:

1.2 Citizenship. What should be the grounds for acquisition, loss and res-
toration of Zimbabwean citizenship? What rights and duties should citizenship confer? ...

1.6 Supremacy of the Constitution. Where there is a conflict between
customary practices and provisions of the constitution, which should pre-
vail? ...

4. Separation of Powers (Pillars of the State). How should the head of state
be chosen? How many terms can the head of state serve? ...

7.7.1 The Right to Life. Should the death sentence remain? Should abor-
tion be allowed? ...

7.7.11 The Right to Vote. What should be the minimum voting age in
public elections: 16 years or 18 years or 21 years? Should voting be by
secret ballot or show of hands or head count? ...

Much the same sets of questions—in English, Ndebele and Shona—
were asked in newspaper adverts which further invited participation in
the process.

The membership of the commission included Justice Godfrey
Chidyausiku, who had recently chaired the investigation into the loot-

ing of the War Veterans' Compensation Fund, as chair; as vice chairs, Anglican Bishop Jonathan Siyachitema, Professor Walter Kamba, former Vice Chancellor of the University of Zimbabwe, and Mrs Grace Lupepe. Kamba chaired the coordinating committee which had two sub-committees: administrative and finance headed by Ibbo Mandaza, media and information chaired by Jonathan Moyo. Of the 395 commissioners, 150 were MPs. The remainder were described as representing interest groups, but this included chiefs, presumed to be ZANU(PF), mayors, at that time all ZANU(PF), as well as a wide range of opposition politicians, church people and NGO representatives. This mix of ZANU(PF), opposition and non-aligned commissioners was quite unprecedented, but ZANU(PF) was over-represented. Margaret Dongo, for instance, accused the commission of duplicating the structures of ZANU(PF), arguing that 'three-quarters are the ruling party's politburo, central committee members, provincial chairpersons, and so-called indigenous business persons aligned to the party'.[77] As we shall see, this led to conflict between the two groups, because the NCA held that anyone who had accepted appointment to the CC should excuse themselves from the NCA.[78]

Like the NCA, the CC appealed for donor funding. While it is not entirely clear how much they received, their projected budget was said to be ZWD 300 million. They were reported to have received funds of ZWD 22.8 million from the Ford Foundation, and ZWD 19 million from the Kellogg Foundation, both channelled through the Southern African Political and Economic Series (SAPES) Trust, which, despite its civil society ties, aligned itself with the government process.[79] Bilateral funding also came from South Korea (ZWD 380,000), Canada (ZWD 4 million) and Australia (ZWD 1.2 million).[80] The UNDP facilitated donations of ZWD 20 million from the Netherlands, Sweden, Norway and Denmark.[81] Both constitutional processes, the NCA and the CC, despite their different originators and membership, were equally recipients of donor funding.

Divide and rule: the politics of polarization

The formation of the Constitutional Commission led to serious divisions within 'civil society', as some groups chose to be incorporated into the state process, while others insisted on remaining autonomous.

Against the background of the government's implicit corporatist approach to NGOs, churches and unions, the opportunity to continue to work within the system was attractive to many organizations. In contrast to NGOs' reluctance to work outside NANGO in the coalitions described earlier, as politics became more polarized some NCA members became more assured in their determination not to cooperate with, and therefore lend legitimacy to, the government's process.

As discussed above, the ZCC had a fraught relationship with the NCA for some time before the formation of the CC. Conflict had first became visible in October 1998, during the NCA march against Zimbabwe's intervention in the Congo war. The ZCC was particularly vulnerable to government pressure at this time, because it needed the regime's support to ensure the smooth functioning of the upcoming World Council of Churches (WCC) meeting, which was to be held in Harare in December 1998. Some of its clerical leaders were thus unwilling to be associated with a protest against the government's foreign adventure. Frustration at this sabotage led the NCA, which had been housed within the ZCC, to move abruptly to new offices in November—a decision taken without notice being given to the ZCC staff who had been working with them. ZCC staff further felt alienated as the funds and computers which their donors had provided were shifted to NCA accounts.

When the government created the CC in March 1999, the ZCC withdrew its membership from the NCA. The ZCC Secretary General described the NCA as a process that had grown beyond the ZCC: 'we wanted to "unpack" the constitution ... [by this time] the understanding of unpacking was lost' and was out of its control; 'they were using our credibility, the actors were being political, there was no way to control them ... Actors in the NCA were exploiting the ZCC.'[82]

While the ZCC's Justice, Peace and Reconciliation (JPR) staff who had originated the NCA project considered remaining within the NCA, they felt there was no mandate for them to do so. ZCC staff emphasized that as the impetus developed for the Zimbabwe Congress of Trade Unions (ZCTU), which was a major player in the NCA, to form a political party, '[i]t was difficult to separate issues from the party and constitutional reform'. The Churches felt threatened. As a key-player said, 'as churches we had to take issues that don't raise too much dust or rock the boat too much, *but the boat was rocking*'.[83] By this time, the two ZCC staff members who had initiated the programme had also left to take better remunerated jobs with international NGOs. The ZCC-NCA break was complete.

The appointment of various high-profile figures to the Constitutional Commission created friction within a wide variety of other organizations and social groups. A three-day People's Constitutional Convention agreed to launch an alternative constitution-writing process that would be 'people-driven' instead.[84] The NCA had resolved that NCA members could not also be Constitutional Commissioners.[85] However, several well-respected individuals previously aligned with the NCA did become commissioners. Law lecturer Ben Hlatshwayo and Commentator Lupi Mushayakarara both moved from the NCA to the CC, and were selected to chair sub-committees.[86] Professor Heneri Dzinotyiweyi of the Zimbabwe Integrated Programme (an NGO-like body which later became a minor opposition party) and Dean of the Faculty of Science at the University of Zimbabwe, who had attended NCA meetings in the past and who also became a sub-committee chair, expressed many people's opinions in saying:

> Boycotting the process creates unnecessary antagonism. We also have our own suspicions but it is better to confront the issue than confront each other. ... There is no balance in the commission yet but we hope the NCA and opposition parties will come and work from within.[87]

Other groups which withdrew from the NCA in order to participate in the CC included the Zimbabwe National Students Union (ZINASU) and the Zimbabwe Union of Journalists (ZUJ).[88] The Anglican Church did not take an official position on the NCA/CC divide but, as we have seen, the Bishop of Harare became Vice Chair of the CC and his cathedral refused to let the NCA hold meetings on their premises.[89] No similarly placed Anglicans held positions within the NCA, although individual parishes and parishioners chose not to follow the Bishop of Harare.[90] Indeed, an Anglican priest, Fr Tim Neill, was widely reported in the press as calling the CC's draft constitution flawed.[91]

The Catholic Church was divided, with the Catholic Commission for Justice and Peace (CCJP) remaining within the NCA, and several of its staff members playing high-profile roles. Its nominal superior, the Zimbabwe Catholic Bishops Conference (ZCBC), supported the commission and called for priests and the laity to make representations to it.[92] Mike Auret, who was about to leave the CCJP and launch a political career, interpreted the bishops' stance cynically: '[They] have no objection to our being on the NCA, but want to hedge their bets.'[93]

The Zimbabwe Human Rights Association (ZimRights), which was at a particularly weak point with deep organizational divisions, was pressurized by the newly elected chair to pull out of the NCA. Members overruled this and insisted on remaining.[94] Zimbabwe Lawyers for Human Rights held a referendum, in which a majority of members advocated staying with the NCA, but a substantial minority did not.[95] The women's movement was seen as being particularly divided, although it eventually formed a coalition to promote women's constitutional interests within both the CC and the NCA.[96]

The NCA-CC split also divided Zimbabwe's fragile academic community. We have seen that SAPES, whose director, Ibbo Mandaza, was a constitutional commissioner, also channelled donor funds to the commission. A row about alleged misappropriation of funds contributed to the increasing polarization between SAPES' weekly *Mirror* newspaper, which along with the *Herald* took a strongly pro-CC line, and the rest of the independent press, which was equally as strongly pro-NCA.[97] While many high-profile Zimbabwean academics arrayed themselves on different sides of the NCA-CC alignment, Jonathan Moyo was by far the most prominent. Moyo, then a professor at Witswatersrand University in South Africa, had gained a strong reputation as a pro-democracy activist in the 'one-party state debate' in the late 1980s, but had been based in the US, Kenya and South Africa for much of the 1990s. As the CC's spokesman, he was responsible for much of the most personalized commentary against the NCA, and the strategic use of state-run media.

Conflicting concepts of constitutionality

The formation of the CC thus created the context for a much more conflict-prone and combative discussion of the constitution. If the government had thought that it could recapture control of the debate, it was mistaken. In August 1999, the Constitutional Commission began a programme of 5,000 meetings, organized by eight provincial teams. While the independent press took great pleasure in detailing the

Constitutional Commission meetings which had low turnouts, many people did address the commissioners and with great forthrightness.[98] As a prominent NCA activist ruefully acknowledged: 'we told people to boycott [the CC hearings] but now they are enjoying voicing their opinions'.[99] In an intriguingly positioned front-page story in the *Herald*, it was reported that in Tsholotsho villagers said that they could not speak freely to commissioners until after the Central Intelligence Organisation (CIO) was disbanded.[100] Meetings with students were also particularly prone to conflict.[101] The Constitutional Commission claimed to have organized 4,321 public meetings attended by 556,276 individuals, as well as 700 special *ad hoc* meetings attended by 150,000 people. In addition, they received 4,000 written submissions and had 16 programmes on Radio 1 [English]; 55 programmes on Radio 2 [Shona and Ndebele]; 2 programmes on Radio 3 [English]; 70 programmes on Radio 4 [minority languages—Tonga, Venda etc.]; as well as 31 programmes on ZBC-TV.[102] Zimbabweans in South Africa and the UK were also consulted. Despite the commission's own overwhelming focus on the flawed Lancaster House constitution, the input that it received emphasized instead the reforms of 1987, which had brought in the executive presidency and provincial governors. Just as the 'non-political' NCA had sparked an intensely political debate, the CC hearings provided a forum in which the current government's policies were explicitly criticized.

From the time that the Constitutional Commission hearings began, the overwhelming topic of conversation was of addressing the problems of the current government, which had led to the economic downturn. The hearings also revealed a thorough understanding of the political manipulation that had occurred. In public hearings the commissioners heard demands that all MPs and cabinet ministers be elected not appointed, that the post of provincial governor be abolished, that the size of the legislature be reduced, that parliament should have responsibility for the budget and more power in general, that presidential powers be reduced, that political party financing be reformed, and that an independent electoral supervisory commission be appointed.[103] This led commissioners to accuse people of using the meetings 'as a platform to present their complaints about the economic problems they are facing, while others think the meetings are held to source their views of the present government and the ruling party'.[104]

In October the CC held a three-day plenary meeting at which, in addition to each provincial team reporting back, special interest groups and political parties also presented their positions, all of which was also broadcast on ZBC and reported in both the state and independent press. It was at this point that clear divergence emerged between the proposals from the opposition parties, interest groups and the general public vis-à-vis the presentation from ZANU(PF), which encompassed an executive presidency as well as a prime minister.[105] These hearings also meant that groups like Gays and Lesbians of Zimbabwe (GALZ), which proposed that the rights of gays and lesbians be enshrined in a Bill of Rights, had access to the electronic media for the first time in five years.[106]

The commission's attempt to prepare a draft constitution after all this publicity led to conflict between the commission and ZANU(PF).[107] Rather than the provincial reports,[108] leading a significant minority of commissioners petitioned President Mugabe, alleging that the draft misrepresented the people's views.[109] The draft prepared by the coordinating committee resembled the submission presented to the commission by ZANU(PF). A particularly controversial aspect was a debate within the 'transitional mechanisms' committee, which was divided as to whether President Mugabe should serve out his current term as president, much less be allowed to contest future elections, if the draft recommended a limit of two five-year terms. The face-saving compromise decided upon was to drop the entire matter of transitional mechanisms, on the basis that it was not included under the commission's mandate, although it was one of the nine thematic committees.[110] Despite a report that twenty-four commissioners dissociated themselves from the draft, a final version was made public at the end of November and a referendum on it was scheduled for February 2000.[111]

After the plenary session in October, the thematic committees had analysed the ten provincial reports. Because these reports had been broadcast publicly and reported in detail in an eleven-part series in the *Herald*, people were well aware of what information the commission received, which meant that everyone had an opinion on whether or not the draft reflected the input. Chisaka's useful analysis suggests that the provincial and the thematic committees 'did a good job' and that it was only when their findings went to the executive that 'people's views were either distorted, ignored or rejected'.[112] Strongly expressed views on the limitations on the powers of the executive and separation of powers between the executive and legislative branches were not included in the draft. For instance, seven out of ten provinces favoured a non-executive president as head of state and an executive prime minister as head of government.

The CC's draft constitution retained the executive presidency and added a prime minister. Eight out of ten provinces wanted the president only to have the power to declare a state of emergency or a state of war after consulting parliament. The draft constitution gave this power to the president in consultation with the prime minister. Seven out of ten provinces said that parliament should have fixed-term limits, but the CC gave the president the power to dissolve parliament as he saw fit. As Chisaka suggests, 'the majority views of those consulted clearly wanted a governmental system that was accountable to them through their elected representatives in parliament … but this was denied them by the commission'.[113]

The very public failure of the draft constitution to reflect the content of people's submissions to the commission in the course of their hearings led to particularly dramatic rejections of the draft.[114] Unsurprisingly, it was criticized by those outside the process, who emphasized that the retention of an executive president was against the people's wishes, and that it retained a large assembly and made no restrictions on the size of the cabinet.[115] More damagingly, it was also criticized from within. Commissioners were particularly critical of the undemocratic way in which the draft had been rushed through their final session. Several commissioners switched sides and urged a 'No' vote.[116]

In one of the most high-profile defections, Bishop Ambrose Moyo of the Evangelical Lutheran Church resigned from the CC in December 1999 on the grounds that the draft constitution did not reflect the views of the people, that the commissioners had had no time to study or debate the draft, and that 'there was no democracy in the manner in which the chairman … processed both the Draft Constitution and the Final Report of the commission'.[117] Several commissioners, including the chair, acknowledged that the draft constitution did not reflect all the views of the people.[118] Two former commissioners launched an unsuccessful legal battle to have the draft reconsidered and the refer-

endum postponed.[119] The draft was even criticized by those who were
expected to support the government—ZANU(PF) and the war veterans—because it did not provide a framework to expedite the land
reform process, although both groups did ultimately advocate a 'Yes'
vote.[120] In a last-ditch effort, the president gazetted some 'corrections
and clarifications' to the draft constitution, the main effect of which
was to introduce a substantive new clause which permitted the state to
exercise compulsory acquisition of agricultural land, and obliged
Britain as the 'former colonial power' to compensate farmers.[121] Erin
McCandless's PhD research reveals the hidden story of the intense
lobbying that led to this result. In a lengthy interview, she is told:

> In the Commission we had one major interest—the Zimbabwe govern-
> ment must take land and not buy it. We tried our best. We lobbied and
> failed. ... There was no land in the constitution. We went back to the
> National Executive, where Hunzvi was chairing. We strategized. We
> decided to demonstrate against the ZANU ministers who were part of the
> Constitutional Commission. We went to Zvogbo ... asking him 'where is
> the land in your constitution?' He said, 'I'll talk to the president and he
> will allow changes to be made.' We moved down Samora Machel Avenue
> singing and chanting. We passed through the Sheraton to Jonathan Moyo's
> office saying 'you are an intellectual ... Why did you let this pass? Where
> is the land?' He said, 'I was also in the bush. I don't want to be frightened.'
> 'You are a sell-out' we told him. [Land Minister] Made walked in and we
> locked them in the room. 'You will not leave' we told them. Members
> from the president's office then came with a message: 'Comrades I have
> heard your cry. I will do something.'[122]

This abrupt change, which went against the previous relatively open
and transparent processes of the Constitutional Commission, influenced the debates in the run-up to the referendum, although these
were also shaped by media campaigns. The CC had run a high-profile
and professional advertising campaign in the six months before the
referendum in both the print and electronic media, even launching a
music video and CD.[123] The NCA, on the other hand, had been effectively blocked from airing programmes or adverts on ZBC airwaves.
Officials claimed that 'political advertising' must have government
approval. Persistent court battles failed to gain the NCA equal access
to ZBC channels.[124] The Media Monitoring Project (MMPZ) reported
that in the week following a high court ruling which required ZBC to

broadcast adverts, there were 22 CC adverts during and after the man news bulletins, and no NCA adverts at all.[125] The MMPZ also observed that the NCA was rarely provided with a right of reply in either news or current affairs broadcasts throughout the referendum campaign period. In a one-week period, it suggested that thirty out of forty-two minutes of television news coverage were allocated to CC officials.[126]

Despite its vociferousness, in retrospect the referendum campaign was relatively peaceful and free of intimidation. Some meetings did break down into violent confrontation, and there were reports that the police were called in to protect commissioners. On the last day before the referendum, two NCA leaders were arrested along with six other members.[127] But in general, the constitutional debate took place in public forums and in the media, drawing into the public sphere many who had not previously participated in political debates, and giving a legitimate platform for discussion of previously taboo subjects.

Who represents the nation?

The NCA-CC debate also catalysed a much broader set of questions about the role of NGOs, trade unions and individual citizens and their relationship to the state. The existence of the NCA challenged the previously dominant rhetoric and practice of the state, which presumed that it must initiate and control such consultations. The state media and the commission's campaign labelled the NCA as political, foreign-funded and anti-unity, because it challenged this premise.

In language reminiscent of 1980s nation-building, the NCA was accused of failing to support 'national consensus-building'[128] and of disrupting a 'national process' when it refused to take part in the CC.[129] In return, the NCA emphasized its demand for a 'stabilizing and unifying constitution-making process'.[130]

The issue of which process was the more legitimate dominated much of their rhetoric. Each accused the other of being less inclusive. The Constitutional Commission launched its public campaign in mid-July with a two-page advert labelled 'The New Democratic Constitution … And a Few of the Questions That You Might Be Asking'. Using a question and answer format, the advert addressed the issues of what the commission was, how commissioners were chosen and most tellingly of all, 'Is the Constitutional Commission in competition with the NCA?' The answer given was:

> The commission is not in competition with the NCA or any other group or individual. Unlike bodies like the NCA and other membership groups like political parties, the commission is a non-partisan body determined to hear and listen to all the views of the people of Zimbabwe and through their organizations such as the NCA. ... What the commissioners will not do is be dragged into a debate or situation that confuses changing the government with changing the constitution ... the commission will take into account even the views of those groups or individuals who are critical of the Commission.

These arguments were replicated in a set of adverts where the NCA and CC squared off against each other, asking, 'Will the new constitution be about our rights ... or theirs?' and 'The new Constitution is for all of us ... so why can't we all have a say in it?' versus 'They say that you should boycott your national process and withhold your views on the new constitution. ... The Constitutional Commission's outreach programme is giving all Zimbabweans a chance to have their views heard and recorded.' The NCA was also attacked for representing foreign or colonial interests. Representatives of the CC repeatedly suggested that a 'No' vote was tantamount to a 'Yes' vote for the Lancaster House constitution, and implied that the NCA was in favour of the latter.[131] Foreign Affairs minister Stan Mudenge asserted on ZBC that 'foreign governments' were working against the constitutional reform process.[132] Jonathan Moyo was quoted as saying, 'this stupid bunch of protesters is being paid and used by overseas donors who do not want to see anything good coming out of this country'.[133] Or again, 'this country would run a high risk of being a non-transparent donor's republic'.[134] An editorial in the *Mirror* claimed, 'The NCA has no local content and is therefore a myth, an international myth about Zimbabwe.'[135] Ironically, as we have already seen, the NCA and CC were both donor-funded, but rebuttal was rarely permitted.[136]

The inclusion of many NCA officials and members in the leadership of the new opposition party, the Movement for Democratic Change, launched in September 1999, led to accusations that the NCA was merely a front for opposition politics:

the new discourse on the quest for an all embracing democratic constitution was suddenly entangled and confused with the old quest for political power pursued under the auspices of an array of failed political parties ... the NCA strategy has been based on a ... premise that the process of constitutional reform should be used along with the current economic crisis in the country to change the government.[137]

Does the NCA still exist? Yes and no depending on what you mean by the NCA. The answer is no if what is meant by the NCA is the organization that was almost formed not too long ago as a loose affiliation of civil society groups, churches, trade unions, academics and human rights lawyers who said they were committed to promoting a non-partisan civic education in favour of democratic constitutional reform. But the answer is yes if by the NCA is meant the de facto secretariat and fundraising arm of the Movement for Democratic Change. That is why the NCA is the first name of the MDC whose full name is NCA-MDC.[138]

But the electorate's rejection of the Constitutional Commission's draft in the February 2000 referendum, with votes of 54 per cent against and 44 per cent in favour, implicitly answered many of these questions.[139] The NCA did represent the opinions of the majority of those who participated in the plebiscite, and was therefore a publicly legitimated voice speaking for the nation.

Conclusion

During the constitutional debate, the regime attempted to continue and enhance the politics of inclusion by claiming for itself the privilege of leading the debate. Its proposals, and the process it created to advance them, appeared participatory and inclusive. Opposition politicians, NGO activists and church people were included on an equal footing with ZANU(PF) stalwarts. At the same time, rhetoric against those who rejected the invitation to participate was increasingly exclusionary and intolerant. In this period after 1997, the ruling party was beset by revelations of scandals, financial crises and declining social services. The constitutional debate was, at least in part, an attempt to regain control of political discourse, even as the state's ability to administer services was weakened. Instead, the public consultations provided a platform for the articulation of devastating critiques of the regime's political and economic policies in public meetings, reported extensively in the state-controlled media.

The regime's attempt to regain control of the constitutional and civic terms of debate by launching the Constitutional Commission had three perhaps unexpected results. Firstly, it succeeded in polarizing and politicizing the debate, which forced groups that had previously avoided 'politics' to take a stand. This forced groups, and individuals, to debate and articulate where they stood vis-à-vis the ruling party and the incipient opposition. Secondly, the CC briefly eclipsed the NCA, holding out the possibility of fair and equal consultation. But the very openness of the process, and the expectations it raised, were its downfall. The publication of the draft constitution revealed the regime's inflexibility and the futility of seeking change from within. Thirdly, the victory of the 'No' camp publicly affirmed its claim to represent the wider citizenry. This fundamental challenge to the premises on which the regime was based set the tone for the confrontation between state and society that developed as soon as the referendum results were announced. LeBas' argument that between 1997 and 2003 Zimbabwe's politics were dramatically reconfigured is without doubt correct, but a close examination of the period 1997–2000 reveals how unexpected this process was, and the complex alliances that emerged and were transformed as part of it.[140]

In 'winning' the referendum, the NCA alliance legitimated the existence of organizations and ideas outside the hegemony of the ruling party/state. In doing so they challenged the party-political conception of the nation. The ideology of unity, the claims to dominance of public discourse, and the control over state institutions were no longer accepted. The voting public (albeit a largely urban selection of the potential electorate) affirmed the claims made by the NCA to speak and act outside the remit of the state. This was a fundamental rejection of the way in which politics had been done since independence.

6

THE POLITICS OF EXCLUSION (2000–2008)

Any political leader who depends on the number of people killed for their political survival cannot last.[1]

Maybe one day the soldiers and the police will say, 'No, we don't want to go out there and beat up the people for nothing.'[2]

After the constitutional referendum of February 2000, the Mugabe government increasingly relied upon nationalism of a particularly unsubtle sort to justify the violence and intimidation directed at its opponents. Zimbabwe's ruling party accused those who rejected it of having forgotten their history and of being influenced by foreign interests. During elections, it resorted to a variety of legislative and administrative stratagems, in further attempts to delegitimize opponents and observers. The rules of the game became dominated by coercion, backed up by the distribution of incentives to select groups, and buttressed by a revivified and exclusionary nationalism. Despite the polarization described in the previous chapter, those who were willing to be mobilized in defence of the regime were rewarded with land, contracts and employment. Individuals and groups that failed to prove their loyalty were excluded socially and politically, and were subject to violent attacks in their homes and workplaces. This polarization extended into villages, churches and schools. From the politics of inclusion, Zimbabwe had moved to a politics of exclusion.

141

This chapter examines the period between 2000 and 2008; as in other chapters, the approach is thematic rather than chronological. It first charts efforts by the regime to rebuild and remobilize the nationalist coalition, which shapes the new opposition's experience of fighting elections. It then demonstrates the ways in which state institutions were used in this process, despite the increasingly difficult economic conditions. We see that despite attempts by the nascent and fragmented opposition to generate alternative discourses, the regime's control of coercion and state institutions, and a powerfully resonant rhetoric gave it the power to resist demands for change. At a regional level, Mugabe is likewise able to harness political rhetoric and successfully portray the MDC as 'a Western stooge',[3] positioning himself effectively even as Zimbabwe's crisis spilled over borders, and neighbours finally insisted on reform.

Despite profound alienation on the part of urban and rural poor, middle classes and some elites, the regime potently harnesses forces, revitalizes alliances and weathers internal and external crisis. For all that its nationalist rhetoric is lacking in subtlety and that economic crisis continued to prevent any developmental gains, the regime proved able to muster enough resources and blustered on, despite all predictions of collapse or reform.

Recreating the nationalist coalition

Despite unprecedentedly widespread attacks across the country, it would be wrong to interpret the politics that shaped the years after the referendum defeat as being solely exclusionary or violent. This period was also about creating support amongst land-poor rural people and unemployed or poorly remunerated urban families. Neither was there 'mindless violence'—elite intellectual forces masterminded much of it and state institutions implemented it.

Many of the strategies deployed echo proposals first made in the 1980s but not implemented then, owing to political costs or a lack of interest. Structurally and rhetorically, ZANU(PF) attempted to recreate the social and political coalition of forces that had supported the liberation war, and to de-legitimize other voices. The party thus drew on both rhetoric and coercion, as well as an ever-decreasing pool of resources. In the 1980s and most of the 1990s, the depoliticization and demobilization of all the social forces had ensured the smooth functioning of the state. The new, mobilized forces of war veterans and party activists rendered this balancing act unstable, forcing groups into conflict with each other as they defended their legitimacy and claims to authority. This period of regime endurance, therefore, is characterized by instability and conflict between those included and those excluded.

The war veterans and land reform

Although the liberation war veterans had demonstrated their power in 1997, they had then receded from public sight. As we have seen, they did make representations about land during the constitutional debate, but had not played a decisive role in the process. The referendum defeat on 14 February 2000 was a turning point. The Zimbabwe National Liberation War Veterans Association (ZNLWVA) released a statement on 15 February that reveals the thinking behind the destabilization programme that emerged: 'As the liberation war veterans of this country, we have done our best to promote the 'YES' vote on the constitutional Draft, not because the Draft favoured our position on all aspects, but because we realised the importance of the draft as being the land issue.'[4] The veterans took issue with the longevity of many of the cabinet ministers and the tendency towards corruption within the government, and the weakness of ZANU(PF) as a party. In particular, they noted that:

> Our own machinery which kept the Chimurenga war going, though disgruntled and depressed, remains our real hope to the cause of our historic revolution. *We advise the party to give these people their rightful place and to put them to use without any delay. The spirit of the revolution, that of 1980, must be revived now* ... the main factor we see as contributing to the NO result is the weakness of the Party's provincial structures, the reluctant mood, the failure to change with the times ... this weakness of the Party structures has watered down our revolutionary aspirations and has proved beyond doubt the *decay within us* and that necessary and immediate steps should be taken *to unify all revolutionary groupings of ZANU(PF) and consolidate the pillars upon which our support and power rests.*[5]

The ZNLWVA's attempts to rebuild the party's coalition commenced immediately. Farm invasions began in Masvingo province on

16 February and quickly spread to the rest of the country.[6] The invasions were later called the fast-track resettlement programme and, more evocatively still, the third *chimurenga*.[7] The war veterans were increasingly incorporated into ZANU(PF)'s party structures, reconstituting the liberationist coalition for a renewed confrontation with those forces who had opposed liberation.[8] While ZANU(PF) experienced divisions and factional infighting, especially around the issue of the presidential succession, its grasp on the state and patronage opportunities prevented any major schisms.[9]

Although the invaders were described as 'war veterans', it became clear that many of this new generation of invaders were either ZANU(PF) cadres or unemployed youths, who 'yoked their identities' to those of the veterans after the referendum defeat of 2000.[10] Sadomba describes small, vulnerable groups of war vets 'calling for reinforcements' and mobilizing peasants, farm-workers and the urban unemployed to support them.[11] Many journalists reported that the invasions were not spontaneous; CIO operatives were involved in planning them and government and army vehicles were used to transport the invaders, suggesting a state-led effort.[12]

McCandless' research reveals a somewhat more complicated story. Some of her informants reported that war veterans met with Army and CIO officials at district and provincial levels to coordinate efforts, with instructions passed down to those on the ground. They also related different interpretations of the 'spontaneity' of the invasions, with some emphasizing the role of political rallies, addressed by senior officials, and others describing a more *ad hoc* process: 'The occupations were not led by anybody—we just organized ourselves, took up our hoes and axes and invaded the farms. War vets and ordinary people were involved'.[13] McCandless and Sadomba's writing offers evidence that the war vets were acting on their own initiative—what Mazarire calls their 'vanguard' role[14]—even though the presence of the invaders was eventually sanctioned from the highest level; President Mugabe publicly condoned their presence on the farms in early March.[15] High court orders to evict the invaders were ignored by police, presumably on the advice of Police Commissioner Chihuri, who was specifically named in the court ruling.[16] In addition to ZNWLVA president Chenjerai 'Hitler' Hunzwi, new leaders emerged, including Joseph

Chinotimba, then an employee of Harare city council, who went on to become a controversial deputy president of the ZNLWVA.

Violence seemed to escalate from mid-March, when reports of attacks on farm-workers and farmers increased. Farmers were driven off their land, or expected to farm only a portion of it, while veterans and others claimed the remainder. In some cases this resulted in a stale-mate and co-habitation; violence erupted in other cases. Commercial farmers were explicitly warned to avoid involvement with Tsvangirai's MDC.[17] Farm-workers were dispersed, often after having their homes and belongings destroyed. In some cases they were promised land. But 30,000 farm-workers were estimated to have been displaced by August 2000.[18] Some peasants and farm-workers were also subjected to quasi-Maoist 're-education' camps on occupied farms.[19] These camps emu-lated the pre-independence *pungwes*, all-night meetings characterized by singing and dancing, which had been the guerrillas' 'chief vehicle for political education' during the liberation war.[20]

As the election approached, those thought to support the opposition, or to be likely to do so, began to be targeted. War veterans disrupted NCA marches in April and May.[21] In justifying police failure to protect marchers, the Commissioner of Police referred to them as 'NCA/MDC', suggesting that they were simply a front for a political rally.[22] Teachers, priests and nuns,[23] activists such as ZimRights members in Marondera[24] and opposition party members were beaten, tortured and killed.[25] An estimated 7,000 teachers fled their homes, shutting 250 pri-mary and secondary schools.[26] The MDC estimated that 10,000 people were displaced[27] while the Human Rights NGO Forum estimated that 13,000 rural people had fled to family in urban areas.[28] The Human Rights NGO Forum identified twenty-nine individuals it believed were killed for political reasons between January 2000 and August 2001.[29]

Unsurprisingly, the rhetoric of this period, as in previous elections and the constitutional debate, revolved around the liberation war and nation-building. Referring to white farmers, the late Border Gezi, Governor of Mashonaland Central, said: 'They now don't appreciate the benefits of the reconciliation policy because we want to redistrib-ute land to the people.'[30] The MDC was portrayed as the 'puppet of white people who wanted to recolonise the country'.[31] President Mugabe accused whites of perpetuating 'vestigial attitudes from the

Rhodesian yester-years, attitudes of a master race, master colour, master owner and master employer'.[32]

The state resumed control over land reform after the June 2000 parliamentary elections. Announcing the 'fast-track' scheme in mid-July, Vice President Msika emphasized that 'impediments' to quick acquisition had been removed, and that beneficiaries would be selected by 'local committees made up of traditional leaders, Councillors, District Administrators, Provincial Administrators, Governors, representatives of War Veterans and other specially appointed individuals'.[33] The 'fast-track' scheme encompassed two main approaches. The scheme allocated land to landless or land-poor families under the designation 'A1' farms, while 'A2' farms were allocated for small-scale commercial farming. By November 2003, 140,866 families had been allocated A1 farms totalling 4.2 million hectares, while there were 14,500 new A2 'commercial' farmers on a total of 2.3 million hectares. This meant that smallholder control of land increased from 56 per cent of the total land area to 70 per cent.[34]

War veterans were given 20 per cent of the land, while MDC supporters and farm-workers were substantially left out of the process.[35] Despite claims that the A2 scheme had 'a deliberate bias towards women',[36] only 5–21 per cent of A2 land went to women, and 12–21 per cent of A1 land. Of the new farmers, 13 per cent were based in town with urban jobs and houses, occupying 34 per cent of the newly allocated land. Rural elites, including chiefs and political leaders, also acquired land in the A2 scheme; poor rural households made up 87 per cent of beneficiaries, and received 66 per cent of the total land allocated. Few of the new resettlement areas had access to schools, clinics or basic infrastructure.

But despite the fast-track programme having an 'elaborate institutional framework', as Masiiwa notes, 'events unfolding on the ground were beyond any logical comprehension'.[37] The regime responded decisively to concerns about misappropriation of land by commissioning a series of 'audits' which detailed political interference in the process. Mugabe himself stated emphatically that no man could own more than one farm. Moyo outlines the 'corrections' which followed from these reports:

> rationalisation of the records of land acquired and beneficiaries; repossessing multiple and oversized (consolidated) land allocations; reversing

fraudulent land allocations; replanning land allocations and the land use requirements to cater for specialist enterprises (forestry, wildlife, dairy and irrigation); streamlining the administrative procedures of land committees and central government interventions; resolving land boundary disputes; building the legal and administrative capacities to complete the formal acquisition of land, (including administrative court hearings and 'compensation' processes); allocating enforceable land tenure documents ('permits' and long leases), and so forth.[38]

In defending the programme, Moyo speaks of the re-assertion of order after a period of chaos, and other scholars have shown that formal land-use policies and planning continued to be salient within resettlement areas, in the behaviour of settlers and war veterans, who measured out plots and enforced bans on riverine cultivation, just as the state had done.[39] These accounts suggest that the technocratic and 'high modernist' tendencies of the state's developmental agenda so dominant in the 1980s (and the colonial era) were subdued but not entirely supplanted.

At the same time, land seizures continued sporadically,[40] as did contestation among '*chefs*' over properties, challenging claims that the process benefited the poor.[41] And as the rainy season approached in 2005, reports increasingly suggested that many farmers were unable to prepare their land for planting, lacking fuel, inputs and draught power unless they had access to off-farm income.[42] Even retired General Zvinavashe questioned the viability of land reform-led development, given the inability of farmers to access diesel.[43] Considering the depth of the economic crisis facing Zimbabwe in 2005, it is unsurprising that resettlement farmers found it difficult to accrue the necessary resources to prepare their land.

These issues of land security and productivity generated high-level responses from the government. Firstly, Reserve Bank Governor Gono suggested that the recent land invasions were the result of 'indiscipline' and claimed that the government had a 'zero tolerance' policy on land invasions.[44] The Minister of Information was quick to clarify that this referred only to those farmers 'without an offer letter', not those who had been officially resettled.[45] Secondly, tensions within the agriculture ministry emerged, with the deputy minister attributing the production decline to the lack of expertise and commitment among newly resettled farmers. His boss, Joseph Made, toed the official line, insisting that declining production was the result of drought and 'illegal sanctions imposed by Britain and her allies'.[46] As this suggests, divisions existed between and within government ministries, but the political line prevailed.

Despite the 'success' of the land invasions, government attempts to reconstruct the nationalist alliance were not unchallenged. The mobilization of the war veterans was, as Kriger shows, the culmination of their demands over two decades for compensation and inclusion.[47] However, the war veterans themselves remained divided and claims to the liberation mythology continue to be contested. After Chenjerai 'Hitler' Hunzwi's death in 2001, the leadership of ZNLWVA was hotly contested between factions.[48] The new resources also intensified competition from other groups for equal support, especially those claiming to be 'war vets' but not officially recognized as such: cadres, collaborators (*mujibas* and *chimbwidos*) and war widows.[49] Ex-political detainees also demanded compensation, which they were granted in 2005.[50]

But not all war veterans wish to be included in this process. The Zimbabwe Liberators' Platform (ZLP), an alternative grouping of veterans, was afforded a great deal of press coverage within and outside Zimbabwe, in an effort to construct an alternate legitimacy for anti-ZANU(PF) liberation-based perspectives.[51] Wilfred Mhanda, the chair of the new body, said:

> The farm occupations could have been a demonstration if they had been spontaneous. ... But this demonstration is illegal because it was denounced by courts of law, which are the custodians of law in this country. ... We want to convince the people that war veterans are members of society who should not be seen as working against the interests of the country.[52]

Erin McCandless' interviews with war veterans also reveal their concerns with the allegations of abuse of power: 'some even described the need for a "Chimurenga 3½"—the removal of politicians from the land and redistribution to the rural poor'.[53] Sadomba, indeed, depicts the relationship between the war veterans and what he calls the 'elite ruling oligarchy' as deeply contested, and portrays ZANU as having hijacked the war veterans' revolution and co-opted their leaders.[54]

Heroes, history and the media

The regime's own emphasis on liberation war history inevitably led to the credentials of newly prominent figures being challenged. Jonathan Moyo was accused of running away from training at Mgagao camp in Tanzania after six weeks; Chenjerai Hunzwi was alleged to have spent the struggle in Poland training to become a medical doctor; Joseph Chinotimba was revealed to have been a refugee, not a soldier, in Mozambique in late 1979.[55] These revelations further challenged the regime's claims to the only legitimate inheritors of the liberation war legacy.

The politics of choosing heroes also intensified. Vice President Joshua Nkomo's death in 1999 brought this debate to the forefront of political dialogue. The spontaneity of grief and the huge turnout at Nkomo's funeral were in sharp contrast to the stilted and artificial nature of other ceremonial events. While it was important politically that Mugabe recognize him as 'national hero' (and thereby entitled to be buried at the National Heroes' Acre in Harare), many in Matabeleland were said to be calling for him to be buried there.[56] Public pressure spread through the media for streets to be named after him;[57] and in the lead-up to the 2002 election, Bulawayo airport, the road leading to it and a local college were renamed in Nkomo's honour.[58] In contrast, ZANU(PF) failed to recognize Ndabaningi Sithole, leader of the original ZANU, as a hero after his death in 2000. Following the death of Henry Hamadziripi and other Karanga ex-fighters from Masvingo province who were not given hero status, it was suggested that ethnic tensions and liberation war divisions still mattered more than being 'pioneer war veterans',[59] further contradicting regime claims as to the coherence and simplicity of the liberation war legacy.

The propagation of official nationalism also took more banal forms. In 2001, government schools, many of which had retained their names from the Rhodesian era, were adumbrated to rename themselves after indigenous heroes and leaders.[60] More substantively, the secondary school curriculum was twice revised: in 2001, following recommendations of a government commission which effectively made history an optional subject; and again in 2002, making history compulsory for all secondary students. Barnes describes the reformed curriculum as focus-

149

ing narrowly on Zimbabwean history, testing students on their ability to recall facts and dates, rather than analysing events as in earlier, more comparative approaches to the subject.[61] While the mobilization of thousands of youth into 'national service' has been most noted for the levels of political violence it generated, it was also designed to teach them 'patriotic history' and incorporate them firmly into the official mythologies, while also providing resources and the promise of employment.[62]

More material representations were also made towards Matabeleland, with unfulfilled promises made that reparations would be forthcoming for victims of the Matabeleland conflict.[63] Funds were also promised to the now much delayed Matabeleland-Zambezi Water Project, which had come to symbolize the lack of development in the south-west.[64]

On a less symbolic level, new laws were introduced in 2001, designed to regulate and limit access to citizenship.[65] Although the immediate impact of these laws was to limit the eligibility of candidates, nominees and voters in elections, this move was also highly significant in creating and reinforcing ideas about 'outsiders' and foreigners versus 'authentic' and 'patriotic' Zimbabweans implicitly ensconced within the nationalist coalition. The instrumentalism thus drives an exclusionary and exclusive conception of who is a legitimate participant in political life.

This new nationalism was also driven through the state-run media and cultural policies, building on the experience of the Constitutional Commission's campaign. Intertwining policy decisions came together under the direction of erstwhile academic Jonathan Moyo to shape profoundly the information and cultural environment in Zimbabwe after 1999. This nexus of academics and media proved very powerful. 'Ministerial historians' and 'media historians' worked together to put 'history at the centre of politics' in Zimbabwe, although historian Terence Ranger argued that the new patriotic history did little more than reify simplistic narratives of resistance to colonialism.[66]

Media and popular culture became the main vehicles for this message. The regime sought both to control media content, and to suppress newspapers that it could not control. The *Daily News*, which gained in readers and popularity throughout 2000, was, as a daily paper, in immediate competition with the state's main mouthpiece, the *Herald*. This put the *Herald* staff under some pressure. Bornwell

Chakaodza, who was editor of the *Herald* during the 2000 elections, provides a particularly frank account of the *Herald*'s role: 'we went out of our way [to promote the ruling party] and abandoned all professional ethics as you know them'. Chakaodza asserted that it was clear that the editorial position during the elections did not agree with the general mood in the country and that 'I was conscious of being an editor who lacked credibility with readers and advertisers ... also circulation had nosedived resulting in the flight of advertisers'.[67] Chakaodza was fired after the June 2000 election.

Although newspapers have been important, the radio remains dominant in rural areas, and the MDC's inability to access this medium handicapped it. In 2000, the party was allowed to run English-language adverts on ZBC's Radio 3, which aims primarily at young urban dwellers, but was refused access to the indigenous-language—and predominantly rural—audience of Radio 2.[68] The MDC challenged ZBC in the Supreme Court, alleging that both Zimpapers, which owns the Herald, and the ZBC was violating section 23 of the constitution—freedom of expression. The Supreme Court issued an interim ruling to this effect and ordered ZBC and Zimpapers to distribute news and general information impartially and without bias, although this ruling had little effect on that election.[69] In the 2005 election the situation changed somewhat. The Media Monitoring Project of Zimbabwe's research showed that on ZTV (formerly ZBC) and Radio Zimbabwe and Power FM (formerly Radio 2 and 3) 85 per cent of campaign stories covered the activities of ZANU (PF) and 15 per cent the MDC. While coverage of ZANU(PF) was generally positive, that of the MDC was neutral.[70] In addition, new broadcasting regulations facilitated access to the media via paid advertisements.[71]

Despite this progress, newspapers continued to face challenges. Ncube reports that 365 journalists were arrested between 2000 and 2006.[72] The *Daily News* was attacked directly and indirectly by the state through economic threats, intimidation, allegations of assassination plots, and the bombing of its printing press.[73] In 2001, it overtook the *Herald* as the most read paper in Zimbabwe.[74] It was finally forced to shut in September 2003 after it failed to gain registration under the Access to Information and Protection of Privacy Act (AIPPA).[75] The *Weekly Tribune* was similarly closed in July 2004. Ibbo Mandaza's *Mirror*, now the only daily independent paper, tended to support government policy, but retained a critical edge on some issues.[76] In 2005, however, reports circulated that the controlling shares in the *Mirror* had been acquired by the CIO, and that Mandaza had been removed.[77]

Attempts to start independent radio stations were crushed by the state, which closed down the Capital Radio broadcasts, accusing them of operating illegally.[78] When the broadcasters challenged the ZBC monopoly provided for by the Broadcasting Act, the Supreme Court struck the latter down as unconstitutional. The state responded by using the Presidential Powers (Temporary Measures) Act to put in place a Statutory Instrument to regulate the issuing of licences, which gave the minister personal control of the process.[79] The Minister of Information also claimed that Capital Radio would not be given a licence under the new regulations because all the directors of the corporation were white, and one was British.[80] In response, the broadcasters moved to shortwave broadcasts from outside the country, which were periodically jammed. Community radio stations were also unable to obtain licenses, despite a long-standing presence and support from churches and other community groups.[81]

Email, an increasingly important tool for activists, was also targeted. In March 2000, an act was rushed through parliament which enabled the state to order internet service providers (ISPs) to 'intercept or monitor communications or suspend services to individuals in the interests of national security or the maintenance of law and order'.[82] In practice, however, the government seemed to lack both the resources and technology to implement this.[83]

Music—with its potential to reach both urban and rural masses— also received the carrot and stick treatment. Those whose recordings were deemed too political were given little airplay, and some claimed they had been banned.[84] In late 1999, Thomas Mapfumo released *Chimurenga Explosion*, with two songs, 'Disaster' and 'Mamveme', which became popular in the crucial first half of 2000 but were interpreted as criticisms of the regime. Despite rumours that these songs had been banned from airplay, Banning Eyre's attempt to track down the truth of this was unsuccessful. DJs insisted to him that there had been no such proscription, although Mapfumo himself was sure of it, and gave this as one of the reasons he left the country.[85] Mapfumo has not kept silent, however, and has issued unambiguous calls for Mugabe to go.[86] Albums published after 2000 seemed more and more explicitly political, although Maurice Vambe challenges simplistic readings of these songs, proposing that 'in its attempt to enact an overthrow of the ZanuPFs official narrative of independence, Mapfumo's song is muted and survives within the limited and limiting ideological boundaries of a cultural nationalist discourse that his lyrics are meant to interrogate'.[87] Other artists have walked a careful line. Several of Oliver Mtukudzi's songs were interpreted by fans as oblique critiques, but he refrained from public statements until 2005, after a performance in honour of the new Vice President Joyce Mujuru was interpreted as showing his support for ZANU(PF). He issued the following uncompromising words: 'I wish to place on record and make absolutely clear that I am not a ZANU PF supporter. I am a loyal Zimbabwean who believes in a true and tolerant democracy', pointing out that he had agreed to perform in private, for a relative, not at a public or party-political event. He further took the opportunity to criticize the 'government's monopoly of the airwaves' and its use to 'restrict airplay of artists who they see as unsupportive of its policies', which he called 'a gross abuse of human rights'.[88]

At the same time, pro-government artists came out of retirement, dusting off their old liberation songs in support of the 'Third Chimurenga', and ministers revealed hidden talents.[89] Jonathan Moyo was credited with producing a series of 'patriotic' and 'pan-African' albums.[90] An existing popular musician, Andy Brown, was accused of being 'bought off' with funding for a recording studio and released songs 'in praise of the government's controversial farm-seizure policy'.[91] Wonderful Bere describes the process by which aspirant young singers were 'enticed' into studios and drawn into performing and recording pro-government songs.[92] Airplay for these and other pro-government tunes was ensured by new broadcasting regulations that required 75 per cent local content,[93] although reports claimed that these musicians' sales and audiences had declined, suggesting that 'indigenization' was not popular with consumers.[94] Although in 2005 the MDC attempted to compete by producing its own CD, it was denied airplay.

Perhaps Moyo's most effective scheme, developing from the Constitutional Commission media strategy, was the promotion of a series of jingles—mostly about land—which saturated radio and tele-vision.[95] Video clips of ZANLA ex-combatants also became regular features on ZTV. In tune with these cultural manifestations, the idea of national dress, a recurring theme from the 1980s, resurfaced in the form of a new 'national fabric', showcased at 'patriotic' music events and 'indigenous' beauty pageants.[96] And in a sign of top-level approval, Solomon Mutsvairo, who wrote the lyrics of the national anthem intro-duced in 1994 and was described as the 'architect of the current arts revolution', was the only living Zimbabwean honoured with an award at the 2005 Heroes' Day ceremony. Along with the late Finance Minister, Bernard Chidzero, he was awarded the Order of the Star of Zimbabwe.[97] Yet, we should not assume that this deluge of patriotism and catchy jingles was uniformly successful. Bere discusses how even 'urban grooves'—a genre that he claims was 'controlled' and 'politi-cized' by the state—embodied critiques of the state project.[98] Reflec-ting on the national anthem and twenty-four years of independence, Everjoice Win muses, 'The trust in our leaders, our former "com-rades", is broken. No revolutionary song, no matter how many times it's played, will mend it.'[99] As this lament suggests, while many did buy into the resurgent, exclusive nationalism, others who might have felt allegiance had been alienated.

The new opposition and elections

The main reason for the vigorous remobilization of ZANU(PF)'s sup-port base was the new momentum in electoral politics, following the challenges of the independent candidates in 1996–7 and the results of the referendum in February 2000.

In 1998, the independent candidates formed a political party led by Margaret Dongo, known as the Zimbabwe Union of Democrats (ZUD).[100] It was expected to be the main challenger to ZANU(PF) in the 2000 elections, and had the undeniable benefit of being led by a bona fide war veteran. However, following personality clashes exacer-bated by CIO infiltration, the party split into two camps in mid-1999.[101] Thus, it seemed that opposition in Zimbabwe would continue to be fragmented and divided.

But then, in 1999, the Zimbabwe Congress of Trade Unions (ZCTU) announced that it would begin the process of forming a political party, which became the Movement for Democratic Change (MDC). This was by no means an inevitable outcome. The ZCTU had adopted a conciliatory approach to the state, typified by their acceptance of the tripartite bargaining schemes. Yet in 1997, they responded to the public mood by successfully organizing the anti-tax demonstrations, which continued into 1998. Several key members of the ZCTU were prominent members of the National Constitutional Assembly (NCA). After the president banned stay-aways and other demonstrations at the end of November 1998, the ZCTU withdrew from the tripartite negotiations on a social contract between employers, workers and the state. Workers' interests began to be pursued through more overtly political means.[102]

In February 1999, the ZCTU called for a 'strong, democratic and organized movement of the people' which would 'recognize and protest the discrete and independent role and mandate of the various associations of working people, including the labour movement, informal traders associations and peasant farmers association'. This National Working Peoples' Convention (NWPC) resolved to 'implement a vigorous and democratic political movement for change'.[103]

The Movement for Democratic Change (MDC) was launched in September 1999 to an estimated 15,000-member audience at Rufaro stadium, most of whom seemed to be organized groups of workers bussed in by various unions. In view of later claims that the MDC was white-dominated, or a front for Rhodesian attitudes, it is worth noting that there were only a handful of whites in the audience, all of whom were long-standing activists from the NGO sector.[104]

The MDC leadership contained many of the individuals who had moved onto the public stage through the NCA, such as Welshman Ncube and Lovemore Madhuku of the University of Zimbabwe, Mike Auret who had just resigned as director of the Catholic Commission for Justice and Peace (CCJP), and Paul Themba Nyathi, the Zimbabwe Project director.[105] David Chimhini, formerly the ZimRights director, became the MDC's executive director. Although the dominance of these educated, NGO-aligned activists led to suggestions that 'key working-class leaders' were sidelined, Morgan Tsvangirai and Gibson Sibanda, the secretary general and president of the ZCTU respectively, were president and secretary general respectively of the new party.[106]

The links between the ZCTU, the NCA and the MDC created problems and opened all three to attack.[107] As we have seen, the Zimbabwe

Council of Churches (ZCC) used this development as an after-the-fact justification for its withdrawal from the NCA.[108] Morgan Tsvangirai gave up his leadership of the NCA in order to avoid accusations of it being partisan, which would alienate the other opposition parties, although he retained his post as secretary general of the ZCTU.[109]

Perhaps inevitably, these links still caused conflict. The NCA was accused of 'behaving like an opposition party'.[110] However, after the NCA's referendum victory, this potential weakness became a strength, as a much wider and more diverse membership adhered to the MDC, in reaction to the dramatically proven ability of the NCA-MDC team to win a convincing victory. It was in this post-referendum, pre-election period that many of the previously apolitical white voters began attending MDC meetings and joined the party. Prominent candidates from Margaret Dongo's ZUD also joined after attempts to create a voting coalition between the MDC and ZUD failed.[111]

The MDC then represented a broad coalition—the first nationally grounded opposition party to challenge ZANU(PF)—with bases in unions, business, academia and NGOs, and support from the urban electorate and the rural residents in Matabeleland and Manicaland. But the hard-fought election campaigns, discussed below, tested the resilience of this disparate base. These were not campaigns fought on issues, but 'between "good" and "evil". On the one side it looked like a mortal combat between "patriots" and "traitors"; on the other side it appeared a fight to the death between "tyrants" and "democrats"'.[112] Having weathered many tensions, the MDC's support base was soon disillusioned and the leadership factionalized. In 2005, the MDC divided into two factions: one centred around Tsvangirai and the other around Arthur Mutambara and Welshman Ncube. Although the proximate cause of the divide was the decision by Tsvangirai to boycott the 2005 Senate elections, it reflected deeper tensions between factions within the party, which was buffeted by attacks on all sides.[113]

Violence and intimidation were common during election periods, although in most areas this diminished on the actual election day. In 2000, voters were forced to attend rallies. In Bulawayo shops and churches were forced to close when rallies took place.[114] Polling agents and candidates were kidnapped, beaten and 'disappeared';[115] others hid or abandoned their constituencies in the face of violence.[116] In October 2000, Shari Eppel of Amani Trust reported:

18,000 civilians have been affected by human rights violations this year. The violations include approximately 2,500 assaults, more than 1,100 properties destroyed or substantially damaged, the displacement of over 10,000 people, the detention or abduction of approximately 600 people, in addition to thousands of other human rights violations involving death threats and assault threats, interference with the rights to vote, associate and express opinions.[117]

Over 90 per cent of the perpetrators were associated with ZANU(PF). President Mugabe granted clemency to perpetrators of all politically motivated crimes, except murder and rape, although this was later found to be in breach of the African Charter on Human and Peoples' Rights.[118]

Supporters and perceived supporters of the MDC were also attacked, abducted and detained in large numbers in 2002.[119] Polling agents were frequent targets, as were sitting MPs, both before and after the election days.[120] Amani Trust reported an increase in reported violence from June 2001, with injuries conforming to 'the types of injuries seen in systematic torture': beatings, including on the soles of feet, electric shock, mock drownings, sexual torture, forced sexual intercourse, sexual humiliation and psychological torture.[121] A total of 150 people were reported killed in political violence between April 2001 and the March 2002 elections.[122]

Beyond the specifics of these attacks was a broader atmosphere of fear and intimidation. The introduction of the Public Order and Security Act (POSA) in early 2002 led to hundreds of MDC rallies and meetings being banned.[123] In a move reminiscent of Ndabaningi Sithole's arrest for treason before the 1995 elections, Tsvangirai was arrested before the 2002 presidential elections and also charged with treason. Although he was acquitted in 2004, the case was doubtless effective in stoking negative publicity and organizational tensions within the MDC.

The atmosphere of coercion increased with the presence of youths (known as 'Green Bombers'), trained in the National Service camps, manning roadblocks and blocking access to rural areas.[124] As the Commonwealth Observers noted, 'Members of [the Youth Militias] were responsible for a systematic campaign of intimidation against known or suspected supporters of the main opposition party, the

Movement for Democratic Change, MDC. The violence and intimidation created a climate of fear and suspicion.'[125] Many individual voters also reported having their ID cards confiscated, to prevent them voting.[126] This, coupled with apparent impunity for ZANU(PF) actions, as the police failed to lay charges or investigate claims of violence, rendered the election unfree and unfair in the eyes of many participants and observers.[127] In the 2005 parliamentary elections, less violence was reported in the pre-election period, and the voting days were peaceful, but violent reprisals were reported in the post-election period. It was important for the regime to win a two-thirds majority in parliament 'through an election that would have regional, if not international, legitimacy'.[128] But once positive reports had come from neighbouring countries, violence was unleashed, with the NGO Human Rights Forum documenting assaults, murders and forced evictions.[129] By contrast, the Senatorial elections in 2005, being uncontested in many areas, exhibited relatively low levels of violence.

Despite most of these elections being hard-fought and marked by violence, ZANU(PF) succeeded in retaining control of parliament and the presidency, as well as the reintroduced Senate. In 2000, the MDC won fifty-seven parliamentary seats, mainly in Harare, Matabeleland and parts of Manicaland, while ZANU retained sixty-two seats, mainly in Mashonaland. With twenty appointed seats, plus ten traditional chiefs in parliament, ZANU was in firm control of the legislative branch of government, even though in some areas over 80 per cent of the electorate had supported the opposition. In 2002, it also retained control of the executive, with President Mugabe being re-elected with 1,688,939 votes to Tsvangirai's 1,254,930, giving Mugabe about 55 per cent of the vote. The parliamentary elections of 2005 further reinforced this trend, with the MDC winning forty-one seats and seventy-eight seats going to ZANU(PF), giving it, with its thirty appointed seats, a two-thirds majority in the House. The MDC's seats again clustered in Harare, Bulawayo and Matabeleland. Jonathan Moyo, expelled from ZANU(PF), won Tsholotsho as an Independent. ZANU also took control of the newly reintroduced Senate following the November 2005 elections, which were marked by a partial MDC boycott and exceptionally low turnout. In Harare, it would have been easy to miss the election entirely—polling booths erected in shopping centres were conspicuously lacking queues, and many candidates in the ZANU(PF) heartlands were elected unopposed.

These election results cannot be taken at face value, but neither can they be interpreted as simply the result of violence and intimidation. As the sections below show, the regime expanded and consolidated control over the electoral process and other state institutions.

Consolidating control: state institutions

We have seen how the government regulation of the media and control of other state institutions was used to shape public culture and discourse. At the same time, state institutions tasked with running the elections and maintaining other state functions between elections became increasingly politicized.

Electoral institutions

As we examine the evolution of electoral legislation and institutional design, we observe a shift from *ad hoc* or reactive strategies to more permanent changes designed to ensure regime dominance, following Norma Kriger's convincing argument that this process of formalizing legislation, apparently in response to the SADC guidelines, was in fact camouflage for codification of existing practice.[130]

The 2000 and 2002 elections were run, as before, by the Director General, the Elections Directorate and the Electoral Supervisory Commission (ESC). In 2000, however, the ESC was a less willing accomplice than in the past. Frustration with the conduct of the local council elections in 1998 and 1999 led to much more open criticism.[131] The long-time chair, former Anglican Bishop Peter Hatendi, resigned in protest at government obstruction in January 2000.[132] The remaining three members were also much more public about their predicament, and called for an independent body to be set up to oversee the elections.[133] When, a week before the 2000 nomination court was to sit, the ESC had not received details of constituency boundaries or polling stations, they complained that the Elections Directorate was 'not cooperative'.[134] After this point, concerns were also expressed at the militarization of the ESC. A 'prominent war veteran' and retired army colonel, Sobuza Gula-

Ndebele, was appointed to replace Hatendi just days before the election.[135] In 2002 Douglas Nyikayaramba, a retired brigadier in the Zimbabwe National Army, was appointed as the ESC's chief executive officer,[136] followed by another former brigadier, Kennedy Zimondi.[137] When the Zimbabwe Electoral Commission (ZEC) replaced the ESC in the run-up to the 2005 parliamentary elections, it too was chaired by a former war veteran and army lawyer turned civilian judge, Justice George Chiweshe.

As discussed in Chapter 4, the 1995 election and subsequent by-elections had provided clear evidence that past electoral rolls were not accurate. A UN Electoral Assistance Mission assessed the electoral roll in December 1999 and calculated that between 10 and 20 per cent of the names on the voters' roll were deceased and that as many as 2 million voters—40 per cent of the electorate—had moved constituency since 1995 without being re-registered.[138] A study carried out by a local NGO on the municipal elections in July 1999 gave similar results.[139] Ministry officials said that 5.1 million out of a potential 5.5 million voters had been registered between January and March 2000. The voters' roll was opened for inspection in June, and many mistakes were found: voters who claimed to have registered were not there, others found discrepancies in their ID numbers and name-spelling, while others noted that the names of many deceased voters were still present on the list. A supplementary roll was created for those who were registered between April and June, although it was in fact mainly a list of those who found themselves not on the roll and re-registered.[140]

One complaint was that, unlike in previous elections, no receipt or voter's card was issued to prove that one had indeed registered. Ironically, in the 1995 election the issuing of such cards had been a big controversy and many people complained about it.[141] However, the lack of proof of registration was now an issue, because many people claimed to have registered but their names did not appear on the roll. Despite these problems, registration did seem to function better in this election than in 1995, when there were many stories of people entirely unable to register—long queues etc. In this election one needed a National ID (or temporary ID) or passport to register and to vote. It was widely reported that ZANU(PF) activists and war veterans seized upon this and were forcing people—especially farm-workers, but also rural people more generally—to hand over their identification documents in exchange for ZANU(PF) membership cards.[142]

In 2002 the process of creating the voters' roll was decidedly opaque. The voters' roll inspection, which started on 19 November and was expected to end on 9 December, was extended until 19 December.[143] The roll was then supposed to close on 27 January, but was then without advertisement or legal sanction extended until 3 March.[144] Media reports suggest that registration continued only in rural ZANU(PF) heartlands. This situation was legalized after the fact, through a presidential order.[145]

A further problem was that, unlike in previous elections, no receipts or voters' cards were issued to prove that one had indeed registered. The lack of proof of registration was now even more of an issue, because again many people claimed to have registered but their names did not appear on the roll. In these elections, again, one needed a National ID (or temporary ID) or passport to register and to vote. During both the 2000 and 2002 elections, there were reports that ZANU(PF) activists, youth militias and war veterans were forcing people to hand over their identification documents if they could not produce up-to-date ZANU party cards or chant ZANU slogans.[146] The Registrar General's office, responsible for issuing IDs, was reported to be refusing to issue new or replacement IDs until after the election.[147]

In the presidential elections of 2002, controversy also followed the Registrar General's requirement for voters to prove that they lived in the constituency.[148] This requirement disqualified many 'lodgers'— people informally sharing houses or backyard shacks in the high-density areas of Harare and Chitungwiza, who were unable to produce water or electricity bills in their names. In rural areas, residence was said to be validated by headmen, who would accompany voters to polls, raising the issue of ruling party influence, as most headmen were believed to be ZANU(PF). A sample of the roll suggested that 'only 50 per cent of the voters whose names appeared on the roll actually lived at the addresses given, and up to 1.8 million of the names should not have been there'.[149]

For the 2005 elections, these stringent residency requirements were incorporated into the new Electoral Act.[150] The voters' roll for the parliamentary and Senate elections was open for registration in May and July

2004. The MDC argued that the urban registration process was under-advertised, and that it was much easier for rural residents to meet the residency requirements, skewing the roll towards rural voters.[151] Despite the massive population movements caused by slum-clearance Operation Murambatsvina in May and June 2005, after the March parliamentary elections the voters' roll was not revised for use in the November Senate elections. But the Senate elections seem to have been marked as much by apathy as by misconduct. With the MDC divided over whether or not to contest elections, many seats were uncontested. Turnout was low, with under 20 per cent of registered voters participating, and there were few reports of violence or rigging.

Eligibility to vote, defined by citizenship, continued to be hotly contested. In 2001, the Citizenship Act was amended to require further proof of renunciation of citizenship. Previously Zimbabweans had been required to renounce their citizenship to Zimbabwean authorities, but the new act required that they renounce it to the authorities of the second citizenship, and provide documentary evidence that they had done so.[152] This regulation affected many descendants of Malawian, Zambian and Mozambican immigrants,[153] but was widely thought to be targeting whites. The Registrar General was empowered to make unilateral changes to the electoral roll.[154] A court ruling in January stated that the Registrar General could not remove voters from the voters' roll without giving them notice and the right to appeal.[155] The law was then changed by Gazette (i.e. not through parliament), such that the Registrar General was directed to create a list of citizens who had either renounced their Zimbabwean citizenship or who were deemed to have lost their citizenship with the introduction of the new law.[156] This list was to be kept at each polling station, and 'any person whose name appears on the list ... shall not be entitled to vote at the election, notwithstanding that his name appears on the roll for any constituency', unless the voter could prove that he had successfully appealed or had an appeal pending.[157]

Many of those who complied by renouncing their other citizenships nevertheless received letters from the Registrar General notifying them that there was reason to believe they were not entitled to be registered, and giving them seven days from the date of the notice to object.[158] Some of those receiving such letters, including Garfield

Todd, the former PM, found that it had been delivered on or after the last date for appeal.[159] The names of many other voters, such as opposition MPs, in addition to the alleged dual citizens registered on a list made available in January, were not on the roll issued shortly before the election.[160] If that was not enough, it was also discovered that registration had continued in some rural areas after the official closing date, without any public announcement.[161]

Postal ballots proved equally problematic. Whereas the Electoral Act had provided for Zimbabweans away from their constituencies—whether abroad or elsewhere in the country—to vote by postal ballot, on 7 June 2000 the president amended the act so that only military serving outside Zimbabwe, diplomatic staff posted overseas, constituency registrars, presiding officers and polling officers could take advantage of postal ballots.[162] This disenfranchised Zimbabweans overseas and people serving as monitors during elections in constituencies other than their own.[163] Both of these groups, especially Zimbabweans in the UK and South Africa, had been highly critical of the regime during the Constitutional Commission hearings, and were thought to support the MDC.

In 2000, postal ballots issued to nearly 6,000 military personnel serving in the DRC were later ruled invalid by the Supreme Court, on the grounds that the Registrar General had not complied with the regulations.[164] The intended recipients had not signed the ballot application forms or the signatures had not been witnessed.[165] In some constituencies in Mutare there were also questions about people voting more than once, either through multiple postal ballots or once with a postal ballot and once in person.[166] Restrictions on Zimbabweans overseas, or outside their constituencies, were re-enforced in the 2002 and 2005 elections, depriving the growing diaspora of access to postal ballot voting, although military personnel continued to be able to vote.[167]

All of these factors made it increasingly difficult for many Zimbabweans to participate in the polls. In the 2000 election turnout was relatively high, at 2.5 million voters or 48 per cent of the electorate. Despite this, observers still estimated that about 10 per cent of potential voters were turned away, either because their names were not on the electoral roll or because they were at the wrong polling station.[168] Although polling hours were extended in the 2002 election, the Zimbabwe Election Support Network estimated that over 360,000 voters were turned away from polling booths. Turnout in this election was 70 per cent in the rural areas but only 40 per cent in the towns and cities.[169] In 2005 the parliamentary elections turnout was reported to be 10 per cent higher than in 2000, with 2.7 million voters, but between 10 and 25 per cent of prospective voters were turned away.[170] The MDC estimated that 133,000 voters attempted to participate on election day but were unable to do so, and also that there were discrepancies in numbers of voters reported and the numbers of votes cast in some polling areas.[171] Attempts to untangle this puzzle were stymied by the ZEC's refusal to release polling station data.

Preparatory to the 2005 elections, the Delimitation Commission again took up its previous tactics of adding government supporting areas to 'opposition' constituencies. Khabela Matlose describes bluntly how the Commission 'decreased urban constituencies and increased rural constituencies. Three (3) constituencies were deducted from urbanized Harare, Bulawayo and Matebeleland South Provinces, while rural provinces of Manicaland, Mashonaland East and Mashonaland West gained one constituency each.'[172] Given ZANU(PF)'s difficulty in winning seats in Harare and Matabeleland, versus its relative strength in rural Mashonaland, this appears to be straightforward gerrymandering: increasing the number of constituencies that were winnable for ZANU(PF). In addition, Harare South, held by opposition MPs since 1995, had its boundaries extended into rural areas, as did Manyame Constituency: 'pockets of ZANU(PF) supporters, particularly around military bases and resettled land allocated to ZANU(PF) supporters, are islands in predominantly MDC territory'.[173] These areas were not just rural, they were also areas that had been resettled since 2000.[174]

The presence of international observers and local monitors had been one of the major controversies in elections since 2000. Although electoral law did not specifically provide for monitors, in the 1995 election the ESC had asked civil society groups to assist them as monitors.[175] In 2000 NGOs trained 20,000 monitors in preparation, and invited international observers to join them.[176] Just before the election, however, new regulations were gazetted. While the ESC could appoint Zimbabweans as monitors, the Elections Directorate would 'on the recommendation of the Ministry of Foreign Affairs' only accredit foreign observers after the payment of USD 100.[177]

The ESC, with former ZANU(PF) politician Elaine Raftopoulos as acting chair, took the Registrar General to court, alleging that, by claiming the power to accredit foreign observers, he had usurped the ESC's role.[178] As this case went to court, the government quickly appointed Gula-Ndebele head of the ESC. The High Court subsequently ruled against the ESC, saying that there was no constitutional reason that the Registrar General's office ought not to have responsibility for accrediting observers.[179] On the same day, a press statement was released stating that no further foreign observers would be accredited, meaning that only a few hundred already accredited EU and Commonwealth observers would be in the field.[180] However, after much negotiation, the Zimbabwe and World Councils of Churches (ZCC/WCC) and Congress of South Africa Trade Unions (COSATU) delegations were accredited with one day to spare before the election, but other groups were excluded, including the National Democratic Institute (NDI), the International Republican Institute (IRI) and Oxfam Canada.[181]

In 2002 and 2005, the government was more proactive. The General Laws Amendment Bill brought in before the 2002 election obstructed both local and foreign organizations from monitoring/observing elections in Zimbabwe: 'no individual may monitor any elections unless they are accredited by the Registrar-General's Office which would provide training and accreditation of the monitors'.[182] In a parliamentary debate, Justice Minister Chinamasa justified this move by stating that: 'We cannot allow people who are our enemies to come to our soil. Those organisations and countries who come with the prejudicial view that Zanu PF will not win the election will not get the privilege to tread on our soil.'[183]

In January, President Mugabe announced that the following organizations were welcome to send observers:

The Organisation of African Unity/Africa Union (OAU/AU); the Southern Africa Development Community (SADC); the Common Market for East and Southern Africa (Comesa); the Economic Community of West African States (Ecowas); the Non-Aligned Movement (NAM); the Commonwealth, excluding the United Kingdom; the joint ACP-EU delegation (excluding the United Kingdom) and led by the ACP; the National Association for the Advancement of Coloured People (NAACP) from the United States of America; individuals and countries to be invited in their own capacities include the Federal Republic of Nigeria.[184]

The World Council of Churches/All Africa Council of Churches/ Zimbabwe Council of Churches were also allowed to observe, on the condition that they did not include delegates from certain countries including Canada, the US, Britain, Germany, Holland, Australia and Denmark.[185] In the 2005 parliamentary and Senate elections, the Minister of Foreign Affairs invited observers from the UN, regional organizations, SADC countries, a select group of ten African countries, India, Indonesia, Iran, Malaysia, Brazil, Jamaica, Venezuela and Russia, and liberation movements from South Africa, Mozambique, Tanzania, Namibia and Sudan.[186]

Zimbabwean civic organizations provided the ESC with highly critical reports on the 2000 elections,[187] and subsequently attempts were made to limit the role played by civic organizations in providing monitors. This led to Churches and NGOs being barred from conducting civic education in the lead-up to the 2002 elections, although this was overturned in court on procedural grounds.[188] The government's response was to reintroduce essentially the same requirements as regulations, that is through presidential gazetting.[189] In the end, only a few hundred civic society-trained monitors were accredited, and most of the monitors trained and accredited by the ESC were civil servants;[190] the Electoral Act introduced in 2004 formalized this for the 2005 elections.[191] In this way, civic groups were legally excluded, and the government retained its claim as the sole authority that could legitimate the elections, which conformed to its anti-NGO policy, and guaranteed its party's victory.

Looking beyond elections

Although control of the elections machinery was central to ZANU(PF)'s institutional strategy, as in previous decades it was coupled with control over other political institutions—parliament, the judiciary, the military and traditional authorities.

The entrance of growing numbers of opposition MPs into parliament changed the tone of debate markedly. Many of the older 'backbench' generation, who had criticized executive power in previous parliaments, had either chosen not to seek re-election or been denied the opportunity. ZANU(PF) backbenchers, therefore, tended to be more supportive of their ministerial colleagues, and the level of party-political invective increased, as substantive debate on issues decreased. This was by no means complete. In the newly created portfolio committees, cross-party cooperation did occur, and was sometimes reflected on the floor of the house in critical reports on legislation.[192] Provisions to return parliament to a bicameral legislature through the creation of a Senate were introduced in mid-2005. Although allegedly intended to ensure legislative scrutiny, in practice this simply created new patronage opportunities for party elites—as many other 'traditional' sources (travel abroad, access to lucrative business opportunities) dried up.[193]

The regime also set out to politicize the judiciary.[194] As we have seen, the independent candidates, the ZCTU, the NCA, the media and the opposition parties had effectively used the courts to seek redress against discriminatory government policies. Despite everything, the Supreme Court had retained a strong reputation for independent rulings. In 1999 Supreme Court Justices McNally, Muchechetere and Sandura adopted a more progressive position when faced with allegations of torture and a military which ruthlessly ignored court orders, asking the president to confirm that the military had no right to detain civilians, that the government would not tolerate torture and to affirm the role of the police and courts.[195] Mugabe's reaction to this was to accuse the judges of playing politics:

> some of our judges have shocked us by behaving in a manner unbecoming of their status. In their overreaction they forgot that their professional role as judges was to sit in and hear cases and pass judgement on them on the evidence before them. ... In accordance with our Constitution and the principle of the separation of powers the Judiciary has no constitutional right whatsoever to give instructions to the president on any matter as the four judges purported to do. ... Surely if Judges assume both a judicial and quasi-political role, what suffers is in effect their Judicial function. In those circumstances the one and only honourable course open to them is that of quitting the bench and joining the political forum where their political views would not offend against our Constitution and the principles of justice we should uphold.[196]

Judicial rulings on the land invasions further contested the ruling party's policies. In reaction, the government began sidelining independent judges, replacing them with those more acceptable to the regime.

Chief Justice Gubbay was forced to resign after coming under attack for rulings challenging land acquisitions, and overturning a presidential decree which banned candidates defeated in the June election from contesting the results in court.[197] Other senior judges were similarly encouraged to resign by the Attorney General. Those targeted included not only four white High Court judges—Smith, Blackie, Gillespie and Devitte—but also the Supreme Court judges—Sandura, Muchechetere, Ebrahim and McNally—of whom only one was white.[198] While several of the threatened judges resisted the pressure, others resigned, often citing personal reasons.[199] Many of the senior, long-serving judges were also approaching retirement age, and resigned at sixty-five rather than seeking to extend their terms. As the remaining judges refused to resign, the numbers of Supreme Court Justices were increased from five to eight, with three judges promoted from the High Court.[200]

The appointment of High Court Justice Chidyausiku as Chief Justice, above the more senior judges of the Supreme Court, presumably as a reward for his work on the Constitutional Commission, suggested that this was not so much a racial purge as a party-political one.[201] Chidyausiku, a former ZANU(PF) minister, chaired several politically sensitive commissions, and has a record of ruling in favour of the ruling party—decisions which were frequently overturned by higher courts.[202] Lawyer Ben Hlatshwayo also appeared to have been rewarded for his support of the Constitutional Commission with an appointment to High Court.[203] The Solidarity Peace Trust reported further inducements:

> The new Chief Justice of the Supreme Court Godfrey Chidyausiku, the Judge President of the High Court Paddington Garwe, High Court Judge Ben Hlatshwayo ... and at least ten of the other seventeen High Court judges have taken prime agricultural estates seized from commercial farmers through the government's controversial land reform program.[204]

Observers also began to report that membership of the police, army and public service was being politicized from 2001 onwards, although both Gerald Mazarire and Miles Tendi called for a more nuanced interpretation of these claims.[205] In April, Border Gezi announced: 'If you want to work for the Government, you should be prepared to support ZANU (PF).'[206] As JoAnn McGregor demonstrated for Matabeleland, 'the ruling party has tried to insert itself within and gain more control over the local state at district and provincial levels'.[207] Throughout the country, those who were not thought to be sufficiently loyal to ZANU(PF) were sidelined or forced out of local government and the prison service under pressure from the party hierarchy.[208] Police officers were purged and removed from positions of authority.[209] Chihuri, the Police Commissioner, made his position clear by declaring '[m]any people say I am Zanu PF. Today I would like to make it public that I support Zanu PF because it is the ruling party.'[210] Army officers were similarly warned against supporting the MDC,[211] and were promised 100 per cent pay increases immediately before the election.[212] And in the aftermath of the 2002 elections, there were many reports that army units were deployed throughout the country.[213]

The Traditional Leaders Act, first debated in 1998 and finally enacted in 2000, 'brought the chiefs back in', giving them increased powers and new monthly allowances.[214] The implementation of this Act has not been smooth. Bill Kinsey's research reveals the ambiguity and confusion over the new powers and authority vested in traditional leaders. Examining the experiences of resettlement villages, which had had only elected leaders since independence, he notes:

> Villagers clearly liked the democratic aspects of electing village chairmen and preferred a system where anyone could stand; and they could select whomever they liked. They also cited neutrality and impartiality as inherent in this system and felt the elected chairman was a unifying force for the village. Proponents of the traditional system, in contrast, slated elections for creating chaos and causing 'instability' in leadership ... they also tended to see a more traditional system as insurance against excessive politicisation and hence inherently more representative. And they liked the fact that the new leaders were being trained.[215]

In these villages, Kinsey argues, the introduction of 'traditional' leadership generated cleavages and divides, rather than any artificial or natural unity.[216]

In 2004, allowances to traditional and local leaders were dramatically increased, and their jurisdiction over crimes enlarged. Chiefs' monthly allowances were doubled from ZWD 500,000 to 1 million, while those for village heads were to quadruple from ZWD 10,000 to 40,000 per month.[217] In both 2003 and 2004, promises were made that chiefs would receive loans to purchase duty-free vehicles, as well as other benefits such as the electrification of their homesteads.[218] As we have already seen, this corresponded with an increasing role for chiefs and headmen during elections.[219] Chiefs were also beneficiaries of the Fast Track Land Reform. Moyo notes that in addition to land, chiefs were also allocated 'vehicles and farming inputs, purportedly to enhance their leadership role and capacities in the agrarian reform process'.[220] Chiefs also increased their influence by arrogating to themselves the right to identify landless peoples in their own communities and by extending their authority into the new resettlement areas, especially where these were contiguous with the communal areas, or where they had been allocated farms.[221]

Chiefs were further mobilized in 2005 to organise a series of 'biras' or cleansing ceremonies, 'to celebrate the country's Silver Jubilee and reclamation of their land' and 'to pay homage to thousands of Zimbabwe's gallant sons and daughters—both living and dead—and the nation's spirits for liberating the country from the chains of colonial bondage'.[222] In this way, chiefs became a key element in the regime's ideological project of linking recent land resettlement to the liberation war, while also responding to long-standing demands on the part of war veterans for the spirits of their fallen comrades to be brought home and put to rest.[223]

Changing state and society relations: the cupboard is bare

The intense electoral politics both reflected and affected shifts within broader state-society relations. As we have already seen, during elections ZANU offered 'sweeteners' to its traditional supporters. Yet this was of limited effectiveness. Other than land, it had few resources to distribute. But it also mounted a parallel action to discredit, sideline or re-incorporate those groups whose access to non-state-derived resources rendered them potentially autonomous of the state. The ruling party's enduring scepticism that Churches, NGOs and unions were on their side took on the nature of a self-fulfilling prophecy. The more it targeted them and accused them of being unfaithful, the less they had to lose by aligning themselves with the opposition and their donors. But under the barrage of attacks and declining economic conditions, Zimbabwe's civic organizations were increasingly unable to articulate an effective counter-message. The public space and voice they had briefly claimed between 1998 and 2000 was closed off.

The economic crisis, building during the 1990s and hitting consumers with particular hardships after 1997, profoundly shaped the politics of this period. Levels of poverty doubled between 1995 and 2003, while Zimbabwe's GDP declined by 30 per cent between 1997 and 2003.[224] The production of export crops was initially hard hit by land reform, as established farmers pulled out, crops went unharvested and new farmers were unable to maintain production levels. Eddie Cross, an economic analyst allied to the MDC, described the situation in mid-2005:

> Almost all indicators point to a disastrous agricultural season—tobacco sales are expected to reach a maximum of 65,000 tonnes (down from 85,000 tonnes in 2004), maize output has fallen to one third of national demand, oilseed crops are down very substantially and other major agricultural sectors are all showing a downturn in output—fruit, sugar, tea, coffee, horticulture, meat products and milk are all in very short supply.[225]

Drought and food shortages in the years following 2002 left between 1.2 and 4 million Zimbabweans in need of food aid in 2005–6.[226] Urban families began to need support as well, with hyperinflation reaching 411 per cent in October 2005, when Zimbabwe's Consumer Council estimated that a family of six needed ZWD 11.6 million for a month's basic goods.[227] Consumer prices continued to skyrocket, wiping out any savings and making planning or budgeting impossible, with inflation rates calculated in thousands of per cents, rather than hundreds, from 2006 onwards. A substantial wage increase given to domestic workers immediately prior to the 2005 parliamentary elections had to be revoked when employers laid staff off, unable to afford the increase out of their own wages.[228] Unemployment at this point was estimated to be 70 per cent, but even those with jobs struggled as salaries declined and work dried up.

Declining inward resource flows were shaped as much by politics as economics. Tourism revenues dropped markedly after 2000, as did international investment. Targeted sanctions were imposed by the EU and Australia in 2002 and the US in 2003, with New Zealand and Canada bringing in similar policies in subsequent years. These focused on freezing assets and blocking international travel by named individuals. In addition, arms embargoes were brought in to prevent Zimbabwe from importing weaponry that might be used against the civilian population. Although these targeted sanctions were not designed to close off trade, restrictions on access to loans and aid affected government and NGO budgets.

Remittances from the growing diaspora became an increasingly important source of foreign exchange, but much of this was channelled into the black market through middlemen with foreign accounts, rather than through formal money transfer schemes like Western Union or Zimbabwe-based bank accounts. The inevitable foreign exchange shortage impacted on fuel imports, creating periodic fuel shortages from 2000 onwards, with knock-on effects in most sectors. Attempts to 'float' the Zimbabwe dollar partially in October 2005 were designed to redirect foreign exchange into the formal banking system, making it available to the state. An official devaluation of 66 per cent still did not match the parallel market rate.

Deprived of donor funds, and with decreasing investment and disappearing tourist dollars, the Mugabe government decided to 'look East', searching for loans, investment and tourists from China, Malaysia and Indonesia. Although loans were forthcoming for the electricity authority,[229] and new buses alleviated some transport difficulties, much of the growth in China-Zimbabwe trade reflected exports of unprocessed tobacco and imports of cheap consumer goods. Dubbed '*zhing-zhong*' by consumers, they were ridiculed for their poor quality. Industry representatives reported that thirty-five textile firms closed between 2002 and 2005, unable to compete against imports.[230]

Other industries were affected by lack of inputs, both imported and domestic. The number of bakeries in Zimbabwe reduced from 300 in 2000 to only sixty in 2005.[231] Price controls on consumer staples, but not on the inputs, made the production of bread uneconomic unless sold on the parallel market.[232] Given flour shortages and the rising cost of bread, Zimbabweans were shocked to read reports that Leo Mugabe, later to become a government MP, had been arrested for attempting to smuggle flour out of the country.[233] Decreasing purchasing power, daily increases in food and a concomitant lack of goods purchasable in the formal economy made life increasingly difficult for urban working-class and poor Zimbabweans, while an elite few benefited from profiteering, smuggling and the black market. Police and youth militias were deployed to try to 'fix' prices and bring 'order' to markets, in operations that sometimes seemed more like looting.[234]

As these pressures mounted, any lingering rhetoric of reconciliation was replaced by claims that whites had not reciprocated the offer of reconciliation offered to them. They were instead the 'real enemy'.[235] In a BBC interview, President Mugabe said:

> Yes, some of them are good people, but they remain cheats. They remain dishonest. They remain uncommitted even to the national cause. It is as if we are running a government of two communities, they on their own not wanting to get truly integrated into the social frame, but just wanting all the time to oppose government.[236]

By 2002, the number of whites was only half that in 1992, making up just 0.5 per cent of the population.[237] The Commercial Farmers Union (CFU), which had been close to ZANU(PF) until the 1998 land designations, wavered between attempting to maintain its position of non-confrontational interaction with government ministries and using the courts to seek redress, reflecting the presence of two camps within its membership. MDC members pressured the CFU to pursue legal action against the unconstitutional land seizures. Other groups of farmers, notably tobacco growers, producing mainly for export, emphasized the economic realities and urged the farm community to seek ways of compromising with the ruling party.[238] At the same time, individual farmers continued to contest land acquisitions in the courts, winning occasional battles, but very much sidelined from power. Frustrated by these attempts, the government repeatedly amended the Land Acquisition Act in reaction to court judgements, and introduced the Protection of Rural Land Occupiers Bill.[239] Finally, in September 2005, the constitution was amended such that all agricultural land acquired for resettlement became state property, and it became unconstitutional to contest acquisitions in court.[240]

Urban workers and white businesspeople were also obvious targets. As we have seen, during the 2000 election, white farmers and businesspeople were thought to be providing much of the MDC's financial support. In addition, the overwhelming urban vote for the MDC revealed to ZANU(PF) that they had lost the support of many workers. As Mugabe said to the Central Committee in July 2000:

With all price controls done away with in the spirit of liberalisation; with our policies and programmes generally failing or being quite slow to yield positive results; with all our safety nets simply failing, it was difficult to see how the Party would ever escape the winter of urban discontent and the harsh political verdict that this brings about in electoral terms. Little wonder then that the bulk of the support and vote for the opposition came from urban or peri-urban dwellers, chiefly from among the unemployed or frustrated youths. Little wonder then that a significant part of the opposition leadership draws from the trade union and tertiary student leadership. Indeed it should not be wondered why the most trenchant criticism against the Party emanated from both the high and low-density suburban dwellers, including professionals whose incomes are being eroded daily, as well as owners of indigenous businesses whose concerns are either struggling or have already succumbed to the negative performance of the economy.[241]

Mugabe clearly identified the grievances of voters, and set out to resolve them through two interconnected campaigns—anti-business and pro-labour—which coalesced into an attempt to intimidate white business owners, and at the same time convince urban labourers that ZANU(PF) could again be an ally in their fight for better working conditions. Immediately after the 2000 election, intense violence permeated urban areas, perpetrated by the army and police.[242] In early 2001, this tactic shifted towards trying to regain the sympathy of urban voters and counteract the influence of the ZCTU. This first took the form of an attempt to gain control of the ZCTU, sanctioning war veteran involvement in labour disputes, and the reinvigoration of a splinter umbrella union.

ZANU(PF) moved to take advantage of the vacancies within the ZCTU caused by the resignations of Tsvangirai and Sibanda. These power struggles were the continuation of earlier conflicts within the leadership of the ZCTU, in that some aspirant ZCTU leaders had tried to align with the ruling party by adopting its proposed social contract—which Tsvangirai's faction had rejected.[243] The social contract advocated by the ruling party was intended to put an end to labour disputes and stay-aways, and return labour relations to a more consensual framework. As the ZCTU's leadership election approached, ZANU(PF) was alleged to have paid up membership dues for unions in arrears, so that they could vote.[244] In the end, the pro-MDC slate retained control of the ZCTU, but ZANU(PF) had succeeded in factionalizing and dividing the workers.[245]

In early 2001, workers were encouraged to forward complaints to a newly formed ZANU(PF) labour committee. War veterans, led again by Joseph Chinotimba, further claimed the right to arbitrate labour disputes at a series of companies, as they had done at independence, before the formation of the ZCTU.[246] After complaints from several foreign governments, the Labour Ministry finally clamped down on the veterans, alleging that rogue elements had gone beyond ZANU(PF)'s intentions and were merely extorting money from companies.[247] Instead, several new judges were appointed to the Labour Relations Tribunal, in an attempt to clear the backlog in cases.[248]

Chinotimba then moved to resuscitate the Zimbabwe Federation of Trade Unions (ZFTU), a pro-ZANU splinter union originally formed in 1998, as a vehicle for further anti-ZCTU campaigning.[249] Government support enabled ZFTU leadership to visit workplaces and forcefully encourage the formation of splinter unions.[250] That these efforts made any headway at all on the shop-floors must be taken as evidence of labour weakness and divisions. Shop-floor grievances were real, and neither the ZCTU nor the MDC had developed strongly rooted allegiances among the workers. Low levels of democracy within unions also kept pro-ZANU leaders in place, even where workers were solidly MDC, which made them available for ZANU(PF)'s 'infiltration' tactics during the ZCTU elections.[251] Complementing this focus on union organizations was a discursive strategy that blamed local business—alleged to be conspiring with shadowing international forces—for shortages of goods and fuelling the inflationary demand for foreign currency.[252] Just as with the divisions artificially created in other sectors, this 'divide and rule' strategy generated confusion and tensions on the shop-floor, effectively weakening the labour voice.

Church-state relations, strained during the constitutional debate, further ruptured in the 2000s. During the referendum, churches had been on the verge of calling for a 'No' vote, when they were persuaded to back away from such a stand.[253] Church voices were then little heard during the lead-in to the 2000 election. The few individual church leaders who spoke out against violence were attacked. Pius Ncube, Catholic Archbishop of Matabeleland, and Evangelical Lutheran Bishop Ambrose Moyo, who had aligned themselves publicly with the NCA and spoken out against violence in the pre-election period, were both reported to be on a CIO hitlist.[254] Mugabe accused Pius Ncube of causing the party's defeat in the election:

> In Matabeleland, I think what we saw was tribalism and ethnicity emerging. We happen to know that some leaders of the MDC alongside leaders of the Church and names such as that of Archbishop Ncube of the Catholic Church have been mentioned banded together and used reasons that emerge from the history and the conflict situation and could want the people of Matabeleland to believe that the government is not attending to their own needs in as much as it is attending to the needs of other regions.[255]

> The most insidious side of the resurgence of white power came by way of the pulpit and in the human form of church figures who did not hesitate to 'render unto God' things that belonged to Caesar. Especially in suburban parishes and in rural Matabeleland, prayers became full-blooded politics and congregations became anti-Zanu (PF) political communities.[256]

Ncube's fellow bishops and the CCJP were less outspoken, but did condemn government-condoned violence, particularly in the aftermath of the election.[257] Without naming either the war veterans or party leaders by name, the Catholic Bishops Conference challenged the ruling elite's claim to power as liberators:

> Let us remind each other that no one person or group of persons liberated this country alone. The great majority of Zimbabweans, because of their love for freedom and sense of justice, liberated it through their sacrifices. … It is the duty of the government to ensure the nation is not held at ransom by a few. … We urge the government to allow the law enforcement agents to perform their duties without interference so that there is a sense of security in the country.[258]

The war veterans responded to this criticism bluntly. Joseph Chinotimba said: 'The war veterans are championing a noble cause. If the churchmen think we are wrong they should mind their own problems and stop provoking us.'[259]

After the 2000 election, we see ZANU(PF) attempting to get the church back on side. The Anglican Church saga played out in a dramatic fashion on the front pages of newspapers, while Bishop Ncube proved to be fodder for the gossip columns. The retirement of Mugabe's ally Siyachitema from the Anglican Diocese of Harare led to a campaign to replace him.[260] Tim Neill had been an outspoken critic of the government's constitutional draft, and was perceived as NCA-aligned; he contested the election, as did the little-known Nolbert Kunonga, who was allied with pro-ZANU(PF) priests in the diocese. Neill's appointment would have made him the only white Anglican bishop, but he lost the election, amid allegations of racism.[261] His public conflict with his Church led to his removal, after he was accused of 'tarnishing the Church's name' by making internal conflict public.[262] Kunonga, as Bishop of Harare, did little to assuage concerns when his first public statements were seen as repeating ZANU(PF) propaganda from the pulpit.[263] In a controversial speech, he said:

> You are sick to think the Western political and economic interests are your interests. You are sick to think the Western world is interested in removing corrupt governments. They are here to look for puppets to put in government ignorant African political leaders who can easily be manipulated. ... We do accept that Zimbabwe is a symbol of the land of freedom where all people of all races, creeds and nationalities could live together. But it is not a land for all people to govern. *It is only for indigenous Africans to govern.* ... Is interest in human rights in Zimbabwe not a tactical selfdefence mechanism against grabbing of land by the Government? ... We live in a sick country. It is a neurotic nation where the young Africans are losing national identity, sense of history, African feeling and selfpride. *The sad thing is most of my priests are religious uncle Toms, puppets, parrots and religious fakers. Refuse to be ignorant and greedy. I am attacking the brainwashed preachers.*[264]

Although many members of Kunonga's congregation did not support his partisan stand, or how he ran the diocese, their attempts to challenge him through Anglican church law were unproductive.[265] By contrast in Bulawayo, Roman Catholic Bishop Ncube was calling openly for Mugabe's removal: 'We're all praying that the Lord will soon take Mugabe away. Everyone is fed up with him. .... We're all hoping against hope that something will happen. He's a very, very evil man. The sooner he dies the better.'[266] Conveniently, evidence appeared implicating Ncube in a sexual affair, and he resigned in 2007.

Other Churches were more interested in aligning themselves with ZANU. The Apostolic faith responded positively to regime overtures. During the 2000 election, the populist Governor of Mashonaland Central, Border Gezi, made several very public appeals to his *Vapostori* brethren.[267] Although some members of the Church criticized him for bringing politics—and the media spotlight—into their worship,[268] their leader encouraged all members of his flock to vote for the first time, because 'we were told by the Holy Spirit that this country would be ruled by a black'.[269] Gezi's untimely death in April 2001 led Apostolic leaders to make even more public statements of support to the president and ruling party.[270] In early 2002, there were reports that 'hundreds of members of the Apostolic Faith sect [led by their pastor Godfrey Nzira] descended on MDC offices at Makoni shopping centre and later attacked the home of Fidelis Mhashu, the MP for Chitungwiza'.[271] And later that year, Nzira and other church leaders met to affirm their support for Mugabe and his government.[272]

Through all of this, mainline churches continued to be important providers of election monitors and observers through the CCJP, ZCC and the Evangelical Fellowship (EFZ). Indeed, the ZCC, caught up in the euphoria of the 2000 elections, was not only highly critical of the ruling party, but claimed credit for launching the NCA and indirectly the MDC.[273] But after 2000, it seemed to retreat into confusion and quiescence in response to intimidation and co-option.[274] Although Bishop Moyo became the new president of the ZCC, replacing retiring Anglican Bishop Siyachitema, his more outspoken tendencies did not manifest themselves.[275] The ZCC, ZCBC and EFZ leadership instead became embroiled in futile attempts to mediate between the MDC and ZANU(PF): 'You limit people's suffering if ZANU(PF) and MDC are working together ... the issue is that they should not burn each others' houses down, but act like they do in parliament ... they should mirror what happened in parliament in the townships.'[276]

However, many pastors and individual church people felt abandoned by their leaders and set up alternative institutions. The churches in Manicaland, for example, were deeply involved in providing shelter and food to victims of political violence displaced during the elections and land invasions. They, and churches in Bulawayo, organized broad ecumenical coalitions which publicly condemned the violence.[277] A national initiative, the Zimbabwe National Pastors' Conference (ZNPC), founded in 2002, brought together these groups and others to discuss the challenges they faced during the economic and political crisis.[278] Many of their members are from smaller, charismatic and evangelical churches, often perceived as 'apolitical'. They struggled to respond to the economic and political crisis that surrounded them and their parishioners—situations that had not been explored in their pastoral training, which was often limited. Gaining confidence as a group, these ministers began to speak publicly and critically on political and social issues,[279] but more importantly supported each other in facing divisions in their congregations, violence directed at themselves and their families, and other challenging situations.[280]

NGO staff, by contrast to the isolated pastors, tend to be well-educated and linked into international networks. Unsurprisingly, then, they became a primary target in the regime's attacks on external forces accused of undermining Zimbabwe's autonomy and democracy. In 1999, Mugabe accused NGOs of 'trying to create political figures out of the opposition'.[281] By the time of the 2000 elections, government attacks had become more explicit: 'NGOs should leave politics to locals.'[282]

For a few months in 2001, the more developmental roles of some international NGOs were disrupted when they were threatened by war veterans.[283] Others were accused of helping to create artificial food shortages and distributing MDC propaganda and party cards with food.[284] Local government officials were also warned against working with NGOs. According to a newspaper report, the Minister of Local Government, Public Works and National Housing said that councils:

> should look for alternative ways of raising funds but warned the councils against accepting money from nongovernmental organisations, which had political agendas. He said a number of NGOs with political agendas had invaded rural areas to promote their own agendas and were not interested in development programmes. A number of NGOs were being used to campaign for MDC in rural areas. The Government has warned that it would not hesitate to cancel licences for those found undertaking political activities instead of focusing on developmental work. Some of these organisations come to you with a packaging which looks good but the contents would be satanic. Do not accept such type of assistance.[285]

Other explicit attacks on local NGOs included demands that unregistered organizations 'urgently stop their operations' until 'regularized'.[286] NGOs were also affected by POSA, the public order law, which was used to ban their meetings. NGO workshops and meetings continued to be visited by CIO agents, either asking questions or posing as 'participants'.[287] As the crisis intensified, the key actors behind the Pastors' Conference contributed to the creation of the Christian Alliance, a broader coalition of church organizations which itself provided a secretariat for the Save Zimbabwe campaign. This latter group, organized in 2006, brought together a wide range of organizations to present a more public and critical stance towards governance issues, but effectively framed their message within a strongly Christian tone and style. Its prayer meetings, which blurred the lines between protest and prayer, were repeatedly targeted by police; and in 2007, attacks on a meeting led to the arrest and torture of many participants, and the death of an NCA activist. But Save Zimbabwe is also credited with putting the Zimbabwe crisis squarely back on the international agenda at a critical point.[288]

Despite such pressure from the regime, some aspects of NGO activity increased, even while others contracted in the face of the decreasing donor funds. HIV/AIDS work expanded, as donors continued to support humanitarian aid. Some interesting coalitions also emerged, such as the campaign to make 'feminine hygiene products' affordable, which linked women's NGOs and female parliamentarians.[289] Although there was a certain sense of 'pulling together' and unity under attack, which made such NGO alliances possible, there were also practical impediments. Experienced NGO staff were increasingly leaving the country in search of better remunerated jobs. Newer activists lacked the shared history of engagement. Straitened resources also limited time and ability to travel and network. But NGOs trying to organize simple things like newspaper supplements also found themselves caught up in politics. Some NGOs were unwilling to advertise support in the opposition-aligned *Daily News*, but only in government-run *Herald* and *Sunday Mail*; while others refused to give money to the government-linked papers, and would only publish in *Daily News*, an obvious barrier to inter-NGO networking.[290] Clearly, it would be a mistake to assume that all NGOs were aligned with the MDC, or distanced from the government.

While the ruling party tried to hold onto some allies, it also briefly pursued a new tactic, facilitating the formation of new 'liberation-based' organizations. Several new groups which appeared to be more or less strongly linked to ZANU(PF) appeared on the scene: Inyika Trust was described as a land rights association,[291] the National Debate Association (NDA) promoted civic discussion,[292] while Heritage Zimbabwe was said to be a cultural association.[293] In addition, like the policy of forming rival trade unions, a 'high-density' residents' association was proposed to contest the growing influence of the 'white-dominated' Combined Harare Residents Association.[294]

A more concerted strategy to bridge these two extremes was also underway. Throughout 2002–3, a newly reinvigorated NANGO and its member NGOs were involved in a process of consultation about the preparation of new legislation to regulate the activities of NGOs. NANGO described its relationship with the government as 'more proactive ... we went to government with high-powered delegation—mostly lawyers—and said they couldn't do it on their own'.[295] The NGOs hired consultants to draw up proposed legislation, which was then submitted to the ministry. But the government's NGO bill, introduced in 2003, bore little resemblance to the NGO's proposed draft. The bill instead banned NGOs from receiving foreign funding for 'governance' issues, at a time when many donors would only fund humanitarian or governance programmes. Despite NGO lobbying and consultative meetings with ministers and parliamentary committees, the bill was passed in 2004. Unusually, however, it did not receive presidential assent nor was it gazetted, leaving NGOs in legal limbo.

Like other strategies, government policies towards urban residents had both incorporative and exclusionary elements. The Ministry of Local Government reacted to the election of MDC mayors and councillors in Bulawayo, Masvingo, Chegutu, Mutare, Kariba and Harare by removing powers from the cities and blocking their efforts at reform.

In Harare, the government was forced to run council elections in 2002, after three years of an appointed commission.[296] An MDC mayor and councillors were elected in forty-four out of forty-five wards, although two white MDC councillors were forced into the courts to prove that they were citizens before being able to take up their seats.[297] The new mayor, Elias Mudzuri, won over 80 per cent of the vote with 262,275 votes against 56,796 for the ZANU(PF) candidate.

The next year, the executive mayor had been forced out of his office, and a number of councillors suspended, while others resigned in protest.[298] The deputy mayor took control of the city, only to defect to ZANU(PF).[299] Then in 2004, an appointed commission was again imposed to run Harare. Other towns and cities had similar experiences: the Chegutu MDC mayor was removed from office a few months later, through the vote of ZANU(PF) councillors who had been accused of corruption, even though they did not have the legal power to do so.[300] In 2005, the Minister of Local Government also suspended the MDC mayor of Mutare and took control of Chitungwiza, alleging that the MDC mayor had failed to deal with burst water and sewage mains, or to pay water bills.[301] The appointment of provincial governors for Harare and Bulawayo added an additional level of governmental control on top of their elected councils.[302]

In the early 2000s, informal sector workshops and tuckshops selling repackaged staple goods and vegetables proliferated, backyard shacks and cottages were built, and hot food was sold on the streets of the central business district (CBD).[303] Relaxation of regulations on urban agriculture was extended, and some parts of the state even embraced the cause enthusiastically.[304] At the same time, councils seemed less and less able to provide basic services. In 2004 and 2005, Harare's eastern suburbs such as Mabvuku and Tafara frequently went for weeks without piped water, forcing women to collect it by the bucketful from vleis and shallow wells.[305] In April 2005, soon after the election, electricity cuts also became common, as generators broke down and foreign exchange shortages prevented the importation of spare parts.[306] In Harare and Chitungwiza, rubbish collection periodically ceased[307] and the supply of electricity and water became infrequent in certain parts of the towns. Raw sewage leaking near homes was a major concern in a number of Harare's suburbs, in Bulawayo and Chitungwiza.[308] While the cities' supply of electricity could not be blamed on the municipalities, problems of water provision and quality were a result of the lack of investment, but also due to lack of foreign exchange for sourcing the requisite chemicals.

The housing situation did not improve either. Land allocated for residential accommodation in Harare decreased each year between 2000 and 2005. The number of building plots (known locally as 'stands') allocated dropped from 1,999 in 1999, to 854 in 2000, 555 in 2001, and 560 in 2003.[309] In Bulawayo, 60,000 people were on the waiting list, with only a few hundred new stands being serviced each year.[310] Those without housing continued to turn to backyard shacks: in 2005 these were estimated at '34,000 backyard extensions compared to 27,000 legally recognised and approved dwellings' in Mutare, and '64% of the housing stock' in Victoria Falls.[311]

Despite these failures and the deterioration of the urban environment, attempts to regulate and control the burgeoning informal sector
and to enforce the now ancient urban by-laws were not entirely abandoned. In 2000, houses built on land adjacent to the Harare suburb of
Kambuzuma were demolished.[312] In 2001, the unelected commission
running Harare issued notices that backyard shacks would be demolished if not regularized. It was estimated that there were 145,000
illegal structures in Harare at that time, which would render 500,000
people homeless if they were destroyed.[313] Meanwhile vendors who
had been allocated space at a flea market in the Central Business
District (CBD) and had been paying monthly rentals were also threatened with eviction;[314] a crackdown on food vendors and tuckshops was
announced.[315] Unsuccessful attempts were made in 2002 and 2003 to
remove illegal settlements that had arisen on peri-urban plots during
the land invasions and been sanctioned by aspiring ZANU(PF) candidates.[316] A second phase of clean-ups began in 2004, when street people in Harare were 'rounded up' after reports of attacks and rapes on
passers-by.[317] The next month, an unplanned mosque in Rugare, one of
the smallest and oldest townships, was destroyed by the city council.[318]
In August 2004, the Minister of Local Government again began
attempts to evict the Porta Farm settlement by force, until restrained
by a Court Order, as in 1995, requiring the provision of 'suitable [ser-
viced] permanent homes'.[319] In their years at Porta Farm, the residents
had built houses, toilets and schools, and many children were scheduled to sit exams, which would have been disrupted by the move to an
unserviced 'holding camp'.[320]

This series of events in 2004, accompanied by newspaper articles
criticizing the state for failing to repair potholes, replace traffic lights and
remove rubbish,[321] seems to have led to the seemingly innocuous
announcement of 'Operation Murambatsvina' (Drive Out Rubbish) by
the commission running Harare in October 2004: 'We have launched this
operation to rid the CBD of illegal vendors, street families and those
parking their cars in undesignated places.' The commission stated that
'Murambatsvina' was intended 'to spruce up the image of the city'.[322]

Although little action was taken until May, after the parliamentary
elections, it became clear that this was not a random aberration, but an
agenda—to roll back the clock. Murambatsvina began with an

announcement that commuter omnibus terminuses had been removed from the city centre, so that routes would terminate on the edge of the CBD. Initially, this seemed little to worry about—such an announcement had been made time and time again during the 1990s, with little impact. But then flea markets, workshops and informal vendors had their stalls destroyed and goods confiscated.[323] After this, the operation began to move into residential areas. Areas targeted for destruction included not just 'squatter camps'—those occupying public land illegally and in semi-sanctioned locations like Porta Farm—but also illegal use of privately owned land as workshops and backyard cottages, extensions and shacks.[324] Residents were also warned off cultivating public land.[325] Although there were reports that this directive had been rescinded, as the planting season began in October, the city council again warned residents against cultivating in 'undesignated' areas.[326]

The UN's Tibaijuka Report used official government data to estimate that 569,685 individuals were displaced and 97,614 lost their primary source of livelihood, arriving at an estimate of 650,000 to 700,000 people directly affected and 2.1 million indirectly affected.[327] Although some vendors re-appeared in the cities in the following month,[328] and some squatter camps re-established themselves,[329] for the most part those affected had few options. Many families were sleeping in the open, some had been removed to transit camps, others found family to stay with, or managed to travel—or had been moved—to rural areas. Churches, especially in Manicaland and Bulawayo, took in many of the homeless. Although this 'clean-up' was far more extensive than previous efforts, it too presumed the need for orderly, modern cities. Many of the victims were told to go to their rural homes. As the senior police officer in Harare, Edmore Veterai, said: 'No one in Zimbabwe comes from nowhere. Everybody belongs somewhere.'[330] While this has generally been interpreted as reflecting an instrumentalized concern with belonging, typical of the exclusionary politics of identity seen in other African states,[331] political discourse surrounding the clean-up also articulated a concern about those without secure jobs or property being allowed to participate in urban politics despite allegedly 'not being stakeholders'. This was explicitly linked to the 1995 extension of the urban franchise to non-rate-payers, which itself evoked Rhodesian-era debates about the qualified franchise, and linked to less well-defined concerns about productivity and contribution of 'good citizens'.[332] Rhetorically, at least, the 'clean-up' was also related to the larger economic crisis. Informal traders were accused of hoarding goods and 'causing' food shortages.[333] The clean-up also targeted foreign exchange dealers, and was framed as part of an anti-corruption campaign, as well as a campaign against illegal activities.[334] Both informal traders and foreign exchange dealers were seen to have been depriving the government of revenue. The 'clean-up' was also an attempt to force consumers out of the informal sector and parallel markets, and into tax-paying shops and banks.[335]

Operation Garikai/Hlalani (Rebuilding and Reconstruction), the delayed carrot extended to urban households, started in July 2005 with the goal of providing new houses. Peri-urban farms were being developed, and houses constructed using technology previously disallowed such as rammed earth bricks, and on smaller plots. But like other similar operations, deadlines were missed, and many were still without shelter as the rains arrived in November.[336]

The rural informal sector was the next to be targeted. Informal mining had long been a source of income for poor rural and peri-urban Zimbabweans, despite concerns about its environmental impact. Like other sectors, artisanal mining had been tolerated and even encouraged, as a response to unemployment. But increased levels of smuggling during the currency crisis made the sector an attractive target. According to Mawowa, in 2007 it was estimated that more than 15 tons of gold (worth over USD 400 million) were smuggled out of the country annually between 2002 and 2007.[337] Clearly, this revenue imperative was an important driver of Operation Chikorokoza Chapera, which brought together the police and the Reserve Bank to displace the miners and incarcerate strikingly high numbers of them.[338]

Yet mining was also the unexpected saviour of the regime. Diamonds discovered in Marange in 2006 provided new sources of income for the state, but far more importantly new patronage flows, as not only the police, but also the army were able to muscle in on the amazing profits to be made.[339] First the state encouraged small-scale miners to flood into the area, and then it attempted to exclude them. Although the extreme brutality of these attacks exposed the regime to more negative media, especially from international human rights groups, these strategies do seem to have been successful in yoking both high-ranking and lower-level members of the security apparatus into the regime's project, just as the DRC and farms had in previous years.[340]

Conclusion

After the loss of the constitutional referendum, the ZANU(PF) regime faced unprecedented economic and political constraints, yet it moved to take advantage of new opportunities and maintained itself in power when many expected it to decline and fall. The increasing economic difficulties as the decade wore on proved a real threat to the regime's discursive and material strategies. Without land and diamonds, not to mention the 'look East' strategy, Zimbabwe's coffers would indeed have been bare. But the regime's remarkable survival should not be attributed solely to bribery and patronage. Renewed discursive strategies and institutional control continued, even as the crisis escalated.

Zimbabwe's political and economic landscape was transformed in this 'short decade'. The countryside looked different with new homesteads and different cropping strategies, while in urban areas both prosperity and poverty transformed shopping areas and suburbs. Yet the strategic use of sweeteners and material rewards could not hide the depths of the country's infrastructural collapse, most evident in the gradual decline of electricity provision, water treatment, road surfaces, schools and hospitals, and dramatically revealed by 2008's cholera epidemic.

But despite all this, the opposition and civil society struggled to define themselves and their position within the state. Exclusionary strategies targeting racial groups, opposition party supporters, NGOs and church people left them vulnerable to violent attack. By the end of this period, most high-level NGO staff had been attacked or arrested at least once, while many grass-roots supporters had experienced threats and abuse, if not worse. NGOs struggled to get their voices heard, as institutions were politicized and transformed so as to exclude their voices, and deny them space in which to operate. The newly mobilized political sphere proved difficult for them to navigate.

186

7

THE POLITICS OF 'WINNER TAKES ALL' (2008–2014)

We are a nation that believes
A hero is a fighter, AK47 adorned
Must have marked or smeared our lives with blood
Killed or died to liberate us
We are a nation that must change
See
Other heroes who touch our nerves
Flow in our veins like blood
Like life[1]

In 2008, after years of turmoil and economic decline, ZANU(PF) experienced its first electoral defeat in parliamentary elections. Yet, five years later they roared back into near-full control of Zimbabwe's politics. Explaining this remarkable turnaround is both straightforward and complicated, reflecting the paradoxical nature of politics in these years. The opposition winning more seats than the incumbent party in the parliamentary election was unprecedented, as were the levels of violence that accompanied the run-off of the presidential election. At the height of Zimbabwe's inflation, infrastructural collapse and health crisis, it seemed impossible that the stand-off between government and opposition could continue.

The creation of the Global Political Agreement (GPA) provided for a government of national unity, and the dollarization of Zimbabwe's economy stabilized the worst of Zimbabwe's political and economic crisis, but did little to resolve it. With ZANU in its weakest position for decades, the GPA and its power-sharing agreement became the means to stave off political defeat. ZANU's re-animation of the nationalist coalition, which had seemed near impossible earlier, proved successful, but left a fragmented party and a vulnerable polity.

Focusing on 2008–13, this chapter first sets out the conjunction of events in 2008 that produced the Global Political Agreement—unprecedented economic and health crises concatenated by the parliamentary and presidential elections. The violence of the run-off election created pressure for a 'power-sharing agreement' intended to make time and space for institutional reconfiguration, in particular the rewriting of the constitution so as to provide a platform for more equitable party politics. However, the power-sharing agreement instead enabled ZANU to regain the political high ground. Zimbabwe confirms Bratton's dictum that 'power sharing does not work well when an intransigent rump of incumbent leaders control the intact parts of a moderately strong state'.[2]

This chapter explores this concept first from the perspective of the political parties, and then from that of civil society, which finds itself constrained and sidelined. Like previous power-sharing attempts, the constitutional and legal institutions that arrived with the 'unity government' did little to give the opposition or civil society access to power. Instead they created space in which the dominant party was able to re-assert itself. As a result, the 2013 election itself was not particularly violent. Rather we saw ZANU confidently re-assuming control of the state apparatus, as they have done since 1980, while also successfully appealing to a new nationalist coalition. The final section of the chapter explores how the shifts in political power also catalyse shifts in discourse within political and civil society, as the material and discursive strategies capitalize on the distributionalist and mobilizationist practices, generating a more fractured and febrile political domain.

Unlike ZANU's flawed attempts to regain discursive and political dominance in 2000, which was in many ways a 'relaunch' of old policies from the 1980s, we see how new strategies and a more coherent narrative rally around institutional innovations and economically advantageous alliances. Civil society finds itself sidelined and impotent as politics becomes more mobilized and factionalized. 'Winner takes all' politics dominates the political environment: there is little to lose from political mobilization, and potentially everything to gain. This exacerbates tensions and factionalization, and intensifies the high stakes of spoils politics played out across the sectors. At the same time, the crisis also rose higher and higher up the agendas of Zimbabwe's neighbours and donors. Rather than diminishing tensions and accommodating demands from contesting groups, as per the theories that shaped its adoption in post-war European democracies, Zimbabwe's power-sharing ratcheted up friction and intensified demands for representation, recognition and access to state power.

Responding to crisis: a (re)turn to power-sharing

Probably the only point of genuine cross-party agreement in 2008 was that the electoral stalemate and economic crisis needed urgent resolution. In response to both domestic and regional pressure, a series of never fully realized institutions were created, most of which lacked autonomy and resources to function effectively or gain legitimacy.

ZANU gambled—for the most part successfully—that it could use the Global Political Agreement (GPA) and 'inclusive government' agreement, which provided the framework for these institutional innovations, to re-establish itself. Despite appearing to be a more robust model of power-sharing, the GPA's implementation followed a similar pattern to the experiences of the 1980s—not so much giving the opposition access to power, as providing space for the dominant party to re-assert itself. Indeed, Brian Raftopoulos, whose knowledge and understanding of the agreement is second to none, sums it up as a 'battle for the state'.[3] ZANU's gamble paid off, while the MDC, divided into two factions and squeezed between short-term and long-term interests, was the loser.[4]

This process must be understood against the backdrop of Zimbabwe's return to relative economic stability. The long-running economic meltdown reached its nadir in 2008, with inflation calculated in millions, even trillions, of percentage points. Formal businesses were increasingly unable to function, with many shutting down. Unemployment was conservatively estimated at 80 per cent. The limited purchasing power of the devalued Zimbabwe dollar fuelled smuggling along all of Zimbabwe's borders. Fidelis Duri documents how smuggling seemingly took over the economy in Mutare's high density suburbs as price-controlled Zimbabwean goods were smuggled over the border for sale in Mozambique, in return for hard currency or second-hand clothes; he observed that: 'nearly every homestead … had become a tuckshop with posters at the gates advertising various commodities, most of which had been sourced … from Mozambique'.[5] Tellingly, he also notes that smuggling 'accelerated' after Operation Murambatsvina disrupted other informal sector activities. None of this was unprecedented in Zimbabwe, but its scale indicated how profoundly the economy was being transformed.

The 2008 cholera outbreak, which spread rapidly through Zimbabwe and had a higher than usual mortality rate, provided further vivid evidence, if that were needed, of how badly basic services—water, sewerage and health—had broken down.[6] Meanwhile the outflow of asylum-seekers and migrants was depriving Zimbabwe of its best and brightest—an estimated 1–3 million having left since 2000. Their remittance flows—estimated at around USD 1 billion in 2009— proved crucial in keeping the state functioning, and keeping their families housed and fed,[7] but was creating new challenges for neighbouring South Africa, which received by far the greatest number of exiles. Botswana, too, was increasingly willing to express its concern over events in Zimbabwe, and the domestic repercussions. This 'regionalization' of Zimbabwe's crisis played a key part in generating pressure for reform and accommodation on the part of Zimbabwe's leaders.

The final element in this unholy concatenation was the so-called 'harmonized' 2008 elections, in which the presidential, Senate, parliamentary and local votes were held on 29 March. These elections provide further evidence of how significant control over electoral institutions continues to be to ZANU(PF)'s strategies. Given their previous track record this should not be surprising, yet in 2008 ZANU actually lost the popular vote; only because of their continued control over electoral institutions was it able to retain power.

Expectations for the elections were not optimistic, despite reforms to electoral laws bringing them into line with SADC's criteria and intended to improve transparency and accountability. Activists had been anticipating that a new constitution would be negotiated before the election, and the failure to do so worried many. Although the creation of the Zimbabwe Electoral Commission (ZEC) in 2005 had supposedly provided for a more autonomous and depoliticized administration of elections, the reality was reminiscent of its predecessor the ESC's behaviour in the early 1990s—lacking strong, authoritative leadership, the commissioners proved hesitant and unwilling to rock the boat.[8]

Despite these inauspicious circumstances, the first stage of the elections went generally well. Turnout was low, but so was violence, and there were few reports of irregularities. Under electoral guidelines, poll observers had been able to report the counts, and in most cases the results were tabulated and posted publicly on the door of the polling station. However, with an apparent news blackout on the vote and reports of recounts, questions began to be raised about transparency. The results were not formally released until 2 May, although educated guesses had been made based on the data posted at polling stations and relayed across the county by mobile phone. The MDC's success in the parliamentary vote—thirty-six seats between the two MDC formations to ZANU's twenty-four—meant that they controlled the legislature. Although it was accepted that Morgan Tsvangirai had won the presidential election—an unprecedented result—the official results gave him less than 50 per cent of the vote; many questions were raised about the reliability of those results, given the unexplained delay.[9] Under the new rules, a run-off election was required.

The tension of the weeks after the election, while the nation waited anxiously, set the stage for a violent and unstable run-off. With the second stage of the presidential election set for 27 June, an unprecedented attack began on opposition supporters and NGOs, and indeed election officials, with thousands of incidents of politically motivated violence in April and May. The Zimbabwe Election Support Network (ZESN) described the situation as 'war-like', while Masunungure talks of the election as having been 'militarized'.[10] A deeper contrast to the first stage could not be imagined. Freedom of association and movement were constrained in many areas, and there was little coverage of the opposition or radio or television. Information sources were clearly targeted, with NGOs harassed and reports of cellphones being checked at roadblocks for 'political' messages; a campaign called 'Operation take down your Satellite Dish' tried to prevent voters from getting 'wrong' information.[11]

On 22 June, with unprecedented violence directed towards opposition supporters, Morgan Tsvangirai withdrew from the election. The vote went ahead, with very high numbers of spoiled ballots and very low turnout. Unsurprisingly, President Mugabe was re-elected president, despite most observers and analysts raising very serious concerns about the legitimacy of the election.[12]

For all that the elections were hotly contested, two aspects are striking in the parliamentary results: firstly the low turnout, and secondly the distance between competitors in most, but not all, constituencies. Although it is difficult to measure turnout, given the uncertainties of the electoral register, the available data suggest that turnout in most constituencies was exceptionally low. Most constituencies reported turnouts of between 30 and 40 per cent or lower, with less than 1 per cent reporting turnouts over 50 per cent. But equally striking is the margin of victory in the parliamentary elections. Although Masunungure notes that the MDC made significant headway in areas that had previously reliably voted for ZANU in previous elections, and ZANU's share of the national vote decreased markedly from 2005,[13] in the constituencies that ZANU won, it still won by substantial margins. The same was true on the whole for the MDC, despite its divisions, revealing a polity which remained traumatized, polarized and disaffected.

The Global Political Agreement (GPA) thus needs to be understood as a response to these multiple crises, to Mugabe's intransigence in holding the elections despite the failure to first agree a new constitution, and the improbable ability of the regime to declare itself baldly the winner of the run-off election. But the GPA was also driven by South Africa's domestic concerns—especially the fear of continued migrant flows— and the growing and unprecedented number of other regional leaders no longer willing to turn a blind eye.[14] It is significant that ZANU(PF), which for so long had called the shots in regional politics and blithely ignored attempts to rein them in, was finally compelled to accept the SADC intervention. But President Mbeki's apparent distrust of the MDC and the implications of MDC victory for the ANC's own 'liberation' credibility also conditioned this response. As a result, civil society was sidelined from the process and its concerns only half-heartedly acknowledged.[15] Like South Africa's first attempts at 'quiet diplomacy' in the region in the early 2000s,[16] this was a high-level, closed process, driven by the concerns of neighbouring states not to be seen to legitimize 'regime change'. But with the effects on those neighbouring states too big to ignore, stability was the main goal, and indeed that is what was achieved, particularly in terms of the economy. But the origins of the GPA explain its limitations—few enforceable commitments, limited elite buy-in and scant public involvement—as well as the peculiar dynamics that it generated for Zimbabwe's public sphere.

Living under the GPA: the re-strengthening of political parties

Power-sharing agreements are intended to distribute power to all players, and in doing so to reduce the 'winner takes all' logic that leads to destructive spoils politics. As a result, they have been a popular policy recommendation in response to post-Cold War political conflicts in Africa.[17] Yet, as Mehler observed, they also risk over-endowing political players with power, to the point where the decision-making becomes tightly bound by the formal partners in the agreement.[18]

In Zimbabwe, not only did power-sharing narrow the inner circle of decision-makers, but in doing so it gave ZANU the means to continue and maintain its strategy of control over state institutions, and use that to advance its own political interests. Derek Matyzak pithily notes, 'Mugabe had conceded power in only three areas'—yet even these were abrogated within days of the agreement being signed. The first point limited the number of ministers the president could appoint to thirty-one, but forty-one were appointed (along with Permanent Secretaries, Diplomats, the Attorney General, the Police Commissioner and the Governor of the Reserve Bank).[19] Although sixteen of the ministers were to be nominees from the combined MDC formations, and all appointments made by Mugabe were to be made 'in consultation with' Morgan Tsvangirai, in practice this was ignored. ZANU ministers were appointed to key ministries such as Defence and Security, with the MDC allocated junior ones for the most part, with little power. Indeed, neither the GPA negotiations nor the lived experience of the GPA showed much evidence of good faith in power-sharing. Instead, it saw ZANU resisting institutional reforms, especially those aimed at bringing transparency to issues of resource management (land) and revenue (mining). Although some ministries and sectors found scope for cooperation, the initial months after the agreement was signed were marked by attacks on MDC legislators, sixteen of whom found themselves arrested or facing charges, in a strategy that seemed to be aimed at reducing their parliamentary majority.[20] In one intriguing interlude, the MDC's Innocent Gonese brought a private member's bill to parliament, which would have amended the much hated Public Order and Security Amendment Act (POSA). Although ZANU(PF) MPs initially allowed the bill to progress to its second reading, in an apparent act of bipartisan support, it was later shut down by party elites.[21]

The one significant ministry that the MDC did hold was that of Finance, and Tendai Biti's tenure there did bring much-needed respite to the economic crisis, as he pushed through the potentially controversial dollarization of the economy, which halted the unmanageable hyperinflation. Given ZANU's strong discourses on economic sovereignty, dollarization might have been difficult to justify politically. Announced as it was by a ministry headed up by the MDC, it may have proven easier to accept. Zimbabwe's treasury benefited from resource flows from mining and the revival of agriculture—particularly tobacco sales to China—and the resumption of humanitarian aid from the US and EU, despite continuing levels of public debt and limited investment. Although no simple success story, the improvement from hyperinflation was notable, and policies that were adopted had clear political agendas. In Bulawayo, the highly symbolic yet long-stalled Matabeleland-Zambesi Water Project (MZWP) was briefly resurrected. Historically promoted by independent-minded politicians courting local support, it was 'depoliticized' by government taking it over and claiming to have secured Chinese funding. Yet, as in the past, this sort of big symbolic project was talked about more than actually carried through. More successful politically were the schemes that promised—or provided—individualized benefits. In this vein, the fast-track land reform remained the most successful political gambit, with accounts of rural life recording former MDC supporters returning to the ZANU fold.[22] Party connections were also crucial, not just in terms of accessing land, but also in getting access to inputs, technical advice and markets, all of which contribute to higher crop production and incomes.[23] Despite the challenges faced by many farmers—and continued insecurity—land distribution had a huge and lasting effect on lives and opportunities in rural Zimbabwe.[24] Yet uncertainty and opacity continued. The GPA's promise of a land audit to identify those holding multiple farms was never taken up. And even as some farmers prospered, insecurity beset others, with continuing reports of farm seizures by well-connected elites, and contestations on the ground among beneficiaries. In urban areas, the distribution of plots for houses and access to markets for the growing numbers of informal sector vendors were also highly politicized.[25]

The implementation of the Indigenization Act, which had been passed before ZANU lost control of parliament, suggested an attempt to expand and replicate the political benefits of fast-track land disbursements into mining and banking, while also reinforcing the 'sovereignty' theme of ZANU's discourse. Indigenization proved a minefield of negotiations and exemptions, just as it had in the 1990s, amid much confusion and claims that potential international investors walked away from the country. More effective, politically speaking at least, was the establishment of Community Share Ownership Trusts in mining areas, which have enabled the construction of schools, clinic buildings and other infrastructure in some districts, although these schemes have tended to be top-down and state-led.[26] Mkodzongi, though, demonstrates how chiefs have contested these agreements and sought to advance local interests and resource management in Mhondoro-Ngezi: 'although indigenization is a contested process, underpinned by class, ethnicity and gender, it has brought benefits to local farmers and businesses at a time when the government cannot support them'.[27]

Although the brutal attacks that had typified attempts to control artisanal mining gradually reduced after 2009, the mining sector remained highly politically and economically significant, with ZANU positioned to capture and exploit windfalls as never before. Suspicions that substantial diamonds were sold illicitly and the revenues channelled back into the CIO and the military were reinforced by a detailed report from Global Witness, cited by Tendai Biti in parliament, as he sought to explain budgetary shortfalls.[28] Despite no longer controlling the treasury, ZANU(PF) and the security sector ensured that political elites and other power-brokers were positioned to take advantage of financial opportunities, maintaining key revenue flows.

This apparent sidestepping of the formal state raises significant questions for our understanding of Zimbabwe's politics, given the use that ZANU has historically made of its control of state machinery. Norma Kriger suggests that ZANU's control of formal institutions was no longer central to its political gameplan, with informal or parallel structures now more significant than control of the state.[29] Yet the outcome of the 2013 election suggests that the state remains significant.[30] Although ZANU's economic resources proved important in the campaign period, the manipulation of voter registration and the electoral rolls remains central, and as Raftopoulos sets out, new forms of state penetration and social relations determine access to material resources in the new dispensation.[31]

The politics of the GPA period cannot be reduced to simply the control over the security complex, important as these 'deep state' institutions continue to be.[32] The violence surrounding the 2008 elections had alienated even ZANU(PF)'s strongest supporters in the region. It was clear that such strategies were no longer acceptable, and major institutional changes were promised by the GPA. However, in practice it was only the constitution (significant as that was) and electoral laws (passed in 2012) that were really reformed. Brian Raftopoulos suggests that a more subtle form of politics was also being played out: 'ZANU(PF) largely kept the energies of the MDCs concentrated on the single issues of constitutional reform [while] the former concentrated its activities on election preparations from early on in the GPA'.[33]

The same could, of course, be said for civil society, as we shall see in the next section, with donors keen to support the 'neutral' constitutional process, but unwilling to disburse funds for preparatory work around elections. The GPA ensured that the actual process of drafting was firmly in the hands of political parties, with civil society reduced to lobbying and 'educating'. Taking nearly four years rather than the expected eighteen months, the Constitutional Parliamentary Committee (COPAC) took over the political stage, revealing divisions within as well as between the political parties.[34] Bryan Sim's doctoral thesis provides a telling insight into the negotiations, based on an interview he carried out with one of the drafting team:

> We [the drafters] were not actually part of the negotiations, but the MDC-T negotiators did an incredibly poor job. Every time ZANU(PF) said 'No, no we want this', they would knuckle under. And even after ZANU(PF) had agreed to something, [they would later say] we have reconsidered, we want further concessions and the MDC-T negotiators did not seem to have the balls to say 'Okay, if you are going to back down on that one, we are going to take back all those concessions we made and

we will start again'. They [MDC-T] would just start from concessions that were already made and work back. [35]

However, the process dramatically portrayed in the fly-on-the-wall documentary 'Democrats' revealed the negotiators to be working under substantial pressure, from both sides. [36]

Having begun work soon after the signing of the GPA, COPAC delivered a draft—supposedly agreed by all parties—in July 2012. Yet in August ZANU revealed a new draft, which contained few of the reforms agreed earlier. More negotiations followed, leading to a new agreed draft in January 2013, approved by parliament and put to a referendum on 16 March.

Benefiting from a good turnout, and support from both parties as well as some segments of civil society, 93 per cent voted in favour of the new draft. While the final constitution was doubtless an improvement on the much-amended and unlamented Lancaster House edition, little progress had been made on implementing its provisions when a long-anticipated election was called for July 2013. Despite apparent promises in the GPA of a better environment for this crucial election, little had changed in terms of the media, freedom of assembly, and other restrictions that had hampered opposition parties and civil society in previous election campaigns. Instead of taking time to bring restrictive legislation into line with the constitution, the nation went straight into the election with the legislative framework untouched. Ironically, Mugabe was even able to bulldoze the election date of his choice, through the newly installed Constitutional Court.

And so, despite a number of changes to the electoral system, the institutional framework of the 2013 election exposed the exact same weaknesses as in every previous election. Voter registration proved the area of most concern: in particular, there were substantial discrepancies between the numbers registered in urban versus rural areas, and considerable numbers of younger voters were not able to register. On polling day, far more voters were turned away in urban areas than in rural ones. [37] The well-honed tactics used in previous elections to disenfranchise opposition voters seemed to be directly replicated, both in the involvement of the controversial Israeli firm NIKUV, also linked to contested elections in other states, and in ZEC's claimed inability to produce an electronic electoral roll before the polls. [38]

But the election results cannot be explained simply by backroom shenanigans. Both parties went into the Government of National Unity (GNU) thinking that they could use it to advance their interests. But for the MDC—divided and weakened—attempts to win back institutional control from ZANU failed.[39] As Cheeseman and Tendi argue, 'ZANU-PF refused to make space for new political players, giving rise to the politics of continuity'.[40] The MDC struggled with the experience of being in government, yet not in power, while the news media promoted ZANU and portrayed the MDC as out of touch and irrelevant. The MDC's struggles with local government proved particularly fertile material for the press. During the election itself, the state media were even more partisan, with 91 per cent of stories about ZANU(PF) portraying them in a positive light, as against 89 per cent of those about the MDC being negative.[41] The effects of this were reflected in opinion polls and focus groups, which revealed growing voter discontent over the period of the GPA. Susan Booysen's analysis of polls that she and others conducted reveals a dramatic and consistent loss of support for the MDC, even as ZANU(PF) regained people's trust.[42] And anyone who has lived in a 'have-not' region will recognize the compulsion to 'back the winner' that Matyszak identified as early as 2010.[43]

The MDC was also inadequately resourced for the campaign, especially in comparison to ZANU, which seemed to have no shortage of resources. Zamchiya cites a source from within the civil service alleging that although the Minister of Finance (Biti, MDC) had released funds for political parties, the Minister of Justice (Chinamasa, ZANU) refused to disburse the monies, leaving the MDC unable to fight the election effectively.[44] ZANU, on the other hand, went into the 2013 elections far more coherently than it had done in 2008, when many party elites had been at odds and candidates had been imposed during nominations. Tendi argues that Mugabe's campaign was consciously 'slick, well-funded, united and peaceful', in full awareness that the election needed to avoid the overt violence that had marred 2008.[45] Its message was also clear: linking patriotic history, fast-track land reform and indigenization of the economy. Julia Gallagher's focus groups, carried out after the election, reinforce the effectiveness of this campaign strategy—particularly that people had benefited under the GNU, and that these benefits were seen as deriving from ZANU's policies, rather than those of the MDC.[46] As Brian Raftopoulos argues, the 2013 election result revealed the reconfiguration of Zimbabwe's political economy—new economic and political dynamics to which the MDC was unable to respond adequately.[47] The results—61 per cent for Mugabe in the presidential campaign and 158 out of 210 seats for ZANU(PF) in the parliamentary results—reveal the scale of its defeat.

Living with the GPA: the marginalization of civil society

Although civil society organizations were all but excluded from the negotiation of the GPA, and much of its subsequent dynamics, Zimbabwe's NGOs did benefit from the relative calm that was restored by the signing of the agreement and the creation of the inclusive government. The final months before the election had proven particularly challenging for NGOs, although these same experiences were also a key element driving pressure for some sort of resolution. In particular, attacks on the church-led Save Zimbabwe campaign had drawn international attention and catalysed commitments from SADC and other international groups for a resolution to the stalemate; while shortly before the inclusive government was announced, Jestina Mukoko and two other staff members of one of the most forthright NGOs, the Zimbabwe Peace Project, were abducted, detained without charge or or access to lawyers, and tortured. Garnering widespread outrage domestically and internationally, these events seemed to set the high-water mark.

Despite the environment remaining tense, Michael Aeby reported that after the signing of the GPA the larger and more prominent organizations experienced a decrease in the raids and arrests which had disrupted their operations in previous months.[48] This does not mean that NGOs were left alone, but rather that attempts to constrain the operation of NGOs reverted to somewhat more subtle patterns familiar from the past. Despite the failure to bring the new NGO Act into effect, a number of senior NGO staff were charged with operating unregistered NGOs. Mukoko was again caught up in this harassment, as were the directors of Zimbabwe Lawyers for Human Rights (ZLHR) and Gays and Lesbians of Zimbabwe (GALZ).[49] ZimRights leaders were also caught up in a long-running legal battle, which accused them of illegal action. Macdonald

Lewanika of the Crisis Group interprets this attack as instrumental: aimed at preventing ZimRights from organizing electoral monitors in the 2013 elections. Tellingly, the 2003 NGO Act remained unimplemented, and was never signed into law by the president.

Despite the lessening in overt attacks on their activities, NGOs struggled under the power-sharing agreement. What Cornelius Ncube had previously described as 'counter-hegemonic' NGOs suddenly found their allies were now in government, and indeed making policy as ministers. This left some NGOs in the uncomfortable position of criticizing policies that their friends in government supported, even while those same allies were still under attack from ZANU. For others who were aspiring to remain in some sense 'neutral', it did not help that MPs and ministers were seen to be using their NGO connections to try to bolster their own positions. At the same time, NGO leaders felt crowded out by the professional politicians: 'One of the unfortunate effects of the GPA is that it has taken power away from the ordinary citizens to the 3 principals [Mugabe, Tsvangirai, and Mutambara].'[50] After several years of being important players, suddenly agenda-setting was being undertaken by politicians rather than civil society, a common effect of power-sharing.[51]

Nowhere was this more evident than in the way that constitution-making dominated available space and time once COPAC—the Constitution Parliamentary Select Committee—was established in accordance with the GPA's commitment to the creation of a new constitution. Unlike the civil society-initiated process of 1998–2000, this time political parties were the driving force, and reluctant to cede space or authority to civic groups. It helped that donor money—which had become scarce in the lead-in to the GPA—was available for constitutional work, but as one activist reported, 'constitution making has ascended over everything else'. Although there had been unsuccessful attempts to agree a new constitution before 2008, the GPA's commitment to writing a new constitution meant that the constitutional process was being led by the GPA through parliament and it catalysed divisions within civil society. Whereas in 1998 civil society had led the process, now it was being dragged along by the political parties. Michael Aeby relates how the NCA's refusal to accept COPAC's legitimacy led to the collapse of the network's structures, and weakened its ties with allied organizations, as well as dividing some groups down the middle.[52]

A related existential challenge for NGOs was how best to engage with the strange nature of the unity government, which was further complicated by the split within the MDC, percolating through civil society as well. Having worked very hard to develop a strategy of 'non-engagement',[53] NGOs were suddenly being expected to engage with the state, yet 'the state' itself had been rendered ambiguous. This complicated relations with ministries, where senior and junior ministers might contradict each other. On top of the polarization between the MDC and ZANU, divisions within the MDC severely tested the ZCTU and NGOs, as their counterparts and allies took up opposing positions. In Bulawayo, where the Mutambara/Ncube faction held seats, pressure on NGOs to align with one faction or the other was particularly challenging.

These challenges were exacerbated by the brain drain and a generational shift. While many civil society veterans of the 1980s and 1990s—often with roots back to the liberation period—had stuck with their organizations through the early 2000s, by the time the unity government was formed many had left the sector. Some had fled persecution and threats to their families, while others moved to better remunerated jobs in South Africa or elsewhere in the region, which would allow them to support their families. The effects of this were stark—with many organizations headed up by relatively young and inexperienced staff, in a period which required great reserves of skill and patience.[54] The NGO leaders who had developed networks and worked together in the 1990s to create the NCA had decades of trust and shared understanding between them, but this newer generation lacked such experiences. These networks had also been most successful when coalesced around clear and agreed objectives and strategies, which were profoundly lacking in post-2008 Zimbabwe. Nonetheless donors were eager to support networks, clusters and coalitions, in the interest of scaling up efforts of relatively small groups. Probably the highest profile 'new' network was CISOMM, which brought civil society groups together to 'monitor' the implementation of the constitution. But these attempts to re-inscribe themselves in the constitutional process failed to generate much enthusiasm.

Having been excluded from the GPA, civil society was vocal in demanding that it be included in those aspects of the deal which dealt with peace-building and reconciliation, although the agreement's obligation to 'consider' a mechanism for dealing with past injustices and trauma reflected a process driven more by pragmatism than any real interest in resolving conflicts. Unsurprisingly, the GPA's engagement with civil society demands for some form of 'truth and reconciliation' was minimal. The oddly titled 'Organ for National Healing, Reconciliation and Integration' (ONHRI) was created, with co-chairs from each of the three parties, but again minimal civil society input. Despite some hope that the 'organ' might bring some calm to the turbulent atmosphere, its failure to take on any meaningful activities has given rise to more cynical interpretations. Shari Eppel goes so far as to suggest that 'it might even be said that the organ's primary reason for existing has been to prevent any meaningful, official developments' in transitional justice.[55] Given the uneasy balance of powers during the inclusive government—and continuing cases of politically motivated violence—it is hard to imagine that even the best designed institution could have made any progress. Student projects—of which there seem to have been many—give a strong sense of how divided and partisan attitudes to ONHRI and to reconciliation remained.[56] On the other hand, Eppel is rather more positive about the role played by JOMIC—a panel intended to oversee and ensure the implementation of the GPA—describing it as 'a credible structure capable of balanced interventions after political violence', commenting that it has taken on functions that might have been considered to be within ONHRI's purview.[57] The relatively apolitical nature of JOMIC enabled it to engage, in ways that ONHRI simply could not. In Zimbabwe's highly politicized environment, political violence, reconciliation and other such discourses remained the preserve of the opposition, and acknowledgement of them by state institutions would have opened them up to unanswerable questions.

Despite this sometimes hostile and always unstable environment, NGOs in Zimbabwe continued work, with some significant shifts in focus. Long accused of being 'only in Harare' and 'out of touch' with the grass roots, especially in rural areas,[58] some NGOs made concrete moves towards bridging the divide between 'advocacy' and 'projects'. While this has been something of a 'holy grail' for years, the role of the grass-roots women's network within the women's coalition is a good example of this being put into practice. Likewise, the Zimbabwe Peace

Project brought the grass-roots members of church organizations and others into the front line of advocacy work, leveraging their strengths into effective monitoring of human rights violations.

Despite terrain that might be considered deeply unfavourable to new ventures, a handful of new organizations did establish themselves in the mid-late 2000s, often with explicit community and/or governance focus, probably shaped by the constraints on donor funding, which limited most aid to humanitarian or good governance projects. Given the heightened political tensions, peace-building proved particularly popular. Other areas of operation included more technocratic and depoliticizing fields, such as support for parliamentarians and their institutions. At the other end of the spectrum, Women of Zimbabwe Arise (WOZA) lost donor support for its intransigent position vis-à-vis the GPA and COPAC. It continued its strategy of mass organizing and public marches, but this approach had little popularity with other groups until 2014, when Itai Dzamera's Occupy Africa Unity Square movement claimed the spotlight. Although NGO leaders expressed solidarity and support for these more confrontational strategies—especially when leaders were detained or disappeared—few chose to emulate them. Beset by uncertainty, ambiguity and factionalism, for the most part Zimbabwean NGOs reverted to strategies of pragmatism.

Discourse, power and material strategies re-asserted

The shifts in the public sphere and political power generated by the GPA also catalysed changes in national discourse within political and civil society. These are most vividly captured in the approaches of political elites to church and traditional leaders. Zimbabwe's religious groups—an area of remarkable growth during the crisis—proved to be fertile ground for politicians seeking allies. The rise of 'mega-churches' and tele-evangelism promoting a hard-hitting 'gospel of prosperity' did not slacken under the relative stability of the GNU. Instead, from 2009 onwards the rise of local superstar pastors running massive campaigns and airing programmes on YouTube and digital channels led Chitando et al. to speak of 'a prophetic craze' in these years, and one which did not shy away from ties to local politics and politicians.[59] Most blatantly, Obadiah Msindo of the Destiny of Africa Network—one of the older

203

'megachurches'—repeated his campaign stunt of promising ZANU(PF) supporters houses in exchange for their vote, and denying that there was any problem with this. Although the Pentecostal churches seemed to be the most buoyant during this period, a striking image of the 2013 election campaign showed the Mugabes attending Vapostori worship, with the president dressed in white robes and carrying a wooden staff, showing that followers of the Apostolic faith too were being courted. Intriguingly, Zamchiya reports that Morgan Tsvangirai's wife, Elizabeth Macheka, used election rallies to suggest that the MDC, and in particular Tsvangirai, was 'heaven-ordained' to rule.[60]

Although the Zimbabwe Christian Alliance sought to mobilize a more activist approach to the GPA, their activities decreased when they lost donor support. For the most part, church leaders and donors alike were more comfortable with activities focused on 'peace-building' and 'healing'. While the Zimbabwe Council of Churches commented critically on the exclusion of faith-based organizations from COPAC, it restrained its comments primarily to a call for peace.[61] And the main church networks came together with NANGO and other NGOs to form a 'Church and Civil Society Forum' focused on the implementation of the constitution's proposals regarding national healing and reconciliation.

In many ways, then, the mission or 'traditional' churches and church-based NGOs took the GPA as an opportunity to retreat from politics and avoid politicization. This strategy was aided when Nolbert Kunonga, the high-flying Anglican ally of President Mugabe, was excommunicated from the Anglican Communion in 2008. Although he sought to retain control of Anglican parishes and properties, the Supreme Court cut this attempt short in November 2012. With one informant suggesting that 'the bishops have become risk averse because of the backlash when they stand up', we see a pattern similar to that which typified the 1980s and 1990s, with church leaders seeking to 'not rock the boat'.[62]

Traditional chiefs, on the other hand, used their considerable skills and social capital to position themselves effectively, despite their often prickly relationship with the ruling party. At risk of being sidelined as land reforms were consolidated, chiefs used the existing Traditional Leaders Act in the context of land reform 'to recast their authority in the areas, renegotiate boundaries and reclaim alienated ancestral lands',[63] albeit with differing levels of success in different parts of the country. Sinclair-Bright highlights the ability of traditional chiefs to expand their areas and incorporate new resettlement areas, including those of former farm-workers, into their sphere of influence in Mazowe,[64] while Mujere's account of Gutu politics reveals more conflict with other authorities.[65] Zamchiya tells us of traditional leaders mediating farmers' access to seeds and fertilizer, which were 'personalized' as gifts from Mugabe, reinforcing the ties between chiefs and party in rural areas in the lead-in to the 2013 elections.[66] Mkodzongi notes that 'indigenization' policies further strengthened the position of traditional leaders, such that in areas with mineral deposits 'chiefs have become powerful political figures'. In Mhondoro, he shows how chiefs further 'instrumentalized' their posi-tions by demanding 'ritual performances' before mineral extraction begins. These claims serve dual purposes—both legitimizing their claims to autochthony and bringing material benefits.[67]

The 2013 constitution further bolstered chiefs' authority in resettle-ment areas—the result of a ZANU(PF)-led amendment to the COPAC draft, under pressure from the chiefs, who marshalled their consider-able political influence.[68] Sinclair-Bright notes, however, that despite the amendment, chiefs were not 'being gazetted'—that is, they were not given clear authority over communities in the new resettlement areas. Instead, she observes, 'the amendment ... placed them once more in a dance of negotiations with the state and ZANU PF concern-ing the extent of their power and the degree to which they remained in an interdependent but asymmetrical relationship with them'.[69] As a result, chiefs also resented the constitution's new provisions which made it illegal for them to be members of political parties, blocking their aspirations to position themselves firmly within ZANU, even as their numbers in parliament were increased.

While churches and chiefs proved fertile ground, ZANU continued to position its elite as the rightful leaders and liberators of the state via 'patriotic history', its discourses coming to emphasize sovereignty and self-reliance. In this, its target audience was partly neighbouring coun-tries, whose influence within SADC shaped regional political dynam-ics, although it also sought to portray the MDC as unacceptable leader-ship material.

In his systematic and perceptive account of the Zimbabwe national project,[70] Ndlovu-Gatsheni argues that there is also an obsession with creating a 'patriotic citizenship' articulated through regime-and party-controlled institutions.[71] Yet this risks giving it more credit than it deserves, as attempts to shape 'the good citizen' have proved ambiguous. Rather than a clearly thought out ideology, or even consistent hero-worship, the regime's rhetorical approach has more often been *ad hoc* and responsive, if sometimes heavy-handed. It has rarely been carried out with much conviction, and Ndlovu-Gatsheni's conceptualization downplays the extent to which such policies remained unevenly implemented in the first decades of independence, only to be returned to after 2000's political crisis. Let us take the example of the Nkomo monument. This long-promised statue was to grace the streets of Bulawayo and signal a more inclusive form of nation-building—surely one of the most significant monuments erected in post-independence Zimbabwe. Yet, when first unveiled in 2010 it was met with a chorus of complaints. First, it was criticized for being too small, then it was alleged that it had been designed by a North Korean artist. Further, it was said that Nkomo's family had not been involved in the planning. Within days the statue was taken down, and then eventually re-erected on a higher plinth.[72]

How could any regime which takes symbolism and nation-building seriously get something so wrong? Even if we assume that the regime saw attempts to woo the 'dissident city' as essentially futile, the slap-dash manner in which this was handled signals incompetence as much as political ill-will. In Harare proposals likewise emerged to rename the 'KGVI' barracks—meaning King George VI—after the late General Tongogara, a towering figure of the liberation war, who died in 1979. What is striking about this is less the decision to honour Tongogara—a key rival of Mugabe—and more that a high-profile army barracks had continued to be named after a British monarch for more than thirty years after Zimbabwe became a republic and twelve years after it withdrew from the Commonwealth. Rather than a subtly master-minded scheme of nation-building, we see a lacklustre approach with moments of farce.

Of course, when the state chose to prosecute perceived slights, the costs to individuals could be high, as is seen in the case of Owen Maseko, who was arrested in 2010 after his art exhibition was accused of 'undermining the authority of the President'.[73] ZLHR reported there were 'about 80' cases in the courts over 'undermining' or 'insulting' the president, even though the Constitutional Court ruled that some sections of the Criminal Law (Codification and Reform) Act Chapter 9.23 that deal with insulting the president were unconstitutional. Court records also reveal many cases of 'subversion'—which are generally thrown out or result in no conviction—typically revealing harassment rather than persecution. Despite the undoubted impact on individuals, these cases show the state reactively performing its desire to discipline cultural representation, rather than any thought-through attempt to create justiciable laws and enforce them uniformly.

Public discourse, however, was not simply grounded in display and memorialization. We see its effects most clearly when we examine how it intertwined with interest groups and material politics as above, explaining why civil society and opposition groups proved unable to marshal an effective counter-narrative. In 2013, ZANU's electoral strategy was able to build on its strategies of distribution and mobilization in both urban and rural areas. Faced with these effective uses of material politics, as well as convincing rhetorical strategies, the MDC failed to present an alternative vision that was compelling and attractive enough to win the discursive war. But these material strategies, although politically astute and useful in the short term, moved politics further into the realm of rent-seeking and spoils politics.

Conclusion

The GPA that ran from 2008 to 2013 created the appearance of a hiatus from the intense political battles, but underneath the institutional facade of unity, political factionalization deepened. Although the GPA limited and contained the extremes of political violence and economic crisis, ZANU was able to capitalize on it by building a new coalition of supporters. Yet the ZANU win in 2013 also revealed the depths of factionalization as party elites struggled to ensure their candidates' position in the succession debate, and to access the benefits of state control. As long-time observer Michael Bratton noted, 'power-sharing served mainly to defer a political crisis rather than resolve it'.[74]

In these dynamics we can perceive the shift from the demobilized politics of nationalist coalition-building to a mobilized—and potentially unstable—winner takes all politics. The co-ops, militias and rural community groups reflect the mobilized urban and rural dynamic that had been left to atrophy at independence. This remobilization of Zimbabwe's politics also heralds the increasingly zero-sum nature of the new political dispensation. As Chris Allen observed, winner takes all politics requires a strong leader, able to control political and economic resources and prevent a downward spiral into spoils politics.[75] The battle to win the 2013 election, harnessing all resources for this goal, provided a momentary point of coherence for ZANU. As Norma Kriger argued: 'the different factions in ZANU PF are held together chiefly by a shared vested interest in preventing the "opposition" parties in the [inclusive government], and in particular, the MDC-T, from coming to power as a result of democratising reforms'.[76] However, once the 2013 election was won, and ZANU back in firm control of the state, the question of who would succeed Mugabe ascended to the top of the agenda. The leadership dispute intensified with vituperative mud-slinging and formerly powerful party leaders being sidelined or even ejected from the party.[77] Allegations of corruption, and worse, rapidly landed on them, revealing the costs of defection.

The party of course had long had its divides. Some factions had already reached the conclusion that they had no chance to seize power, and decided strategically to de-couple. As the former commander of ZIPRA (ZAPU's armed wing), and a long-serving Home Affairs Minister, Dabengwa's liberation legacy and political profile gave him a strong base on which to position himself, when he defected in 2008. It is striking, however, that since that decision, some verified and some rumoured reports have repeatedly surfaced of attempts to draw him back into the fold. Likewise, Jonathan Moyo's remarkable ability to enter and leave the ruling party not just once but twice reveals the continuing flexibility and contingency of the ruling coalition, which has not forgotten its origins.

The increasing factionalization within both the MDC and ZANU(PF) also affected civic groups. This could be seen first in Matabeleland, where the public sphere has long had a distinct register, but the political shifts since 2000 seemed to drive it even further in new directions.

The MDC split was particularly severely felt in Matabeleland, with key political leaders and their local supporters forced into difficult compromises. Likewise, Dabengwa's efforts to revive ZAPU split political allegiances within ZANU(PF). An NGO activist in Bulawayo explained the difficulties of balancing ties to both MDC factions: 'if you say you will work with all pro-democratic forces, you are accused of selling out'. To him, this signalled a more serious moral failing: 'that "sellouts" that is ZANU language ... we need a new political culture of tolerance'.[78] But even the most self-aware NGOs found themselves caught up in and sometimes complicit in the dominant registers of political discourse in Zimbabwe. Indeed, on the whole, civil society, like other sectors, failed to offer a successful challenge to these discursive practices, finding themselves instead firmly embedded in the dominant political norms and behaviour.

8

WRITING ZIMBABWE'S POLITICS

May the foolishness of our leaders and all this violence pass from us. We do not deserve it. It is not a time in our history that we would wish to honour. Our destiny should not be measured in brutality, rape, crime and malice. It should instead be measured in dance, song, beauty, and the celebration of life, not death.[1]

At independence, the Mugabe regime consolidated its electoral victory, taking control of state institutions, appealing to people's desire for peace and development, and ensuring its monopoly on the use of violence through control of the coercive mechanisms of state. In those first years its willingness to deploy force against civilians was clearly signalled. In doing so, it shaped both the new state and the nation of Zimbabwe, constructing a set of understandings, norms and expectations that enabled its party to retain political control for over thirty-five years.

As the years wore on, the ZANU project struggled amidst economic and political uncertainty, and appeared to be wavering. The state institutions became weakened, as politicization and graft overwhelmed professionalism. Rumours and confusion spread over what was legal, and what illegal. Citizens uprooted from their homes no longer knew what to expect from their elected representatives or security forces. Norms and expectations relating to state action and service provision had been shattered. Few activists or opposition politicians in Zimbabwe have not been detained by police at least once, many have suffered far more. And those convicted were treated as criminals, denied the legitimacy of acting on political principle, or moral cause.[2] The painful legacies of abuse of authority, torture and loss, intensified by the continued refusal of perpetrators and their apologists to acknowledge these, permeate victims' consciousness and weaken the foundations of the polity.

By the end of the period covered in this book, it seemed inconceivable that the ageing generation of nationalist politicians could hold on any longer. But attempts by church people, NGOs, labour and community activists to imagine and articulate an alternative set of norms have been stymied. This failure to articulate fully a convincing alternative account of Zimbabwean citizenship and nationhood led Tendi to speak of Zimbabwe's intellectual space having been 'ceded' to the nationalist public intellectuals.[3] The resurgence of the ZANU project, its conceptualization of Zimbabwe's nationhood and its willingness to marshal violence in its interests reveal its continuing potency, even at times of great instability. It remains to be seen how this newly mobilized coalition will respond as the party searches for a successor to its president, and as new economic challenges confront them.

This concluding chapter draws out the interconnections that link together the main themes of nationalism, demobilization, post-liberation politics and struggle to capture the state and represent the nation across these turbulent years of a young polity.

Nationalism: a way of doing politics

The argument of this book has been that the basis of the regime's power over society is not simply coercion, but a tightly welded together fusion of ideology, coercion, material interests and state control attempting to incorporate society within the regime's hegemonic framework. But it also remains a nationalist project at its heart. It might seem easy to dismiss this nationalism as purely instrumental, but that would be to deny its staying power and effectiveness, and ability to reform and reconfigure itself—what Beresford calls the 'sticky' nature of nationalism in post-liberation states.[4] The political struggle in Zimbabwe has been over control of the state, but this is inescapably welded to the right to represent the nation.

The continuing salience of nationalism becomes easier to understand when we think of it as not just an ideological project but also as an organizing principle, a way of doing politics. Nationalism is not some abstract or unproblematic force, but one that needs to be examined critically, so that we can understand what is meant by nationalism and how it shapes politics. Indeed, nationalism needs to be 'complicated', much as Luise White has recently argued, advocating moving beyond thinking of the Rhodesian project as being one of 'racism'.[5] To do otherwise risks engendering equally facile perceptions of the nationalist movements which resisted it. The failure to complicate the Rhodesian project risks allowing simplistic accounts of nationalism to endure. While the regime's own narrative relies on an account of nationalism that is simplistically anti-colonial, Brian Raftopoulos reminds us of the radical democratic notions that also lay at the heart of it.[6] Historical and sociological studies also continue to reveal the intense diversity of experiences of the liberation war. Nationalist movements were loose coalitions which brought together widely divergent experiences and expectations. To quote again from Aristide Zolberg, the nationalist parties that emerged from this struggle were *'partis unifiés'*—unified parties, not single parties.[7] Nationalism thus shaped political dynamics because of the nature of support and the parameters of counter-organization.

Tim Scarnecchia has argued convincingly that since at least the 1950s, the most powerful epithet that could be deployed in Zimbabwe was and continues to be 'sell-out'.[8] Evoking notions of sovereignty and disloyalty, this simple term serves to reinforce the need for unity, which proved a remarkably resilient and pervasive discursive construct. The treason charges filed against Morgan Tsvangirai make 'sense' when we remember the number of other leaders of the opposition who were similarly accused of treason in the 1980s and 1990s, to little international outcry. It would have been more surprising if similar tactics had not been deployed against Tsvangirai.

Anti-colonial nationalist parties often see themselves as having 'earned' the right to be the sole representatives of the people. In Zimbabwe, two countervailing pressures combined to render this a particularly potent force. The Rhodesian state itself, in attempting to quell, infiltrate and destroy the nationalist movement, made leaders

213

particularly suspicious of those who did not toe the line. At the same time, external pressures for 'unity' within the nationalist movement in order to gain acceptance from the international system—which could only cope with one recognized party—further generated pressures for conformity behind a single leadership. Incubated under settler-colonial violence, nationalism came to fetishize unity for its own survival, while after independence unity served to protect those who had committed war crimes and violence against comrades.

The politics of demobilization

Thinking of nationalism as an organizing principle harnessing unity helps explain how and why Zimbabwe was so easily demobilized in the years after independence, but also why authoritarian rule proved so durable. Matombo and Sachikonye pose this puzzle very neatly:

> On the face of it, Zimbabwe represents a paradox. It is a society that 'liberated' itself from settler colonial rule through an arduous armed struggle accompanied by high levels of political mobilisation. The level of political consciousness rose in both rural and urban areas and was evident during the first independence elections in 1980. However, more than a quarter of a century later, authoritarianism appears to have demobilised the wider population to the extent that mobilisation has been replaced by despondency and fear, apathy and withdrawal.[9]

The answer to this paradox is that authoritarianism did not just 'demobilize' people through fear or violence (although this did happen). Demobilization was the means through which authoritarianism organized itself in the Zimbabwean context. Like Matombo and Sachikonye, I found it puzzling that so many activists accepted this shift. I once asked Paul Themba Nyathi to explain how this happened and I recall the sadness in his eyes, and the sigh in his voice as he said 'we laid down our advocacy', evoking at once the tiredness and loss of the liberation struggle, and the pain of remembering how they had placed faith in the new government.[10]

Often analysts of Churches and NGOs speak of them being 'co-opted' into the state's agenda, but this term may obscure more than it clarifies. Studies of peasants and workers remind us that the construction and maintenance of hegemony depends on James Scott's words:

'not a shared ideology but a common material and meaningful frame-work for living through, talking about and acting upon social orders characterised by domination'.[11] Thinking in terms of a 'common frame-work' in which NGOs and the state operate helps make sense of some of these dynamics. In some of the cases discussed earlier, NGOs are denied agency by a potent range of forces. But in others, the impetus for inclusion comes from the NGO itself. More often it is a mix of the two, with NGOs seeking to develop a relationship with civil servants and MPs or local government, but not necessarily seeing this as a threat to their autonomy. Zimbabwe's church people and NGO leadership often have strong personal ties to political figures and civil servants, with whom they may have been at school or in the trenches, both metaphorical and physical. Until 2000 only two NGOs had ever been formally threatened with closure, and both of those had effectively repositioned themselves, suggesting that their strategies proved suc-cessful for a time.

The discourse of unity was not limited to marshalling civil society. We saw similar tactics also when it came to dealing with political par-ties—there can be few other cases of a country ruled both by one ruling party for thirty years and under three purported governments of national unity. Of course none of them was ever 'unified', but this strategy is compelling and attractive because it fits neatly with the nor-malized pattern of organization and discourse. And this is also why NGOs and opposition parties used these same discourses of unity and development in attempting to position themselves and legitimate their role within the public sphere, strategically deploying what James Scott, harnessing Gramsci, called 'reciprocal manipulation' of the hegemonic discourse. As Scott points out, Gramsci's notion of hegemony is often misunderstood as an elite theory of civil society, in which subordinate classes are unable to see that they are being exploited. Against this reading, Scott argues that 'the very process of attempting to legitimate a social order by idealizing it always provides its subjects with the means, the symbolic tools, the very ideas for a critique that operates entirely within the hegemony'.[12]

Demobilization was also facilitated by a discourse of depoliticiza-tion, often itself predicated on norms of 'development'. This was well documented in both urban and rural policy-making. Often seen as a simple continuity of colonial norms and beliefs, the reliance on technocratic approaches also reflected a need to depoliticize decisions in order to sustain and justify demobilization. The stability that most—but not all—enjoyed in the 1980s and 1990s was only possible because of demobilization and top-down decision-making, removing all but the thinnest veneer of popular participation in politics.

Discursive depoliticization

Although the Zimbabwean government has become infamous for its use of 'patriotic history'[13] to justify its excesses and defend its hold on power, this only happened some twenty years after independence. Prior to that, discursive politics put much more weight on 'unity' and 'development'. Taking liberation discourse seriously any earlier would have opened it up to critique and contestation, creating space for counter-narratives and counter-mobilizations. Perhaps out of fear of delving too deeply into liberation history when it remained close to people's memories, memorialization was predominantly a distant process, formalized and formulaic. The relationship with the past is handled gingerly. Only many years after independence have state resources been deployed to explore the memories and material remains of the struggle.

Instead 'liberation discourse' was modulated and diminished in the first decades after 1980. 'Development' filled the gap that was left, dominating government agendas to the extent that obvious 'nation-building' strategies such as the rewriting of textbooks and curricula were simply not prioritized. Thus performative acts of statehood tended to be technocratic and reinforce the colonial legacy, rather than transform it. Even as memorialization of Rhodesian heroes was replaced with that of Mbuya Nehanda, and a select few liberation war heroes, there seems to have been no real sense of urgency, and little public participation. This reflects the confidence of the new regime, which seems to have felt little need to waste resources grandstanding. But it also enabled the construction of a simplistic, monolithic conception of 'the struggle' precluding complicated messy accounts that might emerge from closer examination. Instead, 'development' becomes a way of bringing diverse interest groups onside—a sort of political lowest common denominator. But the 'development' that became such a cherished feature of the new state came from a very particular perception and angle—focused on production for export and modernization, rather than a celebration or support of the peasant producers who had been the key supporters of the liberation war.

NGOs, Churches and producer groups all found their own roles to play in this fundamentally state-led project of 'bringing development'. While states which had gained independence earlier inherited few autonomous institutions and an anaemic middle class (the colonial project having been explicitly designed to prevent their emergence), the new regime in Zimbabwe found itself grappling with colonial-era organizations, liberation-movement support movements and a growing number of groups wanting to 'bring development'. The turn to development enabled the regime to corral them all, while depriving them of both discursive and practical autonomy. The focus on 'development' in their discourse and practice is striking, both explaining and justifying their apolitical stance. Even as the state used 'development' to justify its policies, so too NGOs used the language of development to depoliticize their own positions, redeploying its useful ambiguities.

The limits of liberation

Thinking about mobilization and demobilization rather than focusing simply on liberation discourse further helps us to clarify the continuing saliency of the liberation war in shaping Zimbabwe into a 'post-liberation state', which at times risks being overstated. While Zimbabwe is one of a number of countries that came to independence after an armed liberation struggle, it did not gain independence 'at the barrel of a gun'. There was no military victory, no occupied territory and no armed takeover of the capital city. This is not to deny the importance of the armed struggle, but to nuance our understanding of its influence on contemporary politics.

Zimbabwe's liberation movement was successful in forcing the colonial powers and settler regime to the negotiating table, and it emerged with a constitutional arrangement not entirely to their liking. In this, the similarities to transitions in Namibia and South Africa are evident. And as Gavin Williams pointed out: 'Constitutions arise from political compromises rather than primarily reflecting broad discussions of the principles that should govern political arrangements.'[14] In the language of 'political settlements', Zimbabwe's transition created foundational agreements, but did not generate consensus or ideological congruity. There was no meeting of minds, but the negotiated agreement that formed the basis of the Lancaster House constitution retained the influence of important political and economic segments of the old regime. This 'reconciliation' became part of both the narrative of and the institutional basis for the newly independent state, even if its embrace was always half-hearted and contingent. On the one hand it was a legal requirement, but it also reflected the reality on the ground—of continuity of people, of institutions and of a certain colonial-style bureaucratic culture. These differences become more apparent when we compare Zimbabwe not to countries which underwent similar negotiated transitions, but to one like Eritrea where power literally was seized in 1991 'with the barrel of the gun'. Here, the people were never fully demobilized, and the transitional constitution never enacted. As a result, even limited pluralism has been a chimera.[15] Perhaps the real puzzle is South Africa, where despite a pacted or negotiated transition, social movements have never fully demobilized and protest remains central to the political repertoire.[16]

Thinking about the nature of the transition helps explain both why the regime needed to demobilize its supporters, and why this was done with so little compunction for the interests of the poor, both rural and urban. Demobilization was necessary because without it other groups would themselves mobilize, and that dynamic threatened the precarious hold on power. This was most visible in the case of labour, where strikes broke out across sectors in the first year of independence (a pattern also seen in many other newly independent African states). But it was also very evident in rural areas, where Jocelyn Alexander first noted the demobilization of local party structures;[17] likewise when communal area farmers resettled themselves onto vacant commercial farmland, only to find themselves 'cleared' with little concerns for their needs or claims. The 'cooperative' models of both urban and rural urban housing remained weak, while agricultural policies rewarded production for export, rather than subsistence. Promises made to fighters and civilians during the struggle need to be met, but it is the state, controlled by the liberation elite, which prioritizes and accommodates the demands for meeting developmental goals.

Spoils politics and the gatekeeper state

In Zimbabwe, we see the potent combination of the nationalist-liberationist belief that no one else can speak for the nation, harnessed to the logic of what Chris Allen terms the centralizing—bureaucratic state, trying to prevent descent into destructive spoils politics.[18] Allen linked the challenge of African politics to rapid decolonization and the clientelist crisis that emerged. Strong leaders took control in order to 'manage' clientelism rather than risk its descent into 'spoils' politics. Writing in 1995, he was cautiously optimistic that countries like Zimbabwe, Namibia and Eritrea might follow a distinct path, with more participation and less centralization. Instead, they have in fact come to epitomize his typology, with the liberationist ethos reinforcing the pressures for centralization and control, rather than providing a countervailing force.

Insights from scholars of the colonial state—Fred Cooper and Crawford Young—add to our thinking about trajectories.[19] Cooper and Young highlight the dependence of colonial and post-colonial states on export-import nodes in order to generate revenue for the fiscus, given the difficulty experienced by such states in imposing direct taxation.[20] Cooper, in particular, focused on the structural tendency within extractive colonial states to erect and control 'the gate' while also discouraging the creation of an autonomous middle class. Although Zimbabwe inherited the centralized Rhodesian state, which had emerged from a decade of sanctions, it does not fit Cooper's model of a 'gatekeeper state' perfectly. It maintained a strong reliance on exports from both the agricultural and mining sectors, but it also successfully levied income taxes and sales taxes, giving its exchequer an unusually diversified tax base for an African state. But while Zimbabwe was less of an extractive gatekeeper state than many, the liberationist ethos and nationalist pattern of organizing meant that even groups like NGOs and churches, which were not necessarily reliant on the state financially, felt bound up with it and tied to the state project. Where colonial states simply denied the middle class space to emerge as an autonomous power,[21] post-colonial regimes used diverse ideational and material strategies to ensure that the middle class 'straddled' the border between state and civil society.

Broadening gatekeeper politics to take into account a 'cultural' element, where the regime's control is not purely institutional but reinforced by norms and practices, helps explain its durability in the face of liberalizing reforms designed explicitly to break this stranglehold. It also helps explain the 'winner takes all' or zero-sum politics that continue to dominate in many African states, with little to be gained from positioning oneself outside, whether institutionally or culturally. The nature of the gatekeeper state is that power is contained and centralized, both institutionally and normatively. ZANU's realization that it had almost lost control of the state in 2008 made its struggle to retain it all the more powerful—driven by both the material demands of those reliant on its patronage networks and the pride of those who felt they had earned the right to represent the people.

Understanding Zimbabwe

This book started from the premise that as students of African politics our first task is to understand, before we seek to predict or explain. In making a case for an interpretative approach to the study of politics, I am aware that others who have lived through these times or used different methodologies will have taken away different messages. By definition, interpretative studies will not prove replicable, although we can hope that they are convincing. Yet it remains important to foreground concerns about the deployment of knowledge, power and methodological choice in research. Such concepts are rightly central to contemporary debates within African Studies, but despite their weight and significance my personal 'hermeneutical turn' was shaped as much by mundane experiences on the ground, which raised methodological concerns about how we study politics, as by epistemological concerns.

Shortly after I first arrived in Zimbabwe as an undergraduate student, the government announced its 'ESAP' budget—the introduction of economic liberalization and stabilization to a previously 'controlled' economy. International news media and academic reports from other countries suggested that 'riots' and 'unrest' would inevitably result. As we sat on the grass at the University of Zimbabwe, listening to a transistor radio broadcasting the announcement, we felt a certain unease that the peaceful scene around us might erupt. But Zimbabwe reacted calmly to this major ideological shift. There were critics, to be sure, as well as those who welcomed policies that promised to relieve the chronic shortages of transport, cement and factory parts. But for the most part, structural adjustment policies were implemented with little resistance, even from those organizations that worked with the most affected groups.

With hindsight, we can see connections between the economically straitened times and the emergence of the MDC as a viable opposition party some eight years later, but that path was by no means simple or straightforward. Writing Zimbabwe back into studies of African politics highlights the importance of studying how structural and cultural forces interact. The picture painted in the previous chapters is one of a state shaped in the colonial period and carrying with it the baggage not just of colonial institutions and norms, but also of contestation and exclusion over who are the rightful rulers of that state. We have seen how the politics of these states moved from an 'inclusionary' model, prioritizing coalitions—with importance exceptions—to one in which exclusion and mobilization increasingly dominated. The shift to spoils politics revealed the factionalization and centrifugal tendencies that had continued to underlie the facade of stability.

It would be a brave scholar indeed who dared predict where Zimbabwe is going at this fragile and febrile point. While the institutions, practices, norms and discourses explored in the preceding pages will continue to resonate through Zimbabwe's politics, their trajectory is as yet undetermined. But we might usefully ask where the study of Zimbabwean politics is heading. The teaching and training of political scientists has been a particular casualty in most African universities, starved of resources and pressured into the equally sterile tracks of administrative or consultancy-driven research. Notwithstanding resolute efforts by a small number of under-resourced colleagues in Zimbabwe's universities and think tanks, political science has remained a weak and vulnerable discipline in Zimbabwe and across much of the continent. Despite this unpromising context, the study of Zimbabwean politics has seen a remarkable flourishing—in history, literature, popular culture, law, anthropology, agrarian and urban studies, as well as new theoretical approaches drawing increasingly on post-structuralism and decolonialism, driven in the main by Zimbabwean scholars. This diversity, creativity and commitment can only bode well for the study of Zimbabwean politics, and also for the Zimbabwean political landscape itself.

NOTES

1. UNDERSTANDING ZIMBABWEAN POLITICS

1. Chenjerai Hove, 'Collapse of Law: Collapse of Conscience', *Palaver Finish* (Harare: Weaver, 2002), 10.
2. Gavin Williams, *Fragments of Democracy: Nationalism, Development and the State in Africa* (Cape Town: HSRC Press, 2003); Sam Nolutshungu, 'Fragments of Democracy: Reflections on Class and Politics in Nigeria', *Third World Quarterly* 12.1 (1990).
3. Chris Allen, 'Understanding African Politics', *Review of African Political Economy* 65 (1995); Charles Taylor, 'Interpretation and the Sciences of Man', in Charles Taylor, ed., *Philosophy and the Human Sciences*, vol. 2 (Cambridge: Cambridge University Press, 1985).
4. Timothy Mitchell, 'Society, Economy and the State Effect', in George Steinmetz, ed., *State / Culture: state formation after the cultural turn* (Ithaca, NY: Cornell University Press, 1999), 86–7.
5. David Blair, *Degrees in Violence: Robert Mugabe and the Struggle for Power in Zimbabwe* (London: Continuum, 2003); Martin Meredith, *Mugabe: Power and Plunder in Zimbabwe* (Oxford: Public Affairs, 2002); Stephen Chan, *Robert Mugabe: a life of power and violence* (London: I. B. Tauris, 2003); Paul Moorcraft, *Mugabe's War Machine* (London: Pen and Sword, 2012).
6. Jean-François Bayart, *The State in Africa*, translated by Mary Harper, Christopher and Elizabeth Harrison (London: Longman, 1993).
7. Abiodun Alao, *Mugabe and the Politics of Security in Zimbabwe* (Montreal and Kingston: McGill-Queen's University Press, 2012); Daniel Compagnon, *A Predictable Tragedy: Robert Mugabe and the Collapse of Zimbabwe* (Philadelphia, PA: University of Pennsylvania Press, 2011).
8. I draw here in particular on John Gaventa, *Power and Powerlessness: Quiescence and Rebellion in an Appalachian Valley* (Urbana, IL: University of Illinois, 1982); Steven Lukes, *A Radical View* (Basingstoke: Macmillan, 1974);

Antonio Gramsci, 'State and Civil Society', in Quintin Hoare and Geoffrey Nowell Smith, eds, *Selections from the Prison Notebooks of Antonio Gramsci* (New York: International Publishers, 1971).

9. Allen, 'Understanding African Politics', 302–20.

10. Frederick Cooper, *Africa since 1940: The Past of the Present (New Approaches to African History)* (Cambridge: Cambridge University Press, 2002).

11. See the debate on continuities in Terence Ranger, 'Nationalist historiography, patriotic history and the history of the nation: the struggle over the past in Zimbabwe', *Journal of South African Studies* 30.2 (2004), 220; Joost Fontein, 'Shared Legacies of the War: Spirit Mediums and War Veterans in Southern Zimbabwe', *Journal of Religion in Africa* 36.2 (2006), 168.

12. Colin Stoneman and Lionel Cliffe, *Zimbabwe: Politics, Economics and Society* (London: Pinter, 1989).

13. See for example Ibbo Mandaza, 'The State and Politics in the Post-White Settler Colonial Situation', in Ibbo Mandaza, ed., *Zimbabwe: the Political Economy of Transition, 1980–1986* (Dakar: CODESRIA, 1986), 55.

14. Patrick Bond, *Uneven Zimbabwe* (Trenton, NJ: Africa World Press, 1998) esp. ch. 6.

15. On ZANU and socialism, see for example 'ZANU(PF) to decide soon on new party ideology, says Mahachi', *Herald*, 29 January 1991, 3; 'ZANU(PF) leaders debate need to update socialism', *Herald*, 23 March 1991, 1; 'Chidzero speaks on new thrust: investors assured of commitment to marker economy', *Financial Gazette*, 28 March 1991, 1; 'Mutasa makes U-turn on socialism', *Financial Gazette*, 28 March 1991, 1; R. G. Mugabe, 'President calls for full debate on socialism', *Financial Gazette*, 28 March 1991, 4; 'Socialism not for now: Chidzero', *Sunday Mail*, 28 April 1991, 1.

16. Hevina Dashwood, *Zimbabwe: the Political Economy of Transition* (Toronto: University of Toronto Press, 2000).

17. Jonathan Moyo, 'State Politics and Social Domination', *Journal of Modern African Studies* (1992), 329; see also his *Politics of the National Purse* (Harare: SAPES Trust, 1992).

18. These comments refer mainly to Herbst's well-known monograph *State Politics in Zimbabwe* (Harare: University of Zimbabwe Publications, 1990). In a much less well-known article, Herbst does engage with ideological politics, but even here he is concerned with how ideology influences policy (i.e. the 'socialist' debate), not how ideology is used to bolster support for the regime: 'The Consequences of Ideology', in Simon Baynham, ed., *Zimbabwe in Transition* (Almqvist & Wiksell, 1992).

19. Some of the most optimistic accounts include: Masipula Sithole, 'Zimbabwe's eroding Authoritarianism', *Journal of Democracy* 8.1 (1997), 127–41; John Makumbe, 'Is there a civil society in Africa?' *International*

Affairs 74.2 (1998), 305–16; Richard Saunders, 'The Press, Civil Society and Democratic Struggles in Zimbabwe', paper presented to the conference on national identity and democracy, Cape Town, March 1997; Richard Saunders, *Never the Same Again: Zimbabwe's Growth towards Democracy, 1980–2000* (Harare, 2000); Alfred G. Nhema, 'Post-settler state-society relations in Zimbabwe: the rise of civil society and the decline of authoritarianism', in Sandra J. MacLean, Fahimul Quadir and Timothy M. Shaw, eds, *Crises of Governance in Asia and Africa* (Aldershot: Ashgate, 2001).

20. Sara Rich Dorman, 'Inclusion and Exclusion: NGOs and Politics in Zimbabwe', unpublished PhD thesis, Dept. of Politics, University of Oxford, 2001.

21. Sara Rich Dorman, 'Studying Democratization in Africa: A Case Study of Human Rights NGOs in Zimbabwe', in Tim Kelsall and Jim Igoe, eds, *Between a Rock and a Hard Place, African NGOs, Donors, and the State* (Durham, NC: Carolina Academic Press, 2005), 33–59.

22. Robert Rotberg, 'Africa's Mess, Mugabe's Mayhem', *Foreign Affairs* 79.5 (2000), 47–61; Martin Meredith, *Mugabe: Power and Plunder in Zimbabwe* (New York: Public Affairs, 2002); David Blair, *Degrees in Violence: Robert Mugabe and the Struggle for Power in Zimbabwe* (London: Continuum, 2003).

23. Stephen Chan, *Robert Mugabe: A Life of Power and Violence* (London: I. B. Tauris, 2003); Abiodun Alao, *Mugabe and the Politics of Security in Zimbabwe* (Montreal and Kingston: McGill-Queen's University Press, 2012); Michael Auret, *From Liberator to Dictator: An Insider's Account of Robert Mugabe's Descent into Tyranny* (Cape Town: David Philip, 2009); Daniel Compagnon, *A Predictable Tragedy: Robert Mugabe and the Collapse of Zimbabwe* (Philadelphia, PA: University of Pennsylvania Press, 2011).

24. Michael Bratton, *Power Politics in Zimbabwe* (Boulder, CO: Lynne Rienner, 2014).

25. Erin McCandless, *Polarization and Transformation in Zimbabwe: Social Movements, Strategy Dilemmas and Change* (Lanham, MD: Lexington Books, 2011); Adrienne LeBas, *From Protest to Parties: Party-Building and Democratization in Africa* (Oxford: Oxford University Press, 2011).

26. See also Angelique Haugerud, *The Culture of Politics in Modern Kenya* (Cambridge: Cambridge University Press, 1997); Michael Schatzberg, 'Power, legitimacy and "democratisation" in Africa', *Africa* 63.4 (1993); Darren Hawkins, 'Democratization Theory and Nontransitions: Insights from Cuba', *Comparative Politics* 33 (2001), 441–61.

27. Richard Werbner, 'Smoke from the Barrel of a Gun: Postwars of the dead, memory and reinscription in Zimbabwe', in Richard Werbner, ed., *Memory and the Postcolony* (London: Zed Books, 1998), 77.

28. Terence Ranger, *Peasant Consciousness and Guerrilla War in Zimbabwe* (London: James Currey, 1985); Jocelyn Alexander, JoAnn McGregor and

Terence Ranger, *Violence and Memory* (London: James Currey, 2000); Ranger, 'Nationalist historiography, patriotic history and the history of the nation', 215–34.

29. Lene Bull Christiansen, *Tales of the Nation; Feminist Nationalism or Patriotic History? Defining National History and Identity in Zimbabwe* (Uppsala: NAI, 2004).

30. Sabelo J. Ndlovu-Gatsheni, ed., *Mugabeism? History, Politics and Power in Zimbabwe* (New York: Palgrave Macmillan, 2015); Sabelo J. Ndlovu-Gatsheni, *Do 'Zimbabweans' Exist?* (Bern: Peter Lang, 2009); Blessing-Miles Tendi, *Making History in Mugabe's Zimbabwe* (Bern: Peter Lang, 2010); Blessing-Miles Tendi, 'Patriotic History and Public Intellectuals Critical of Power', *Journal of Southern African Studies* 34.2 (June 2008), 379–96. And on the region as a whole, see Henning Melber, *Limits to Liberation in Southern Africa* (Uppsala: NAI, 2003); Henning Melber, *Understanding Namibia* (Hurst & Co., 2014).

31. Norma Kriger, *Guerrilla Veterans in Post-War Zimbabwe: Symbolic and Violent Politics, 1980–1987* (Cambridge: Cambridge University Press, 2003).

32. Rudo B. Gaidzanwa, 'Grappling with Mugabe's Masculinist Politics in Zimbabwe: A Gender Perspective', in Sabelo J. Ndlovu-Gatsheni, ed., *Mugabeism? History, Politics and Power in Zimbabwe* (Basingstoke: Palgrave Macmillan, 2015); Sita Ranchod-Nilsson, 'Gender Politics and the Pendulum of Political and Social Transformation in Zimbabwe', *Journal of Southern African Studies* (2006); Everjoice Win, 'When Sharing Female Identity is Not Enough: Coalition Building in the Midst of Political Polarisation in Zimbabwe', *Gender & Development* 12.1 (May 2004), 19–27; Sheelagh Stewart, 'Working with a Radical Agenda: The Musasa Project Zimbabwe', *Gender and Development* 3.1 (1995), 30–35.

33. Michael Drinkwater, 'Technical Development and Peasant Impoverishment: Land Use Policy in Zimbabwe's Midlands Province', *Journal of Southern African Studies* 15.2 (1989), 287–305; Jocelyn Alexander, 'Things Fall Apart, the Centre Can Hold', in Ngwabi B. Bhebe and Terence Ranger, eds, *Society in Zimbabwe's Liberation War* (Harare: University of Zimbabwe Publications, 1995); Joseph Chaumba, Ian Scoones and William Wolmer, 'From Jambanja to Planning: The Reassertion of Technocracy in Land Reform in South-Eastern Zimbabwe?' *Journal of Modern African Studies* 41.4 (December 2003), 533–54.

34. C. Sylvester, 'Zimbabwe's 1985 Elections: a Search for National Mythology', *Journal of Modern African Studies* 24.1 (1986), 246; C. Sylvester, 'Unities and disunities in Zimbabwe's 1990 election', *Journal of Modern African Studies* 28.3 (1990), 375–400; C. Sylvester, 'Simultaneous Revolutions: the Zimbabwe Case', *Journal of Southern African Studies* 16.3 (1990).

35. Brian Raftopoulos, *Race and Nationalism in a Post-Colonial State* (Harare: SAPES Trust, 1996).

36. Blair Rutherford, *Working on the Margins* (Harare: Weaver, 2001); Björn Lindgren, *The Politics of Ndebele Ethnicity* (Uppsala: Uppsala University, 2002); Werbner, 'Smoke from the Barrel of a Gun'; Eric Worby, 'Tyranny, Parody and Ethnic Polarity: ritual engagements with the state in north western Zimbabwe', *Journal of Southern African Studies* 24.3 (September 1998), 561–78.

37. B. Beckman, 'The Liberation of Civil Society: Neo-Liberal Ideology and Political Theory', *Review of African Political Economy* 58 (1993), 20–33.

38. Chenjerai Hove, *Palaver Finish* (Harare: Weaver, 2002); see also Chenjerai Hove, *Rainbows in the Dust* (Harare: Baobab, 1998); and Chenjerai Hove, *Shebeen Tales* (Harare: Baobab, 1994).

2. THE POLITICS OF LIBERATION (1965–1980)

1. Chenjerai Hove, 'Shades of Power: colonial and post-colonial experiences of a writer', *Palaver Finish* (Harare: Weaver, 2002), 56.

2. Sudipta Kaviraj, 'In Search of Civil Society', paper presented to the SOAS politics seminar, London, 20 October 1999.

3. For a more detailed comparative exploration, see Sara Rich Dorman, 'Post-Liberation Politics in Africa: examining the political legacy of struggle', *Third World Quarterly* 27.6 (September 2006), 1085–1101.

4. Masipula Sithole, *Struggles within the Struggle*, 2nd edn (Harare: Rujeko, 1999); Sabelo J. Ndlovu-Gatsheni, *Do 'Zimbabweans' Exist?: Trajectories of Nationalism, National Identity Formation and Crisis in a Postcolonial State* (Bern: Peter Lang, 2009); Sabelo J. Ndlovu-Gatsheni, *The Zimbabwean Nation-State Project: A Historical Diagnosis of Identity* (Uppsala, 2011); Tim Scarnecchia, 'The "Sellout Logic" in the Formation of Zimbabwean Nationalist Politics, 1961–1964', in Sarah Helen Chiumbu and Muchapara Musemwa, eds, *Crisis! What Crisis?* (Cape Town: HSRC Press, 2012).

5. Terence Ranger, 'Nationalist historiography, patriotic history and the history of the nation: the struggle over the past in Zimbabwe', *Journal of Southern African Studies* 30.2 (June 2004), 215–34; Teresa Barnes, '"History Has to Play Its Role": Constructions of Race and Reconciliation in Secondary School Historiography in Zimbabwe, 1980–2002', *Journal of Southern African Studies* 33.3 (September 2007), 633–51.

6. Gerald Mazarire, 'Reflections on Pre-Colonial Zimbabwe c.850–1880s', in Brian Raftopoulos and A. S. Mlambo, eds, *Becoming Zimbabwe* (Harare: Weaver, 2009), 1–2.

7. Enocent Msindo, *Ethnicity in Zimbabwe* (New York: University of Rochester Press, 2012).

8. Sabelo J. Ndlovu-Gatsheni, 'Mapping Cultural and Colonial Encounters, 1880s-1930s', in Raftopoulos and Mlambo, *Becoming Zimbabwe*, 39–74. David James Maxwell, *Christians and Chiefs in Zimbabwe: A Social History of the Hwesa People, c.1870s-1990s* (Edinburgh: Edinburgh University Press for the International African Institute, International African Library 20, 1999), 142–6 captures the later stages of this particularly well.

9. Maxwell, *Christians and Chiefs in Zimbabwe*; T. O. Ranger, 'Missionaries, Migrants and the Manyika: The Invention of Ethnicity in Zimbabwe', in Leroy Vail, ed., *The Creation of Tribalism in Southern Africa* (London: James Currey, 1989), 118–51.

10. Elizabeth Schmidt, *Peasants, Traders and Wives: Shona Women in the History of Zimbabwe, 1870–1939* (Harare: Baobab Books, 1996); Norma J. Kriger, *Zimbabwe's Guerrilla War: Peasant Voices* (Cambridge: Cambridge University Press, African Studies series 70, 1992).

11. James R. Hooker, 'Welfare Association and other Instruments of Accommodation in the Rhodesias between the World Wars', *Comparative Studies in Society and History* 9 (1966); Ngwabi Bhebe, *B. Burumbo: African Politics in Zimbabwe 1947–1958* (Harare: College Press, 1989); Jane Farquar, *Jairos Jiri: the Man and his Work 1921–1982* (Gweru: Mambo Press, 1987); T. O. Ranger, *The African Voice in Southern Rhodesia 1898–1930* (London: Heinemann, 1970).

12. I. R. Hancock, 'The Capricorn Africa Society in Southern Africa', *Rhodesian History* IX (1978); I. R. Hancock, *White Liberals, Moderates and Radicals in Rhodesia, 1953–1980* (London: Croom Helm, 1984); Hardwicke Holderness, *Lost Chance* (Harare: Zimbabwe Publishing House, 1985), 122–35; Michael O. West, *The Rise of an African Middle Class: Colonial Zimbabwe, 1898–1965* (Bloomington, IN: Indiana University Press, 2002).

13. For discussions of the politics of this period, see West, *Rise of an African Middle Class*, 203–35; and Ngwabi Bhebe, 'The Nationalist Struggle, 1957–1962', in Canaan Banana, ed., *Turmoil and Tenacity: Zimbabwe 1890–1990* (Harare: College Press, 1989), 50–115.

14. Sithole, *Struggles within the Struggle*, 4.

15. André Astrow, for example, develops this theory at some length in *Zimbabwe: A revolution that lost its way?* (London: Zed Books, 1983), 82–90.

16. Msindo, *Ethnicity in Zimbabwe*, 192–9.

17. Sithole, *Struggles within the Struggle*.

18. David Moore, 'The Ideological Formation of the Zimbabwean Ruling Class', *Journal of Southern African Studies* 17.3 (1991), 488–95; David Moore, 'The Contradictory Construction of Hegemony in Zimbabwe', unpublished PhD thesis, York University, 1990; Zvakanyorwa Wilbert Sadomba, *War Veterans in Zimbabwe's Revolution: Challenging Neo-Colonialism and Settler and International Capital* (Woodbridge: Boydell & Brewer, 2011).

19. Josephine Nhongo-Simbanegavi, *For Better or Worse? Women and ZANLA in Zimbabwe's Liberation Struggle* (Harare: Weaver, 2000); Tanya Lyons, *Guns and Guerrilla Girls: Women in Zimbabwe's Liberation Struggle* (Trenton, NJ: Africa World Press, 2004); see also Sita Ranchod-Nilson, 'This too is a way of fighting: Rural women's participation in Zimbabwe's Liberation War', in Mary Ann Tetreault, ed., *Women and Revolution in Africa, Asia, and the New World* (Columbia, SC: University of South Carolina Press, 1994); and Leda Stott, *Women and the Armed Struggle for Independence in Zimbabwe* (Edinburgh: Centre of African Studies, 1990).

20. Sithole, *Struggles within the Struggle*, esp. ch. 4–5; see also Luise White, *The Assassination of Herbert Chitepo: Texts and Politics in Zimbabwe* (Bloomington, IN: University of Indiana, 2003).

21. Scarnecchia, 'The "Sellout Logic"', 226.

22. See David Moore, 'The Zimbabwe People's Army: Strategic Innovation or more of the same?', in Ngwabi Bhebe and Terence Ranger, eds, *Soldiers in Zimbabwe's Liberation War* (Harare: University of Zimbabwe Publications, 1995), 73–86; also Emmerson Mnangagwa, 'The Formation of the Front for the Liberation of Zimbabwe', in Banana, ed., *Turmoil and Tenacity*, 140–42; and Mnangagwa, 'The formation of the Zimbabwe People's Army', in Banana, ed., *Turmoil and Tenacity*, 143–6.

23. Thanks to Takura Zhanghaza for making this point to me.

24. *Free and Fair? The 1979 Rhodesian Election*, Parliamentary Human Rights Group (May 1979), 26. The British parliamentary observers were told by a Special Branch officer that there were 10,000–15,000 UANC and 1,500–3,000 ZANU auxiliaries. Contemporaneous Rhodesian army papers consulted by Luise White give lower numbers of 8,000 UANC and 1,500 ZANU.

25. *Free and Fair?*; David Martin, 'Sithole guerrillas "fly to Amin for training"', *Observer* (UK), 13 August 1978; Martha Honey, 'Sithole and Muzorewa "training guerrillas"', *Guardian* (UK), 17 February 1978.

26. Personal communication, 9 August 2004.

27. Claire Palley, *The Rhodesian Election* (London: Catholic Institute for International Relations, 1979), 3–4, 9; *Free and Fair?*, 41–4.

28. Terence Ranger, *Peasant Consciousness and Guerrilla War in Zimbabwe* (London: James Currey, 1985).

29. Kriger, *Zimbabwe's Guerrilla War*.

30. David Lan, *Guns and Rain: Guerrilla and Spirit Mediums in Zimbabwe* (London: James Currey, 1985).

31. David Maxwell, *Christians and Chiefs in Zimbabwe* (Edinburgh: Edinburgh University Press, 1999), 139–40.

32. Jocelyn Alexander, JoAnn McGregor and Terence Ranger, *Violence and Memory* (London: James Currey, 2000). See also Jocelyn Alexander, 'Things Fall Apart, the Centre Can Hold', in Ngwabi Bhebe and Terence Ranger,

eds, *Society in Zimbabwe's Liberation War* (Harare: University of Zimbabwe Publications, 1995), 176–9, 161.

33. Mike Kesby, 'Arenas for Control, Terrains of Gender Contestation: Guerrilla Struggle and Counter-Insurgency Warfare in Zimbabwe 1972–1980', *Journal of Southern African Studies* 22.4 (1996), 574.

34. Brian Wood, 'Trade Union Organisation and the Working Class', in Colin Stoneman, ed., *Zimbabwe's Prospects: issues of race, class, state and capital in Southern Africa* (London: Macmillan, 1988), 286; Brian Raftopoulos, 'The Labour Movement in Zimbabwe 1945–65', in Brian Raftopoulos and Ian Phimister, eds, *Keep on Knocking: a History of the Labour Movement in Zimbabwe 1900–97* (Harare: Baobab, 1997), 55–90.

35. Ian Phimister and Brian Raftopoulos, '"Kana sora ratswa ngaritswe": African Nationalists and Black Workers—The 1948 General Strike in Colonial Zimbabwe', *Journal of Historical Sociology* 13.3 (2000), 289–324.

36. Brian Raftopoulos, 'Nationalism and Labour in Salisbury', *Journal of Southern African Studies* 21.1 (1995), 79–93.

37. Terence Ranger, 'Legitimacy, Civil Society and the State in Africa', 1st Alexander Visiting Professor Lecture presented at the University of Western Australia, 2 December 1992, 23.

38. Raftopoulos, 'The Labour Movement in Zimbabwe 1945–65', 87.

39. For discussion of these laws and their impacts, see Freek Schiphorst, 'Strength and Weakness: the Rise of the Zimbabwe Congress of Trade Unions and the Development of Labour Relations, 1980–1995', PhD thesis, Leiden, 2001, 37–57; and Julie Brittain and Brian Raftopoulos, 'The Labour Movement in Zimbabwe 1965–1980', in *Keep on Knocking*, 97–102.

40. Brittain and Raftopoulos, 'The Labour Movement in Zimbabwe 1965–1980', 94.

41. Schiphorst, 'Strength and Weakness', 43.

42. Tim Scarnecchia, *The Urban Roots of Democracy and Political Violence in Zimbabwe* (New York: University of Rochester Press, 2008).

43. John Pape, 'Chimurenga in the *kia*: domestic workers and the liberation struggle', in Brian Raftopoulos and Tsuneo Yoshikuni, *Sites of Struggle: Essays in Zimbabwe's Urban History* (Harare: Weaver, 1999), 257–71.

44. K. H. Wekwete, 'Development of urban planning in Zimbabwe', *Cities* (1988), 60.

45. Carole Rakodi with Penny Withers, *Land, Housing and Urban Development in Zimbabwe: markets and policy in Harare and Gweru*, Final Report on ESCOR Project R4468 (Cardiff: University of Wales, 1993), 50.

46. Ennie Chipembere, 'Smith and the City', UDI 40th anniversary conference, Cambridge (September 2005).

47. Diana H. Patel, 'Government Policy and Squatter Settlements in Harare,

Zimbabwe', in R. A. Obudho and Constance C. Mhlanga, eds, *Slum and Squatter Settlements in Sub-Saharan Africa* (New York: Praeger, 1988), 207.

48. Patel, 'Government Policy and Squatter Settlements', 208; see also Rakodi with Withers, *Land, Housing and Urban Development*, 79.

49. P. A. Hardwick, 'The Transportation System', in George Kay and Michael Smout, eds, *Salisbury: A Geographical Survey of the Capital of Rhodesia* (London: Hodder and Stoughton, 1977), 100–101.

50. D. Mazambani, 'Peri-urban cultivation within Greater Harare', *Zimbabwe Science News* 16.6 (June 1992).

51. Palley, *Rhodesian Election*, 14–15.

52. Thomas Turino, *Nationalists, Cosmopolitans, and Popular Music in Zimbabwe* (Chicago: University of Chicago Press, 2000), 195.

53. James Muzondidya, 'Sitting on the fence or walking a tightrope? A political history of the coloured community in Zimbabwe, 1945–1980', unpublished PhD thesis, University of Zimbabwe, 2001.

54. Michael O. West, 'Indians, India, and Race and Nationalism in British Central Africa', *South Asia Bulletin* XIV.2 (1994), 97.

55. Muzondidya, 'Sitting on the fence or walking a tightrope?'

56. Busani Mpofu, 'The struggles of an "undesirable" alien community in a white settler colony: the case of the Indian minority in Colonial Zimbabwe, with particular reference to the city of Bulawayo, *c*.1890–1963', unpublished MA thesis, University of Zimbabwe, 2005, 32–5.

57. J. K. Seirlis, 'Undoing the United Front? Coloured Soldiers in Rhodesia 1939–1980', *African Studies* 63.1 (2004), 73–94; Muzondidya, 'Sitting on the fence or walking a tightrope?', 259–69.

58. Muzondidya, 'Sitting on the fence or walking a tightrope?', 218.

59. Although it is worth noting Alan Cousin's argument that there are 'clear elements of continuity in white ideology in Rhodesia during the period 1958–1972 and also in structures of power'. Alan Cousins, 'State, Ideology and Power in Rhodesia, 1958–1972', *International Journal of African Historical Studies* 24.1 (1991), 63.

60. A. S. Mlambo, *White Immigration into Rhodesia: from occupation to federation* (Harare: University of Zimbabwe Publications, 2002); Angela Davies, 'From Rhodesian to Zimbabwean and Back: White Identity in an African Context', PhD thesis, University of California, 2001, 22–80.

61. Davies, 'From Rhodesian to Zimbabwean', 210 (emphasis in the original).

62. For a discussion of myth-making, see John Day, 'The Creation of Political Myths', *Journal of Southern Asian Studies* 2.1 (1975), 52–65; for an emphasis on the role of literature, see Davies, 'From Rhodesian to Zimbabwean', 34–46; David Maughan Brown, 'Myths on the March: the Kenyan and Zimbabwean Liberation Struggles in Colonial Fiction', *Journal of Southern*

African Studies 9.1 (1982), 93–117; Preben Kaarsholm, 'From Decadence to Authenticity and Beyond: Fantasies and Mythologies of War in Rhodesia and Zimbabwe, 1965–1985', in Preben Kaarsholm, ed., *Cultural Struggle and Development in Southern Africa* (Harare: Baobab, 1991), 33–60; Anthony Chennells, 'Rhodesian Discourse, Rhodesian Novels and the Zimbabwe Liberation War', in Bhebe and Ranger, eds, *Society in Zimbabwe's Liberation War*, 102–29; Luise White, 'Precarious Conditions: A Note on Counter-Insurgency in Africa after 1945', *Gender and History* 16.3 (2004), 603–25.

63. Luise White, 'Civic virtue, young men and the family: conscription in Rhodesia 1974–1980', *International Journal of African Historical Studies* 37.1 (2004), 103–21; Josiah Brownell, *Collapse of Rhodesia: Population Demographics and the Politics of Race* (London: I. B. Tauris, 2010); Josiah Brownell, 'The Hole in Rhodesia's Bucket: White Emigration and the End of Settler Rule', *Journal of Southern African Studies* 34.3 (September 2008), 591–610.

64. Ch. 7 of Peter Godwin and Ian Hancock's *Rhodesians Never Die* (Oxford: Oxford University Press, 1993) captures the ambiguity of this odd transitional period particularly well.

65. Palley, *Rhodesian Election*; *Free and Fair?*; see also Luise White, *Unpopular Sovereignty: Rhodesian Independence and African Decolonization* (Chicago, IL: University of Chicago Press, 2015), 245.

66. Angus Selby, 'Commercial Farmers and the State: Interest Group Politics and Land Reform in Zimbabwe' (University of Oxford, 2006).

67. I. R. Hancock, *White Liberals*, 28.

68. Ruth Weiss with Jane Parpart, *Sir Garfield Todd and the Making of Zimbabwe* (London: I. B. Tauris, 1999); Guy Clutton-Brock, *Cold Comfort Confronted* (London: Mowbray, 1972); Guy Clutton-Brock, *The Cold Comfort Farm Society* (Gweru: Mambo Press, 1970); Donal Lamont, *Speech from the Dock* (Stowmarket: Kevin Mayhew, 1977); Kenneth Skelton, *Bishop in Smith's Rhodesia* (Gweru: Mambo Press, 1985), 109.

69. Hancock, *White Liberals*, 200; Ian Linden, *The Catholic Church and the Struggle for Zimbabwe* (London: Longman, 1980); Michael Lapsley, *Neutrality or Co-option? Anglican Church and State from 1964 until the Independence of Zimbabwe* (Gweru: Mambo, 1986), 75.

70. Interview, Mike Auret, CCJP, 14 September 1995; R. H. Randolph, *Dawn in Zimbabwe: The Catholic Church in the New Order: a report on the activities of the Catholic Church in the Zimbabwe for the five years, 1977–1981* (Gweru: Mambo Press, 1985), 173–4.

71. Terence Ranger, *Are we not also men? The Samkange Family and African Politics in Zimbabwe: 1920–64* (London: James Currey, 1995), 88–93.

72. C. D. Watyoka, *25 Years of Struggle* (Harare: Zion Christian Church, 1991).

73. Carl F. Hallencreutz, 'Council in the Crossfire: ZCC 1964–1980', in Carl F. Hallencreutz and Ambrose M. Moyo, eds, *Church and State in Zimbabwe* (Gweru: Mambo Press, 1988), 57–9.

74. Watyoka, *25 Years*, 10–11.

75. Hallencreutz, 'Council in the Crossfire', 60–61.

76. Skelton, *Bishop in Smith's Rhodesia*, 102.

77. Lapsley, *Neutrality or Co-option?*, 75.

78. Ibid., 73.

79. David Maxwell, 'The Church and Democratization in Africa: the Case of Zimbabwe', in Paul Gifford, ed., *The Christian Churches and the Democratisation of Africa* (Leiden: Brill, 1995), 112; Watyoka, *25 Years*, 19.

80. David Martin and Phyllis Johnson, *The Struggle for Zimbabwe: the Chimurenga War* (London and Boston: Faber, 1981).

81. T. O. Ranger, *African Voice*, 235.

82. Ian Phimister, 'The combined and contradictory inheritance of the struggle against colonialism' in Stoneman, ed., *Zimbabwe's Prospects* (1988), 8.

83. See, for example, Nathan Shamuyarira, 'An overview of the struggle for unity and independence', in Banana, ed., *Turmoil and Tenacity*, 13–24.

84. Christine Sylvester, 'Simultaneous Revolutions: the Zimbabwe Case', *Journal of Southern African Studies* 16.3 (1990).

85. Zolberg's analysis of Sékou Touré's thinking about unity makes for particularly worthwhile reading in this context: Aristide Zolberg, *Creating Political Order: The Party States of West Africa* (Chicago: Rand McNally, 1966), esp. 44–7. Ruth Iyob's study of the Eritrean national struggle emphasizes the use made by the Ethiopian regime of 'unity' to discredit the Eritrean nationalist project: Ruth Iyob, *The Eritrean Struggle for Independence* (Cambridge: Cambridge University Press, 1995), esp. 47–58.

86. Juan Linz, *Totalitarian and Authoritarian Regimes* (Boulder, CO: Lynne Rienner, 2000), 229, citing William J. Foltz, *From French West Africa to the Mali Federation* (New Haven, CT: Yale University Press, 1965), 143, citing Léopold Senghor; see also Zolberg, *Creating Political Order*, 51–2.

87. This point was made by the late Stanley Trapido in a paper on 'African and Afrikaner Nationalism', which was unfortunately never published.

88. Linz, *Totalitarian and Authoritarian Regimes*, 166.

89. Mahmood Mamdani, 'State and Civil Society in Contemporary Africa: Reconceptualizing the Birth of State Nationalism and the Defeat of Popular Movements', *Africa Development* XV (1990), 55; see also Ernest Wamba-dia-wamba, 'Discourse on the National Question', in I. G. Shivji, *State and Constitutionalism: an African debate on democracy* (Harare: SAPES Trust, 1991), 63.

3. THE POLITICS OF INCLUSION (1980–1987)

1. Chenjerai Hove, 'Zimbabwe's Lost Visions', *Palaver Finish* (Harare: Weaver, 2002), 21.

2. Sugata Bose and Ayesha Jalal, 'Nationalism, democracy and development', in Sugata Bose and Ayesha Jalal, eds, *Nationalism, Democracy and Development* (Delhi: Oxford University Press, 1997), 1.

3. Ronald Weitzer, 'Continuities in the Politics of State Security in Zimbabwe', in Michael G. Schatzberg, *The Political Economy of Zimbabwe* (New York: Praeger, 1984), 82; George Hamandishe Karekwaivanane, 'Legal Encounters: Law, State and Society in Zimbabwe, c.1950–1990' (University of Oxford, 2012).

4. Terence Ranger, 'Legitimacy, Civil Society and the State in Africa', 1st Alexander Visiting Professor Lecture presented at the University of Western Australia, 2 December 1992, 23.

5. Mahmood Mamdani, 'State and Civil Society in Contemporary Africa: Reconceptualizing the Birth of State Nationalism and the Defeat of Popular Movements', *Africa Development* XV (1990), 49.

6. See Chapter 2; also Immanuel Wallerstein, 'Voluntary Organisations', in J. S. Coleman and Carl Rosberg, *Political Parties and National Integration in Tropical Africa*, 2nd printing (Berkeley: University of California Press, 1966), 318–38.

7. Lloyd Sachikonye, 'The national-state project and conflict in Zimbabwe', in Liisa Laakso and Adebayo Olukoshi, eds, *Challenges to the Nationstate in Africa* (Uppsala: Nordiska Afrikainstitutet, 1996), 140.

8. Norbert Tengende, 'Workers, Students and the Struggles for Democracy: State-Civil Society Relations in Zimbabwe', unpublished PhD thesis, Roskilde University, 1994, 153.

9. 'Address to the nation by the Prime Minister: The wrongs of the past must stand forgiven and forgotten', *Herald*, 18 April 1980, 4.

10. Brian Raftopoulos, 'Beyond the House of Hunger: Democratic Struggle in Zimbabwe', *Review of African Political Economy* 54, 64; but see also Victor de Waal, *The Politics of Reconciliation* (London: Hurst & Co., 1990).

11. Ibid.

12. Henning Melber, *Understanding Namibia* (London: Hurst & Co., 2014); Sara Rich Dorman, 'Born Powerful? Authoritarian Politics in Eritrea and Zimbabwe', in Kalowatie Deonandan, Dave Close and Gary Prevost, eds, *From Revolutionary Movements to Political Parties: Cases From Africa and Latin America* (New York: Palgrave Macmillan, 2008).

13. Ibbo Mandaza, 'The state and politics in the post-white settler colonial situation', in Ibbo Mandaza, ed., *The Political Economy of Transition* (Dakar: CODESRIA, 1986), 54.

14. Sachikonye, 'The national-state project', 142.
15. Richard Werbner, 'Smoke from the Barrel of a Gun: Postwars of the dead, memory and reinscription in Zimbabwe', in Richard Werbner, ed., *Memory and the Postcolony* (London: Zed Books, 1998), 79.
16. Sioux Cumming, 'Post-colonial urban residential change in Harare', in Lovemore Zinyama, Daniel Tevera and Sioux Cumming, eds, *Harare: the Growth and Problems of the City* (Harare: University of Zimbabwe Publications, 1993).
17. Rukudzo Murapa, 'Race and the Public Service in Zimbabwe 1890–1983', in Michael G. Schatzberg, ed., *The Political Economy of Zimbabwe* (New York: Praeger, 1984),
18. Weitzer, 'Continuities in the Politics of State Security in Zimbabwe', 84–5.
19. Suzanne Dansereau, 'Legacy of Colonialism in Zimbabwe's Labour Utilization Model: Mineworkers' Wages, Skills, and Migration', in Brian Raftopoulos and Lloyd Sachikonye, *Striking Back: The Labour Movement and the Post-colonial State in Zimbabwe 1980–2000* (Harare: Weaver, 2001), 258.
20. Tor Skålnes, *The Politics of Economic Reform in Zimbabwe: continuity and change in development* (Basingstoke: Macmillan, 1995); Carolyn Jenkins, 'The Politics of Economic Policy-making in Zimbabwe', *Journal of Modern African Studies* 35.4 (1997); Jeffrey Herbst, *State Politics in Zimbabwe* (Harare: University of Zimbabwe Publications, 1991).
21. Jenkins, 'Politics of Economic Policy-making in Zimbabwe', 588.
22. Ruth Weiss, *Zimbabwe and the New Elite* (London: I. B. Tauris, 1994); Angela Davies, 'From Rhodesian to Zimbabwean and Back: White Identity in an African Context', unpublished PhD thesis, University of California, Berkeley, 2001.
23. N. C. G. Mathema, *Newspapers in Zimbabwe* (Lusaka: Multimedia Zambia, 2001), 17.
24. See Jan Raath's interesting story on the government's failure to reappoint Norman in 1985: 'Harare quick to heal rift with its white farmers', *Times* (UK), 5 August 1985.
25. Christine Sylvester, 'Unities and disunities in Zimbabwe's 1990 election', *Journal of Modern African Studies* 28.3 (1990), 376.
26. 'We must be vigilant and united, says President', *Herald*, 3 January 1981, 1.
27. Karekwaivanane, 'Legal Encounters'.
28. 'Unity is prosperity, says Minister', *Herald*, 18 October 1982, 1.
29. 'No one party state, yet, Mugabe pledges', *Herald*, 5 August 1982, 1.
30. 'Unity of Party and state our objective—Zvobgo', *Herald*, 2 November 1981, 1.

31. Joseph Hanlon, 'Destabilisation and the battle to reduce dependence', in Colin Stoneman, ed., *Zimbabwe's Prospects* (London: Macmillan, 1988); Michael Evans, 'The security threat from South Africa', in Stoneman, ed., *Zimbabwe's Prospects*.

32. Tengende, 'Workers, Students and the Struggles for Democracy', 254.

33. CCJP/LRF, *Breaking the Silence, Building True Peace* (Harare: CCJP/LRF, 1997), 157–8. See also Lawyers Committee on Human Rights, *Zimbabwe: Wages of War* (New York: Lawyers Committee, 1986); ZimRights, *Choosing the Path to Peace and Development: Coming to Terms with Human RightsViolations of the 1982–1987 Conflict in Matabeleland and Midlands Provinces* (Harare: ZimRights, 1999).

34. See for instance Lloyd Sachikonye, *When a State Turns on its Citizens* (Johannesburg: Jacana, 2011), 15–17.

35. CCJP/LRF, *Breaking the Silence*, 45–6.

36. Richard Werbner, *Tears of the Dead: the Social Biography of an African family* (Edinburgh: Edinburgh University Press, 1991), 162.

37. 'Muzorewa arrested', *Herald*, 2 November 1983, 1; 'Why Muzorewa being detained—Premier', *Herald*, 4 November 1983.

38. 'New grounds for the detention of Muzorewa', *Herald*, 5 November 1983, 1.

39. 'Bishop's Zaire link exposed', *Herald*, 19 November 1983, 1.

40. The perspective of the guerrillas-turned-dissidents is best described in Jocelyn Alexander, 'Dissident perspectives on Zimbabwe's Post-Independence War', *Africa* 68.2 (1998); Norma Kriger gives the most detailed account of the whole process: *GuerrillaVeterans in Post-war Zimbabwe* (Cambridge: Cambridge University Press, 2003).

41. Alexander, 'Dissident perspectives'.

42. Weitzer, 'Continuities in the Politics of State Security in Zimbabwe', 543 (italics in the original).

43. 'Division will destroy us, says Mugabe', *Herald*, 18 October 1982.

44. Björn Lindgren, 'The Politics of Ndebele Ethnicity: origins, nationality and gender in southern Zimbabwe', PhD dissertation, Uppsala University, 2002, 151.1.

45. For 'official' accounts of this process, see ch. 13–17 of Canaan Banana, ed., *Turmoil and Tenacity: Zimbabwe 1890–1990* (Harare: College Press, 1989).

46. 'One picture worth a thousand years', *Herald*, 3 November 1981, 1.

47. 'Graffiti man faces deportation', *Herald*, 18 December 1981, 1.

48. For a useful discussion of this metaphor, see Michael Schatzberg, 'Power, legitimacy and "democratisation" in Africa', *Africa* 63.4 (1993).

49. For an interesting analysis of this tendency in Malawi, see Stanslaus Muyebe and Alexander Muyebe, *The Religious Factor within the Body of*

Political Symbolism in Malawi, 1964–1994 (Florida: Universal Publishers, 1999).

50. 'Maiden Speech for new MP,' *Herald*, 1 June 1990, 2.

51. 'Names changed: Colonial legacy wiped out in 32 centres', *Herald*, 21 April 1982, 1; 'Getting to the root of Zimbabwe's place-names', *Herald*, 3 May 1982, 4; 'New names to give Zimbabwe true identity', *Herald*, 23 April 1985, 1. As we shall see in Chapter 5, this process was restarted after the 2000 election.

52. Jan Raath, 'New names for old in Zimbabwe', *Times* (UK), 24 April 1985.

53. 'Cities, towns' streets renamed', *Herald*, 7 March 1990, 1, 3.

54. 'War memorial to be smashed', *Herald*, 18 November 1981, 1.

55. 'Political subjects to be placed on new curriculum', *Herald*, 13 November 1981, 6.

56. Fay Chung, 'Education: revolution or reform', in Colin Stoneman, ed., *Zimbabwe's Prospects* (London: Macmillan, 1988), 118–32; Teresa Barnes, 'Reconciliation, Ethnicity and School History in Zimbabwe, 1980–2002', in Brian Raftopoulos and Tyrone Savage, *Zimbabwe: injustice and political reconciliation* (Johannesburg: Institute for Justice and Reconciliation, 2004), 140–59.

57. 'Let's develop a national dress', *Herald*, 6 December 1983, 1.

58. Thomas Turino, *Nationalists, Cosmopolitans, and Popular Music in Zimbabwe* (Chicago: University of Chicago Press, 2000), 321.

59. Maurice Taonezi Vambe, 'Popular songs and social realities in post-independent Zimbabwe', *African Studies Review* 43.2 (2000), 75.

60. Welshman Ncube, 'The post-unity period: developments, benefits and problems', in Banana, *Turmoil and Tenacity* (1989), 312.

61. Norma J. Kriger, *Zimbabwe's Guerrilla War: Peasant Voices* (Cambridge: Cambridge University Press, African Studies series 70, 1992), 140.

62. 'Who is a hero—ZAPU?' *Herald*, 16 September 1982, 7.

63. 'Who is a hero', *Zimbabwe Mirror*, 23 July 1999.

64. Werbner, 'Smoke from the Barrel of a Gun', 91.

65. Karen M. Lee, 'The Historical Development of Zimbabwe's Museums and Monuments', unpublished MPhil thesis, University of St Andrews, 1995, 75–91; Peter J. Ucko, 'Museums and sites: cultures of the past within education—Zimbabwe, some ten years on', in Peter G. Stone and Brian L. Molyneux, eds, *The Presented Past: Heritage, Museums, and Education* (London: Routledge in association with English Heritage, 1994), 237–82.

66. Joost Fontein, *Silence of Great Zimbabwe: Contested Landscapes and the Power of Heritage* (London: UCL Press, 2006).

67. Ucko, 'Museums and sites', 246–56.

68. Jill Crystal, 'Authoritarianism and its Adversaries in the Arab World', *World Politics* 46 (1994), 288, also 280–81.

69. See for instance Robert G. Mugabe, 'Welcoming address by the Right Honourable Prime Minister', in 'Let's Build Zimbabwe Together: Report on Conference Proceedings, Zimbabwe Conference on Reconstruction and Development' (Salisbury: ZIMCORD, 23–27 March 1981).

70. Diana Auret, *A Decade of Development* (Gweru: Mambo/CCJP, 1990), 17; for an overview of successes and challenges in education reforms, see also Claudia Madzoke, 'Education', in *Social Policy and Administration in Zimbabwe* (Harare: School of Social Work, 1995), 173–89.

71. Jean Lennock, *Paying for Health* (UK: Oxfam, 1994), 6.

72. Hevina Dashwood, *Zimbabwe: the Political Economy of Transition* (Toronto: University of Toronto Press, 2000), 43–6.

73. UNDP, Poverty Reduction Forum, Institute of Development Studies, *Zimbabwe Human Development Report 1998*.

74. 'Paweni likely to face trial by end of July', *Herald*, 8 June 1984, 1; 'PM calls for overhaul of tender system', *Herald*, 12 June 1984, 1, 5; 'Paweni corruption hearing begins', *Herald*, 24 July 1984, 1, 3; 'Paweni bribed me: mystery man', *Herald*, 26 July 1984, 1, 15; see also Andrew Meldrum, 'Food relief fraud in Zimbabwe', *Guardian* (UK), 5 June 1984; 'Two convicted in Zimbabwe bribery scandal', *Times* (UK), 14 September 1984; 'Zimbabwe aid swindler jailed for 15 years', *Times* (UK), 15 September 1984. Brian Raftopoulos kindly brought this incident to my attention.

75. Herbst, *State Politics in Zimbabwe*; Stephen Burgess, *Smallholders and Political Voice in Zimbabwe* (New York: University Press of America, 1997).

76. James Scott, *Seeing like a State* (New Haven, CT: Yale University Press, 1998).

77. Jocelyn Alexander, '"Squatters", Veterans and the State in Zimbabwe', in Amanda Hammer, Brian Raftopoulos and Stig Jensen, eds, *Zimbabwe's Unfinished Business* (Harare: Weaver, 2003), 85–91.

78. Jocelyn Alexander, 'The State, Agrarian Policy and Rural Politics in Zimbabwe', unpublished PhD thesis, University of Oxford, 1993; William Munro, *The Moral Economy of the State: Conservation, Community Development and State-making in Zimbabwe* (Ohio: Ohio University, 1998); Donald S. Moore, *Suffering for Territory: Race, Place and Power in Zimbabwe* (Harare: Weaver, 2005); Marja Spierenburg, *Strangers, Spirits and Land Reforms* (Leiden: Brill, 2004).

79. Moore, *Suffering for Territory*, 78.

80. Robin Palmer, 'Land reform in Zimbabwe, 1980–1990', *African Affairs* 89.355 (1990), 169–71.

81. Bill Kinsey, 'Land reform, growth and equity: emerging evidence from Zimbabwe's resettlement programme', *Journal of Southern African Studies* 25 (1999), 173–96; J. G. M. Hoogeveen and B. H. Kinsey, 'Land Reform, Growth and Equity: Emerging Evidence from Zimbabwe's Resettlement

Programme—A Sequel', *Journal of Southern African Studies* 27 (2001), 126–36.

82. ODA, 'Land resettlement in Zimbabwe: a preliminary evaluation', Evaluation report EV 434, September 1988.

83. Palmer, 'Land reform in Zimbabwe', 175.

84. Jocelyn Alexander, 'State, Peasantry and Resettlement in Zimbabwe', *Review of African Political Economy* 21.61 (1994), 334.

85. Palmer, 'Land reform in Zimbabwe', 173–4.

86. Weitzer, 'Continuities in the Politics of State Security in Zimbabwe'.

87. 'Create Unity, Mutumbuka urges 5000 head-masters', *Herald*, 13 November 1981, 3.

88. 'Nhongo urges unity of sexes for progress', *Herald*, 27 January 1982, 3.

89. 'Breakthrough in battle to unite all businessmen', *Herald*, 28 January 1982, 1.

90. 'Workers told to unite', *Herald*, 27 January 1982, 2; 'Unite or be disowned, warns top ZCTU man', *Herald*, 29 January 1982, 11; 'Workers' unity is vital', *Herald*, 3 May 1982, 4.

91. 'Clothing unions' merger "is valid"', *Herald*, 3 February 1982, 4.

92. 'Unity vital—Townsend', *Herald*, 6 November 1981, 15. Townsend was chair of the Mashonaland Farmers Association, and was speaking in support of the establishment of a National Commercial Farmers Union.

93. Teresa Barnes, 'The Heroes' Struggle: Life after the Liberation War for four ex-combatants in Zimbabwe', in Ngwabi Bhebe and Terence Ranger, eds, *Soldiers in Zimbabwe's Liberation War* (Harare: University of Zimbabwe Publications, 1995), 128–9.

94. See for example Barnes, 'The Heroes' Struggle'; also Jeremy Brickhill, 'Making Peace with the Past: War Victims and the Work of the Mafela Trust', in Bhebe and Ranger, eds, *Soldiers in Zimbabwe's Liberation War*, especially notes 11 and 12. More recent interview research also confirms this: Erin McCandless, 'Rights or Redistribution … and other strategic dilemmas facing Zimbabwean Social Movements', PhD dissertation, American University in Washington, 2005.

95. Norma Kriger, 'Les vétérans et le parti au pouvoir: une coopération conflictuelle dans la longue durée', *Politique Africaine* 81 (2001), 81; quotations from the author's original English version of text.

96. Norma Kriger, 'The War Victims Compensation Act', *Journal of African Conflict and Development* 1 (2000); Author's MS, n.p.

97. Kriger, 'Les vétérans et le parti au pouvoir', 91.

98. Zvakanyorwa Wilbert Sadomba, *War Veterans in Zimbabwe's Revolution: Challenging Neo-Colonialism and Settler and International Capital* (Woodbridge: Boydell & Brewer, 2011), 98–107; Kriger, 'Les vétérans et le parti au pouvoir', 82.

99. 'NGOs must keep in step with government', *Herald*, 1 May 1984, 3.

100. Revd Canaan Banana, 'Official Opening', in Val Thorpe and John Vekris, 'Workshop on the Effects of ESAP on Zimbabwean NGOs and their Services' (Harare, 20–24 March 1995), 4.

101. Interview, Paul Themba Nyathi, 18 September 1995.

102. Brian Raftopoulos, 'The State, NGOs, and Democratization', in Sam Moyo, John Makumbe and Brian Raftopoulos, *NGOs, the State and Politics in Zimbabwe* (Harare: SAPES Trust, 2000), 45.

103. Sheila White, 'A New Voice in Rural Welfare', *Herald*, 27 November 1981, 13; 'Teaching good management by Voice', *Herald*, 1 February 1984, 6; 'Voluntary body sets up 1000 pre-schools', *Herald*, 29 July 1985, 3.

104. 'Advert for National Director', *Herald*, 18 November 1981, 23; conversations with Zebediah Gamanya, July 1991.

105. Michael O. West, 'Nationalism, Race and Gender: The Politics of Family Planning in Zimbabwe, 1957–1990', *Social History of Medicine* (1994), 459–65.

106. Brian Raftopoulos and Jean-Paul Lacoste, 'From Savings Mobilisation to Micro-Finance: An Historical Perspective on the Zimbabwe Savings Development Movement', paper presented at the SARIPS Colloquium 2001 on 'Social Policy and Development in Southern Africa', Harare, 23–26 September 2001.

107. Michael Bratton, 'Non-governmental organizations in Africa: can they influence public policy', *Development and Change* 21 (1990), 96–9.

108. Raftopoulos and Lacoste, 'From Savings Mobilisation to Micro-Finance', 10.

109. Interview, Sally Zimbiti, SHDF, 19 September 1995.

110. Raftopoulos and Lacoste, 'From Savings Mobilisation to Micro-Finance', 10.

111. See for example 'Why the outcry over curfew, premier asks Church', *Herald*, 18 April 1984, 1; '[editorial] Church and State', *Herald*, 19 April 1984, 6; 'Stop the gossip, President tells Church', *Herald*, 8 May 1984, 1; 'Church accused of double standards', *Herald*, 20 February 1986, 1.

112. Diana Auret, *Reaching for Justice: The Catholic Commission for Justice and Peace Looks Back at the Past Twenty Years 1972–1992* (Gweru: Mambo Press, 1992), 215–17; Interviews with Nick Ndebele, former CCJP Director, 27 September 1999; and with Mike Auret, former CCJP Chair and Director, 14 September 1995 and 28 September 1999.

113. Paul H. Gundani, 'The Catholic Church and National Development in Independent Zimbabwe', in Carl F. Hallencreutz and Ambrose M. Moyo, eds, *Church and State in Zimbabwe* (Gweru: Mambo Press, 1988), 215.

114. Interview, John Bakila Sibanda, Christian Care, 26 September 1995.

115. Dexter M. Chavunduka, Gerrit Huizer, Tholakele D. Khumalo and Nancy Thede, *Khuluma Usenza: The Story of O.R.A.P. in Zimbabwe's Rural Development* (Bulawayo: ORAP, 1985), III.

116. 'Dismantle ORAP system', *Herald*, 22 March 1985, 3.

117. Interview, Nomalanga Zulu, ORAP, 17 February 1997.

118. Zimbabwe Project Trust Annual Report (1998), 5.

119. Interview, Paul Themba Nyathi, 18 September 1995.

120. Ibid.

121. Sara Rich Dorman, 'NGOs and State in Zimbabwe: implications for civil society theory', in Björn Beckman, Anders Sjögren and Eva Hansson, eds, *Civil Society and Authoritarianism in the Third World* (Stockholm: PODSU, 2001); Sara Rich Dorman, 'Studying Democratization in Africa: A Case Study of Human Rights NGOs in Zimbabwe', in Tim Kelsall and Jim Igoe, eds, *Between a Rock and a Hard Place, African NGOs, Donors, and the State* (Durham, NC: Carolina Academic Press, 2005), 33–59.

122. David Lan, *Guns and Rain: Guerrilla and Spirit Mediums in Zimbabwe* (London: James Currey, 1985), 226–7; Terence Ranger, *Peasant Consciousness and Guerrilla War in Zimbabwe* (London: James Currey, 1985), 291–2; 296.

123. David Maxwell, *Christians and Chiefs in Zimbabwe* (Edinburgh: Edinburgh University Press, 1999), 211; Alexander, 'The State, Agrarian Policy and Rural Politics in Zimbabwe', 181.

124. Kriger, *Zimbabwe's Guerrilla War*, 214.

125. A. H. J. Helmsing, 'Transforming rural local government: Zimbabwe's post-independence experience', Environment and Planning C (1990: 8), 101.

126. Alexander, 'The State, Agrarian Policy and Rural Politics in Zimbabwe', 183; see also Marja Spierenburg, *Strangers, Spirits and Land Reforms* (Leiden: Brill, 2004), 40–45.

127. John Makumbe, *Democracy and Development in Zimbabwe: Constraints of Decentralisation* (Harare: SAPES Trust, 1998), esp. ch. 6.

128. Alexander, 'The State, Agrarian Policy and Rural Politics in Zimbabwe', 184.

129. In addition to the reforms discussed above, Government of Zimbabwe (GOZ), Customary Law and Primary Courts Act, 1981; GOZ, Communal Lands Act, 1982; Jocelyn Alexander, 'Chiefs and the State in Independent Zimbabwe', paper presented to the conference on Chieftaincy in Africa, St Antony's College, Oxford, 9 June 2001.

130. Pius S. Nyambara, 'The Politics of Land Acquisition and Struggles Over Land in the 'Communal' Areas of Zimbabwe: The Gokwe Region in the 1980s and 1990s', *Africa* 22.3 (2001), citing the Rukuni report.

131. Helmsing, 'Transforming rural local government', 103–4.

132. Blair Rutherford, *Working on the Margins: Black Workers, White Farmers in Postcolonial Zimbabwe* (Harare: Weaver, 2001), 52; Arild Schou, 'The Adaptation of Quasi-Citizens to Political and Social Marginality: Farm Workers in Zimbabwe', Forum for Development Studies no. 1, June 2000, 44; see also, GOZ. No 21 Local Authorities Election Laws Amendment Act, 1997; and for a discussion of the implications of the act: ZESN, 'Rural District Council Elections, Urban Council by Elections and Hurungwe by Election 2002 Report'.

133. Helmsing, 'Transforming rural local government'; Schou, 'The Adaptation of Quasi-Citizens', 47–8. An informant also reported that in Marondera a vocational college lecturer had been appointed as a special interest councillor to 'represent' farm-workers: personal communication, 1 September 2004.

134. For accounts of the Ulere Motor Transport System, which brought volunteer workers from Nyasaland and Zambia, see Steven C. Rubert, *A Most Promising Weed* (Ohio: Centre for International Studies, 1998), 30–41; and Peter Scott, 'Migrant Labour in Southern Rhodesia', *Geographical Review* 44.1 (1954), 29–48.

135. Rutherford, *Working on the Margins*, 211.

136. Cumming, 'Post-colonial urban residential change in Harare'; on 'block-busting' in Bulawayo, see Busani Mpofu, 'The struggles of an "undesirable" alien community in a white settler colony: the case of the Indian minority in Colonial Zimbabwe, with particular reference to the city of Bulawayo, c.1890–1963', unpublished MA thesis, University of Zimbabwe, 2005, 96–9.

137. Carole Rakodi, 'The production of housing in Harare, Zimbabwe', *Trialog* XX (1989), 7–13, cited in Lovemore Zinyama, 'The evolution of the spatial structure of Greater Harare'; see also Colleen Butcher, 'Urban Low-income Housing: a Case Study of the Epworth Settlement Upgrading Programme', in Zinyama, Tevera and Cumming, *Harare*, 66.

138. Diana Auret, *Urban Housing: a national crisis?* (Gweru: Mambo Press/CCJP, 1995), 16.

139. Miriam Grant, 'Movement Patterns and the Medium Sized City', *Habitat International* 19.3 (1995), 360.

140. Deborah Potts with C. C. Mutambirwa, 'High-density housing in Harare', *Third World Planning Review* 13 (1991), 2.

141. Potts with Mutambirwa, 'High-density housing', 7–10.

142. Auret, *Urban Housing*, 17; Potts with Mutambirwa, 'High-density housing'.

143. Potts with Mutambirwa, 'High-density housing', 10; see also Diana H. Patel, 'Government Policy and Squatter Settlements in Harare, Zimbabwe', in R. A. Obudho and Constance C. Mhlanga, eds, *Slum and Squatter Settlements in Sub-Saharan Africa* (New York: Praeger, 1988), 210.

144. Patel, 'Government Policy and Squatter Settlements', 210; see also Diana Patel, *Chirambahuyo* (Gweru: Mambo Press, 1983).

145. Patel, 'Government Policy and Squatter Settlements', 210.

146. Michael Bourdillon, *Poor, harassed, but very much alive: an account of the street people and their organization* (Gweru: Mambo Press, 1991).

147. Butcher, 'Urban Low-income Housing'.

148. N. Horrell, 'The potential growth of urban squatter settlements in the capital city of Zimbabwe', unpublished report, cited in David Drakakis-Smith, 'The changing economic role of women in the urbanization process', *International Migration Review* 18 (1984), 1284.

149. Lovemore Zinyama, 'The evolution of the spatial structure of Greater Harare', in Zinyama, Tevera and Cumming, eds, *Harare*, 25.

150. Potts with Mutambirwa, 'High-density housing', 21.

151. Deborah Potts, 'City life in Zimbabwe at a time of Fear and Loathing: urban planning, urban poverty and Operation Murambatsvina', in G. Myers and M. Murray, eds, *Cities in Contemporary Africa* (Basingstoke: Palgrave Macmillan, 2006).

152. David Drakakis-Smith, 'Strategies for Meeting Basic Food Needs in Harare', in Jonathan Baker and Poul Ove Pedersen, eds, *The Rural-Urban Interface in Africa* (Uppsala: NAI, 1992), 276.

153. Beacon Mbiba, *Urban Agriculture in Zimbabwe* (Aldershot: Avebury, 1995), 88–93; see also Carole Rakodi, *Harare* (Chichester: John Wiley, 1995), 171–3; and Beacon Mbiba, 'Institutional responses to uncontrolled urban cultivation in Harare: prohibitive or accommodative?' *Environment and Urbanization* 6.1 (1994).

154. *Herald*, 16 November 1992, 3, cited in Mbiba, *Urban Agriculture*, 92.

155. Mbiba, *Urban Agriculture*, 95; see also David Drakakis-Smith, Tanya Bowyer-Bower and Dan Tevera, 'Urban poverty and urban agriculture', *Habitat International* 19 (1995), 189–91.

156. Amin Kamete, 'Restrictive Control of Urban High-density Housing in Zimbabwe', *Housing, Theory and Society* 16 (1999), 143.

157. Nancy E. Horn, *Cultivating Customers: market women in Harare, Zimbabwe* (Boulder, CO: Lynne Rienner, 1994).

158. 'Ban on sadza to go nation-wide', *Herald*, 21 November 1983, 1; see also Rakodi, *Harare*, 72–3.

159. Naison D. Mutizwa-Mangiza, 'Urban Informal Transport Policy: the Case of Emergency Taxis in Harare', in Zinyama, Tevera and Cumming, *Harare*; see also Rakodi, *Harare*, 81.

160. 'Vagrancy swoop', *Herald*, 19 November 1983, 1.

161. Peggy Watson, *Determined to Act* (Harare: WAG, 1998).

162. 'Councils get go ahead to order urban clean up', *Herald*, 1 July 1986.

163. Brian Raftopoulos, *Problems of Research in a Post-colonial State: the Case of Zimbabwe* (Harare: ZIDS, 1988), 7.

164. Lloyd Sachikonye, quoted in Richard Saunders, 'Association and Civil Society in Zimbabwe', paper presented to the conference on the Historical Dimensions of Democracy and Human Rights in Zimbabwe, September 1996, 18.

165. Saunders, 'Association and Civil Society', 2.

166. 'New group to spearhead social change', *Herald*, 11 March 1982, 4; see also 'ZIDS—the herald of socialism', *Herald*, 3 April 1982, 7; and 'Stormy ZIDS Bill passage', *Herald*, 15 February 1984, 5.

167. T. V. Sathyamurthy, 'Moving Spirit', *Guardian* (UK), 17 September 1982.

168. Raftopoulos, *Problems of Research*, 21.

169. Raftopoulos, *Problems of Research*, 23.

170. Address by his Excellency the President, Cde R. G. Mugabe, on the Occasion of the Heroes Burial of Dr B. T. G. Chidzero and Heroes' Day Commemoration, National Heroes Acre, Harare, 12 August 2002.

171. David Moore, 'The Zimbabwean "organic intellectuals" in transition', *Journal of Southern African Studies* 15 (1988), 104.

172. Quoted in Richard Saunders 'Life in Space—the new politics of Zimbabwe', *Southern Africa Review of Books* (January/February 1993), 19.

173. Tengende, 'Workers, Students and the Struggles for Democracy', 194–5.

174. Angela Cheater, 'The University of Zimbabwe: University, National University, State University or Party University', *African Affairs* 90 (1991), 189–90.

175. Tengende, 'Workers, Students and the Struggles for Democracy', 235.

176. Ibid., 234.

177. Brian Wood, 'Trade Union Organisation and the Working Class', in Colin Stoneman, ed., *Zimbabwe's Prospects: issues of race, class, state and capital in Southern Africa* (London: Macmillan, 1988), 291.

178. See Richard Saunders, 'Striking Ahead: Industrial Action and Labour Movement Development', in Brian Raftopoulos and Lloyd Sachikonye, *Striking Back: The Labour Movement and the Post-colonial State in Zimbabwe 1980–2000* (Harare: Weaver, 2001), 135–42 for a discussion of the strikes of 1980–81 and the politics surrounding them.

179. Shadur and Schiphorst both emphasize how long-standing but non-ZANU unionists were sidelined and replaced by those with less formal unionist credentials: Mark Shadur, *Labour Relations in a Developing Country: a case study of Zimbabwe* (Aldershot: Avebury, 1994), 99–107; Freek Schiphorst, 'Strength and Weakness: the Rise of the Zimbabwe Congress of Trade Unions and the Development of Labour Relations, 1980–1995', PhD thesis, Leiden University, 2001, 61.

180. Abisha Kupfuma, ZCTU Secretary-General, cited in Schiphorst, 'Strength and Weakness', 67.

181. 'Workers told to unite', *Herald*, 27 January 1982, 2; 'Unite or be dis-owned, warns top ZCTU man', *Herald*, 29 January 1982, 11; 'Workers' unity is vital', *Herald*, 3 May 1982, 4; 'Clothing unions' merger "is valid"', *Herald*, 3 February 1982, 4.

182. Miles Larmer, 'The political role of the trade union movement in Zambia and Zimbabwe after independence', paper presented to Southern Africa History and Politics Seminar, Oxford, 22 January 2001.

183. Tengende, 'Workers, Students and the Struggles for Democracy', 257.

184. Schiphorst, 'Strength and Weakness', 81–6.

185. Richard Saunders, 'Trade Union Struggles for Autonomy and Democracy in Zimbabwe', unpublished MS.

186. Hallencreutz and Moyo, *Church and State*.

187. David Maxwell, 'The Church and Democratisation in Africa: the case of Zimbabwe', in Paul Gifford, ed., *The Christian Churches and the Democratization of Africa* (Leiden: Brill, 1995), 109.

188. 'Help us create socialism, PM tells Church', *Herald*, 1 May 1982, 1. Interestingly, however, this position was not held by all members of the government. Simba Mubako, then the Minister of Justice, suggested that '… any close alliance with any political ideology could lead the church into over-looking injustices perpetuated under that system … too close a relationship with the government brought the church into disrepute'. 'Church must fight injustice—Mubako', *Herald*, 9 August 1982, 1.

189. 'State policy gets bishops' blessing', *Herald*, 29 November 1982, 1.

190. 'Church leaders must respond to Government', *Herald*, 26 January 1981, 8.

191. 'Don't preach subversion, clergy told', *Herald*, 27 January 1982, 1.

192. 'We support the state, say churches', *Herald*, 29 January 1982, 11.

193. Per Nordlund, 'Organising the Political Agora: Domination and Democratisation in Zambia and Zimbabwe', PhD thesis, Uppsala University, 1996, 143.

194. Auret, *Reaching for Justice*, 137–8; personal communication, John Stewart, 15 August 2001.

195. 'Help us create socialism, PM tells Church', *Herald*, 1 May 1982, 1.

196. 'Churches urged to spread socialism', *Herald*, 2 March 1982, 4.

197. 'Stop lies from the pulpit—Muzenda', *Herald*, 10 March 1982, 7.

198. 'Church urged to help build socialism', *Herald*, 4 August 1982, 11.

199. 'Church battling to fulfil social role—Hatendi', *Herald*, 23 August 1982, 9.

200. Peter Hatendi, 'Celebrations which point towards unity', *Herald*, 21 April 1982, 4.

201. 'Church probes charge by president', *Herald*, 10 November 1981, 3; '[Editorial] Visionary dilemma', *Herald*, 10 November 1981, 6; '[Letter

to the editor] WCC charges must get serious consideration', *Herald*, 16 November 1981, 8; Carl Hallencreutz, 'Ecumenical Challenges in Independent Zimbabwe', in Hallencreutz and Moyo, *Church and State*, 267.

202. 'Church probes charge by president', *Herald*, 10 November 1981, 3.

203. Carl Hallencreutz, 'Church and State in Zimbabwe and South Africa', in Carl F. Hallencreutz and Mai Palmberg, eds. *Religion and Politics in Southern Africa* (Uppsala: Scandinavian Institute of African Studies, 1991), 159–65.

204. Hallencreutz, 'Ecumenical Challenges', 275.

205. See for example '200 sect children immunised', *Herald*, 17 September 1985, 5; Donald Mackay and Plaxedes Motsi, 'Some contemporary trends in Independent Churches in Zimbabwe: the cases of ZCC and AACJM', in Hallencreutz and Moyo, *Church and State*, 369–70; also Maxwell, 'The church and democratization in Africa', 124.

206. 'Development of Korsten village on the cards', *Herald*, 15 March 1990, 1.

207. See for example, 'Why the outcry over curfew, premier asks Church', *Herald*, 18 April 1984, 1; '[Editorial] Church and State', *Herald*, 19 April 1984, 6; 'Stop the gossip, President tells Church', *Herald*, 8 May 1984, 1; 'Church accused of double standards', *Herald*, 20 February 1986, 1.

208. Cited in N. C. G. Mathema, *Newspapers in Zimbabwe* (Lusaka: Multimedia Zambia, 2001), 7–8.

209. Richard Saunders, 'Information in the Interregnum: The Press, State and Civil Society in Struggles for Hegemony, Zimbabwe 1980–1990', unpublished PhD thesis, Carleton University, 1992, 112.

210. Saunders, 'Information in the Interregnum', 248–9. See also Stanford Mukasa's account of this period, based on his personal experience as a journalist in the 1980s: 'Press and Politics in Zimbabwe', *African Studies Quarterly* 7.1–2 (2003).

211. Saunders, 'Information in the Interregnum', 250–53; see also Jan Raath, 'Nkomo Associate ousted from editorship', *Times* (UK), 1 August 1985.

212. 'Protest at reporter's expulsion', *Times* (UK), 8 September 1986.

213. The original story is 'Mass murder in Matabeleland: the evidence', *Sunday Times* (UK), 8 April 1984; Peter Godwin's account of this period is in his autobiography, *Mukiwa: a white boy in Africa* (London: Macmillan, 1996).

214. Jan Raath, 'Zimbabwe rejects UK "propaganda"', *Times* (UK), 20 July 1984; see also 'Harare says reports disproved', *Times* (UK), 12 May 1984; and 'Papers accused', *Times* (UK), 16 June 1984.

215. Saunders, 'Information in the Interregnum', 353.

216. Saunders, 'Information in the Interregnum', 357–8; on the role of Geoff

Nyarota and the *Chronicle* in exposing Willowgate, see Saunders, 'Information in the Interregnum', 418, 420.

217. 'Gazette in takeover by businessmen', *Herald*, 29 September 1989, 1; Saunders, 'Information in the Interregnum', 357–8.

218. Colin Stoneman and Lionel Cliffe, *Zimbabwe: Politics, Economics and Society* (London: Pinter, 1989), 79.

219. Christine Sylvester, 'Zimbabwe's 1985 Elections: a Search for National Mythology', *Journal of Modern African Studies* 24.1 (1986), 246.

220. See, for instance, Tony Rich, 'Legacies of the past? The results of the 1980 election in Midlands province, Zimbabwe', *Africa* 52 (1982), esp. 50–52; and the Report of the Election Commissioner, Sir John Boynton MC, 'Southern Rhodesia Independence Elections 1980' (Salisbury, March 1980) 12–13.

221. 'ZAPU offices gutted: 32 hurt in demos', *Herald*, 19 June 1984, 1; 'Mass demos in Midlands claim two lives', *Herald*, 21 June 1984, 1.

222. 'ZAPU ban extended to 2nd Province', *Herald*, 20 June 1984, 1.

223. Jan Raath, 'Bloody weekend for Zimbabwe', *Times* (UK), 26 February 1985; 'Zimbabwe violence kills 10', *Guardian* (UK), 26 February 1985; Andrew Meldrum, 'Mugabe men shot "muzorewa officials"', *Guardian* (UK), 27 February 1985; Glenn Frankel, '5 Muzorewa backers shot in Zimbabwe', *Washington Post*, 27 February 1985.

224. For a more detailed account of the election, see Masipula Sithole, 'The general elections 1979–1985', in Ibbo Mandaza, ed., *The Political Economy of Transition, 1980–1986* (Dakar: CODESRIA, 1986).

225. Tandeka Nkiwane, 'Opposition Politics in Zimbabwe: the Struggle within the Struggle', in Abdebayo Olukoshi, *The Politics of Opposition in Africa* (Uppsala: Nordiska Afrikainstitutet, 1998), 92.

226. Kriger, *Zimbabwe's Guerrilla War*, 217–18.

227. Jocelyn Alexander, 'The State, Agrarian Policy and Rural Politics in Zimbabwe: Case Studies of Insiza and Chimanimani Districts, 1940–1990', unpublished DPhil thesis, University of Oxford, 1993, 181.

228. Makumbe, *Democracy and Development in Zimbabwe*, 22.

229. Makumbe, *Democracy and Development*, 76.

230. Ronald Weitzer, 'In Search of Regime Security: Zimbabwe since Independence', *Journal of Modern African Studies*, 22.4 (December 1984), 557.

4. THE POLITICS OF DURABILITY (1987–1997)

1. Chenjerai Hove, 'Zimbabwe's Lost Visions', *Palaver Finish* (Harare: Weaver, 2002), 22.

2. Richard Saunders, 'Trade Union Struggles for Autonomy and Democracy

in Zimbabwe', unpublished MS; Richard Saunders, 'Association and Civil Society in Zimbabwe', paper presented to the conference on the Historical Dimensions of Democracy and Human Rights in Zimbabwe, September 1996; John Makumbe, *Democracy and Development in Zimbabwe: Constraints of Decentralisation* (Harare: SAPES Trust, 1998); Masipula Sithole, 'Zimbabwe's Eroding Authoritarianism', *Journal of Democracy* 8.1 (1997), 127–41.

3. Padraig Carmody and Scott Taylor, 'Industry and the Urban Sector in Zimbabwe's Political Economy', *African Studies Quarterly* 7.2–3 (2003).

4. Naison D. Mutizwa-Mangiza, 'Urban Informal Transport Policy: the Case of Emergency Taxis in Harare', in Lovemore Zinyama, Daniel Tevera and Sioux Cumming, eds, *Harare: the Growth and Problems of the City* (Harare: University of Zimbabwe Publications, 1993), 97–108.

5. Patrick Bond, *Uneven Zimbabwe: A Study of Finance, Development, and Underdevelopment* (Trenton, NJ: Africa World Press, 1998).

6. Hevina Dashwood, *Zimbabwe: the Political Economy of Transition* (Toronto: University of Toronto Press, 2000), 107.

7. Ibid., 4.

8. Ibid., 110.

9. Deborah Potts with Chris Mutambirwa, '"Basics are not a luxury": perceptions of structural adjustment's impact on rural and urban areas in Zimbabwe', *Environment and Urbanization* 10.1 (1998), 55–75.

10. 'Housing crisis deepens as money runs out', *Insider*, May 1992.

11. Carmody and Taylor, 'Industry and the Urban Sector'.

12. A. S. Mlambo, *The Economic Structural Adjustment Programme: The Case of Zimbabwe, 1990–1995* (Harare: University of Zimbabwe, 1997); Nazneen Kanji and Niki Jazdowska, 'Structural Adjustment and Women in Zimbabwe', *Review of African Political Economy* 56 (1993), 11–26.

13. 'Five thousand students in Mashonaland West stay in "bush-boarding" facilities', *Herald*, 14 July 1999, 6.

14. Helen Jackson, *AIDS action now: information, prevention and support in Zimbabwe* (Harare: AIDS Counselling Trust, 1988), 114–16; 'Council to combat Aids', *Herald*, 7 October 1989, 5.

15. UNAIDS/WHO, *Zimbabwe Epidemiological Fact Sheet* (UNAIDS/WHO, 2000), 3.

16. See discussions in Jeffrey Herbst, *State Politics in Zimbabwe* (Harare: University of Zimbabwe Publications, 1991), 135; Tor Skålnes, *The Politics of Economic Reform in Zimbabwe: continuity and change in development* (Basingstoke: Macmillan, 1995), 79.

17. 'If Strive was Leo?', *Independent*, 14 February 1997. On indigenization more broadly, see also Brian Raftopoulos and Sam Moyo, 'The Politics of Indigenisation in Zimbabwe', *East African Social Science Review* XI. 2 (1995),

17–32; and Scott Taylor, 'Race, Class and Neopatrimonialism in Zimbabwe', in Richard Joseph, ed., *State, Conflict and Democracy in Africa* (Boulder, CO: Lynne Rienner, 1999).

18. 'Hazy images shroud proposed Harare terminal', *Independent*, 7 March 1997; 'Airport forex negotiations underway', *Independent*, 20 September 1996; Iden Wetherell, 'Zimbabwe airport furore', *Mail & Guardian*, 30 May 1997.

19. 'Telecel project goes ahead despite tender suspension', *Independent*, 4 April 1997; Lewis Machipisa, 'Cellular man Strive gets his day in court', *Mail & Guardian*, 23 September 1997.

20. Vincent Kahiya, 'Ministers cash in on housing fraud', *Independent*, 25 April 1997, 1–2; 'VIPS in "luxury homes" scandal', *Horizon*, July 1997, 14–15.

21. GOZ, Report of the Commission of Inquiry into the Administration of the War Victims Compensation Act (Chapter 11.16), May 1998.

22. 'Magistrate remands Hunzvi in Custody', *Herald*, 28 November 1998; 'Hunzvi's relatives appear in court', *Herald*, 1 December 1998; 'Hunzvi bail application ruling set for Monday', *Herald*, 12 December 1998; 'High Court dismisses Hunzvi's bail application', *Herald*, 15 December 1998; 'Hunzvi's last ditch bail bid dismissed', *Herald*, 19 December 1998; 'Hunzvi refused bail for the fourth time', *Herald*, 31 December 1998; Tonderai Katswara, 'Court grants Hunzvi $50,000 bail, set other conditions', *Herald*, 16 January 1999; Dumisani Ndlela, 'Amnesty for war fund looters?', *Independent*, 19 March 1999; 'Hunzvi's trial postponed indefinitely', *Daily News*, 20 July 1999, 5.

23. Graham Tipple, 'Transformations in Zimbabwe', unpublished MS (1999), 2.

24. Diana Auret, *Urban Housing: a national crisis?* (Gweru: Mambo/CCJP, 1995), 39.

25. 'Backyard shacks spring up in Mutoko, Murehwa', *Herald*, 13 June 1990, 2.

26. Minister Chikowore in address to parliament, *Herald*, 4 August 1994, cited in Auret, *Urban Housing*, 1.

27. 'Presentation by Minister J. L. Nkomo'; 'Discussion with the Minister'; Chenjerai Chisaka and Regis Mtutu, 'Housing for all: between a dream and the reality', in the special issue on Housing and Shelter, *Social Change and Development* 47 (May 1999), 3–6 and 15–16.

28. Carole Rakodi with Penny Withers, *Land, Housing and Urban Development in Zimbabwe: markets and policy in Harare and Gweru*, Final Report on ESCOR Project R4468 (Cardiff: University of Wales, 1993), 226, citing the *Herald*, 22 February 1993.

29. This term was coined by Graham Tipple: see Ann Schlyter, *Multi-habitation: urban housing and everyday life in Chitungwiza, Zimbabwe* (Uppsala: Nordiska Afrikainstitutet, 2003), 7.

30. *Sunday Mail*, 23 October 1994, cited in Auret, *Urban Housing*, 1.
31. See for instance Michael Bourdillon, *Poor, harassed, but very much alive: an account of the street people and their organization* (Gweru: Mambo Press, 1991), 90–97; 'State to house street children', *Daily Gazette*, 22 June 1993; 'Streetkids rounded up', *Daily Gazette*, 3 November 1994; 'New home for streetkids', *Sunday Mail*, 15 January 1995; 'ZimRights condemns rounding up of squatters', *Herald*, 20 February 1997, 8.
32. In July 1991 I was taken to 'view' the sites at Mbare, Porta Farm and Epworth; see also 'Porta Farm Disaster', *Insider*, December 1991; Auret, *Urban Housing*, 71; Carole Rakodi, *Harare* (Chichester: John Wiley, 1995), 74–6.
33. Rakodi, *Harare*, 75; Charles Rukuni's *Insider* also notes that 'Considerable preparation has been done secretly, with piped water laid on, roads constructed and shelters of poles, hessian sacks and black plastic built': 'Porta Farm Disaster', *Insider*, December 1991.
34. GOZ, Minister of Local Government, Rural and Urban Development, 'Squatter Policy', Local authority circular no. 160, 6 October 1992.
35. Michael Auret, *Churu Farm: A chronicle of despair* (CCJP, 1994).
36. Auret, *Churu Farm*, 14–15.
37. 'ZimRights complains of fate of families', *Herald*, 15 December 1994.
38. Amin Kamete, 'Transit or concentration camps? Revisiting state responses to urban homelessness in Harare, Zimbabwe', unpublished paper, no date, 5; see also 'City Fathers cut off Porta Farm lifeblood in squatter war', *Horizon*, October 1995, 15.
39. Joan Brickhill, 'Investigating the Impact of Urban Agriculture in Harare, Zimbabwe', IDRC, 15 May 1998.
40. For data on this from Harare, see T. C. Mbara and D. A. C. Maunder, 'The initial effects of introducing commuter omnibus services in Harare, Zimbabwe', Transport Research Library, 1996.
41. 'Commuters relive '80s public transport blues', *Herald*, 15 February 1999, 11.
42. Nancy E. Horn, *Cultivating Customers: market women in Harare, Zimbabwe* (Boulder, CO: Lynne Rienner, 1994), 24, 64. See also 'Councillors be serious', *Insider*, June 1992.
43. Amin Kamete, 'Restrictive Control of Urban High-density Housing in Zimbabwe', *Housing, Theory and Society* 16 (1999), 143.
44. Kamete, 'Restrictive Control', 143–4.
45. *Herald* 1998, cited in Kamete, 'Restrictive Control', 144.
46. A. Chimhowu, D. Tevera, N. Chimbetete, S. Gandure, 'Urban Solid Waste Management in Zimbabwe', in D. Conyers, G. Matovu, D. Tevera, eds, *The Challenges and New Innovations in Urban Solid Waste Management: Issues and Policy Options* (Harare: MDP, 2002), 20.

47. Interview, Simon Pitt, former independent councillor, Harare, 21 November 2005.
48. Amin Kamete argues that the urban areas were 'ruling party strongholds' until 2000, but he ignores the campaigns contested by independent candidates. Amin Kamete, 'The Rebels Within: Urban Zimbabwe in the Post-Election Period', in Henning Melber, ed., *Zimbabwe's Presidential Elections 2002* (Uppsala: Nordiska Africainstitutet, 2002), 31–47.
49. Interviews, November 2005, Residents Association Members.
50. Andrew Rusinga, 'Government under pressure to review economic reforms', *Africa Information Afrique*, 20 October 1993.
51. Watson Daika, 'Consumers suffering without food subsidies', *Africa Information Afrique*, 18 August 1993.
52. '1993: Year of the Capitalist', *Horizon*, December 1993, 21.
53. 'State orders a blackout on strike', *MISA*, 28 August 1996; 'Civil servants strike to continue', *Independent*, 30 August 1996; 'Civil Servant strike costs $120 million', *Independent*, 30 August 1996; John Vekris, 'Chronicle of two strikes', *Social Change and Development*, February 1997, 3–7, 29.
54. 'Government slated for its handling of strike', *Independent*, 15 November 1996; Vekris, 'Chronicle of two strikes', 3–7, 29.
55. 'Strikes spread countrywide', *Independent*, 8 November 1996; Vekris, 'Chronicle of two strikes', 3–7, 29.
56. 'General Strike in Zimbabwe', *ICFTU*, 12 November 1996; Vekris, 'Chronicle of two strikes', 3–7, 29.
57. 'Hospitals turn away patients', *Independent*, 10 January 1997; Vekris, 'Chronicle of two strikes' 29; 'Nurses demand reinstatement', *Standard*, 31 October 1999; 'Dismissed nurses, doctors demand five years pay', *Financial Gazette*, 20 April 2001.
58. Research notes, July 1997; 'More strikes ahead?', *Standard*, 13 July 1997, 1.
59. 'ZCTU bills strike the most successful ever', *Financial Gazette*, 11 December 1997; Never Gadaga, 'Rage at police attacks in Zimbabwe', *Mail & Guardian*, 11 December 1997; Chris McGreal, 'Zimbabwe's "unholy alliance": black workers, white farmers', *Mail & Guardian*, 17 December 1997.
60. Zimbabwe Human Rights NGO Forum, 'A Consolidated Report on the Food Riots', 19–23 January 1998.
61. Norbert Tengende, 'Workers, Students and the Struggles for Democracy: State-Civil Society Relations in Zimbabwe', unpublished PhD thesis, Roskilde University, 1994, 446; see also 'War veterans' constitution', *Herald*, 1 May 1989, 3.
62. Erin McCandless, 'Rights or Redistribution … and other strategic dilemmas facing Zimbabwean Social Movements', PhD dissertation, American University in Washington, 2005, ch. 5.

63. 'Meetings with war vets turn nasty', *Herald*, 21 July 1997, 1, 8, 11; 'Ex-combatants loot ZANU(PF) headquarters', *Herald*, 14 August 1997, 1, 9; 'War veterans threaten to seize white-owned land', *Independent*, 29 August 1997, 12.

64. 'Meetings with war vets turn nasty', *Herald*, 'Angry Zimbabwean War Veterans Chase Ministers', *PANA*, 20 July 1997.

65. Although there are indications that at least one leader of the riots was detained and charged. 'War vet leader released from police custody', *PANA*, 4 January 1998; Zvakanyorwa Wilbert Sadomba, *War Veterans in Zimbabwe's Revolution: Challenging Neo-Colonialism and Settler and International Capital* (Woodbridge: Boydell & Brewer, 2011).

66. McCandless, 'Rights or Redistribution', ch. 5.

67. Iden Wetherell, 'Mugabe and the sudden rebellion', *Mail & Guardian*, 12 December 1997; Lewis Machipisa, 'Zim's MPs flex muscles over higher taxes', *Mail & Guardian*, 3 December 1997.

68. 'Discontent emerging over Zimbabwe's veteran's levy', *PANA*, 30 November 1997.

69. 'Proposed Levy draws unprecedented fire', *Financial Gazette*, 4 December 1997.

70. 'Political tension hovers over Heroes' Day', *Financial Gazette*, 7 August 1997; 'Fears rise about youths disrupting Zimbabwe Day', *PANA*, 15 April 1998; 'Pressure groups attack govt over Unity Day', *Independent*, 24 December 1998; Daniel Manyandure, 'The Flame has Died', *Standard*, 18 April 1999; 'Is the Unity accord still alive?', *Standard*, 17 December 2000.

71. 'Bob Mugabe's wailers silenced', *Standard*, 25 March 2001; Jan Raath, 'Mugabe lost in love while Zimbabwe smoulders', *Mail & Guardian*, 2 November 1996; 'New globetrotting record', *Standard*, 15 October 2000; 'Mugabe's foreign trips gobble $10 billion', *Independent*, 21 January 2000; Editorial cartoon, *Independent*, 7 November 1997; Basildon Peta, 'Grace Mugabe charters Boeing 737 for SA trip', *Independent*, 8 August 1997, 1.

72. Raftopoulos and Moyo, 'Politics of Indigenisation in Zimbabwe', 23–4.

73. Skålnes, *Politics of Economic Reform*, 101.

74. Brian Raftopoulos, 'The State, NGOs, and Democratization', in Sam Moyo, John Makumbe and Brian Raftopoulos, *NGOs, the State and Politics in Zimbabwe* (Harare: SAPES Trust, 2000).

75. For example, 'National Strike cripples economy for second day', SAPA-AFP, 4 March 1998; Andrew Meldrum, 'Zimbabwe strikers ignore Mugabe threat', *Guardian* (UK), 4 March 1998, 12.

76. Ruth Weiss, *Zimbabwe and the New Elite* (London: I. B. Tauris, 1994), 183; see also Brian Raftopoulos, *Race and Nationalism in a Post-Colonial State* (Harare: SAPES Trust, 1996), 87.

77. Brian Raftopoulos, 'Nationalism, Violence and Politics: an outline of an overview of Zimbabwean politics', speaking at the Britain–Zimbabwe Society Research Day, Oxford, 3 June 2000.

78. 'Leaders told to rise above village politics', *Herald*, 24 December 1998.

79. C. Sylvester, 'Unities and disunities in Zimbabwe's 1990 election', *Journal of Modern African Studies* 28.3 (1990), 388.

80. 'ZANU(PF) suspends independents: "Let's unite and organise to win"', *Herald*, 18 March 1995, 1, 5; 'Problems can be solved through unity', *Herald*, 21 July 1999.

81. 'Kangai warns people of Chipinge … Vote ZANU(PF) or there will be no development', *Herald*, 25 March 1995, 5.

82. ZCC, *ZCC Annual report 1994–1995*, 5 July 1995, 60; 'Resign or lose posts, ZAPU councillors told', *Herald*, 18 September 1985, 3, as cited in Jocelyn Alexander, 'The State, Agrarian Policy and Rural Politics in Zimbabwe: Case Studies of Insiza and Chimanimani Districts, 1940–1990', unpublished DPhil thesis, University of Oxford, 1993, 294.

83. 'Reconciliation policy may be revisited: President', *Sunday Mail*, 28 February 1999. This remark seems particularly ominous when compared with Mugabe's pre-Gukurahundi remarks that Zimbabwe must 'revise its policy of national reconciliation'. Joseph Hanlon, 'Mugabe warns of a purge of opponents', *Guardian* (UK), 24 December 1981.

84. 'Party to ensure that Unity day celebrations take place countrywide', *Herald*, 23 December 1998; 'Provinces name changes: too little, too late', *Standard*, 9 November 1997; 'President calls on Party leaders to end factionalism', *Sunday Mail*, 13 December 1998.

85. ZCC, *ZCC Annual report 1994–1995*, 5 July 1995, 60–64.

86. United Parties, *Manifesto* (n.p., n.d.), 2.

87. Stephen Ndlovu and Stanley Gama, 'Dongo launches political party', *Sunday Mail*, 20 December 1998.

88. Jocelyn Alexander, 'State, Peasantry and Resettlement in Zimbabwe', *Review of African Political Economy* 21.61 (1994), 338.

89. 'Mugabe backs down to western demands for legal land reform', *SAPA*, 3 March 1998.

90. Robin Palmer, 'Mugabe's land grab in regional perspective', paper presented to the Conference on Land Reform in Zimbabwe—the Way Forward, SOAS, London, 11 March 1998.

91. Andrew Rusinga, 'Land redistribution threatens reconciliation', *AIA*, 15 October 1993.

92. Jonathan Moyo, *Voting for Democracy: Electoral Politics in Zimbabwe* (Harare: University of Zimbabwe, 1992), 149.

93. John Makumbe and Daniel Compagnon, *Behind the Smokescreen: The Politics of Zimbabwe's 1995 General Elections* (Harare: University of Zimbabwe Publications, 2000), 220.

94. Moyo, *Voting for Democracy*, 147.

95. 'Commission now better equipped to supervise poll', *Herald*, 27 March 1995.

96. 'ESC Sworn in', *Herald*, 7 July 1994; 'Political parties lambast poll team', *Daily Gazette*, 8 July 1994.

97. Makumbe and Compagnon, *Behind the Smokescreen*, 285.

98. Maxie Matavaire, 'Elections free, not fair', *Sunday Gazette*, 23 April 1995; Ramson Muzondo, '1995 elections unfair', *Sunday Gazette*, 13 August 1995; 'Election was unfair: ZCC', *Herald*, 21 August 1995; and 'State Press snaps at watchdog's "unfair poll" verdict', *Horizon*, July 1995, 9.

99. Interview, Fidelis Mhashu, 17 June 1997.

100. Research notes, Supreme Court, 21 July 1997.

101. See for example the debate on ex-combatant teachers in Parliamentary Debates, 8 and 9 May 1991, and the extensive coverage in the *Herald*: 'Spotlight on pay for ex-combatant teachers', *Herald*, 8 May 1991, 5; 'MPs urge fair deal for teachers', *Herald*, 10 May 1991, 1; 'MPs now debate with supporting documentary evidence', *Herald*, 12 May 1991, 7.

102. 'Gara scolds mum MPs', *Financial Gazette*, 22 March 1991, W3; Barnabas Thondhlana, 'MPs call for better communication with government', *Zimbabwe Independent*, 5 September 1997, 11.

103. 'School fees: the MPs may say no, chef!', *Financial Gazette*, 22 March 1991, W9; 'MPs in no mood to back Chung on school fees', *Herald*, 22 November 1991, 1; 'Backbench MPs' stand on new school fees disputed', *Herald*, 28 November 1991, 1.

104. 'MPs block passage of Sports Bill', *Herald*, 25 April 1991, 1; 'Kwidini runs into barrage of queries on Sports Bill', *Herald*, 26 April 1991, 1; Parliamentary Debates, 7 May 1991, 9 May 1991; 'MPs now debate with supporting documentary evidence', *Herald*, 12 May 1991, 7.

105. Jimu Simbwi, 'To Cde President with Love', *Moto*, 120, January 1993, 5.

106. 'MPs again refuse to pass governors pay', *Herald*, 3 October 1992, 5; 'MPs vote for governors' salaries', *Herald*, 8 October 1992, 1, 9.

107. See for example 'MPs defy government over airport deal', *Financial Gazette*, 22 May 1997, 1, 2; Barnabas Thondhlana, 'Government to get tough with MPs over controversial airport funding', *Independent*, 23 May 1997, 3; Francis Murape, 'Mugabe's Winter of Discontent', *Mail & Guardian*, 13 June 1997, 10; Barnabas Thondhlana, 'Government defies parliament over airport', *Standard*, 27 July 1997, 1.

108. 'Another attempt to short-circuit parliament', *Standard*, 27 July 1997, 6; 'Yet another stand-off in Parliament?', *Standard*, 10 August 1997, 9.

109. Barnabas Thondhlana, 'MPs call for better communication with government', *Independent*, 5 September 1997, 11.

110. 'Backbenchers break ranks and vote with "indis"', *Horizon*, July 1997, 6.

111. 'Parliament moves to break links with colonial dressing', *Daily News*, 22 July 1999.

112. 'Era of openness at full tide', *Standard*, 11 May 1997, 6; 'Parliamentary reform panel comes to Harare', *Financial Gazette*, 20 November 1997.

113. Welshman Ncube, 'Controlling Public Power: the role of the constitution and the legislature', *Legal Forum*, 9 August 1997, 20.

114. 'MPs shed culture of fear', *Horizon*, July 1997, 6–8.

115. See 'Fired: but is Mavhaire really alone?', *Insider*, April 1998; 'Who is Dzikamayi Mavhaire?', *Insider*, April 1998.

116. For an early discussion of some key cases in the 1980s, see Richard Sklar, 'Reds and Rights: Zimbabwe's Experiment', in Dov Ronen, ed., *Democracy and Pluralism in Africa* (Boulder, CO: Lynne Rienner, 1986). On parliamentary resistance to judicial autonomy, see 'Supreme Court judges hit back at Mutasa over Smith ruling', *Herald*, 10 November 1989, 1; and 'Cabinet backs court in Smith's pay row', *Herald*, 22 November 1989, 1.

117. Adrian de Bourbon, 'Are magistrates independent?', *Legal Forum*, 1 December 1989, 7.

118. Geoff Feltoe, 'Deciding not to decide: case note on the case of *Holland & Ors v the Minister of Public Service, Labour and Social Welfare*, S-15–97', *Legal Forum*, 43–5.

119. On the executive's use of legislative power to reverse judicial decisions, see *inter alia* Welshman Ncube, 'Controlling public power: the role of the constitution and the legislature', *Legal Forum*, 9, 3 (1997), esp. 18–20; and Karla Saller, *The Judicial Institution in Zimbabwe* (Cape Town: Siber Ink, 2004), 2–4.

120. Jocelyn Alexander, 'Chiefs and the State in Independent Zimbabwe', paper presented to Conference on Chieftaincy in Africa, St Antony's College, Oxford, 9 June 2001, 10.

121. GOZ, Traditional Leaders Act, 1998.

122. Alexander, 'Chiefs and the State in Independent Zimbabwe', 12.

123. For example, interviews with Cont Mhlanga, Amakhosi Theatre Productions, 26 September 1995; and with Auret, CCJP, 14 September 1995; similar observations recorded by Tengende, 'Workers, Students and the Struggles for Democracy', 294–5; see also Welshman Ncube, 'The Post-unity Period: Development, Benefits and Problems', in Canaan Banana, ed., *Turmoil and Tenacity: Zimbabwe 1890–1990* (Harare: College Press, 1989), 309.

124. See for instance the collection of essays in Ibbo Mandaza and Lloyd Sachikonye, eds, *The One Party State and Democracy: the Zimbabwe Debate* (Harare: SAPES Trust, 1991).

125. See for instance Charles Samupindi, 'One party system has failed in

Africa', *Herald*, 26 June 1990, 4; Charles Samupindi, 'The one party state and some economic effects', *Herald*, 27 June 1990, 8.

126. 'No one-party state by law—President', *Herald*, 28 September 1990, 1; 'No move on one-party issue', *Herald*, 3 October 1990, 1.

127. Ncube's discussion of these claims and counter-claims is instructive. Welshman Ncube, 'The Post-unity Period', 320–24.

128. Sylvester, 'Unities and disunities', 386; see also '[Editorial] Let us make sure we remain a united nation', *Herald*, 22 December 1989, 10; 'Democracy boosted by unity—President', *Herald*, 1 January 1990, 1; ZANU(PF) election manifesto reprinted in the *Herald*, 5 March 1990, 2–3; also, adverts throughout March 1990, including 'ZANU(PF) Harare Province Unity gave us victory', advertising Nelson Mandela's attendance at an election rally, *Herald*, 3 March 1990, 8. Another Harare province rally advert concluded in large print: 'Let us all remain united! Let us all prepare ourselves for the new decade of unity, peace and development by voting ZANU(PF) ... Vote ZANU(PF) for Unity, Peace and Development!' *Herald*, 24 March 1990, 3.

129. 'Farmers, traders deny backing ZUM', *Herald*, 9 March 1990, 1; 'ZUM sees nothing wrong in getting aid from anyone', *Herald*, 12 March 1990, 1.

130. 'General Election a real test for unity—President', *Herald*, 17 March 1990, 1, 5.

131. 'Tekere plotting coup', *Herald*, 19 March 1990, 1.

132. 'Farmers, traders deny backing ZUM', *Herald*; 'Farm leaders and business back president and party', *Herald*, 16 March 1990, 1, 7.

133. 'Farm leaders and business back president and party'.

134. Sylvester, 'Unities and disunities', 376.

135. Moyo, *Voting for Democracy*, 77–8.

136. 'Magoche faction launches democratic party, *Sunday Mail*, 29 September 1991, 1; 'ZUM announces new executive', *Herald*, 30 October 1991, 5; 'Who is who in ZUM', *Sunday Mail*, 10 November 1991, 1.

137. *Forum Party of Zimbabwe & ORS* v. *Minister of Local Government*, Judgement No. S-129–97 ZLR 1997 (2); 'Supreme Court dismisses appeal by Forum Party', *Herald*, 15 August 1997; Tandeka Nkiwane, 'Opposition Politics in Zimbabwe: the struggle within the struggle', in Adebayo Olukoshi, ed., *The Politics of Opposition in Africa* (Uppsala: Nordiska Afrikainstitutet, 1998), 103.

138. 'Sithole refused trial date in plot to kill Mugabe', SAPA-AFP, 1 June 1996.

139. 'Sithole says he is innocent of treason charges', *Independent*, 27 June 1997, 1.

140. See for instance Sam Moyo, *The Land Question in Zimbabwe* (Harare:

SAPES Trust, 1995), 257; 'Churu farm: the land blues continue', *SAPEM* 7.1 (October 1993), 9–11.

141. Interview, Isaac Manyemba, Information Secretary, UP, 16 June 1997.

142. Research notes, Supreme Court, 30 July 1997; *United Party* v. *The Minister of Justice, Legal and Parliamentary Affairs*, ZLR 1997 (2) 254, Judgement no. SC 139–97, 30 July and 5 September 1997; 'Fifteen-seat threshhold for public funding "unconstitutional"', *Herald*, 6 September 1997, 1, 3.

143. *Dongo* v. *Mwashita & ORS*, Judgement no. HH-106–95, ZLR 1995 (2) 228 (H), 13 & 27 July and 10 & 30 August 1995. Interview, Margaret Dongo, ZUD, 17 June 1997.

144. Interview, Margaret Dongo, ZUD, 17 June 1997; interview, Kempton Makamure, ZUD, 16 June 1997.

145. Research notes, Supreme Court of Zimbabwe, 21 July 1997; interview, Priscilla Misihairambwi, 18 June 1997; 'Court rules Misihairabwi had right to contest poll', *Herald*, 8 August 1997, 1, 17.

146. *Fidelis George Mhashu* v. *Tichakunda Chiroodza & Chitungwiza Town Council & Andrew Jiri & ZANU (PF) & Minister of Local Government, Rural and Urban Development*, High Court Judgement HH 43–97; interview, Fidelis George Mhashu, 17 June 1997.

147. Tendayi Kumbula, 'Press freedom in Zimbabwe', in Festus Eribo and William Jong-Ebot, eds, *Press Freedom and Communications in Africa* (Trenton, NJ: Africa World Press, 1997), 179.

148. 'ZBC fires DJ for rapping police action', *Financial Gazette*, 18 December 1997.

149. Richard Saunders, 'The Press and Popular Organization in Zimbabwe', unpublished paper, 15.

150. Maurice Taonezi Vambe, 'Popular songs and social realities in post-independent Zimbabwe', *African Studies Review* 43.2 (2000), 78.

151. Ibid., 80–81.

152. Banning Eyre, *Playing with Fire: fear and self-censorship in Zimbabwean Music*, Freemuse.org (2001), 57.

153. Ezra Chitando, *Singing Culture: A study of gospel music in Zimbabwe* (Uppsala: Africainstitutet, 1992), 62.

154. Schiphorst's evidence suggests that some of the corruption scandals must have been stage-managed by ZANU(PF).

155. Freek Schiphorst, 'Strength and Weakness: the Rise of the Zimbabwe Congress of Trade Unions and the Development of Labour Relations, 1980–1995', PhD thesis, Leiden University, 2001, 124.

156. Albert Musarurwa, 'The labour movement and the one-party state', in Mandaza and Sachikonye, eds, *The One Party State and Democracy*, 152–3.

157. Tengende, 'Workers, Students and the Struggles for Democracy', 354.

158. 'ZCTU drops plans to be in parliament', *Herald*, 3 September 1990.
159. Tengende, 'Workers, Students and the Struggles for Democracy', 184.
160. Tengende, 'Workers, Students and the Struggles for Democracy', 437–8; Per Nordlund, 'Organising the Political Agora: Domination and Democratisation in Zambia and Zimbabwe', PhD thesis, Uppsala University, 1996, 184.
161. Nordlund, 'Organising the Political Agora', 184.
162. Ibid., 190.
163. *In re* Munuhumeso & Ors 1994 (1), ZLR 49 (S); Nordlund identifies this as '… the most substantial advancement of democratic rights in Zimbabwe since independence', in 'Organising the Political Agora', 200.
164. Schiphorst, 'Strength and Weakness', 121–2.
165. For a discussion of this shift, see Paris Yeros, 'Labour Struggles for Alternative Economics in Zimbabwe: Trade union nationalism and Internationalism in a Global Era', unpublished MS, 2000.
166. Nordlund, 'Organising the Political Agora', 200–201; Schiphorst, 'Strength and Weakness', 125–8.
167. 'Fire gutted offices', SAPA-AFP, 5 March 1998.
168. 'Tens of thousands defy Mugabe in Zimbabwe anti-government strike', SAPA-AFP, 3 March 1998; Andrew Meldrum, 'Zimbabwe strikers ignore Mugabe threat', *Guardian* (UK), 4 March 1998, 12.
169. 'Basildon Peta, 'Demo ban unconstitutional', *Independent*, 1 August 1997; 'ZCTU defies ban', *Independent*, 11 December 1998.
170. 'ZCTU man detained', *Herald*, 7 October 1989, 5.
171. Arthur Mutambara, 'The One Party State, Socialism and Democratic Struggles in Zimbabwe: A Student Perspective', in Mandaza and Sachikonye, eds, *The One Party State*, 140–41.
172. 'Closure of UZ long overdue', *Herald*, 6 October 1989, 6; 'University council backs closure of campus', *Herald*, 7 October 1989, 1.
173. Ngoni Chanakira, 'Academic Freedom in Higher Institutions of Learning in Zimbabwe', *SAPEM*, April 1991, 30–31; Angela Cheater, 'The University of Zimbabwe: University, National University, State University or Party University', *African Affairs* 90 (1991), 200–203.
174. L. M. Sachikonye, Democracy, Civil Society, and the State: *Social Movements in Southern Africa* (Harare: SAPES Trust), 151.
175. Tengende, 'Workers, Students and the Struggles for Democracy', 508.
176. Ibid., 517.
177. Discussions with SRC member (1996–7) and students (1996–9).
178. Bond, *Uneven Zimbabwe*, 153.
179. Tengende, 'Workers, Students and the Struggles for Democracy', 321.
180. Solmon Zwana, 'The Churches in Higher Education: Their Impact on

Contemporary Social Issues in Zimbabwe', paper presented at New College, University of Edinburgh, 8 June 2005.

181. Solomon Zwana, 'Struggles and Strides: Religion and Politics in the Evolution of Church Related Universities in Zimbabwe—the Case of Africa University', April 2005, 1–26.

182. Interview, Murombedzi Kuchera, ZCC Secretary General, 11 September 1995.

183. Diana Auret, *Reaching for Justice: The Catholic Commission for Justice and Peace Looks Back at the Past Twenty Years 1972–1992* (Gweru: Mambo Press, 1992), 225.

184. Interview, Mike Auret, former CCJP Chair and Director, 14 September 1995.

185. 'Churches, laymen from Zimbabwe and South Africa speak out', *Sunday Mail*, 20 August 1995, 1, 4; 'Demo against homos in city', *Sunday Mail*, 17 September 1995, 1.

186. 'Wedding costs taxpayers $3 million', *Independent*, 28 August 1996.

187. Interviews, Mike Auret, 14 September 1995, 28 September 1999; 'Auret snubbed bishops over strife report', *Sunday Mail*, 1 August 1999; 'Catholic Commission accused of politicking', *Sunday Mail*, 6 July 1997; CCJP/LRF, *Breaking the Silence: Building True Peace. A Report on the Disturbances in Matabeleland and the Midlands, 1980–1988* (Harare: CCJP/LRF, February 1997).

188. Dumisani Muleya, 'Auret resigns from CCJP', *Independent*, 2 July 1999.

189. David Maxwell, 'Catch the Cockerel Before Dawn: Pentecostalism and Politics in Post-Colonial Zimbabwe', *Africa* 70.2 (2000).

190. Maxwell, 'Catch the Cockerel'.

191. Dumisani Ndlela, 'ZANU (PF) seeks spiritual help', *Horizon*, July 1997, 11, 42.

192. Ibid., 11, 42.

193. Although in 1997 the Registrar General claimed that a law to 'reduce the number of churches' was being drafted: cited in Oskar Wermter, 'Police to enforce ten commandments? A look at Church and State in Zimbabwe', *Moto*, February 1998, 8. Students, labour and NGOs were the subject of 'pre-emptive' legislation throughout the 1990s in the form of the UZ Act (1990), the Labour Relations Act (1992) and the PVO Act (1995).

194. Sam Moyo, 'Towards an Understanding of Zimbabwean NGOs', paper prepared for the NANGO/MWENGO Self-Understanding Workshop, November 1995.

195. Interview, former volunteer with Street Kids in Production, 25 September 1995.

196. Parliamentary Debates, 16 August 1995, vol. 22 no. 29, 1643–4; interview, Director, NODED, 28 September 1995.

197. Cephas Chitsike, 'Government, NGOs head for show-down', *Sunday Mail*, 13 October 1991, 1, 7.

198. Peggy Watson, *Determined to act: the first 15 years of the Women's Action Group* (Harare: WAG, 1998).

199. Ibid., 13.

200. Ibid., 28.

201. Ibid., 35.

202. Ibid., 45.

203. Interview, Director, WAG, 6 October 1999.

204. Sam Moyo, *NGO Advocacy in Zimbabwe: Systematising an Old Function or Inventing a New Role?* (Harare: ZERO, 1992).

205. Interview, Trustee, WAG, 20 September 1999; other activists expressed similar opinions to me in informal conversations.

206. GOZ, Welfare Organisations Amendment Act, 1995.

207. 'New hope for ailing organisation', *Herald*, 3 September 1982, 7.

208. 'Learning never stops', *Herald*, 3 September 1982, 7.

209. Vincent Chikwari, 'Shamuyarira accused of bid to hijack women's projects', *Financial Gazette*, 30 November 1995; Diana Mitchell, 'Political leaders frustrating women's efforts', *Independent*, 11 October 1996, 23; various discussions with Sekai Holland, 1996–7 and 2013.

210. 'Sekai begins a new struggle', *Herald*, 6 November 1981, 12; and various discussions, 1996–7.

211. GOZ, Government Gazette Extraordinary, vol. LXXIII, no. 59A, 2 November 1995.

212. 'Team of Trustees to run association of women's clubs', *Sunday Mail*, 5 November 1995; 'Newly elected women's clubs council urged to be vigilant', *Sunday Mail*, 9 June 1996; 'Party Women take over NGO', *Independent*, 19 July 1996, 1; various discussions with Sekai Holland, 1996–7; personal communication from Jim Holland, 7 August 2001.

213. Applicants' Heads of Argument, Supreme Court of Zimbabwe, Case no. SC 333/96, 14 October 1996, 2.

214. Judgement no. SC 15/97, Civil Application no. 333/96, Supreme Court of Zimbabwe, 11 February 1997, 9; judgement also reported as *Holland & Ors* v. *Minister of the Public Service, Labour and Social Welfare*, Zimbabwe Law Reports, 1997 (1), 186–96.

215. Interview, Arnold Payne, 26 February 1997; Edgar Moyo, personal communication, 13 July 2005.

216. Derek Gunby, Roger Mpande and Alan Thomas, 'The campaign for water from the Zambezi for Bulawayo', in Alan Thomas, Susan Carr and David Humphreys, eds, *Environmental Policies and NGO Influence: land degradation and sustainable resources management in sub-Saharan Africa* (London: Routledge, 2001), 72–93.

217. Thomas D. Gwebu, 'Urban water scarcity management: civic vs state response in Bulawayo', *Habitat International*, 26 (2002), 430.
218. Interview, Staff member ZCC-JPR, 15 September 1995.
219. ZCC, Annual report 1994–1995, 5 July 1995, 56; research notes, senior church official, ZCC election briefing, 20 June 2000.
220. Research notes, Church–NGO Civic Education Project, Chitungwiza Workshop, 2–3 November 1996; see also Church–NGO Civic Education Project, Harare Province Workshop Report, 18–19 September 1996; Church–NGO Civic Education Project, Chitungwiza Workshop Report, 2–3 November 1996; Church-NGO Civic Education Project, Highfield Workshop Report, 9–10 November 1996.
221. 'NGO–Government Relations: Lessons from India; Challenges for Zimbabwe', 1990, session organized with the Commonwealth secretariat as part of the lead-up to the 1991 Commonwealth Heads of Government Meetings (CHOGM) and a follow-up NEPC and NANGO-sponsored workshop on 'Government of Zimbabwe and NGO Relations in Development' (1993); 'Work together to educate society president tells opposition, NGOs', *Herald*, 28 February 1997, 1.
222. 'NGOs to map out further strategies', *Herald*, 9 March 1991, 3; 'Director of Voice suspended', *Herald*, 17 June 1990; 'Former director awarded full pay and benefits', *Herald*, 26 April 1991, 5.
223. Interview, staff member NANGO, 5 September 1995; NANGO, Constitution, Welfare Organisation no. 221/68; J. B. Kiragu and Sarah Sakupwanya, *Evaluation of NANGO*, 18 October—27 November 1995.
224. The lower figures are from the 1995 Evaluation Report: Kiragu and Sakupwanya, *Evaluation of NANGO*, n.p.; the higher figures are from Sam Moyo, 'The Structure and Characteristics of NGOs', in Sam Moyo, John Makumbe and Brian Raftopoulos, *NGOs, the State and Politics in Zimbabwe* (Harare: SAPES Trust, 2000), 57, and appear to be based on statistics from 1992.
225. NANGO, 'A report of the Northern region general meeting held on 4th September 1996 at the Holiday Inn Crown Plaza Monomatapa Hotel'.
226. J. B. Kiragu and S. Sakupwanya, *Evaluation of NANGO*, 1995; NANGO, 'Report of a workshop on strengthening the planning process within NANGO structures, 2–3 April 1996' (often referred to as the Adelaide Acres report); NANGO, 'Report of a workshop on strengthening the planning process within NANGO structures, 16 July 1998' (often referred to as the Westwood report); G. Madzima, *A Co-ordinated voice for NGOs—The path ahead*, May 1997.
227. 'Officials resign as NANGO goes broke', *Financial Gazette*, 1 August 1998. The members who resigned were Paul Themba Nyathi, Thoko Ruzvidzo, Eunice Njovana, Niki Jazdowska and Priscilla Misihairambwi.
228. E. Maisiri, 'The Fourth NANGO national annual general meeting: Cresta

Oasis Hotel, Harare: January 7, 1995', *NANGO News andViews*, February 1995.

229. 'State to introduce Bill to monitor activities of NGOs', *Herald*, 8 February 1995; interview, Agatha Dodo, NANGO, 4 September 1995.

230. Letter from S. S. P. Matindike, Executive Director of NANGO, to the Hon. Mr J. Nkomo, Minister of Public Service, Labour and Social Welfare, 7 February 1995.

231. Letter from S. S. P. Matindike, Executive Director of NANGO, to the Director of Social Welfare, 9 February 1995.

232. ESS, 'Liberation and Self-reliance through Ecumenical Action based on Radical Christian Commitment', leaflet, *c*.1997.

233. 'New human rights organisation formed', *Herald*, 22 May 1992; for an extended discussion of ZimRights, see Sara Rich Dorman, 'Studying Democratization in Africa: A Case Study of Human Rights NGOs in Zimbabwe', in Tim Kelsall and Jim Igoe, eds, *Between a Rock and a Hard Place: African NGOs, Donors, and the State* (Durham, NC: Carolina Academic Press, 2005), 33–59.

234. Interview, Murombedzi Kuchera, ZCC General Secretary, 11 September 1995.

235. ZimRights. 'New NGO Act Threatens Freedom' (Harare: ZimRights, n.d.).

236. NANGO, 'Amendments to the Social Welfare Organisations Act (PVO) Recommendations by the Task Committee', n.d.

237. ZimRights, 'Report of a Workshop on NGO Activisim held at Adelaide Acres June 17–19, 1996' (Harare: ZimRights, n.d.), 2.

238. Another Working Group on Land also evolved from this process, convened by ZimRights. It organized a workshop on land issues in July 1997.

239. Streets Ahead (an organization working with street children), Housing People of Zimbabwe (an organization working with housing cooperatives), Ecumenical Support Services (an interdenominational church organization), the Zimbabwe Project (a development NGO) and ZimRights (a human rights organization).

240. Campaign for the Repeal of the PVO Act, Fact Sheet no. 1, 'The PVO Act: A History and Analysis'; Fact Sheet no. 2, 'A Case Study: The AWC'; Fact Sheet no. 3, 'NGO Responses to the PVO Act'; Fact Sheet no. 4, 'New legislation? Towards a Consultative Drafting Process' (n.p., n.d.).

241. Campaign for the Repeal of the PVO Act, 'NGO Briefing paper: The Private Voluntary Organisations Act: A widening rift between civil society and the state in Zimbabwe' (n.d.), 5, emphasis added.

242. Campaign for the Repeal of the PVO Act, 'Joint Statement by Non-Governmental Organisations and Concerned Citizens demanding the Repeal of the Private Voluntary Organisations Act 1995', October 1996, ch.93, 2, emphasis added.

243. Research Notes, PVO Act meeting, 29 January 1997.
244. Research Notes, PVO Act meeting, 23 October 1996.
245. Research Notes, ZCC-PVO Act meeting, 13 February 1997.
246. Ibid.
247. Research Notes, PVO Act meeting, 'Unfinished Business', 7 March 1997.
248. Sekai Holland, personal communication, 14 February 1997.

5. THE POLITICS OF POLARIZATION (1998–2000)

1. Daves Guzha, Edgar Langeveldt and Chirikure Chirikure, *State of the Nation* (Harare: Rooftops Promotions Production, performed 9 November 2005).
2. Adrienne LeBas, 'Polarization as Craft: Party Formation and State Violence in Zimbabwe', *Comparative Politics* 38 (2006), 419–38.
3. 'Meetings with war vets turn nasty', *Herald*, 21 July 1997, 1, 8; 'Ex-combatants loot ZANU (PF) HQ', *Herald*, 14 August 1997, 1; 'Compensation demands to continue: Hunzvi', *Herald*, 15 August 1997, 1, 7; GOZ, 'Report of the Commission of Enquiry into the Administration of the War Victims Compensation Act, ch. 11.16, May 1998.
4. Iden Wetherell, 'Mugabe under siege: ending the plunder?', *Southern Africa Report*, March 1998, 16–18.
5. 'Commuters relive '80s public transport blues', *Herald*, 15 February 1999, 11.
6. 'Ordinary workers worse off now than 10 years ago as inflation bites', *Herald*, 24 May 1999, 1.
7. 'ZCTU bills strike the most successful ever', *Financial Gazette*, 11 December 1997; Never Gadaga, 'Rage at police attacks in Zimbabwe', *Mail & Guardian*, 11 December 1997; Chris McGreal, 'Zim's "unholy alliance": black workers, white farmers', *Mail & Guardian*, 17 December 1997.
8. Never Gadaga, 'Violent demos rock Harare', *Mail & Guardian*, 20 January 1998; Pedzisai Ruhana, 'Riots bring hasty reverse on maize prices', *MISA*, 20 January 1998.
9. 'Tens of thousands defy Mugabe in Zimbabwe anti-government strike', *SAPA*, 3 March 1998; 'National strike cripples economy for second day', *SAPA*, 4 March 1998; Iden Wetherell, 'Threats fail to halt Zim's workers', *Mail & Guardian*, 6 March 1998.
10. 'Demo ban unconstitutional—lawyers', *Independent*, 1 August 1997, 8.
11. 'Army deployed to quell food riots', *PANA*, 20 January 1998; 'Military spark panic in Zimbabwe's riot-torn capital', SAPA-AFP, 21 January 1998.
12. Never Gadaga, 'SG of the Zimbabwe Congress of Trade Unions attacked', ZimRights press release, 11 December 1997; 'Union is Strength', *Africa Confidential*, 20 March 1998, 5–6.

13. Lewis Machipisa, 'Zim panic over price rises', *Mail & Guardian*, 29 September 1998; Andrew Meldrum, 'Fuel riots erupt in Zimbabwe', *Guardian* (UK), 5 November 1998; Lewis Machipisa, 'Zim unionists upbeat after massive strike', *Mail & Guardian*, 12 November 1998; 'ZCTU to go ahead with next stayaway', *Independent*, 13 November 1998.

14. 'Housing for all misses 2000 target', *Herald*, 13 August 1999, 10; see also 'City fails to clear housing backlog', *Mirror*, 8 May 1998; 'Dream of housing for all by 2000 crumbles', *Financial Gazette*, 15 August 1997.

15. See for instance Angeline Mushakavanhu, 'A filthy problem', *Standard*, 24 September 2000; 'Virginia Dhliwayo, 'Ratepayers protest over rubbish', *Standard*, 26 November 2000.

16. 'Bulawayo council to meet', *Independent*, 20 April 2000; 'Harare council owed \$120 million: ministers not paying rates', *Independent*, 4 June 1999.

17. See for instance Farai Mutsaka, 'Mutare residents want demo over 4000% rates hike', *Standard*, 7 January 2001; Farai Mutsaka, 'Ratepayers halt payments', *Standard*, 11 February 2001; Chengetai Zvauya, 'Norton residents refuse to pay rates', *Standard*, 22 August 1999.

18. Parliamentary Debates, 25 March 1999.

19. Parliamentary Debates, 6 October 1999.

20. Mercedes Sayagues, 'Zimbabwe peasants seize four farms', *Mail & Guardian*, 26 June 1998; see also Jocelyn Alexander, '"Squatters", Veterans and the State in Zimbabwe', in Amanda Hammer, Brian Raftopoulos and Stig Jensen, eds, *Zimbabwe's Unfinished Business* (Harare: Weaver, 2003), 96–8.

21. 'Mutasa incites farm takeovers', *Standard*, 18 April 1999.

22. Rachel Knight, 'We are tired of promises, tired of waiting: People's power, local politics and the fight for land in Zimbabwe', BA Development Studies, Brown University, RI, December 1999, 25.

23. Knight, 'We are tired of promises', 29.

24. African Rights, 'In the Party's Interest?', Discussion paper 8, 41–2.

25. 'SDF to help orphans and destitutes only', *Herald*, 14 January 1999, 1; 'Inquiry begins into SDF looting', *Herald*, 15 January 1999, 1; 'SDF reels under \$206 million debt', *Herald*, 18 January 1999, 1, 11; see also 'Over Zd42 Million Paid for Poor Pupils: Deputy Minister', *SAPA*, 1 June 1996.

26. 'Scam may have cost DDF \$12 million', *Herald*, 10 April 1999, 1; 'DDF prejudiced of millions of dollars', *Herald*, 21 May 1999, 1; 'DDF allegedly diverted \$100 million', *Herald*, 9 July 1999, 1; 'DDF manager in court for alleged \$300 000 fraud', *Herald*, 24 July 1999, 6; 'As DDF scandal widens, high level graft impoverishes rural folk', *Independent*, 16 July 1999.

27. Brian Hungwe, 'AG's office accused of taking bribes', *Independent*, 8 October 1999.

28. 'Tawengwa and Vingirai arrested', *Herald*, 23 March 2000; 'Tawengwa appears in court', *Herald*, 24 March 2000.

29. 'Massive corruption costs NOCZIM $1.4 bn', *Herald*, 4 February 1999, 1.

30. Wisdom Mdzungairi, 'Ex-NOCZIM Boss, senior staff arrested', *Herald*, 1 March 2000; 'Chihuri consults Mugabe on ministers implicated in NOCZIM/GMB scandals', *Independent*, 3 March 2000.

31. 'Chefs offshore accounts probed', *Financial Gazette*, 6 April 2000.

32. Parliamentary Debates, 24 March 1999, 'Interim Report of the ad hoc committee on the ZBC affairs'.

33. Ibid.

34. 'Mugabe accuses ministers of accepting bribes', *Daily News*, 21 July 1999; 'Sudden anti-corruption drive raises eyebrows', *Independent*, 31 March 2000.

35. Michael Nest, 'Ambitions, Profits and Loss: Zimbabwean Economic Involvement in the Democratic Republic of the Congo', *African Affairs* 100 (2001), 470–71.

36. UN Security Council, 'Report of the Panel of Experts on the Illegal Exploitation of Natural Resources and Other Forms of Wealth of the Democratic Republic of the Congo' (2001), 28; Andrew Meldrum, 'Zimbabwe loans cut off as leak shows war costs', *Mail & Guardian*, 7 October 1999; 'Zimbabwe's Congo intervention in official figure', *Mail & Guardian*, 27 October 1999.

37. 'Inside Zimbabwe Inc', *Focus* 19 (September 2000); UN Security Council, 'Report of the Panel of Experts', 33–6.

38. UN Security Council, 'Report of the Panel of Experts', 34.

39. Andrew Meldrum, 'Zimbabwe loans cut off as leak shows war costs'; 'Netherlands cancels aid to Zimbabwe', *Mail & Guardian*, 29 September 1999.

40. 'Private press editors dismiss government claims', *Daily News*, 4 May 1999, 2.

41. 'Grisly trail of 5th Brigade atrocities exposed', *Mail & Guardian*, 9 May 1997; 'Memories of army atrocities still haunt Matabeleland', *Mail & Guardian*, 13 May 1997; 'The Matabele wounds are still open', *Mail & Guardian*, 21 May 1997.

42. The independent media had run stories on the atrocities in the 1990s, and in 1996–7, but the CCJP report provided a particularly stringent account, and the CCJP's role was, in and of itself, an important story. 'CCJP submits report on Mat atrocities to Mugabe', *Independent*, 21 March 1997; 'Matabele slaughter: CCJP report exposé', *Standard*, 4 May 1997, 1, 4; 'Matabeleland atrocities return to haunt the President: Mugabe battles with past that won't go away', *Financial Gazette*, 15 May 1997, 4; 'Fifth brigade victims demand official apology', *Independent*, 16 May 1997,

1, 2; 'Amnesty challenges Mugabe to atone for Matabeleland rights vio-lations', *Independent*, 23 May 1997; 'Government must not cover up 5 Brigade atrocities, says ZimRights', *Daily News*, 27 September 1999; 'Remains of 5 brigade victims exhumed', *Daily News*, 10 October 1999; 'Mat exhumations help to heal wounds of bereaved', *Financial Gazette*, 11 November 1999.

43. For example, 'Zimbabwe compensation offer', BBC, 12 July 1999; 'Committee on Gukurahundi seeks to meet Mugabe', *Mirror*, 24 March 2000.

44. 'Chihuri admits illegal Act', *Standard*, 19 September 1999.

45. Mark Chavunduka and Ray Choto, Royal Commonwealth Society Meeting, London, 16 April 1999; see also news reports: Andrew Meldrum, 'Mugabe "Foiled Officer's Coup"', *Guardian* (UK), 11 January 1999; Andrew Meldrum, 'Zimbabwe army torture alleged', *Guardian* (UK), 22 January 1999.

46. 'Zim police arrest three journalists', *Mail & Guardian*, 8 February 1999; 'Zimbabwe Mirror journalists further remanded', *Herald*, 2 March 1999.

47. Law and Order (Maintenance) Act (revised edition, 1996), Section 50 (1).

48. 'Charges Against Two Zimbabwean Journalists Dropped', SAPAAFP, 30 April 1999.

49. Chavunduka, speaking at Royal Commonwealth Society, London, 16 April 1999.

50. Mark Chavunduka and Ray Choto, Royal Commonwealth Society Meeting, London, 16 April 1999.

51. 'Daily News records phenomenal growth', *Daily News*, 10 November 2000.

52. 'Dongo asks ZBC to lift news blackout on her', *Standard*, 2 November 1997.

53. On attempts to control ZBC coverage: 'ZBC fires DJ for rapping police action', *Financial Gazette*, 18 December 1997; 'Govt tightens gag on ZBC', *Independent*, 4 December 1998; see also Kristin Skare Orgeret, 'The drum-beat of the nation?' Unpublished dissertation, University of Oslo, 1998, 111–13.

54. Parliamentary Debates, 23 March 1999 and 24 March 1999; 'Interim Report of the ad hoc committee on the ZBC affairs'.

55. Research notes, 28 May 1997, 11 June 1997; see also inter alia NCA, 'The NCA: First Interim Report', 3 July 1997; and T. Mutasah, 'Building a representative and all-inclusive constitution: proposals and strategies', in ESS, 'Tolerance in Zimbabwe: towards a political, cultural and consti-tutional basis', report of a workshop held in Harare, 28 May 1997.

56. NCA, 'Annexure 1: NCA income and expenditure 1998', NCA annual report, 1998.

57. Brian Kagoro, 'The evolution of the NCA', *Agenda* 2.1 suggests that this committee was elected in May 1997; my notes and the meeting's agenda suggest that this was formalized in June. Research notes, 11 June 1997; NCA, 'The NCA: First Interim Report', 3 July 1997.
58. Masipula Sithole, 'Fighting Authoritarianism in Zimbabwe', *Journal of Democracy* 12.1 (2001), 167 and ftn 7, 169.
59. Peter Alexander, 'Zimbabwean workers, the MDC and the 2000 election', *Review of African Political Economy* 27.85 (2000), 389.
60. Munyaradzi Gwisai, 'Constitutional controversy: elected constituent assembly is the only way forward', *Herald*, 14 April 1999, 6.
61. Research notes, 7 September 1997; see also 'Spotlight falls squarely on the constitution', *Financial Gazette*, 11 September 1997.
62. Brian Raftopoulos and Gerald Mazarire, 'Civil society and the constitution-making process in Zimbabwe: NCA 1997–2000', in Kayode Fayemi and Sam Moyo, eds, *Evaluating the Constitutional Process in Zimbabwe* (Harare: SAPES Trust, 2001), 31.
63. The phrase 'panel-beating' is from Dr John Makumbe, speaking at 'Public Meeting: Establishing a Constitutional base for Democratic Practice: lessons from South Africa', Harare, 28 May 1997. For a useful if dated discussion, see John Reid Rowland, 'Amendments to Zimbabwe's constitution: a summary', *Legal Forum*, 6, 2 June 1994, 38–42.
64. NCA [Morgan Tsvangirai], 'Welcome address at the national conference on the Zimbabwe constitutional debate project', Kadoma Ranch motel, 6 September 1997, 3.
65. Masipula Sithole, 'Minister with many portfolios and the NCA', *Agenda*, April 1999.
66. Research notes, Constitutional Assembly Meeting, Kadoma, 7 September 1997.
67. Ibid.
68. Raftopoulos and Mazarire, 'Civil society and the constitution-making process in Zimbabwe', 15.
69. NCA evaluation report, n.d., NCA files, 14; also 'Evaluation of Strategic Process', NCA Annual Report 1998, 40–41; interview, Mrs Kowo, Head of Church and Society ZCC, 7 October 1999.
70. 'Unity of NCA hangs in balance', *Herald*, 8 November 1998; 'Activists hit at govt ban on protest', *Independent*, 7 November 1998.
71. Interviews, ZCC, 7 October 1999; and NCA, 28 September 1999.
72. On the launch of the government's CC: 'Constitutional amendments to involve all—president', *Herald*, 23 February 1999; 'President gives notice to appoint commission', *Sunday Mail*, March 1999, 1, 4; 'Commission of Inquiry into a new constitution for Zimbabwe', advertisement in the *Herald*, 15 June 1999. On the NCA reaction: Daniel Manyandure, 'NCA

won't accept gvt "fraud"', *Standard*, 2 May 1999; Dumisani Muleya, 'NCA vows not to take part in presidential commission', *Independent*, 2 April 1999.

73. Basildon Peta, 'NCA and government discuss the way forward', *Agenda*, November 1998, 6; 'Clashes as constitutional talks breakdown', *Herald*, 26 March 1999; see also Raftopoulos and Mazarire, 'Civil society and the constitution-making process in Zimbabwe', 6–10.

74. 'Church leaders meet over constitutional reform process', *Herald*, 4 March 1999, 4.

75. 'Daunting task for commissioners—Chidyausiku', *Herald*, 8 June 1999, 5.

76. E.g. five (tabloid) pages in English in the *Daily News*, 5 August 1999, 16–21; three (broadsheet) pages in the *Herald*, 5 August 1999, C1, C2, C3; three (broadsheet) pages in Shona in the *Herald*, 21 August 1999, 4, 5, 6.

77. 'ZUD describes CC as a political joke', *Herald*, 6 May 1999, 6.

78. NCA, 'Resolution passed at the Harare NCA assembly', 13 April 1999.

79. 'Constitutional Commission get $20 million from US donor', *Herald*, 24 August 1999, 11; 'Commission concerned about $500,000 demand', *Sunday Mail*, 3 October 1999, 15; '$30m grant for Constitutional Commission approved', *Herald*, 20 September 1999, 9; 'Commission put fund in private bank account', *Daily News*, 7 October 1999, 1; 'CC dismisses allegations of misuse of donor funds', *Mirror*, 8 October 1999, 2.

80. 'Commission receives financial support from Republic of Korea', *Herald*, 6 August 1999; 'Canada pledges $4 million to constitutional commission', *Herald*, 14 August 1999, 1; 'Five countries donate $20.1 million to Constitutional Commission', *Herald*, 6 October 1999, 5.

81. 'Five countries donate $20.1 million to Constitutional Commission', *Herald*, 6 October 1999, 5.

82. Interview, Densen Mafinyani, Secretary General ZCC, 29 September 1999.

83. Interview, ZCC, 7 October 1999.

84. Declaration and resolutions of the 1st People's Constitutional Convention, 18–20 June 1999; 'NCA says constitutional review process in danger of being hijacked', *Daily News*, 20 April 1999, 2.

85. NCA, 'Resolution passed at the Harare NCA assembly', 13 April 1999.

86. Hlatshwayo, who was probably second only to Jonathan Moyo in his prolific public engagements with the NCA, was rewarded with an appointment as a High Court judge in 2001.

87. Dumisani Muleya, 'Unwieldy, accused of partisan bias, Constitutional commission seeks legitimacy', *Independent*, 7 May 1999.

88. 'NCA must stop shifting goalposts', *Herald*, 19 April 1999, 1.

89. 'Anglican Church bars NCA from meeting in cathedral', *Financial Gazette*, 13 August 1999.

90. See, for instance, the letter to the editor entitled 'Church leaders negating spirit of evangelism', *Financial Gazette*, 9 September 1999, 9.
91. 'Church vote rejects constitution', *Daily News*, 28 January 2000, 1, 2.
92. 'Constitutional reforms split Catholic Church', *Financial Gazette*, 5 August 1999; 'Catholic Bishops Divided', *Daily News*, 7 August 1999, 1, 2; 'Church split dramatised, says Wermter', *Standard*, 8 August 1999; 'We are not part of the NCA: CCJP Chairman', *Financial Gazette*, 13 August 1999; 'Catholics protest', *Sunday Mail*, 18 April 1999.
93. Interview, Mike Auret, Director, CCJP, 28 September 1999.
94. 'ZimRights unhappy with NCA decision', *Chronicle*, 26 July 1999, 9; interview, Munyaradzi Bhidi, Acting Director, 13 September 1999; interview, Peter Maregare, Legal Officer, 13 September 1999; interview, Paul Themba Nyathi, former National Council Member, 16 September 1999; interview, David Chimhini, [Former] Director, 4 October 1999.
95. 'Human rights lawyers divided', *Standard*, 2 August 1999; interview, Beverly Hargrove, ZLHR administrator, 28 September 1999.
96. 'Coalition dismisses shift from "No" vote stance', *Daily News*, 24 January 2000; 'Harare women march against draft constitution', *Standard*, 2 February 2000; Interviews, Thoko Matshe, ZWRCN, 30 September 1999 and Selina Mumbengegwi, Women's Action Group, 6 October 1999.
97. 'Commission funds put in private bank account', *Daily News*, 7 October 1999, 1; 'Commission's donor funds misused', *Financial Gazette*, 7 October 1999; 'CC dismisses allegations of mis-use of donor funds', *Mirror*, 8 October 1999, 2; Jonathan Moyo, 'War on discrediting Constitutional Commission still on', *Sunday Mail*, 10 October 1999, 8.
98. For example, 'Citizens cold-shoulder Commission meetings', *Financial Gazette*, 19 August 1999, 5; 'Tough time for Commission team in Chirumanzu', *Daily News*, 20 August 1999; 'Public ignores Constitutional Commission meetings', *Daily News*, 18 August 1999.
99. Interview, Paul Themba Nyathi, NCA Taskforce, 16 September 1999.
100. 'Villagers not free to contribute views', *Herald*, 13 September 1999, 1.
101. 'Govt panel tries to sell itself to sceptical students', *Financial Gazette*, 5 August 1999; 'Chakaredza says older commissioners botched meetings with students', *Daily News*, 22 September 1999, 3; 'Commission meeting abandoned because of UZ rowdies', *Herald*, 4 September 1999, 1; 'Trials, tribulations of Commissioners', *Herald*, 18 September 1999, 1.
102. Plenary Statement by Justice Godfrey Chidyausiku, Constitutional Commission 3rd plenary, 22 October 1999.
103. For example, 'Residents give view on the constitution', *Herald*, 24 August 1999, 1; 'Public not aware of objective of meetings', *Herald*, 25 August 1999, 9; 'Commissioners' job is to reflect people's wishes accurately', *Herald*, 24 September 1999, 6.

104. 'Public not aware of objective of meetings', *Herald*.

105. Dumisani Muleya, 'The public interest versus Zanu PF blueprint', *Independent*, 29 October 1999.

106. 'Gay broadcast sparks heated debate in Zimbabwe', *Mail & Guardian*, 5 November 1999; 'GALZ wants homosexuality enshrined in new constitution', *Herald*, 25 October 1999, 6.

107. 'Storm brewing over constitutional draft', *Independent*, 26 November 1999.

108. 'Read constitutional draft thoroughly', *Herald*, 2 December 1999, 1.

109. 'Commission adopts draft constitution', *Herald*, 30 November 1999, 1.

110. 'Mugabe must resign', *Independent*, 26 November 1999; 'Constitutional commission rift deepens: Moyo said to have threatened to resign', *Herald*, 29 November 1999, 1; 'Commission adopts draft constitution', *Herald*, 30 November 1999, 1.

111. 'Commission adopts draft constitution', *Herald*; 'Draft advocates creation of a national assembly', *Herald*, 30 November 1999, 4; 'Constitutional court will be superior', *Herald*, 30 November 1999, 4; 'New constitution brings electoral commission', *Herald*, 30 November 1999, 4.

112. Chenjerai Chisaka, 'Did the constitution correctly interpret the views of the people?', *Social Change* 50 (June 2000), 3.

113. Chenjerai Chisaka, 'Did the constitution correctly interpret the views of the people?', 19; see also 'NCA Vote No', supplement inserted in the *Financial Gazette*, the *Independent*, the *Standard*, the *Daily News*, the *Eastern Star* and the *Dispatch*, 4 February 2000, which similarly details 'what the people wanted' v. 'what the commission wrote'.

114. '3000 walk out of referendum meeting', *Daily News*, 27 January 2000; 'Tough time for commissioners', *Daily News*, 21 January 2000.

115. 'President quizzes commission again', *Herald*, 10 December 1999, 1, 10; 'Women's coalition wants Constitution adjusted, *Herald*, 16 December 1999, 16; 'Regard draft constitution as a green paper: church leaders', *Herald*, 11 December 1999, 1.

116. 'Commissioner snubs draft constitution', *Chronicle*, 27 January 2000.

117. 'Bishop changes colour on draft constitution', *Chronicle*, 8 February 2000.

118. 'Draft ignored people, says Zvobgo', *Daily News*, 9 February 2000.

119. 'Mushayakarara, Mudzingwa apply for an urgent hearing', *Herald*, 9 February 2000; 'Mushayakarara, Mudzingwa fail to stop referendum', *Herald*, 11 February 2000; 'Last minute bid to stop draft poll fails', *Daily News*, 11 February 2000, 1, 2.

120. 'Party to support draft constitution', *Herald*, 17 December 1999; ZNLWVA, 'The "NO" Vote to the Draft Constitution: which way forward?', 15 February 2000.

121. 'Don't be misled—read for yourself; draft constitution for Zimbabwe; Corrections and Clarifications', advertisement inserted by the Constitutional Commission in the *Mirror*, 28 January 2000.

122. See Erin McCandless, 'Rights or Redistribution … and other strategic dilemmas facing Zimbabwean Social Movements', PhD dissertation, American University in Washington, 2005, ch. 6 for the full quotation and analysis; Zvakanyorwa Wilbert Sadomba, *War Veterans in Zimbabwe's Revolution: Challenging Neo-Colonialism and Settler and International Capital* (Woodbridge: Boydell & Brewer, 2011), 156–61 confirms her account.

123. 'Constitutional commission launches campaign CD', *Herald*, 24 September 1999, 12; ZBC programmes, September–October 1999.

124. 'ZBC defies court order, blocks NCA programmes', *Independent*, 28 January 2000; 'ZBC refutes NCA allegations', *Sunday Mail*, 30 January 2000; 'NCA seeks legal advice to recover funds from ZBC', *Independent*, 10 March 2000, 11; see also the detailed discussion of these negotiations in Raftopoulos and Mazarire, 'Civil society and the constitution-making process in Zimbabwe', 17–18.

125. MMPZ, Media Update 2000/4, 24–30 January 2000.

126. See for example MMPZ, Media Update 2000/13, 9 January 2000, 'Countdown to referendum'; MMPZ, Media Update 2000/4, 24–30 January 2000, 'Referendum on the draft constitution'.

127. 'Top NCA leaders arrested', *Daily News*, 14 February 2000.

128. Jonathan Moyo, 'Is the NCA grouping still existing?', *Financial Gazette*, 30 September 1999, 12.

129. Jonathan Moyo, 'Greatest enemy of truth is myth', *Independent*, 21 May 1999; see also 'NCA subverting constitutional process', *Herald*, 22 June 1999, 8; 'Constitution, let's stop bickering and get moving', *Herald*, 5 July 1999, 6.

130. Welshman Ncube, 'Insults won't deter NCA', *Financial Gazette*, 13 August 1999, 8.

131. Commissioner Walter Kamba, ZTV evening news, 16 January 2000, as reported in MMPZ, Media Update 2000/2, 10–16 January 2000; 'Referendum—What will a no vote mean for the country?', *Herald*, 18 January 2000.

132. ZTV news, 15 January 2000, as reported in MMPZ Update 2000/2.

133. 'Political temperature rises in constitutional debate', *Independent*, 25 June 2000.

134. Jonathan Moyo, 'Is the NCA grouping still existing?'; see also Alexander Kanengoni, 'NCA now experiencing some rude awakening', *Herald*, 26 May 1999, 8.

135. 'NCA demo out to tarnish country's image', *Mirror*, 19 November 1999.

136. 'Commission concerned about $500,000 demand', *Sunday Mail*,

3 October 1999, 15; '$30m grant for Constitutional Commission approved', *Herald*, 20 September 1999, 9; 'CC dismisses allegations of misuse of donor funds', *Mirror*, 8 October 1999, 2; 'Donors reluctant to fund commissions work', *Independent*, 13 August 1999, 3.

137. Jonathan Moyo, 'NCA not interested in changing the constitution', *Independent*, 2 July 1999.

138. Jonathan Moyo, 'Is the NCA Grouping Still Existing?'.

139. Innocent Kurwa, 'Draft Constitution a "fraud"', *Daily News*, 17 February 2001; Tarcey Munaku, 'Referendum results rock ZANU (PF) Foundations', *Daily News*, 17 February 2001.

140. LeBas, 'Polarization as Craft'; Sara Rich Dorman, 'NGOs and the Constitutional Debate in Zimbabwe: From Inclusion to Exclusion', *Journal of Southern African Studies* 29. 4 (2003), 845–63.

6. THE POLITICS OF EXCLUSION (2000–2008)

1. Chenjerai Hove, 'Violence without Conscience', *Palaver Finish* (Harare: Weaver, 2002), 81.

2. Thomas Mapfumo, in an interview with Banning Eyre, 'Thomas Mapfumo releases *Rise Up*', 28 March 2005, http://news.calabashmusic.com/world/lioninwinter.

3. Abiodun Alao, *Mugabe and the Politics of Security in Zimbabwe* (Montreal and Kingston: McGill-Queen's University Press, 2012),128.

4. ZNLWVA, 'The 'NO' Vote to the Draft Constitution: which way forward?', 15 February 2000.

5. Ibid., emphasis in the original.

6. 'War veterans invade farms countrywide', *Herald*, 29 February 2000; Zvakanyorwa Wilbert Sadomba, *War Veterans in Zimbabwe's Revolution: Challenging Neo-Colonialism and Settler and International Capital* (Woodbridge: Boydell & Brewer, 2011), 170–91 provides fascinating detail on this process.

7. Jonathan Moyo, 'Oppositional press put to shame', *Sunday Mail*, 22 April 2001.

8. Erin McCandless, 'Rights or Redistribution … and other strategic dilemmas facing Zimbabwean Social Movements', PhD dissertation, American University in Washington, 2005, ch. 5, citing Chenjerai Hunzwi in the *Sunday Mail*, 27 February 2000; but see also Sadomba, *War Veterans in Zimbabwe's Revolution*, 157, who questions Hunzwi's representativeness.

9. When Mugabe purges the 'Tsholotsho' group from the party in 2005, it is only Jonathan Moyo, having no constituency with ZANU(PF), who leaves and runs as an independent.

10. Donald S. Moore, *Suffering for Territory: Race, Place and Power in Zimbabwe* (Harare: Weaver, 2005), 11.

11. Sadomba, *War Veterans in Zimbabwe's Revolution*, 172.

12. 'Jobless hired to seize farms', *Financial Gazette*, 16 March 2000; Vincent Kahiya, 'Government directs farm invasions', *Independent*, 3 March 2000.

13. McCandless, 'Rights or Redistribution', ch. 6; see also Nelson Marongwe, 'Farm Occupations and Occupiers in the New Politics of Zimbabwe', in Amanda Hammer, Brian Raftopoulos and Stig Jensen, eds, *Zimbabwe's Unfinished Business* (Harare: Weaver, 2003), 180–82.

14. Gerald Chikozho Mazarire, 'ZANU-PF and the Government of National Unity', in Brian Raftopoulos, ed., *The Hard Road to Reform: The Politics of Zimbabwe's Global Political Agreement* (Harare: Weaver Press, 2013).

15. 'War veterans can remain on farms says president', *Herald*, 11 March 2000.

16. 'Police defy high court order to evict war vets', *Financial Gazette*, 23 March 2000.

17. 'Stay out of politics, CFU warned', *Standard*, 2 April 2000.

18. Steve Kibble and Paul Vanlerberghe, 'Land, Power and Poverty: farm workers and the crisis in Zimbabwe' (London: CIIR, 2000), 32–3, 41.

19. Steve Kibble, 'Zimbabwe: the State, Development and Democratization', unpublished paper, 2000.

20. See for instance Lionel Cliffe, Joshua Mpofu and Barry Munslow, 'Nationalist Politics in Zimbabwe, the 1980 elections and beyond', *Review of African Political Economy* 18 (1980), 51–3.

21. 'Police and War Vets Attack NCA', *Standard*, 12 May 2000; 'Havoc in City', *Standard*, 2 April 2000; Zimbabwe Human Rights NGO Forum, 'The Unleashing of Violence: A report on violence against peaceful protestors in Harare', April 2000.

22. ZBC 8 p.m. news bulletin, 6 April 2000, as cited in Zimbabwe Human Rights NGO Forum, 'The Unleashing of Violence', ftn 24.

23. 'Teachers abducted as political tension reaches fever high', *Parade*, June (2000), 3, 7, 13; 'Zanu PF terror targets rural professionals', *Independent*, 26 May 2000; 'Another safe home for fleeing villagers, teachers established', *Daily News*, 29 May 2000; 'War vets blackmail teachers', *Daily News*, 5 June 2000; 'Nun relives ordeal at the hands of ZANU (PF) enforcers', *Daily News*, 22 June 2000; 'ZANU PF mob brutally assaults Catholic priest', *Daily News*, 24 June 2000, 1; 'Threatened teachers flee from 3 schools', *Daily News*, 26 June 2000; numerous personal communications.

24. ZimRights, 'Early warning and Alert: 2', 5 April 2000, especially case no. 1, 'Activist headmaster brutally assaulted by land-grabbers', and case no. 2, 'ZimRights members attacked'.

25. '31 deaths of MDC supporters in political violence', MDC Press release, 22 June 2000; Zimbabwe Human Rights NGO Forum, 'Politically motivated violence in Zimbabwe, 2000–2001', July 2000, 3–5.

26. EU Election Observation Mission Zimbabwe 2000, 'Report of the EU Election Observation Mission on the Parliamentary Elections which took place in Zimbabwe on 24th and 25th June 2000' (Harare/Strasbourg, 4 July 2000), 15.

27. '31 deaths of MDC supporters in political violence', MDC Press release, 22 June 2000.

28. 'Terror reigns in Mberengwa', *Daily News*, 24 June 2000; see also 'Refugees in their own country', *Financial Gazette*, 22 June 2000.

29. Zimbabwe Human Rights NGO Forum, 'Politically Motivated Violence in Zimbabwe 2000–2001', August 2001, 45–8.

30. 'Gezi slams whites for funding MDC', *Herald*, 3 March 2000.

31. 'MDC admits antiZanu (PF) alliance with whites', *Herald*, 10 April 2000.

32. Televised Address by His Excellency the President on the Occasion of Zimbabwe's Twentieth Anniversary, Pockets Hill, Harare, 18 April 2000: transcript of address.

33. Statement Made by Vice President Joseph Msika on Announcing the Accelerated Land Reform and Resettlement Programme 'Fast Track' Approach, 15 July 2000.

34. Sam Moyo, 'Land Policy, Poverty Reduction and Public Action in Zimbabwe', paper presented at the ISS/UNDP conference on Land Reform and Poverty Reduction, 17–19 February 2005, The Hague, Netherlands, citing 'Internal land reform and resettlement progress reports', Ministry of Lands and Rural Resettlement, Government of Zimbabwe.

35. Human Rights Watch, 'Fast Track Land Reform in Zimbabwe', March 2002, 27–30; 'Land reform sidelines farm workers', *Daily Mirror*, 30 April 2003, 1.

36. Mr A. Mawere, 'Governing Policies—A perspective of the Ministry of Lands, Agriculture and Resettlement', in FNF, 'Report on the one-day workshop to review the Land Reform Programme in Zimbabwe', 10 May 2001, 5; see also 'Women sidelined in land reform exercise', *Daily News*, 11 August 2002.

37. Medicine Masiiwa, 'Land Reform Programme in Zimbabwe: Disparity Between Policy Design and Implementation', Institute of Development Studies, University of Zimbabwe, May 2004.

38. Moyo, 'Land Policy, Poverty Reduction and Public Action', 50.

39. Joseph Chaumba, Ian Scoones and William Wolmer, 'From jambanja to planning: the reassertion of technocracy in land reform in south-eastern Zimbabwe?', *Journal of Modern African Studies* 41.4 (2003), 533–4.

40. 'Fresh evictions on farms', *Financial Gazette*, 30 June 2005; 'More farms invaded', *Independent*, 7 October 2005; 'Msika hits out at war veterans', *Mirror*, 29 October 2005, 1; 'Zimbabwe evicts 16 more white farmers', Zim Online, 2 November 2005.

41. 'Chefs ignore order to give up extra farms', *Independent*, 21 May 2004; 'Leo Mugabe loses farm', *Mirror*, 27 October 2005, 1; 'Kereboom Farm dispute spills into court', *Herald*, 27 October 2005; 'Nkomo in farm battle', *Financial Gazette*, 3 November 2005, 4.

42. Bill Kinsey, 'Comparative Economic Performance of Zimbabwe's Resettlement Models', 22; 'Zimbabwe's agricultural production declines', *Herald*, 1 November 2005, 2; 'Avail agricultural inputs on time: Mzembi', *Herald*, 3 November 2005; 'Matabeleland South farmers fail to prepare for rainy season', *Mirror*, 3 November 2005; 'Land preps the worst since independence', *Independent*, 28 October 2005, 4.

43. Blessing-Miles Tendi, 'Ideology, Civilian Authority and the Zimbabwean Military', *Journal of Southern African Studies* 39.4 (December 2013), 829–43.

44. 'Farm invasions not State policy: Gono', *Herald*, 22 October 2005, 8; see also 'Msika hits out at war veterans', *Mirror*, 29 October 2005, 1.

45. 'Matonga clarifies policy on land', *Herald*, 25 October 2005, 2.

46. 'Zim's agricultural production declines', *Herald*, 1 November 2005; 'Made speaks on agricultural production', *Herald*, 2 November 2005; 'Ministers publicly clash over crisis on farms', *Financial Gazette*, 3 November 2005, 1, 31.

47. Norma Kriger, 'Les vétérans et le parti au pouvoir: une coopération conflictuelle dans la longue durée', *Politique Africaine* 81 (2001); see also McCandless, 'Rights or Redistribution', ch. 5.

48. See for instance 'Confusion reigns over war vets leadership', *Daily News*, 8 September 2000; 'War vets power struggle deepens', *Independent*, 8 September 2000; 'War veterans split over election', *Independent*, 14 September 2001; 'Ndlovu threatens to deal with Nyaruwata, Mhlanga', *Mirror*, 14 September 2001.

49. 'War Vets group takes government to court', *Standard*, 6 August 2000.

50. GOZ, Ex-political Prisoners, Detainees, and Restrictees Act (2004); 'Govt to pay $36bn gratuities', *Mirror*, 8 October 2005; see also Norma Kriger, 'Competing Liberation War Histories: suffering, contributions, and heroism', unpublished paper, 2005.

51. See for instance R. W. Johnson, 'Interview: Wilfred Mhanda, former freedom fighter', *Focus*, December 2000; R. W. Johnson, 'How Mugabe came to power', *London Review of Books*, 22 February 2001; David Moore, 'How Mugabe came to power' [letter], *London Review of Books*, 5 April 2001.

52. 'New war vets body attacks Hunzvi executive', *Mirror*, 15 September 2000.

53. McCandless, 'Rights or Redistribution', ch. 6.

54. Sadomba, *War Veterans in Zimbabwe's Revolution*, 224.

55. 'I never saw Moyo in the struggle—Tekere', *Independent*, 27 April 2001;

'Controversy over Hunzvi's hero status', *Independent*, 8 June 2001; 'Chinotimba's credentials questioned', *Independent*, 3 August 2001; 'Chinotimba Attacks General Mujuru', *Standard*, 5 August 2001; 'Chinotimba a fake', *Independent*, 10 August 2001; see also 'The struggle was not about places', *Sunday Mail*, 1 May 2001; 'Talking to Chinotimba— the "true" war veteran', *Daily News*, 6 June 2003, 10.

56. 'Nkomo death sparks trouble', *Standard*, 4 July 1999.

57. Daniel Muleya, 'Streets to be renamed, statue erected to Nkomo', *Independent*, 9 July 1999; 'Airport to be renamed', *Sunday Mail*, 16 December 2001; see also 'Renaming Bulawayo Airport after Nkomo an insult', *Standard*, 23 December 2001.

58. 'Street names change', *Standard*, 23 December 2001.

59. 'What credentials does a hero need?', *Independent*, 30 September 2005.

60. 'Schools challenged to change colonial names', *Herald*, 27 August 2001; 'School names to change', *Herald*, 29 November 2001; 'Most schools propose new names', *Sunday Mail*, 6 January 2002.

61. Teresa Barnes, 'History has to play its part: constructions of race and reconciliation in high school historiography in Zimbabwe, 1980–2004', unpublished MS, 2005; see also 'Minister accused of promoting own books', *Standard*, 9 September 2001.

62. Ranger, 'Nationalist historiography, patriotic history and the history of the nation', 219; Björn Lindgren, 'The Green Bombers of Salisbury: elections and political violence in Zimbabwe', *Anthropology Today* 19.2 (2003), 6–10; see also for instance 'Army behind youth training', *Daily News*, 30 January 2002; 'ZANU PF abandons "Green Bombers"', *Financial Gazette*, 23 May 2002.

63. 'Hundreds throng Heroes' Acre as Moyo is laid to rest', *Herald*, 16 October 1999; 'Mugabe promises to pay Matabeleland victims', *Mail & Guardian*, 18 October 1999; 'Committee on Gukurahundi seeks to meet Mugabe', *Mirror*, 24 March 2000; 'Committee on Matabeleland atrocities suspends operations', *Mirror*, 13 October 2000; 'Gukurahundi genocide compensation in doubt', *Daily News*, 8 January 2001.

64. 'Malaysians fail to turn up for Mat water project', *Independent*, 5 April 2002; '41bln for water project', *Financial Gazette*, 19 June 2003, 1; 'Government to fund Zambezi Water Project', *Daily Mirror*, 16 April 2004; 'MZWP urged to fast-track Zambesi project', *Daily Mirror*, 28 July 2004; 'Dam project gets $152bn', *Herald*, 7 November 2005.

65. 'Zimbabweans team up to fight new Citizenship Act', *Financial Gazette*, 20 December 2001; 'Last minute rush', *Herald*, 5 January 2002.

66. Ranger, 'Nationalist historiography, patriotic history and history of the nation', 218.

67. 'Former Herald editor speaks out', *Standard*, 15 October 2000.

68. 'MDC accuses ZBC of holding back campaign advertisements', *Daily News*, 21 June 2000.

69. 'ZBC ordered to stop propaganda', *Independent*, 16 June 2000.

70. ZESN, 'Report on the Zimbabwe's 2005 General Election', April 2005, 37.

71. GOZ, Broadcasting Services (Access to radio and television during an Election) Regulations, 2005. Statutory Instrument 22 of 2005.

72. Cornelius Ncube, 'Contesting Hegemony: Civil Society and the Struggle for Social Change in Zimbabwe, 2000–2008' (University of Birmingham, 2010), 123.

73. 'Plot to close Daily News', *Daily News*, 21 November 2000; 'War vets besiege The Daily News', *Daily News*, 24 January 2001; 'War veterans "ban" Daily News', *Daily News*, 27 January 2001; 'Press bombed', *Daily News*, 28 January 2001.

74. 'Daily News topples Herald', *Daily News*, 12 July 2001.

75. GOZ, Access to Information and Protection of Privacy Act (2002).

76. The following presents an interesting perspective on this period: Wallace Chuma, 'The Real Ibbo Mandaza', *New Zimbabwe*, 11 December 2009.

77. 'High Court confirms Mandaza ouster', *New Zimbabwe*, 12 October 2005.

78. 'Capitol Radio to be launched soon', *Daily News*, 26 September 2000; 'Moyo warns Capitol Radio', *Daily News*, 3 October 2000; 'Capitol Radio defies government', *Daily News*, 4 October 2000; 'A fresh breath on the air waves', *Standard*, 8 October 2000; 'Moves to extend ZBC monopoly to 2002', *Standard*, 8 October 2000.

79. 'Freeing of airwaves unleashes scramble for radio licences', *Mirror*, 6 October 2000; Dumisani Muleya, 'New broadcasting law grossly restrictive', *Independent*, 6 October 2000; 'Capital Radio judgment reserved', *Daily News*, 10 October 2000; 'Search on Auret's home yields nothing', *Daily News*, 11 October 2000.

80. 'Capital Radio judgement reserved', *Daily News*, 10 October 2000; 'Latest on Capital Radio', *Independent*, 3 November 2000.

81. Radio Dialogue interview, September 2012

82. 'Communications bill seen as draconian', *Independent*, 10 March 2000; Nqobile Nyathi, 'ISPs vow to fight Bill gagging email', *Financial Gazette*, 23 March 2000; Grant Ferrett, 'Outcry at Zimbabwe Internet bill', BBC, 20 March 2000.

83. Interview, Jim Holland, Mango/Zispa, 11 July 2003; but see 'Gvt tightens control of Internet … despite protestations', *Mirror*, 23 October 2005, 2.

84. Wonderful Bere, 'Infectious Beats: Urban Grooves Music's Collusion with the Zimbabwean State', in Toyin Falola and Tyler Fleming, eds, *Music, Performance and African Identities* (London: Routledge, 2012), 78–96;

Wonderful Bere, 'Urban Grooves: The Performance of Politics in Zimbabwe's Hip Hop Music' (New York University, 2008).

85. Banning Eyre, *Playing with Fire: fear and self-censorship in Zimbabwean* (*Music* (Freemuse.org, 2001), 68–74.

86. 'Let Mugabe go safely: Mapfumo', *Daily News*, 27 July 2003; Research Notes, Thomas Mapfumo speaking at the Glasgow Centre for Political Song, June 2003.

87. Maurice Taonezvi Vambe, 'Thomas Mapfumo's Toi Toi in context: popular music as narrative discourse', *African Identities* 2.1 (2004), 97.

88. Oliver Mtukudzi, 'Tuku sets the record straight', press release, 25 March 2005, Tukumusic.com; 'Tuku takes a dig at govt', *Financial Gazette*, 24 March 2005.

89. Maxwell Sibanda, 'Music central tool in Zimbabwe election', freemuse.org, 29 March 2005.

90. 'Moyo records album', *Daily News*, 21 July 2001; 'Music also won liberation struggle', *Sunday Mail*, 7 August 2005; 'Hondo Yeminda album doing well on local market', *Herald*, 8 September 2001; 'Waste of time?', *Insider*, September 2003.

91. Eyre, *Playing with Fire*, postscript.

92. Bere, 'Infectious Beats', 86–7.

93. Dumisani Moyo, 'Re-regulation or over-regulation: broadcasting regulations in Zimbabwe', africafilmtv.com, n.d.; Bere, 'Urban Grooves'.

94. Jennifer Byrne, 'The political music of Zimbabwe' (Glasgow: Centre for Political Song, March 2003); 'ProMugabe musicians suffer crippling boycott', *Independent* (UK), 23 March 2005.

95. Maxwell Sibanda, *Complete control: music and propaganda in Zimbabwe*, freemuse.org, 20 September 2004

96. 'Miss Rural Beauties tour Exhibition Park', *Herald*, 24 August 2005; 'Mashakada steals show', *Herald*, 8 August 2005.

97. 'Silver Jubilee: Zim to honour distinguished individuals', *Herald*, 15 April 2005; 'Zimbabweans set to throng heroes' shrines', *Herald*, 8 August 2005.

98. Wonderful Bere, 'Urban Grooves'.

99. Everjoice Win, 'Celebrating independence—isn't 24 years enough?' Text written in April 2004; personal communication May 2016.

100. 'Dongo launches political party', *Sunday Mail*, 20 December 1998, provides a surprisingly detailed and sympathetic portrait of Dongo's agenda; see also Kempton Makamure, 'It's time we graduated from personality politics', *Independent*, 28 May 1999.

101. 'ZUD claims CIO infiltration', *Standard*, 23 May 1999; 'Things fall apart: Margaret Dongo, Kempton Makamure part ways', *Parade*, September 1999, 3, 43; 'CIO claims victory for splitting Dongo's party', *Independent*, 16 July 1999.

102. 'President uses his powers to amend act: Mass job actions temporarily banned', *Herald*, 28 November 1998; 'ZCTU pulls out of tri-partite talks', *Herald*, 2 March 1999; 'Unions form party to challenge Mugabe', *Mail & Guardian*, 2 March 1999.

103. NWPC, 'Declaration of the National Working Peoples Convention', Harare, February 1999.

104. Research notes, 11 September 1999; 'MDC launched', *Standard*, 12 September 1999.

105. Nyathi, who had been in charge of raising funds for the launch of the MDC, indicated to me that he had intended to remain in the background of the new party, but was unexpectedly exposed (interview, 16 September 1999).

106. Peter Alexander, 'Zimbabwean workers, the MDC and the 2000 election', *Review of African Political Economy* 27.85 (2000), 391.

107. 'No formal links between ZCTU and new party', *Herald*, 16 September 1999, 1.

108. Interview, Densen Mafinyani, ZCC Secretary General, 29 September 1999.

109. Lovemore Madhuku, 'NCA cannot be a member of MDC', *Financial Gazette*, 16 September 1999, 9, 10; 'Tsvangirai quits NCA', *Mirror*, 17 September 1999, 1, 2; 'Tsvangirai resigns from NCA, *Independent*, 17 September 1999, 2; 'NCA denies allegiance to MDC', *Daily News*, 25 September 1999, 5.

110. 'Opposition parties pull out of NCA', *Mirror*, 13 November 1998; 'NCA in policy crisis', *Sunday Mail*, 10 March 2000; 'NCA denies siphoning off $6 billion to MDC', *Daily News*; 'NCA rally in Bulawayo a flop', *Daily News*, 20 September 1999, 1; 'Opposition political parties slam NCA', *Sunday Mail*, 26 September 1999.

111. 'Misihairabwi joins MDC', *Standard*, 5 March 2000; 'ZUD official defects to MDC', *Mirror*, 24 March 2000; 'Mhashu to contest in Chitungwiza East', *Standard*, 20 February 2000.

112. Terence Ranger, 'The Zimbabwe Elections: A Personal Experience', unpublished MS, 19 March 2002, 5.

113. For a useful account of the split, see Adrienne LeBas, *From Protest to Parties: Party-Building and Democratization in Africa* (Oxford: Oxford University Press, 2011); Brian Raftopoulos, 'Reflections on the Opposition in Zimbabwe: The Politics of the Movement for Democratic Change', in Stephen Chan and Ranka Primorac, eds, *Zimbabwe in Crisis: The International Responses and the Space of Silence* (London: Routledge, 2007), 125–47.

114. 'Mugabe rallies flop', *Standard*, 18 June 2000; 'Harare residents snub Mugabe rally—businesses defy orders to close shops', *Financial Gazette*, 22 June 2000.

115. 'Suspected war vets abduct MDC poll agents', *Daily News*, 26 June 2000; 'MDC polling agent abducted in Bulawayo', *Daily News*, 26 June 2000, 17; 'Candidates in hospital after brutal assaults', *Daily News*, 26 June 2000.

116. 'Club monitors fail to locate MDC candidate for Kariba', *Daily News*, 20 June 2000; 'MDC candidate still in hiding despite winning poll', *Daily News*, 29 June 2000; 'MDC candidates flee terror in Gokwe', *Daily News*, 22 June 2000.

117. Shari Eppel, 'Impunity in Zimbabwe', 11 October 2000.

118. GOZ, Clemency Order no. 1 of 2000 (2000); ACHPR 2006, Zimbabwe Human Rights NGO Forum v Zimbabwe (2006), AHRLR, 128.

119. '34 MDC supporters reported missing', *Daily News*, 23 January 2002; '166 arrested during last two days of presidential election', *Herald*, 14 March 2002; 'Five whites, 25 MDC polling agents arrested', *Daily News*, 13 March 2002.

120. 'MDC official abducted', *Daily News*, 1 February 2002.

121. Amani Trust, 'The Presidential Election and the Post-Election Period in Zimbabwe', 10 May 2002, 9–10.

122. Statement from the International Ecumenical Peace Observer Mission on the Zimbabwe Presidential Election 2002, 13 March 2002.

123. GOZ, Public Order and Security Act (2002); 'MDC cries foul as more rallies barred', *Daily News*, 18 February 2002. See 'The Electoral Environment for the March 2005 Parliamentary Elections in Zimbabwe', 23 March 2005, 36–7 for a good discussion of the scope of POSA.

124. Lindgren, 'Green Bombers'; see also Ranger, 'The Zimbabwe Elections'.

125. Preliminary Report of the Commonwealth Observer Group to the Presidential Election in Zimbabwe, 9–10 March 2002.

126. See for instance 'Militia seize hundreds of ID cards', *Independent*, 8 February 2002; on visits after 2002, I continued to hear many accounts of this, especially from pastors and ministers.

127. The Khampepe Report, released only in 2015, further confirms this.

128. Zimbabwe Human Rights NGO Forum (ZHRNF), 'Of Stuffed Ballots and Empty Stomachs: Reviewing Zimbabwe's 2005 Parliamentary Election and Post-Election Period', July 2005, 5.

129. Ibid., 29–37.

130. Norma Kriger, 'Zimbabwe's Parliamentary Election of 2005: The Myth of New Electoral Laws', *Journal of Southern African Studies* 34.2 (2008).

131. 'Recommendations on electoral conduct made', *Herald*, 18 February 1999, 11; 'ESC concerned with by-election delays', *Herald*, 22 February 1999, 6.

132. 'Case for an independent electoral body', *Mirror*, 17 September 1999, 6; 'Polls conduct taxes man of the cloth's patience', *Financial Gazette*,

30 September 1999, 3; 'ESC members protest', *Financial Gazette*, 30 March 2000.

133. 'ESC members protest', *Financial Gazette*, 30 March 2000.

134. 'ESC hamstrung: parties', *Daily News*, 29 May 2000.

135. 'Gula-Ndebele tipped to head ESC', *Independent*, 9 June 2000; 'Key poll role for military', *Financial Gazette*, 31 January 2002.

136. 'Army deployed to supervise poll process', *Independent*, 8 February 2002; 'Soldier seconded to ESC', *Independent*, 15 February 2002.

137. 'Ex-army officer to run polls', *Independent*, 16 July 2004.

138. EU Election Observation Mission, 'Report of the EU Election Observation Mission on the Parliamentary Elections which took place in Zimbabwe on 24th and 25th June 2000', ch. 3, 10.

139. FODEZI, 'The state of the voters' roll: preliminary findings local authority elections' (1999). Interviews, Rashida Fazilahmed, FODEZI, 8 October 1999; Dr Christopher Mushonga, FODEZI, 8 October 1999.

140. See for instance EU Election Observation Mission, 'Report of the EU Election Observation Mission on the Parliamentary Elections which took place in Zimbabwe on 24th and 25th June 2000', ch. 3, 10–11.

141. See for instance 'Israeli-made voters cards cost a fortune', *Sunday Gazette*, 26 March 1995, 1, 3

142. 'Moving the goalposts', *Mail & Guardian*, 24 June 2000; 'Villagers adopt new survival strategies to avoid beatings', *Standard*, 18 June 2000; 'War vets impound farm employees' identity cards', *Daily News*, 20 June 2000.

143. 'Inspection of voters roll extended', *Herald*, 11 December 2001.

144. 'Vote scam exposed', *Financial Gazette*, 7 March 2002; 'Election rigged on a massive scale—ZESN', *Independent*, 14 March 2002; 'Further allegations of Zanu PF rigging', *Daily News*, 7 March 2002.

145. GOZ, Electoral (Presidential Election) (no. 2) Notice, 2002SI 14B/2002; GOZ, Electoral (Presidential Election) (no. 3) Notice, 2002 SI 41A/2002; 'Mugabe in last-ditch poll fraud', *Independent*, 8 March 2002.

146. 'Villagers adopt new survival strategies to avoid beatings', *Standard*, 18 June 2000; 'War vets impound farm employees' identity cards', *Daily News*, 20 June 2000; 'Militia seize hundreds of ID cards', *Independent*, 8 February 2002.

147. 'No new IDs until presidential poll', *Financial Gazette*, 22 November 2001; 'New ID law targets opposition', *Financial Gazette*, 24 January 2002.

148. 'Mudede fails to clarify voter registration requirement', *Daily News*, 3 December 2001.

149. Crisis in Zimbabwe Coalition, 'Zimbabwe Report', June 2002, 20; see R. W. Johnson's analysis of the 2002 electoral roll in Annexure 6 for further detail.

150. GOZ, Zimbabwe Electoral Act, 2004; Kriger, 'Zimbabwe's Parliamentary Election of 2005'.
151. MDC, 'How the elections were rigged', 12 April 2005, 11.
152. GOZ, Citizenship of Zimbabwe Amendment Act, 2001; 'Last minute rush', *Herald*, 5 January 2002.
153. Although a later amendment to the act enabled migrants and children of migrants from SADC countries employed as labourers to 'confirm' their Zimbabwean citizenship. GOZ, Citizenship of Zimbabwe Amendment Act, 2003.
154. 'Gula-Ndebele opposes plans to amend electoral laws', *Daily News*, 3 January 2002.
155. 'Mudede ordered not to tamper with voters' roll', *Daily News*, 4 January 2002.
156. GOZ, Electoral Act (Modification) (no. 2) Notice, 2002; Statutory Instrument 42B of 2002.
157. GOZ, Electoral Act (Modification) Notice, 2002; Statutory Instrument 41D of 2002.
158. 'Thousands won't vote despite renouncing British citizenship', *Daily News*, 4 February 2002.
159. 'Sir Garfield Todd loses right to vote', *Daily News*, 13 February 2002.
160. 'Hundreds missing from voters' roll', *Financial Gazette*, 28 February 2002.
161. 'Election rigged on a massive scale—ZESN', *Independent*, 14 March 2002.
162. *Government Gazette*, 7 June 2000.
163. 'Lawyers attack electoral act amendment on postal votes', *Daily News*, 20 June 2000.
164. 'MDC wins case', *Daily News*, 16 August 2000.
165. 'Opposition cried foul over postal ballots', *Daily News*, 22 June 2000.
166. 'Massive vote fraud alleged in Mutare central', *Daily News*, 27 June 2000; 'Irregularities discovered on postal ballots from DRC', *Herald*, 27 June 2000.
167. GOZ, Electoral Act (Modification) Notice, 2002; Statutory Instrument 41D of 2002.
168. ZCC, 'Report of Ecumenical Peace Observer Mission', n.d., 4, 11.
169. Amani Trust, 'The Presidential Election and the Post-Election Period in Zimbabwe', 12.
170. ZESN, 'Final report on the 2005 Parliamentary Elections', 41–2.
171. MDC, 'How the Elections were rigged', 12 April 2005, 4.
172. Khabele Matlosa, 'Delimitation of electoral boundaries', 8 March 2005; extracted from the EISA Election newsletter no. 19 by www.kubatana.net, 8 March 2005.

173. ZHRNF, 'Of Stuffed Ballots and Empty Stomachs', 24.

174. Ibid., 6.

175. Some groups refused in 1995, because there was no guarantee of independence; see John Makumbe and Daniel Compagnon, *Behind the Smokescreen: The Politics of Zimbabwe's 1995 General Elections* (Harare: University of Zimbabwe Publications, 2000), 230–32.

176. 'ZCC starts training election monitors', *Mirror*, 6 December 1999.

177. GOZ, Election (Amendment) Regulations, 2000 (no. 7); Statutory Instrument 161A of 2000; see also 'Amendments to electoral act gazetted', *Herald*, 21 June 2000, 10.

178. Research notes, 20 June 2000.

179. 'ESC loses case over polls', *Herald*, 22 June 2000.

180. 'Zimbabwe Parliamentary Elections 2000: Accreditation of elections', press release, GOZ, Department of Information, 20 June 2000.

181. Research Notes, 20–22 June 2000; ZCC, 'Report of Ecumenical Peace Observer Mission', n.d., 9; 'UK-sponsored observers barred', *Herald*, 19 June 2000; '216 more election observers barred', *Herald*, 21 June 2000; 'Government bars 40 US observers', *Daily News*, 21 June 2000.

182. 'Gula-Ndebele opposes plans to amend electoral laws', *Daily News*, 3 January 2002.

183. 'Government to bar poll observers from 'hostile states', says Chinamasa', *Daily News*, 26 November 2001.

184. 'Poll observers invited', *Herald*, 29 January 2002.

185. Personal communication, 26 April 2002.

186. 'Zim to bar observers from elections', 22 October 2004; 'Senate Polls: state invites foreign observers', *Herald*, 1 November 2005, 3.

187. 'CCJPZ blames Zanu PF for pre-election violence', *Standard*, 1 October 2000; 'ESC divided over election report', *Independent*, 13 October 2000.

188. 'Govt to ban churches, NGOs from educating voters', Africa Church Information Service, 13 July 2001; 'Statutory body to educate voters', *Sunday Mail*, 1 July 2001; 'MDC wins poll case', *Daily News*, 28 February 2002; see also 'NGOs free to educate voters—ESC', *Financial Gazette*, 31 January 2002.

189. GOZ, Electoral (Amendment) Regulations, 2002 (no. 13); Statutory Instrument 41B of 2002.

190. Brian Raftopoulos, 'Briefing: Zimbabwe's 2002 Presidential Election', *African Affairs* 101 (2002), 420; interview, Densen Mafinyani, ZCC, 23 July 2003.

191. GOZ, Zimbabwe Electoral Act, 2004.

192. As for instance in the case of the Electoral Act, 'Adverse Report of the Parliamentary Legal Committee on the Zimbabwe Electoral Commission Bill'.

193. 'Bill for Senate gazetted', *Herald*, 16 July 2005.

194. Human Rights NGO Forum, 'Politically motivated violence in Zimbabwe, 2000–2001', July 2001, especially sections 5 and 6.

195. 'Supreme Court petitions Mugabe', *Standard*, 31 January 1999.

196. R. G. Mugabe, Broadcast to the Nation, 6 February 1999.

197. 'Mugabe rids bench of Gubbay but not its independence', *Financial Gazette*, 8 March 2001; 'Gubbay triumphs', *Daily News*, 3 March 2001; 'I am not going, says defiant Gubbay: Government insists he must go today', *Herald*, 28 February 2001; 'Moyo insists Gubbay will leave', *Daily News*, 28 February 2001; 'Chief Justice won't go', *Daily News*, 28 February 2001; 'Chief Justice Gubbay quits', *Daily News*, 3 February 2001; 'Poll petition ban unconstitutional', *Herald*, 31 January 2001; 'State loses poll case', *Daily News*, 31 December 2001; 'Chombo plots to oust judges', *Independent*, 26 January 2001; 'Chidyausiku attacks Supreme Court, police', *Daily News*, 9 January 2000; 'Supreme Court judges hit back', *Standard*, 7 January 2001; 'President attacks judiciary', *Financial Gazette*, 14 December 2000.

198. 'Assault on Judges continues', *Standard*, 11 February 2001; 'Supreme Court resumes sitting despite threats', *Daily News*, 14 February 2001; 'Judges refuse to meet Chinamasa', *Independent*, 16 February 2001; 'War Vets to raid Judges homes', *Standard*, 18 February 2001; 'Supreme Court judge Ebrahim refuses to go', *Herald*, 22 February 2001; 'Judges to stay', *Daily News*, 23 February 2001; 'State overtures in asking judges to resign mere courtesy', *Herald*, 23 February 2001.

199. 'Justice Chatikobo resigns', *Independent*, 1 June 2001; 'Justice Devittie stops hearing MDC election petitions', *Herald*, 15 May 2001; 'Why I quit: judge', *Daily News*, 6 October 2001; 'Only two white judges remain', *Herald*, 3 January 2002.

200. 'Supreme Court to have 3 more judges', *Herald*, 27 July 2001; 'Chidyausiku sidelines judges', *Daily News*, 18 September 2001.

201. 'Lawyers move in to block Chidyausiku appointment', *Standard*, 20 May 2001; 'Judge attacks Minister', *Daily News*, 3 October 2001; 'Chinamasa slammed for "simplistic" remarks on judges', *Independent*, 5 October 2001.

202. 'Chidyausiku accused of bias', *Daily News*, 20 September 2001; 'Chidyausiku is Chief Justice', *Daily News*, 21 August 2001; 'Chidyausiku set for new job', *Standard*, 24 June 2001; 'Mugabe man appointed top judge', BBC, 9 March 2001; 'Chidyausiku's record inspires little confidence', *Independent*, 16 February 2001.

203. 'Top black lawyers earmarked for the bench', *Standard*, 4 March 2001; 'MDC to contest Justice Hlatshwayo's appointment in petitions', *Daily News*, 25 June 2001.

204. Solidarity Peace Trust, 'Subverting Justice: the role of the judiciary in denying the will of the Zimbabwean electorate since 2000', March 2005, 17.

205. Mazarire, 'ZANU-PF and the Government of National Unity'; Blessing-Miles Tendi, 'Ideology, Civilian Authority and the Zimbabwean Military', *Journal of Southern African Studies* 39.4 (December 2013), 829–43.

206. *Herald*, 12 April 2001, cited in Human Rights NGO Forum, 'Politically motivated violence in Zimbabwe 2000–2001, A report on the campaign of political repression conducted by the Zimbabwean Government under the guise of carrying out land reform', August 2001.

207. JoAnn McGregor, 'The Politics of Disruption: War Veterans and the Local State in Zimbabwe', *African Affairs*, January 2002.

208. 'War vets besiege [Chiredzi] district administrator's office', *Daily News*, 14 March 2001; 'War vets run show at Kadoma offices', *Daily News*, 12 March 2001; 'Govt purges suspected pro-MDC workers', *Financial Gazette*, 1 March 2001; 'Workers victimised [Matabeleland North]', *Daily News*, 6 March 2001; 'Government accused of "militarising" civil service', *Mirror*, 2 March 2001; 'Prison service suspends 16 alleged MDC supporters', *Daily News*, 6 October 2001; 'Seven more officers fired for allegedly supporting MDC', *Daily News*, 31 October 2001.

209. 'Chihuri violates Police Act', *Standard*, 28 January 2001; 'Police chief told to quit', *Daily News*, 16 January 2001; 'Top cops victimised', *Standard*, 25 February 2001; 'Another cop victimised', *Standard*, 11 March 2001; 'Support for MDC lands detectives in hot water', *Daily News*, 26 September 2000; 'ZRP purge on suspected MDC cops up', *Daily News*, 13 April 2001; 'Chihuri purges top cops', *Financial Gazette*, 14 June 2001; 'Police have an obligation to support Government', *Sunday Mail*, 10 June 2001; see also 'ZRP hit by spate of resignations', *Financial Gazette*, 10 April 2003.

210. 'Police chief told to quit', *Daily News*, 16 January 2001.

211. 'Commander tells soldiers not to vote for Tsvangirai', *Daily News*, 29 May 2001; 'Army chief decampaigns MDC', *Financial Gazette*, 24 May 2001; 'MDC blasts govt over army politics', *Independent*, 1 June 2001; 'Military does not engage in politics', *Herald*, 1 June 2001; 'Army shoots down Tsvangirai', *Financial Gazette*, 10 January 2002, 1, 39; 'Zvinavashe's "treason" slammed', *Independent*, 11 January 2002.

212. 'Mugabe approves 100% pay hike for armed forces', *Financial Gazette*, 4 January 2002; but see also 'Soldiers' pay slashed', *Independent*, 22 March 2002; 'Top army jobs for war vets', *Financial Gazette*, 19 July 2001; 'Army jobs for Zanu PF militia', *Standard*, 23 September 2001.

213. 'Army on high alert, troops recalled', *Financial Gazette*, 7 March 2002; 'Army deployed', *Daily News*, 13 March 2002; 'Defence, Security forces

on full alert', *Herald*, 13 March 2002; 'Zim Army ordered to stay on high alert', *Financial Gazette*, 21 March 2002.

214. GOZ, Traditional Leaders Act (2000).

215. Bill Kinsey, 'Fractionating Local Leadership: Created Authority and Management of State Land in Zimbabwe', in S. Evers, M. Spierenburg and H. Wels, eds, *Competing Jurisdictions: Settling Land Claims in Africa* (Leiden: Brill, 2005), 20.

216. Kinsey, 'Fractionating Local Leadership', 22.

217. 'Chiefs get hefty allowances', *Herald*, 20 April 2004; 'Concern as ZANUPF lures chiefs with perks, money', *Standard*, 9 May 2004.

218. 'Chiefs' benefits to gobble $27.5 b', *Independent*, 15 May 2004; 'Chiefs eat cake with Mugabe', *Standard*, 2 February 2003.

219. 'Observers query chiefs' role in poll', *Financial Gazette*, 24 January 2005.

220. Moyo, 'Land Policy, Poverty Reduction and Public Action', 52.

221. Ibid., 53–4; see also Leila Tafara Sinclair-Bright, 'This Land: Land Reform, Authority, Morality and Politics in Zimbabwe' (Edinburgh, 2016).

222. 'National bira preps reach advanced stage', 22 September 2005; see also 'Celebratory biras reach climax', *Sunday Mail*, 25 September 2005; 'National biras continue to gain momentum', *Herald*, 26 September 2005; 'Make biras annual event', *Herald*, 17 October 2005.

223. See for instance Jeremy Brickhill, 'Making peace with the past: war victims and the work of the Mafela Trust', in Ngwabi Bhebe and Terence Ranger, eds, *Soldiers in Zimbabwe's Liberation War* (Harare: University of Zimbabwe Publications, 1995), 163–73; for a more recent account of such ceremonies, see James L. Cox, 'The Land Crisis in Zimbabwe: A Case of Religious Intolerance?', paper presented at New College, University of Edinburgh, 8 June 2005.

224. IMF statement on the conclusion of 2004 Article IV consultation discussions with Zimbabwe, 31 March 2004.

225. Eddie Cross, 'The Zimbabwe Economy in 2005', 16 June 2005, www.kubatana.net.

226. 'Bleak outlook for vulnerable, say aid workers', *IRIN*, 6 September 2005.

227. 'Family budget surges to $11.6m', *Herald*, 4 November 2005.

228. 'Government backs down on domestic workers' salaries', *Mirror*, 12 May 2005; 'Domestic wage rise will erode RBZ gains: Emcoz', *Herald*, 20 April 2005.

229. 'ZESA gets UDS$10m credit line', *Herald*, 18 October 2005.

230. 'Over 30 textile companies collapse', *Financial Gazette*, 6 October 2005.

231. 'Bakeries face viability problems', *Chronicle*, 6 October 2005.

232. 'Producers evade gazetted prices', *Mirror*, 19 July 2005; '28 Supermarkets fined', *Herald*, 9 May 2005; 'Retailers defy government directive', *Herald*, 28 April 2005.

233. 'Leo Mugabe arrested', *Herald*, 20 October 2005.
234. Jeremy Jones, 'Freeze! Movement, narrative and the disciplining of price in hyperinflationary Zimbabwe', *Social Dynamics* 36.2 (2010), 338–51; see also Solomon Mungure, 'Informal Armed Formations and the State: The Case of Zimbabwe', *Journal of Peacebuilding and Development* 9.2 (2014), 37–41.
235. 'Mugabe criticises "white enemy"', BBC, 14 December 2000.
236. 'Mugabe blasts whites', *Standard*, 22 October 2000.
237. 'Zim's birth rate falls', *Herald*, 22 August 2005.
238. Personal communication, Angus Selby, 30 October 2001; 'CFU faces split over withdrawal of charges', *Daily News*, 18 August 2000; Mercedes Sayagues, 'CFU opens its chequebook to buy peace in Zim', *Mail & Guardian*, 19 May 2000; 'White farmers offer government one million hectares', UN Integrated Regional Information Network, 25 May 2001; 'Commercial farmers break deadlock with government', *Daily News*, 27 July 2001; 'State accepts land offer', *Herald*, 6 September 2001; CFU, 'GoZ/ZJRI implementation launch', 2 November 2001.
239. GOZ, Land Acquisition Amendment Act (2000) (2001); GOZ, Rural Land Occupiers (Protection from Eviction) Act (2001).
240. GOZ, Constitution of Zimbabwe Amendment (no. 17) Act, 2005.
241. Address by the First Secretary and President of Zanu(PF), Cde. R. G. Mugabe, at the Forty-Third Ordinary Session of the Central Committee, 21 July 2000.
242. 'CCJP blasts army attacks', *Financial Gazette*, 22 February 2001; 'Opposition stronghold of St Mary's under siege', *Daily News*, 3 March 2001; 'Riot squad unleashes terror in Chitungwiza', *Daily News*, 5 March 2001; 'Govt incites crackdown on voters', *Independent*, 9 March 2001; 'War vets to storm cities', *Financial Gazette*, 5 March 2001.
243. 'ZCTU officials face expulsion', *Daily News*, 22 January 2001.
244. 'Alleged Zanu PF funding needs probe—ZCTU', *Independent*, 15 December 2000; 'Plot to rig ZCTU poll', *Financial Gazette*, 1 February 2001.
245. 'MDC clash looms at ZCTU congress', *Daily News*, 9 February 2001; 'MDC Zanu PF rivalry scuppers ZCTU Congress', *Mirror*, 17 November 2000; 'Daggers drawn at ZCTU's Masvingo congress', *Independent*, 23 February 2001; 'ZCTU, MDC marriage comes under spotlight', *Mirror*, 23 February 2001; 'Zanu PF suspicious of new ZCTU executive', *Daily News*, 10 March 2001; 'ZCTU faces fresh polls', *Sunday Mail*, 18 March 2001.
246. 'War veterans hired to settle labour dispute', *Daily News*, 28 March 2001; 'War vets to storm cities', *Financial Gazette*, 5 April 2001; 'War veterans force director into hiding', *Daily News*, 9 April 2001; 'War vets

displace ZCTU', *Independent*, 12 April 2001; 'War veterans close shop', *Daily News*, 13 April 2001; 'Company chiefs flee war vets', *Financial Gazette*, 20 April 2001; 'Steel company owner abducted by war vets', *Daily News*, 24 April 2001; 'Ex-fighters raid more companies', *Daily News*, 25 April 2001; 'War vets force NGO to pay ex-workers', *Daily News*, 25 April 2001; 'Joy and celebrations at Zanu-PF headquarters as firms pay-up', *Sunday Mail*, 22 April 2001; 'Hunzvi targets embassies, NGOs', *Financial Gazette*, 26 April 2001.

247. 'Zimbabwe's war vets told to back off', BBC, 16 May 2001; 'State working to stop firm invasions', *Herald*, 17 May 2001; 'Rogue war vets arrested over alleged extortion', *Herald*, 17 May 2001; 'Police hunting for Pasipamire', *Daily News*, 17 May 2001; 'War vets blame govt for chaos', *Independent*, 18 May 2001; 'Workers stage demo', *Herald*, 18 May 2001; 'Blitz on rogue war veterans nets twenty', *Herald*, 18 May 2001; 'Moyo says arrest Moyo', *Daily News*, 22 May 2001.

248. 'Supreme Court to have 3 more judges', *Herald*, 27 July 2001.

249. 'Chinotimba proclaims himself new ZCTU boss', *Daily News*, 12 April 2001; 'Chinotimba continues company raids', *Independent*, 1 June 2001; 'ZFTU latest vehicle for ZANU(PF)'s campaign', *Independent*, 15 June 2001; 'Chinotimba in new raids', *Independent*, 29 June 2001; 'ZFTU vows to intensify raids', *Independent*, 27 July 2001; Lovemore Matombo and Lloyd M Sachikonye, 'The Labour Movement and Democratisation in Zimbabwe', ch. 6 in Björn Beckman, Sakhela Buhlungu and Lloyd Sachikonye, *Trade Unions and Party Politics* (Cape Town: HSRC Press, 2010), 109–30.

250. 'Govt pours money into Chinotimba's union', *Financial Gazette*, 19 July 2001.

251. Personal communication, Miles Larmer, 6 November 2001.

252. Jones, 'Freeze'.

253. Chengetai Zvauya, 'Churches to reject draft constitution', *Standard*, 2 December 1999; 'Christian groups threaten to reject draft constitution', *Daily News*, 13 December 1999; 'Christian community resolves to appeal to constitutional body', *Herald*, 26 January 2000; 'Churches threaten 'No' vote in referendum', *Daily News*, 26 January 2000.

254. 'Mugabe threatens Archbishop', *Daily News*, 3 July 2000; Eunice Mafundikwa, 'After Zimbabwe's divisive poll, ecumenical leader aims for reconciliation', *ENI*, 27 July 2000.

255. '[South African] Bishops warn Mugabe', *Daily News*, 6 July 2000; see also 'Bishop seeks to meet Mugabe', *Standard*, 12 November 2000.

256. Address by the First Secretary and President of Zanu (PF), Cde. R. G. Mugabe, at the Forty-Third Ordinary Session of the Central Committee, 21 July 2000.

257. See for example 'Catholic bishops condemn violence', *Daily News*, 5 June 2000; 'Zimbabwe bishops condemn violence', BBC, 2 May 2001; Zimbabwe Catholic Bishops' Conference Pastoral Letter, May 2001; '"Nation should not be held to ransom by a few", bishops say', *Ecumenical News International*, 8 May 2001; 'Catholic bishops blast government', *Daily News*, 4 May 2001.

258. Zimbabwe Catholic Bishops' Conference Pastoral Letter, Tolerance and Hope, May 2001.

259. 'Mind your own business or else … war vets warn Catholics', *Mirror*, 11 May 2001.

260. 'Anglican Church dispute rages on', *Daily News*, 15 January 2001; 'Kunonga confirmed as Anglican Bishop of Harare', *Herald*, 2 February 2001; 'Committee wants Neill removed from position', *Herald*, 19 January 2001.

261. 'Anglican church meets over objections to newly elected bishop', *Daily News*, 7 March 2001.

262. 'Neill stripped of vicarship', *Daily News*, 9 March 2001; 'Reverend Neill vows to solider on', *Daily News*, 12 March 2001; see also 'Anglican vicar in mysterious accident', *Daily News*, 9 March 2001.

263. 'Kunonga accused of making partisan statements', *Daily News*, 15 May 2001; see also 'Outrage at Bishop's praise for Mugabe', *Telegraph* (UK), 14 May 2001.

264. Weston Kwete, 'New Anglican bishop says West out to control Africa', *Sunday Mail*, 13 May 2001. Emphasis added.

265. Interview, Senior lay member of Harare Cathedral, 21 July 2003.

266. Ncube speaking in Edinburgh, 21 May 2005.

267. ZBCTV evening news, 18 June 2000; picture of Border Gezi at Vapostori meeting, *Herald*, 19 June 2000, 1.

268. 'Church sect demands apology from Gezi', *Daily News*, 21 June 2000.

269. 'Vapostori vote for the first time', *Sunday News*, 25 June 2000.

270. 'Apostolic sect supports President', *Herald*, 3 May 2001.

271. 'Militias on rampage', *Daily News*, 7 January 2002.

272. 'Local churches pledge to back government', *Sunday Mail*, 26 May 2002; 'Churches celebrate thanksgiving day', *Sunday Mail*, 19 May 2002.

273. Research notes, ZCC briefing for election observers, 22 June 2000.

274. Revd Gift Mkwasha, '[letter to the editor] Churches silence on human rights abuse embarrassing', *Daily News*, 15 January 2001; 'Deafening silence on violence is frightening', *Daily News*, 31 January 2001.

275. 'Lutheran Bishop to head Zimbabwe's ecumenical organisation', *Lutheran World Information*, August 2000.

276. Interview, Densen Mafinyani, ZCC, 23 July 2003; 'Zanu(PF)/MDC in church-led talks', *Independent*, 13 June 2003.

277. Interviews, Ray Motsi, Christians Together for Justice and Peace, 7 August 2003; Nicholas Mkaronda, May 2005; see for instance 'Pastoral Statement of the Churches in Manicaland, March 2001', Mutare, 13 March 2001; Christians Together for Justice and Peace, 'The corrupting of Zimbabwe's youth', 14 January 2003; Christians Together for Justice and Peace, 'Statement issued in response to the ZCC communiqué', Bulawayo, 22 July 2003.

278. Jonah Gokova, ZNPC, 30 July 2003 and 7 August 2003.

279. For example, 'A statement from the Harare pastors and clergy', 16 January 2003; ESS/ZNPC, 'Zimbabwe in transition: Challenges for the churches', 25 September 2003; Zimbabwe National Pastors' Conference, statement on 'Operation Restore Order', 29 May 2005.

280. Research notes, ZNPC Mashonaland West Pastors meeting, Chinhoyi, 25 July 2003; Churches working group meeting, 7 August 2003; ZNPC Chitungwiza Pastors meeting, 26–27 October 2005.

281. 'Money won't make leaders: president', Herald, 21 July 1999.

282. 'Chombo warns NGOs against meddling in political activity', Herald, 10 July 2001; see also 'NGOs accused of betraying Government', Chronicle, 4 July 2001, 2.

283. 'SOS closes offices after war vets invasion', Standard, 13 May 2001; 'Canadian aid agency director released by militants', Globe and Mail (Canada), 5 May 2001; 'Hunzvi targets embassies, NGOs', Financial Gazette, 26 April 2001; 'War vets force NGO to pay exworkers', Daily News, 25 April 2001; 'Donor relocates office from Zim', Financial Gazette, 9 August 2001.

284. 'NGO implicated in food scam', Sunday Mail, 8 July 2001, 4; 'State warns NGOs against subversive activity', Herald, 2 July 2001, 8; 'NGOs warned against disorder', Chronicle, 2 July 2001, 2; see also 'State blocks NGO aid', Standard, 18 November 2001.

285. 'State to hand over running of growth points to rural council', Herald, 16 July 2001.

286. 'Notice to all Private Voluntary Organisations not registered', Herald, 13 September 2002, 15; 'Karimanzira urges NGOs to register', Herald, 20 October 2005.

287. Interviews, 2003, 2005; see also NANGO, 'NGOs under surveillance', 21 March 2005, extracted from Issue 3, Zim-NGO Voice by www.kubatana.net.

288. Bertha Chiroro, 'Turning Confrontation in to Critical Engagement: The Challenge of the Inclusive Government to Zimbabwean Civil Society', in Brian Raftopoulos, ed., The Hard Road to Reform: The Politics of Zimbabwe's Global Political Agreement (Harare: Weaver, 2013).

289. 'Group stages demo in Harare', Sunday Mail, 9 March 2003.

290. Interview, NGO activist, 17 July 2003.
291. 'Inyika Trust commends Government on proposed Bill', *Herald*, 9 May 2001; 'Inyika Trust condemns CFU's plans', *Herald*, 11 May 2001; 'Inyika Trust slams judgment', *Herald*, 9 February 2001.
292. 'NCA, NDA clash over interests', *Standard*, 5 November 2000.
293. 'Heritage linked to Jonathan Moyo', *Daily News*, 20 January 2001; 'Heritage Zimbabwe refutes daily's story', *Sunday Mail*, 26 January 2001; 'Heritage Zim hosted Hunzvi mourners', *Independent*, 15 June 2001.
294. 'Zanu PF pushes for formation of rival residents association', *Independent*, 26 January 2001.
295. Interview, Jonah Mudehwe, NANGO, 22 July 2003.
296. 'Mugabe broke the law: Chidyausiku', *Financial Gazette*, 7 February 2002; Chanakira commission calls it a day at last', *Daily News*, 7 March 2002.
297. 'Harare's new Councillors sworn in', *Herald*, 19 March 2002; 'MDC wins mayoral polls', *Daily News*, 15 March 2002; personal communications.
298. 'Chombo ups political stakes for Harare, other cities', *Financial Gazette*, 3 October 2002; 'Mudzuri thrown out', *Herald*, 30 April 2003, 1; 'Chombo's suspension of councillors quashed', *Daily News*, 10 September 2003.
299. She was rewarded with a farm: 'Govt rewards Makwavarara with seized Raffingora farm', *Standard*, 19 September 2004.
300. 'Council passes no-confidence vote', *Financial Gazette*, 7 August 2003, 3; 'Chegutu council fiasco: Chombo accused', *Standard*, 19 October 2003, 3; see also 'Chegutu councillors reinstated', *Mirror*, 8 November 2005.
301. 'State takes over Chitungwiza', *Herald*, 7 November 2005; see also 'Chitungwiza water cut-off', *Herald*, 27 October 2005; 'Chitungwiza mayor learns hard way', *Independent*, 11 November 2005.
302. 'New governors condemned as "white elephants"', *Financial Gazette*, 12 February 2004; Zimbabwe Liberators' Platform, 'Appointment of governors for major cities a retrogressive and costly move', 11 February 2004, *Financial Gazette*, 12 February 2004.
303. 'Office workers turn to street sadza vendors', *Standard*, 23 November 2003; 'Council fails to deal with vendors', *Mirror*, 5 March 2004.
304. 'Urban agriculture thriving', *Herald*, 2 November 2002; 'Zim laws support urban agriculture', *Herald*, 27 June 2004. This was not welcomed by all: 'Urban Farming Threatens Harare Water Sources', *Standard*, 18 January 2004.
305. 'Water blues resurface', *Herald*, 10 May 2004.
306. 'Power cuts to continue', *Mirror*, 29 April 2005; 'Power cuts to continue', *Mirror*, 4 May 2005; 'Power cuts to continue: Zesa', *Mirror*, 31 May 2005.

307. 'Garbage problems haunt Harare suburbs', *Mirror*, 5 January 2005.
308. 'Harare's sewage system falls apart', *Daily News*, 2 June 2003; 'Serious health hazard looms', *Mirror*, 6 February 2004; 'Sewage poses health risk in Byo', *Mirror*, 20 May 2004.
309. 'Harare fails on Housing', *Financial Gazette*, 9 September 2004.
310. 'City councillors slam executive committee', *Chronicle*, 4 November 2004.
311. UN, 'Report of the fact-finding mission', 26.
312. This land was re-allocated to a housing co-op in 2004 in an attempt to drum up political support for ZANU(PF). 'Controversial Aspindale Park finally allocated for housing', *Herald*, 3 October 2005.
313. 'Harare residents condemn council plans to demolish illegal building', *Herald*, 13 March 2001.
314. 'Vendors secure court order barring eviction', *Herald*, 13 March 2001.
315. 'Municipal police demolish tuckshops', *Daily News*, 5 March 2001; 'Harare council moves to regularise tuckshops', *Daily News*, 30 May 2001; 'Council set to crackdown on Harare's illegal food vendors', *Daily News*, 30 May 2001; 'Bulawayo City Council clamps down on vendors', *Daily News*, 14 March 2001.
316. 'Ministry accused of blocking land probe', *Daily News*, 19 March 2003; 'Harare home seekers face billion-dollar losses', *Independent*, 27 May 2005.
317. 'Police round-up street people', *Mirror*, 20 February 2004.
318. 'Council demolished Mosque in Rugare', *Mirror*, 8 March 2004; 'Moslems bitter over destruction of Mosque', *Mirror*, 10 March 2004; 'Council intolerant of other religions', *Mirror*, 9 March 2004; 'Rugare roads need attention', *Mirror*, 10 March 2004.
319. 'Relief for Porta Farm residents', *Mirror*, 2 September 2004; 'Man dies in Porta Farm mayhem', *Mirror*, 3 September 2004; 'Porta residents granted temporary relief', *Mirror*, 7 September 2004.
320. 'Porta farm residents' future bright', *Mirror*, 23 August 2004; 'Porta saga: residents resist directive', *Mirror*, 30 August 2004; 'Porta farm dispute spills into court', *Mirror*, 31 August 2004.
321. See for example 'Residents castigate council', *Mirror*, 3 March 2004; 'Council fails to deal with vendors', *Mirror*, 5 March 2004.
322. 'City council launches cleanliness campaign', *Mirror*, 25 October 2004. *In Annexe 2, the UN's Tibuajika Report provides an excellent account of this process, despite a slightly different chronology: UN, 'Report of the Fact-Finding Mission to Zimbabwe to assess the Scope and Impact of Operation Murambatsvina by the UN Special Envoy on Human Settlements Issues in Zimbabwe, Mrs. Anna Kajumulo Tibaijuka' (2005), 86–91.*
323. 'Furniture makers move ahead of swoop', *Mirror*, 25 May 2005.

324. 'Porta Farm residents' lawsuit against Chombo, Chihuri dismissed', *Mirror*, 18 July 2005; 'Police remove defiant Porta Farm squatters', *Mirror*, 25 July 2005.
325. 'Urban farming banned', *Herald*, 22 June 2005.
326. 'Urban agriculture not banned', *Herald*, 23 June 2005; 'Illegal urban farming', *Herald*, 21 October 2005, 4; 'Harare warns illegal farmers', *Mirror*, 27 October 2005, B2.
327. Tibuajika Report, 32–3.
328. 'Vending resurfaces', *Sunday Mail*, 11 September 2005; 'Police nab 14,706 illegal vendors', *Herald*, 3 October 2005.
329. 'Squatter camps mushrooming again', *Sunday Mail*, 11 September 2005; 'Relocated families return to Harare', *Mirror*, 10 November 2005.
330. *Daily Mirror*, 21 June 2005.
331. Sara Dorman, Daniel Hammett and Paul Nugent, *Making Nations, Creating Strangers* (Leiden: Brill, 2007); Sara Rich Dorman, 'Citizenship in Africa: The Politics of Belonging', in Peter Nyers Engin and F. Isin, eds, *Routledge Handbook of Global Citizenship Studies* (Routledge, 2014).
332. Sara Rich Dorman, '"We Have Not Made Anybody Homeless": Regulation and Control of Urban Life in Zimbabwe', *Citizenship Studies* (2016).
333. 'Police blitz nets 550', *Herald*, 19 May 2005; see also 'Basic good scam exposed', *Herald*, 7 June 2005.
334. 'Murambatsvina meant to develop nation', *Herald*, 19 July 2005; see also 'War against flea market rages', *Mirror*, 21 May 2005.
335. Interview, Mike Davies, 19 October 2005.
336. 'Five months on, blitz victims still homeless', *Independent*, 28 October 2005.
337. Showers Mawowa, 'The Political Economy of Artisanal and Small-Scale Gold Mining in Central Zimbabwe', *Journal of Southern African Studies* 39.4 (2013), 925.
338. Samuel J. Spiegel, 'Legacies of a Nationwide Crackdown in Zimbabwe: Operation Chikorokoza Chapera in Gold Mining Communities', *Journal of Modern African Studies* (2014), 541–70.
339. Richard Saunders, 'Briefing Note: Conflict Diamonds from Zimbabwe', 2009; Tinashe Nyamunda and Patience Mukwambo, 'The State and the Bloody Diamond Rush in Chiadzwa: Unpacking the Contesting Interests in the Development of Illicit Mining and Trading, c.2006–2009', *Journal of Southern African Studies* 38.1 (2012),145–66; Spiegel, 'Legacies of a Nationwide Crackdown in Zimbabwe'.
340. David Towriss, 'Buying Loyalty: Zimbabwe's Marange Diamonds', *Journal of Southern African Studies* 39.1 (March 2013).

7. THE POLITICS OF 'WINNER TAKES ALL' (2008–2014)

1. From Batsirai Chigamba, 'Heroes', September 2008.
2. Michael Bratton, *Power Politics in Zimbabwe* (Boulder, CO: Lynne Rienner, 2014), 99.
3. Brian Raftopoulos, ed., *The Hard Road to Reform: The Politics of Zimbabwe's Global Political Agreement* (Harare: Weaver, 2013).
4. Thys Hoekman, 'Testing Ties: Opposition and Power-Sharing Negotiations in Zimbabwe', *Journal of Southern African Studies* 39.4 (December 2013), 903–20.
5. Fidelis Duri, 'Negotiating the Zimbabwe—Mozambique Border: The Politics of Survival by Mutare's Poor 2000–2008', in Sarah Chiumbu and Muchapara Musemwa, eds, *Crisis! What Crisis?* (Cape Town: HSRC Press, 2012), 129.
6. Muchaparara Musemwa, 'Perpetuating Colonial Legacies: The Post-Colonial State, Water Crises and the Outbreak of Disease in Harare, Zimbabwe, 1980–2009', in Chimbua and Musemwa, eds, *Crisis! What Crisis?*
7. Daniel Makina, 'Migration and Characteristics of Remittance Senders', *International Migration* (July 2013).
8. John Makumbe, 'Theft by Numbers: ZEC's Role in the 2008 Elections', in E. V. Masunungure, ed., *Defying the Winds of Change: Zimbabwe's 2008 Election* (Harare: Weaver, 2009).
9. Ibid.
10. Eldred V. Masunungure, 'A Militarized Election: The June 27 Presidential Run-Off', in *Defying the Winds of Change*.
11. ZESN Electoral Run-off, 'March 29 Harmonized Election Post Mortem' (May 2008), 54–5.
12. Masunungure, *Defying the Winds of Change*.
13. Eldred V. Masunungure, 'Voting for Change: The 29 March Harmonized Elections', in *Defying the Winds of Change*.
14. Simon Badza, 'Zimbabwe's 2008 Harmonized Elections: Regional and International Reaction', in *Defying the Winds of Change*, 149–75.
15. Hoekman, 'Testing Ties'.
16. Martin Adelman, 'Quiet Diplomacy: The Reasons behind Mbeki's Zimbabwe Policy', *Africa Spectrum* 39.2 (2004), 249–76; David Moore, 'A Decade of Disquieting Diplomacy: South Africa, Zimbabwe and the Ideology of the National Democratic Revolution, 1999–2009', *History Compass* 8.8 (2010), 752–67.
17. Andreas Mehler, 'Peace and Power Sharing in Africa: A Not So Obvious Relationship', *African Affairs* 108.432 (2009), 453–73; Bratton, *Power Politics in Zimbabwe*; Nic Cheeseman, 'The Internal Dynamics of Power-Sharing in Africa', *Democratization* 18.2 (2011), 336–65.

18. Mehler, 'Peace and Power Sharing in Africa'.
19. Derek Matyszak, *Law, Politics and Zimbabwe's 'Unity' Government* (Konrad-Adenauer Stiftung, 2010).
20. 'MDC bemoans "victimisation" of its MPs', *Mail & Guardian*, 22 July 2009, last accessed 28 April 2016, http://www.mg.co.za/article/2009-07-22-mdc-bemoans-victimisation-of-its-mps.
21. Paidamoyo Muzulu, 'Posa Bill support withdrawn', *Independent*, 2 December, 2010.
22. Leila Tafara Sinclair-Bright, 'This Land: Land Reform, Authority, Morality and Politics in Zimbabwe' (University of Edinburgh, 2016).
23. Phillan Zamchiya, 'The Role of Politics and State Practices in Shaping Rural Differentiation: A Study of Resettled Small-Scale Farmers in South-Eastern Zimbabwe', *Journal of Southern African Studies* 39.4 (2013), 937–53.
24. Grasian Mkodzongi, 'New People, New Land and New Livelihoods: A Micro-Study of Zimbabwe's Fast-Track Land', *Agrarian South* 2.3 (2013), 1–22; I. Scoones et al., 'The New Politics of Zimbabwe's Lowveld: Struggles over Land at the Margins', *African Affairs* 111 (2012), 527–50; Ian Scoones, 'Zimbabwe's Land Reform: New Political Dynamics in the Countryside', *Review of African Political Economy* (August 2014), 1–16; Gareth D. James, 'Transforming Rural Livelihoods in Zimbabwe: Experiences of the Fast Track Land Reform Programme, 2000–2012' (University of Edinburgh, 2015).
25. Davison Muchadenyika, 'Land for Housing: A Political Resource—Reflections from Zimbabwe's Urban Areas', *Journal of Southern African Studies* (December 2015), 1–20.
26. Showers Mawowa, 'Community Share Ownership (CSOT) in Zimbabwe's Mining Sector: The Case of Mhondoro-Ngezi', Zimbabwe Environmental Law Association (2013); Mark Matsa and Tatenda Masimbiti, 'The Community Share Ownership Trust Initiative as a Rural Development Solution in Zimbabwe: The Tongogara Experience in Shurugwi District', *International Journal of the Humanities and Social Science* 4.8 (2014), 151–63.
27. Grasian Mkodzongi, '"I am a paramount chief, this land belongs to my ancestors": the reconfiguration of rural authority after Zimbabwe's land reforms', *Review of African Political Economy* (November 2015), 1–22.
28. Ray Ndlovu, 'MDC accuses diamond miner of funding shadow Zanu-PF', *Mail & Guardian*, June 2012; 'Financing a Parallel', Global Witness (June 2012), 1–33; David Towriss, 'Buying Loyalty: Zimbabwe's Marange Diamonds', Journal of Southern African Studies 39.1 (March 2013), 99–117.
29. Norma Kriger, 'ZANU PF Politics under Zimbabwe's "Power-Sharing" Government', *Journal of Contemporary African Studies* 30.1 (2012), 11–26.

30. For important analyses of how the formal and informal institutions inter-act, see Samuel J. Spiegel, 'Legacies of a Nationwide Crackdown in Zimbabwe: Operation Chikorokoza Chapera in Gold Mining Communities', *Journal of Modern African Studies* (2014), 541–70; JoAnn McGregor, 'Surveillance and the City: Patronage, Power-Sharing and the Politics of Urban Control in Zimbabwe', *Journal of Southern African Studies* 39.4 (2013), 783–805.

31. Brian Raftopoulos, 'The 2013 Elections in Zimbabwe: The End of an Era', *Journal of Southern African Studies* 39.4 (2013), 980–81.

32. Lloyd M. Sachikonye, 'Continuity or Reform in Zimbabwean Politics? An Overview of the 2013 Referendum', *Journal of African Elections* 12.1 (2013), 178–85.

33. Raftopoulos, 'The 2013 Elections in Zimbabwe'.

34. Sachikonye, 'Continuity or Reform in Zimbabwean Politics?'

35. Bryan M. Sims, 'Conflict in Perpetuity? Examining Zimbabwe's Protracted Social Conflict through the Lens of Land Reform', unpublished PhD thesis, Stellenbosch University, March 2015, 219.

36. Camilla Nielsson (director), film of *Democrats*, 2014.

37. Research and Advocacy Unit, 'Brief report on the 2013 Harmonised Elections', 6 August 2013; ZESN, 'Report on the 31 July Harmonised Elections', 2013.

38. Phillan Zamchiya, 'The MDC-T's (Un)Seeing Eye in Zimbabwe's 2013 Harmonised Elections: A Technical Knockout', *Journal of Southern African Studies* 39 (2013), 959.

39. James Muzondidya, 'The Opposition Dilemma in Zimbabwe: A Critical Review of the Politics of the MDC Parties under the GPA Transitional Framework 2009–2012', in Brian Raftopoulos, ed., *The Hard Road to Reform: The Politics of Zimbabwe's Global Politcal Agreement* (Harare: Weaver, 2013).

40. Nic Cheeseman and Blessing-Miles Tendi, 'Power-Sharing in Comparative Perspective: The Dynamics of 'Unity Government' in Kenya and Zimbabwe', *Journal of Modern African Studies* 48.2 (May 2010), 206.

41. ZESN, 'Report on the 31 July 2013 Harmonised Elections', 46, citing MMPZ.

42. Susan Booysen, 'The Decline of Zimbabwe's Movement for Democratic Change—Tsvangirai: Public Opinion Polls Posting the Writing on the Wall', *Transformation: Critical Perspectives on Southern Africa* 84 (2014), 53–80; Julia Gallagher, 'The Battle for Zimbabwe in 2013: From Polarisation to Ambivalence', *Journal of Modern African Studies* 53.1 (2015), 27–49.

43. Matyszak, *Law, Politics and Zimbabwe's 'Unity' Government*, 97.

44. Zamchiya, 'The MDC-T's (Un)Seeing Eye in Zimbabwe's 2013 Harmonised Elections: A Technical Knockout', 961.

45. Blessing-Miles Tendi, 'Robert Mugabe's 2013 Presidential Election Campaign', *Journal of Southern African Studies* 39.4 (2013), 965.
46. Gallagher, 'The Battle for Zimbabwe in 2013', 40–41.
47. Raftopoulos, 'The 2013 Elections in Zimbabwe'.
48. Michael Aeby, 'Zimbabwe's Gruelling Transition: Interim Power-Sharing and Conflict Management in Southern Africa' (University of Basel, 2015).
49. http://www.hrforumzim.org/alerts/major-reprieve-for-civil-society-as-abel-chikomo-is-acquitted/, last accessed 28 April 2016.
50. Civil society informant, interview, Bulawayo, September 2012.
51. Cheeseman and Tendi, 'Power-Sharing in Comparative Perspective'; Mehler, 'Peace and Power Sharing in Africa'.
52. Aeby, 'Zimbabwe's Gruelling Transition'.
53. Cornelius Ncube, 'The 2013 Elections in Zimbabwe: End of an Era for Human Rights Discourse?', *Africa Spectrum* 48.3 (2013), 99–110.167.
54. Interviews with civil society leaders in Harare and Bulawayo, September 2012.
55. Shari Eppel, 'Repairing a Fractured Nation: Challenges and Opportunities in Post-GPA Zimbabwe', in *The Hard Road to Reform*, 214.
56. Moreblessing Mbire, 'Seeking Reconciliation and National Healing in Zimbabwe: Case of the Organ on National Healing, Reconciliation and Integration (ONHRI)', 2011; Tafadzwa Clifford Gutura, 'An Evaluation on the Effectiveness of the Organ of National Healing, Reconciliation and Integration as a Peacebuilding Mechanism in Zimbabwe. A Case of Mashonaland Central Province' (Bindura, n.d.).
57. Eppel, 'Repairing a Fractured Nation', 238.
58. Cornelius Ncube, 'Contesting Hegemony: Civil Society and the Struggle for Social Change in Zimbabwe, 2000–2008' (University of Birmingham, 2010), 174.
59. Ezra Chitando, Masiiwa Ragies Gunda and Joachim Kugler, *Prophets, Profits and the Bible in Zimbabwe* (Bamberg: University of Bamberg Press, 2013).
60. Zamchiya, 'The MDC-T's (Un)Seeing Eye in Zimbabwe's 2013 Harmonised Elections'.
61. ZCC Pastoral letter, 'Work for peace in Zimbabwe: Pray for it! Speak it! Do it! (Isaiah 60:1–22)', January 2013.
62. Interview with faith-based organization, August 2012; Sara Rich Dorman, '"Rocking the Boat?": Church-NGOs and Democratization in Zimbabwe', *African Affairs* 101.402 (2002), 75–92.
63. Joseph Mujere, 'Land, Graves and Belonging: Land Reform and the Politics of Belonging in Newly Resettled Farms in Gutu, 2000–2009', *Journal of Peasant Studies* 38.5 (2011), 1128; Mkodzongi, 'I am a paramount chief'.
64. Leila Tafara Sinclair-Bright, 'Relationships between Farm Workers and Land Beneficiaries in a New Resettlement Area of Zimbabwe', presented at African Studies Conference, University of Sussex, September 2014.

65. Mujere, 'Land, Graves and Belonging'.
66. Zamchiya, 'The Role of Politics and State Practices'.
67. Mkodzongi, 'I am a paramount chief'.
68. 'Traditional leaders reject draft constitution', *Herald*, www.herald.co.zw/ traditional-leaders-reject-draft-constitution/ 24 Jul 2012, last accessed 28 April 2016; 'Copac draft riles chiefs', www.herald.co.zw/copac-draft-riles-chiefsl-seek-to-meet-president-claus, 3 February 2013, last accessed 28 April 2016.
69. Sinclair-Bright, 'This Land'.
70. Sabelo J. Ndlovu-Gatsheni, *The Zimbabwean Nation-State Project: A Historical Diagnosis of Identity* (Uppsala: Nordic Afrika Institute, 2011); Ndlovu-Gatsheni, *Do 'Zimbabweans' Exist? Trajectories of Nationalism, National Identity Formation and Crisis in a Postcolonial State* (Bern: Peter Lang, 2009).
71. Ndlovu-Gatsheni, *Do 'Zimbabweans' Exist?*
72. 'Nkomo Statue to Be Removed', accessed 27 January 2015, http://www. newzimbabwe.com/news-3319-Nkomo+statue+to+be+removed/ news.aspx; 'Nkomo Statues to Go up Again', accessed 27 January 2015, http://www.newzimbabwe.com/news-5110-Nkomo statues to go up again/news.aspx; '"Nkomo Statue Did Not Meet Our Standards"—The Zimbabwe Independent', accessed 28 January 2015, http://www. theindependent.co.zw/2010/11/18/nkomo-statue-did-not-meet-our-standards/
73. 'Owen Maseko Speaks Out', *Southern Eye*, accessed 28 January 2015, http://www.southerneye.co.zw/2013/11/10/owen-maseko-speaks/. mas
74. Bratton, *Power Politics in Zimbabwe*, 141.
75. Chris Allen, 'Understanding African Politics', *Review of African Political Economy* 65 (1995).
76. Kriger, 'ZANU PF Politics under Zimbabwe's 'Power-Sharing' Government', 13.
77. 'Zimbabwe's ruling party expels former vice-president Mujuru, 3 April 2015, last accessed 28 April 2016, http://mg.co.za/article/2015-04-03-zimbabwes-ruling-party-expels-former-vice-president-mujuru
78. Interview with civil society informant, Bulawayo, September 2012.

8. WRITING ZIMBABWE'S POLITICS

1. Chenjerai Hove, 'Violence without Conscience', *Palaver Finish* (Harare: Weaver, 2002), 81.
2. Jocelyn Alexander, 'The Political Imaginaries and Social Lives of Political Prisoners in Post-2000 Zimbabwe', *Journal of Southern African Studies* 36.2 (June 2010), 483–503.

3. Blessing-Miles Tendi, *Making History in Mugabe's Zimbabwe* (Bern: Peter Lang, 2010), 28.

4. Alexander Beresford, *South Africa's Political Crisis: Unfinished Liberation and Fractured Class Struggles* (London: Palgrave Macmillan, 2015).

5. Luise White, *Unpopular Sovereignty: Rhodesian Independence and African Decolonization* (Chicago, IL: University of Chicago Press, 2015).

6. Brian Raftopoulos, 'The Zimbabwean Crisis and the Challenges for the Left', *Journal of Southern Africa Studies* 32.2 (2006), 203–219.

7. Aristide Zolberg, *Creating Political Order: The Party States of West Africa* (Chicago, IL: Rand McNally, 1966).

8. Tim Scarnecchia, 'The "Sellout Logic" in the Formation of Zimbabwean Nationalist Politics, 1961–1964', in Sarah Helen Chiumbu and Muchapara Musemwa, eds, *Crisis! What Crisis?* (Cape Town: HSRC Press, 2012).

9. Lovemore Matombo and Lloyd M Sachikonye, 'The Labour Movement and Democratisation in Zimbabwe', ch. 6 in Björn Beckman, Sakhela Buhlungu and Lloyd Sachikonye, *Trade Unions and Party Politics* (Cape Town: HSRC Press, 2010), 109–30.

10. Interview, Paul Themba Nyathi, 18 September 1995.

11. James Scott, *Weapons of the Weak* (New Haven, CT: Yale University Press, 1985), 309.

12. Ibid., p. 338.

13. Terence Ranger, 'Nationalist historiography, patriotic history and the history of the nation: the struggle over the past in Zimbabwe', *Journal of South African Studies* 30.2 (2004).

14. Gavin Williams, *Fragments of Democracy: Nationalism, Development and the State in Africa* (Cape Town: HSRC Press, 2003).

15. Sara Rich Dorman, 'Born Powerful? Authoritarian Politics in Eritrea and Zimbabwe', in Kalowatie Deonandan, Dave Close and Gary Prevost, eds, *From Revolutionary Movements to Political Parties: Cases From Africa and Latin America* (New York: Palgrave Macmillan, 2008); Sara Rich Dorman, 'Past the Kalashnikov: Youth, Politics and the State in Eritrea', in Jon Abbink and Ineke van Kessel, eds, *Vanguard or Vandals? Youth, Politics and Conflict in Africa* (Leiden: Brill, 2004), 189–204; Sara Rich Dorman, 'Post-Liberation Politics in Africa: examining the political legacy of struggle', *Third World Quarterly* 27.6 (September 2006), 1085–1101.

16. Robert Mattes and Samantha Richardson, 'Are South Africa's Youth Really a "Ticking Time Bomb"?', Afrobarometer working paper 152 (2015).

17. Jocelyn Alexander, 'Things Fall Apart, the Centre Can Hold', in Ngwabi B. Bhebe and Terence Ranger, eds, *Society in Zimbabwe's Liberation War* (Harare: University of Zimbabwe Publications, 1995).

18. Allen, 'Understanding African Politics.'

19. Frederick Cooper, *Africa since 1940: The Past of the Present (New Approaches*

to *African History*) (Cambridge: Cambridge University Press, 2002); Crawford Young, *The African Colonial State in Comparative Perspective* (New Haven, CT: Yale University Press, 1994).

20. Jeffrey Ira Herbst, *States and Power in Africa: Comparative Lessons in Authority and Control, Princeton Studies in International History and Politics* (Princeton, NJ: Princeton University Press, 2000).

21. Gavin Williams, 'There is no Theory of Petit-bourgeois Politics', *Review of African Political Economy* 3.6 (1976), 84–9; Thomas Lionel Hodgkin, 'The African Middle Class', in Chris Allen and Gavin Williams, eds, *Sub-Saharan Africa* (London: Macmillan, 1982), xxi, 217; Sara Rich Dorman, 'New Year; New Questions', *Democracy in Africa* (2015), last accessed 28 April 2016, http://democracyinafrica.org/new-year-new-questions-sara-rich-dorman/.

BIBLIOGRAPHY

Adelman, Martin, 'Quiet Diplomacy: The Reasons behind Mbeki's Zimbabwe Policy', *Afrika Spectrum* 39.2 (2004), 249–76.

Aeby, Michael, *Zimbabwe's Gruelling Transition: Interim Power-Sharing and Conflict Management in Southern Africa* (PhD thesis, University of Basel, 2015).

Alao, Abiodun, *Mugabe and the Politics of Security in Zimbabwe* (Montreal and Kingston: McGill-Queen's Press, 2012).

Alexander, Jocelyn, *The State, Agrarian Policy and Rural Politics in Zimbabwe: Case Studies of Insiza and Chimanimani Districts, 1940–1990* (DPhil thesis, University of Oxford, 1993).

————, 'State, Peasantry and Resettlement in Zimbabwe', *Review of African Political Economy* 61 (1994), 325–45.

————, 'Things Fall Apart, the Centre Can Hold', in Ngwabi Bhebe and Terence Ranger, eds, *Society in Zimbabwe's Liberation War* (Harare: University of Zimbabwe, 1995), 175–91.

————, 'Dissident Perspectives on Zimbabwe's Post-Independence War', *Africa* 68.2 (1998), 151–82.

————, 'Chiefs and the State in Independent Zimbabwe', paper presented to Conference on Chieftaincy in Africa, St Antony's College, Oxford, 9 June 2001.

————, '"Squatters", Veterans and the State in Zimbabwe', in Amanda Hammer, Brian Raftopoulos and Stig Jensen, eds, *Zimbabwe's Unfinished Business* (Harare: Weaver Press, 2003), 85–91.

————, 'The Political Imaginaries and Social Lives of Political Prisoners in Post-2000 Zimbabwe', *Journal of Southern African Studies* 36.2 (2010), 483–503.

Alexander, Jocelyn, JoAnn McGregor and Terence Ranger, *Violence and Memory* (Oxford: James Currey, 2000).

BIBLIOGRAPHY

Alexander, Peter, 'Zimbabwe Workers, the MDC and the 2000 election', *Review of African Political Economy* 389 (2000), 385–406.

Allen, Chris, 'Understanding African Politics', *Review of African Political Economy* 65 (1995), 302–20.

Astrow, André, *Zimbabwe: a revolution that lost its way?* (London: Zed, 1983).

Auret, Diana, *A Decade of Development* (Gweru: Mambo/CCJP, 1990).

———, *Reaching for Justice: The Catholic Commission for Justice & Peace, 1972–1992* (Gweru: Mambo, 1992).

———, *Urban Housing: a national crisis?* (Gweru: Mambo/CCJP, 1995).

Auret, Michael, *Churu Farm: A chronicle of despair* (Harare: CCJP, 1994).

———, *From Liberator to Dictator: An Insider's Account of Robert Mugabe's Descent into Tyranny* (Claremont: David Philip, 2009).

Badza, Simon, 'Zimbabwe's 2008 Harmonized Elections: Regional and International Reaction', in Eldred Masunungure, ed., *Defying the Winds of Change: Zimbabwe's 2008 Election* (Harare: Weaver Press, 2009), 149–75.

Banana, Canaan S., ed., *Turmoil and Tenacity: Zimbabwe 1890–1990* (Harare: College Press, 1989).

Barnes, Teresa, 'The Heroes' Struggle: Life after the Liberation War for four ex-combatants in Zimbabwe', in Ngwabi Bhebe and Terence Ranger, eds, *Soldiers in Zimbabwe's Liberation War* (Harare: University of Zimbabwe, 1995), 128–39.

———, 'Reconciliation, Ethnicity and School History in Zimbabwe, 1980–2002', in Brian Raftopoulos and Tyrone Savage, eds, *Zimbabwe: injustice and political reconciliation* (Johannesburg: Institute for Justice and Reconciliation, 2004), 140–59.

———, '"History Has to Play Its Role": Constructions of Race and Reconciliation in Secondary School Historiography in Zimbabwe, 1980–2002', *Journal of Southern African Studies* 33.3 (2007), 633–51.

Bayart, Jean-François, *The State in Africa*, translated by Mary Harper, Christopher and Elizabeth Harrison (London: Longman, 1993).

Baynham, Simon, ed., *Zimbabwe in Transition* (Stockholm: Almqvist & Wiksell International, 1992).

Beckman, Björn, 'The Liberation of Civil Society: Neo-Liberal Ideology and Political Theory', *Review of African Political Economy* 58 (1993), 20–33.

Bere, Wonderful, *Urban Grooves: The Performance of Politics in Zimbabwe's Hip Hop Music* (PhD thesis, New York University, 2008).

———, 'Infectious Beats: Urban Grooves Music's Collusion with the Zimbabwean State', in Toyin Falola and Tyler Fleming, eds, *Music, Performance and African Identities* (New York: Routledge, 2012), 78–96.

Beresford, Alexander, *South Africa's Political Crisis: Unfinished Liberation and Fractured Class Struggles* (London: Palgrave Macmillan, 2015).

Bhebe, Ngwabi, *Benjamin Burumbo: African Politics in Zimbabwe 1947–1958* (Harare: College Press, 1989).

———, 'The Nationalist Struggle, 1957–1962' in Canaan Banana, ed., *Turmoil and tenacity: Zimbabwe 1890–1990* (Harare: College Press, 1989) pp. 50–115.

Blair, David, *Degrees in Violence: Robert Mugabe and the Struggle for Power in Zimbabwe* (London: Continuum, 2003).

Bond, Patrick, *Uneven Zimbabwe: A Study of Finance, Development, and Underdevelopment* (Trenton, NJ: Africa World Press, 1998).

Booysen, Susan, 'The Decline of Zimbabwe's Movement for Democratic Change-Tsvangirai: Public Opinion Polls Posting the Writing on the Wall,' *Transformation: Critical Perspectives on Southern Africa* 84 (2014), 53–80.

Bose, Sugata and Ayesha Jalal, 'Nationalism, Democracy and Development', in Sugata Bose and Ayesha Jalal, eds, *Nationalism, Democracy and Development* (Delhi: Oxford University Press, 1997).

Bourdillon, Michael, *Poor, harassed, but very much alive: an account of the street people and their organization* (Gweru: Mambo, 1991).

Bratton, Michael, 'Non-governmental Organizations in Africa: can they influence public policy?', *Development and Change* 21 (1990), 87–118.

———, *Power Politics in Zimbabwe* (Boulder: Lynne Rienner, 2014).

Brickhill, Jeremy, 'Making Peace with the Past: War Victims and the Work of the Mafela Trust', in Terence Ranger and Ngwabi Bhebe, eds, *Soldiers in Zimbabwe's Liberation War* (Harare: University of Zimbabwe, 1995), 163–73.

Brickhill, Joan, 'Investigating the Impact of Urban Agriculture in Harare, Zimbabwe', working paper (Ottawa: International Development Research Centre), 15 May 1998.

Brittain Julie and Brian Raftopoulos, 'The Labour Movement in Zimbabwe 1965–1980', Brian Raftopoulos and Ian Phimister, eds, *Keep on Knocking: A History of the Labour Movement in Zimbabwe 1900–97* (Harare: Baobab, 1997), 97–102.

Brownell, Josiah, 'The Hole in Rhodesia's Bucket: White Emigration and the End of Settler Rule', *Journal of Southern African Studies* 34.3 (2008), 591–610.

———, *Collapse of Rhodesia: Population Demographics and the Politics of Race* (London: I.B. Tauris, 2010).

Burgess, Stephen, *Smallholders and Political Voice in Zimbabwe* (New York: University Press of America, 1997).

Butcher, Colleen, 'Urban Low-income Housing: A Case Study of the Epworth Settlement Upgrading Programme', in Lovemore Zinyama, Daniel Tevera and Sioux Cumming, eds, *Harare: The Growth and Problems of the City* (Harare: University of Zimbabwe, 1993), 61–76.

Carmody, Padraig and Scott Taylor, 'Industry and the Urban Sector in Zimbabwe's Political Economy', *African Studies Quarterly* 7.2/3 (2003), 53–80.

BIBLIOGRAPHY

CCJP/LRF, *Breaking the Silence: Building True Peace. A Report on the Disturbances in Matabeleland and the Midlands, 1980–1988* (Harare: CCJP&LRF, February 1997).

Chan, Stephen, *Robert Mugabe: A Life of Power and Violence* (London: I.B. Tauris, 2003).

Chan, Stephen and Ranka Primorac, eds, *Zimbabwe in Crisis: The International Responses and the Space of Silence* (London: Routledge, 2007),

Chanakira, Ngoni, 'Academic Freedom in Higher Institutions of Learning in Zimbabwe', *SAPEM*, April 1991, 30–31.

Chaumba, Joseph, Ian Scoones and William Wolmer, 'From Jambanja to Planning: The Reassertion of Technocracy in Land Reform in South-Eastern Zimbabwe?', *The Journal of Modern African Studies* 41.4 (2003), 533–54.

Chavunduka, Dexter M., Gerrit Huizer, Tholakele D. Khumalo and Nancy Thede, *Khuluma Usenza: The Story of O.R.A.P. in Zimbabwe's Rural Development* (Bulawayo: ORAP, 1985).

Cheater, Angela, 'The University of Zimbabwe: University, National University, State University or Party University', *African Affairs* 90 (1991), 189–90.

Cheeseman, Nic, 'The Internal Dynamics of Power-Sharing in Africa', *Democratization* 18.2 (2011), 336–65.

Cheeseman, Nic and Blessing-Miles Tendi, 'Power-Sharing in Comparative Perspective: The Dynamics of "Unity Government" in Kenya and Zimbabwe', *The Journal of Modern African Studies* 48.2 (2010), 203–29.

Chennells, Anthony, 'Rhodesian Discourse, Rhodesian Novels and the Zimbabwe Liberation War', in Ngwabi Bhebe and T.O. Ranger, eds, *Society in Zimbabwe's Liberation War* (Harare: University of Zimbabwe, 1995), 102–29.

Chigama, Batsirai, 'Heroes', September 2008, accessed 13 May 2016, http://www.zimbablog.com/2008/09/18/heroes/

Chipembere, Ennie, 'Smith and the City', paper presented at UDI 40th anniversary conference, University of Cambridge, September 2005.

Chiroro, Bertha, 'Turning Confrontation in Critical Engagement: The Challenge of the Inclusive Government to Zimbabwean Civil Society', in Brian Raftopoulos, ed., *The Hard Road to Reform: The Politics of Zimbabwe's GPA* (Harare: Weaver Press, 2013), 117–30.

Chisaka, Chenjerai, 'Did the constitution correctly interpret the views of the people?', *Social Change and Development* 50 (June 2000), p. 3.

Chisaka, Chenjerai and Regis Mtutu, 'Housing For All: between a dream and the reality', *Social Change and Development* 47 (May 1999), 3–6 and 15–16.

Chitando, Ezra, *Singing Culture: A study of gospel music in Zimbabwe* (Uppsala: Africainstitutet, 1992).

Chitando, Ezra, Masiiwa Ragies Gunda and Joachim Kugler, *Prophets, Profits and the Bible in Zimbabwe* (Bamberg: University of Bamberg Press, 2013).

BIBLIOGRAPHY

Chiumbu, Sarah Helen and Muchapara Musemwa, eds, *Crisis! What Crisis?* (Cape Town: HSRC 2012).

Christiansen, Lene Bull, *Tales of the Nation: Feminist Nationalism or Patriotic History? Defining National History and Identity in Zimbabwe* (Uppsala: NAI, 2004).

Chung, Fay, 'Education: Revolution or Reform' in Colin Stoneman, ed., *Zimbabwe's Prospects* (London: Macmillan, 1988),118–32.

Cliffe, Lionel, Joshua Mpofu and Barry Munslow, 'Nationalist Politics in Zimbabwe: the 1980 elections and beyond', *Review of African Political Economy* 18 (1980), 51–53.

Clutton-Brock, Guy, *Cold Comfort Confronted* (London: Mowbray, 1972).

———, *The Cold Comfort Farm Society* (Gwelo: Mambo Press, 1970).

Compagnon, Daniel, *A Predictable Tragedy: Robert Mugabe and the Collapse of Zimbabwe* (Philadelphia, PA: University of Pennsylvania Press, 2011).

Cooper, Frederick, *Africa since 1940: The Past of the Present. New Approaches to African History* (Cambridge: Cambridge University Press, 2002).

Cousins, Alan, 'State, Ideology and Power in Rhodesia, 1958–1972', *International Journal of African Historical Studies* 24.1 (1991), 35–64.

Cox James L., 'The Land Crisis in Zimbabwe: A Case of Religious Intolerance?', paper presented at New College, University of Edinburgh, 8 June 2005.

Crystal, Jill, 'Authoritarianism and its Adversaries in the Arab World' *World Politics* 46 (1994), 262–89.

Cumming, Sioux, 'Post-colonial Urban Residential Change in Harare', in Lovemore Zinyama, Daniel Tevera and Sioux Cumming, eds, *Harare: the Growth and Problems of the City* (Harare: University of Zimbabwe, 1993).

Dansereau, Suzanne, 'Legacy of Colonialism in Zimbabwe's Labour Utilization Model: Mineworkers' Wages, Skills, and Migration', in Brian Raftopoulos and Lloyd Sachikonye, *Striking Back: The Labour Movement and the Post-colonial State in Zimbabwe 1980–2000* (Harare: Weaver Press, 2001), 251–72.

Dashwood, Hevina, *Zimbabwe: The Political Economy of Transition* (Toronto: University of Toronto Press, 2000).

Davies, Angela, 'From Rhodesian to Zimbabwean and Back: White Identity in an African Context' (PhD thesis, University of California, Berkeley, 2001).

Day, John, 'The Creation of Political Myths', *Journal of Southern African Studies* 2.1 (1975), 52–65.

de Bourbon, Adrian, 'Are magistrates independent?', *Legal Forum*, 1 December 1989, 7–8.

de Waal, Victor, *The Politics of Reconciliation* (London: Hurst & Co., 1990).

Dorman, Sara Rich, 'Inclusion and Exclusion: NGOs and Politics in Zimbabwe' (DPhil thesis, Dept. of Politics, University of Oxford, 2001).

————, 'NGOs and State in Zimbabwe: implications for civil society theory', in Bjorn Beckman, Anders Sjögren and Eva Hansson, eds, *Civil Society and Authoritarianism in the Third World* (Stockholm: PODSU, 2001).

————, '"Rocking the Boat?": Church NGOs and Democratization in Zimbabwe', *African Affairs* 101 (2002), 75–92.

————, 'NGOs and the Constitutional Debate in Zimbabwe: From Inclusion to Exclusion', *Journal of Southern African Studies* 29.4 (2003), 845–63.

————, 'Past the Kalashnikov: Youth, Politics and the State in Eritrea', in Jon Abbink and Ineke van Kessel, eds, *Vanguard or Vandals? Youth, Politics and Conflict in Africa* (Leiden: Brill Academic Publishers, 2004), 189–204.

————, 'Studying Democratization in Africa: A Case Study of Human Rights NGOs in Zimbabwe', in Tim Kelsall and Jim Igoe, eds, *Between a Rock and a Hard Place, African NGOs, Donors, and the State* (Durham, NC: Carolina Academic Press 2005), 33–59.

————, 'Post-Liberation Politics in Africa: Examining the Political Legacy of Struggle', *Third World Quarterly* 27.6 (2006), 1085–101.

————, 'Born Powerful? Authoritarian Politics in Eritrea and Zimbabwe', in Kalowatie Deonandan, Dave Close and Gary Prevost, eds, *From Revolutionary Movements to Political Parties: Cases From Africa and Latin America* (New York: Palgrave Macmillan, 2008).

————, 'Citizenship in Africa: The Politics of Belonging', in Peter Nyers and Engin F. Isin, eds, *Routledge Handbook of Global Citizenship Studies* (Oxford: Routledge, 2014), 161–71.

————, 'New Year; New Questions,' *Democracy in Africa*, 2015, accessed 13 May 2016, http://democracyinafrica.org/new-year-new-questions-sara-rich-dorman/.

————, '"We Have Not Made Anybody Homeless": Regulation and Control of Urban Life in Zimbabwe', *Citizenship Studies*, 20.1 (2016), 84–98.

Dorman, Sara, Daniel Hammett and Paul Nugent, eds, *Making Nations, Creating Strangers* (Leiden: Brill, 2007).

Drakakis-Smith, David, 'Strategies for Meeting Basic Food Needs in Harare', in Jonathan Baker and Poul Ove Pedersen, eds, *The rural-urban interface in Africa* (Uppsala: NAI, 1992).

Drakakis-Smith, David, Tanya Bowyer-Bower and Dan Tevera, 'Urban poverty and Urban agriculture' *Habitat International* 19 (1995), 189–91.

Drinkwater, Michael, 'Technical Development and Peasant Impoverishment: Land Use Policy in Zimbabwe's Midlands Province', *Journal of Southern African Studies* 15.2 (1989), 287–305.

Duri, Fidelis, 'Negotiating the Zimbabwe-Mozambique Border: The Politics of Survival by Mutare's Poor 2000–2008', in Sarah Helen Chiumbu and Muchapara Musemwa, eds, *Crisis! What Crisis?* (Cape Town: HSRC 2012), 122–42.

BIBLIOGRAPHY

Eppel, Shari, 'Repairing a Fractured Nation: Challenges and Opportunities in Post-GPA Zimbabwe', in Brian Raftopoulos, ed., *The Hard Road to Reform: The Politics of Zimbabwe's GPA* (Harare: Weaver Press, 2013), 211–50.

Evans, Michael, 'The Security Threat from South Africa', in Colin Stoneman, ed., *Zimbabwe's Prospects* (London: Macmillan, 1988), 218–35.

Eyre, Banning, 'Thomas Mapfumo releases Rise Up', 28 March 2005, http://news.calabashmusic.com/world/lioninwinter.

Eyre, Banning, 'Playing with Fire: Fear and Self-censorship in Zimbabwean Music', Freemuse.org (2001), 68–74.

Farquar, Jane, *Jairos Jiri: the Man and his Work 1921–1982* (Gweru: Mambo Press, 1987).

Feltoe, Geoff, 'Deciding not to decide: case note on the case of Holland & Ors v the Minister of Public Service, Labour and Social Welfare, S-15–97', *Legal Forum* (1997), 43–45.

Fontein, Joost, 'Shared Legacies Of The War: Spirit Mediums And War Veterans In Southern Zimbabwe', *Journal of Religion in Africa* 36.2 (2006), 167–99.

——————, *Silence of Great Zimbabwe: Contested Landscapes and the Power of Heritage* (London: UCL Press Ltd, 2006).

Gaidzanwa, Rudo B., 'Grappling with Mugabe's Masculinist Politics in Zimbabwe: A Gender Perspective', in Sabelo J. Ndlovu-Gatsheni, ed., *Mugabeism? History, Politics and Power in Zimbabwe* (New York: Palgrave Macmillan, 2015), 157–80.

Gallagher, Julia, 'The Battle for Zimbabwe in 2013: From Polarisation to Ambivalence', *Journal of Modern African Studies* 53.1 (2015), 27–49.

Gaventa, John, *Power and Powerlessness: Quiescence and Rebellion in an Appalachian Valley* (Urbana, IL: University of Illinois Press, 1982).

Gramsci, Antonio, 'State and Civil Society', in Quintin Hoare and Geoffrey Nowell Smith, eds, *Selections from the Prison Notebooks of Antonio Gramsci* (New York: International Publishers, 1971).

Grant, Miriam, 'Movement Patterns and the Medium Sized City', *Habitat International* 19.3 (1995), 357–69.

Gunby, Derek, Roger Mpande and Alan Thomas, 'The campaign for water from the Zambezi for Bulawayo', in Alan Thomas, Susan Carr and David Humphreys, eds, *Environmental Policies and NGO Influence: Land Degradation and Sustainable Resources Management in Sub-Saharan Africa* (London: Routledge, 2001), 72–93.

Gundani, Paul H., 'The Catholic Church and National Development in Independent Zimbabwe', in Hallencreutz, Carl and Ambrose Moyo, eds, *Church and State in Zimbabwe* (Gweru: Mambo, 1988), 215–49.

Gutura, Tafadzwa Clifford, 'An Evaluation on the Effectiveness of the Organ of National Healing, Reconciliation and Integration as a Peacebuilding

Mechanism in Zimbabwe. A Case of Mashonaland Central Province' (Master's dissertation, Bindura University of Science Education, n.d).

Guzha, Daves, Edgar Langeveldt and Chirikure Chirikure, *State of the Nation*. A Rooftops Promotions Production, performed 9 November 2005, Harare, Zimababwe.

Gwebu, Thomas D., 'Urban water scarcity management: civic vs state response in Bulawayo', *Habitat International* 26 (2002), 417–31.

Hallencreutz, Carl, 'Church and State in Zimbabwe and South Africa', in Carl F. Hallencreutz and Mai Palmberg, eds, *Religion and politics in Southern Africa* (Uppsala: Scandinavian Institute of African Studies, 1991), 159–65.

Hallencreutz, Carl and Ambrose Moyo, eds, *Church and State in Zimbabwe* (Gweru: Mambo, 1988).

Hammar, Amanda, Brian Raftopoulos and Stig Jensen, eds, *Zimbabwe's Unfinished Business* (Harare: Weaver Press, 2003).

Hancock, I.R., 'The Capricorn Africa Society in Southern Africa', *Rhodesian History* IX (1978), 41–62.

———, *White Liberals, Moderates and Radicals in Rhodesia*, 1953–1980 (London: Croon Helm, 1984).

Hanlon, Joseph, 'Destabilisation and the battle to reduce dependence', in Colin Stoneman, ed., *Zimbabwe's Prospects* (London: Macmillan, 1988).

Hardwick, P.A., 'The Transportation System', in George Kay and Michael Smout, eds, *Salisbury: A Geographical Survey of the Capital of Rhodesia* (London: Hodder and Stoughton, 1977), 94–112.

Haugerud, Angelique, *The Culture of Politics in Modern Kenya* (Cambridge: Cambridge University Press, 1997).

Hawkins, Darren, 'Democratization Theory and Nontransitions: Insights from Cuba', *Comparative Politics* 33 (2001), 441–61.

Helmsing, A.H.J., 'Transforming rural local government: Zimbabwe's post-independence experience', *Environment and Planning; C. Government & Policy* (1990), 87–110.

Herbst, Jeffrey, *State Politics in Zimbabwe* (Harare: University of Zimbabwe, 1991).

———, 'The Consequences of Ideology' in Simon Baynham, ed., *Zimbabwe in transition* (Stockholm: Almqvist & Wiksell International, 1992).

———, *States and Power in Africa: Comparative Lessons in Authority and Control* (Princeton, N.J.: Princeton University Press, 2000).

Hodgkin, Thomas Lionel, 'The African Middle Class', in Chris Allen and Gavin Williams, eds, *Sub-Saharan Africa* (London: Macmillan, 1982).

Hoekman, Thys, 'Testing Ties: Opposition and Power-Sharing Negotiations in Zimbabwe', *Journal of Southern African Studies* 39.4 (2013), 903–20.

Holderness, Hardwicke, *Lost Chance* (Harare: Zimbabwe Publishing House, 1985).

BIBLIOGRAPHY

Hoogeveen, J. G. M. and B. H. Kinsey, 'Land Reform, Growth and Equity: Emerging Evidence from Zimbabwe's Resettlement Programme–A Sequel', *Journal of Southern African Studies* 27,(2001), 126–36.

Hooker, James R., 'Welfare Association and other Instruments of Accommodation in the Rhodesias between the World Wars', *Comparative Studies in Society and History* 9 (1966), 51–63.

Horn, Nancy E., *Cultivating customers: market women in Harare, Zimbabwe* (Boulder, CO: Lynne Rienner, 1994).

Hove, Chenjerai, *Shebeen Tales* (Harare: Baobab, 1994).

———, *Rainbows in the Dust* (Harare: Baobab, 1998).

———, *Palaver Finish* (Harare: Weaver, 2002).

Iyob, Ruth, *The Eritrean Struggle for Independence* (Cambridge: Cambridge University Press, 1995).

James, Gareth D., *Transforming Rural Livelihoods in Zimbabwe: Experiences of the Fast Track Land Reform Programme, 2000–2012* (PhD thesis, University of Edinburgh, 2015).

Jenkins, Carolyn, 'The Politics of Economic Policy-making in Zimbabwe', *Journal of Modern African Studies* 35.4 (1997), 575–602.

Jones, Jeremy, 'Freeze! Movement, narrative and the disciplining of price in hyperinflationary Zimbabwe', *Social Dynamics* 36.2 (2010), 338–51.

Kaarsholm, Preben, 'From Decadence to Authenticity and Beyond: Fantasies and Mythologies of War in Rhodesia and Zimbabwe, 1965–1985' in Preben Kaarsholm, ed., *Cultural Struggle and Development in Southern Africa* (Harare: Baobab, 1991), 33–60.

Kamete, Amin, 'Restrictive Control of Urban High-density Housing in Zimbabwe', *Housing, Theory and Society* 16 (1999), 136–51.

———, 'The Rebels Within: Urban Zimbabwe in the Post-Election Period', in Henning Melber, ed., *Zimbabwe's Presidential Elections 2002* (Uppsala: Nordiska Africainstitutet, 2002), 31–47.

———, 'Transit or concentration camps? Revisiting state responses to urban homelessness in Harare, Zimbabwe', unpublished paper, n.d., 5.

Kanji, Nazneen and Niki Jazdowska, 'Structural Adjustment and Women in Zimbabwe', *Review of African Political Economy* 56 (1993), 11–26.

Karekwaivanane, George Hamandishe, *Legal Encounters: Law, State and Society in Zimbabwe, c. 1950–1990* (DPhil thesis, University of Oxford, 2012).

Kaviraj, Sudipta, 'In Search of Civil Society', paper presented to the SOAS Politics Seminar, London, 20 October 1999.

Kesby, Mike, 'Arenas for Control, Terrains of Gender Contestation: Guerrilla Struggle and Counter-Insurgency Warfare in Zimbabwe 1972–1980', *Journal of Southern African Studies* 22.4 (1996), 561–84.

Kibble, Steve, 'Zimbabwe: the State, Development and Democratization', unpublished paper, 2000.

BIBLIOGRAPHY

Kinsey, Bill, 'Land reform, growth and equity: emerging evidence from Zimbabwe's resettlement programme', *Journal of Southern African Studies* 25 (1999), 173–96.

————, 'Fractionating Local Leadership: Created Authority and Management of State Land in Zimbabwe', in S. Evers, M. Spierenburg and H. Wels, eds, *Competing Jurisdictions: Settling Land Claims in Africa* (Leiden: Brill Academic Publishers, 2005).

Knight, Rachel, '"We are tired of promises, tired of waiting": People's power, local politics and the fight for land in Zimbabwe' (Dissertation, Brown University, 1999).

Kriger, Norma J., *Zimbabwe's Guerrilla War: Peasant Voices* (Cambridge: Cambridge University Press, 1991).

————, 'The War Victims Compensation Act', *Journal of African Conflict and Development* 1 (2000). Author's MS, n.p.

————, 'Les vétérans et le parti au pouvoir: une coopération conflictuelle dans la longue durée', *Politique Africaine* 81 (2001), 80–100.

————, *Guerrilla Veterans in Post-War Zimbabwe: Symbolic and Violent Politics, 1980–1987* (Cambridge: Cambridge University Press, 2003).

————, 'Zimbabwe's Parliamentary Election Of 2005: The Myth Of New Electoral Laws', *Journal of Southern African Studies* 34.2 (2008), 359–78.

————, 'ZANU PF Politics under Zimbabwe's "Power-Sharing" Government', *Journal of Contemporary African Studies* 30.1 (2012), 11–26.

Kumbula, Tendayi, 'Press Freedom in Zimbabwe', in Festus Eribo and William Jong-Ebot, eds, *Press Freedom and Communications in Africa* (Trenton, NJ: Africa World Press, 1997), 157–82.

Lamont, Donal, *Speech from the Dock* (Suffolk: Kevin Mayhew, 1977).

Lan, David, *Guns and Rain: Guerrilla and Spirit Mediums in Zimbabwe* (London: James Currey, 1985).

Lapsley, Michael, *Neutrality or Co-option? Anglican Church and State from 1964 until the Independence of Zimbabwe* (Gweru: Mambo, 1986).

Larmer, Miles, 'The political role of the trades union movement in Zambia and Zimbabwe after independence', paper presented to Southern Africa History and Politics Seminar, Oxford, 22 January 2001.

Lawyers Committee on Human Rights, 'Zimbabwe: Wages of War' (New York: Lawyers Committee, 1986).

LeBas, Adrienne, 'Polarization as Craft: Party Formation and State Violence in Zimbabwe', *Comparative Politics* 38 (2006), 419–38.

————, *From Protest to Parties: Party-Building and Democratization in Africa* (Oxford: Oxford University Press, 2011).

Lee, Karen M., 'The Historical Development of Zimbabwe's Museums and Monuments', (MPhil thesis, University of St Andrews, 1995).

Linden, Ian, *The Catholic Church and the struggle for Zimbabwe* (London: Longman, 1980).

BIBLIOGRAPHY

Lindgren, Björn, 'The Green Bombers of Salisbury: Elections and Political Violence in Zimbabwe', *Anthropology Today* 19.2 (2003), 6–10

———, *The Politics of Ndebele Ethnicity: Origins, Nationality and Gender in Southern Zimbabwe* (PhD dissertation, Uppsala University, 2002).

Linz, Juan, *Totalitarian and Authoritarian Regimes* (Boulder, CO: Lynne Rienner, 2000).

Lukes, Steven, *Power: A Radical View* (Basingstoke: Macmillan, 1974).

Lyons, Tanya, *Guns and Guerrilla Girls: Women in Zimbabwe's Liberation Struggle* (Trenton, NJ: Africa World Press, 2004).

Madzoke, Claudia, 'Education', in *Social Policy and Administration in Zimbabwe* (Harare: School of Social Work, 1995), 173–89.

Makina, Daniel, 'The Impact of Regional Migration and Remittances on Development: The Case of Zimbabwe', Open Society Initiative for Southern Africa working paper, 2009.

Makumbe, John, 'Public Meeting: Establishing a Constitutional Base for Democratic Practice: lessons from South Africa', Harare, 28 May 1997.

———, *Democracy and Development in Zimbabwe: Constraints of Decentralisation* (Harare: SAPES, 1998).

———, 'Is there a civil society in Africa?', *International Affairs* 74.2 (1998), 305–16.

———, 'Theft by Numbers: ZEC's Role in the 2008 Elections', in Eldred Masunungure, ed., *Defying the Winds of Change: Zimbabwe's 2008 Election* (Harare: Weaver Press, 2009).

Makumbe, John and Daniel Compagnon, *Behind the Smokescreen: The Politics of Zimbabwe's 1995 General Elections* (Harare: University of Zimbabwe, 2000).

Mamdani, Mahmood, 'State and Civil Society in Contemporary Africa: Reconceptualizing the Birth of State Nationalism and the Defeat of Popular Movements', *Africa Development* XV (1990), 47–70.

Mandaza, Ibbo, 'The State and Politics in the Post-White Settler Colonial Situation', in Ibbo Mandaza, ed., *Zimbabwe: the Political Economy of Transition, 1980–1986* (Dakar: CODESRIA, 1986), 51–65.

———, ed., *Zimbabwe: the Political Economy of Transition, 1980–1986* (Dakar: CODESRIA, 1986).

Mandaza, Ibbo and Lloyd Sachikonye, eds, *The One-Party State and Democracy* (Harare: SAPES, 1991).

Marongwe, Nelson, 'Farm Occupations and Occupiers in the New Politics of Zimbabwe', in Amanda Hammar, Brian Raftopoulos and Stig Jensen, eds, *Zimbabwe's Unfinished Business* (Harare: Weaver Press, 2003), 155–91.

Martin, David and Phyllis Johnson, *The Struggle for Zimbabwe: The Chimurenga War* (London: Faber Boston, 1981).

Masiiwa, Medicine, 'Land Reform Programme in Zimbabwe: Disparity

BIBLIOGRAPHY

Between Policy Design and Implementation', Institute of Development Studies, University of Zimbabwe, May 2004.

Masunungure, Eldred V., ed., *Defying the Winds of Change: Zimbabwe's 2008 Election*, (Harare: Weaver Press, 2009).

Mathema, N.C.G., *Newspapers in Zimbabwe* (Lusaka: Multimedia Zambia, 2001)

Matombo, Lovemore and Lloyd M. Sachikonye, 'The Labour Movement and Democratisation in Zimbabwe', in Björn Beckman, Sakhela Buhlungu and Lloyd Sachikonye, eds, *Trade Unions and Party Politics: Labour Movements in Africa* (Cape Town: HSRC Press), 109–30.

Matsa, Mark and Tatenda Masimbiti, 'The Community Share Ownership Trust Initiative as a Rural Development Solution in Zimbabwe: The Tongogara Experience in Shurugwi District', *International Journal of the Humanities and Social Science* 4.8 (2014), 151–63.

Matyszak, Derek, *Law, Politics and Zimbabwe's 'Unity' Government* (Harare: Konrad Adenauer Stiftung and Research Advocacy Unit, 2010).

Maughan-Brown, David, 'Myths on the March: the Kenyan and Zimbabwean Liberation Struggles in Colonial Fiction', *Journal of Southern African Studies* 9.1 (1982), 93–117.

Mawowa, Showers, 'The Political Economy of Artisanal and Small-Scale Gold Mining in Central Zimbabwe', *Journal of Southern African Studies* 39.4 (2013), 921–36.

———, 'Community Share Ownership (CSOT) in Zimbabwe's Mining Sector: The Case of Mhondoro-Ngezi', Working Paper, ZELA 2013.

Maxwell, David, 'The Church and Democratisation in Africa: the case of Zimbabwe', in Paul Gifford, ed., *The Christian Churches and the Democratization of Africa* (Leiden: Brill, 1995), 108–29.

———, *Christians and Chiefs in Zimbabwe: A Social History of the Hwesa People, c.1870s-1990s* (Edinburgh: Edinburgh University Press for the International African Institute, 1999).

———, 'Catch the Cockerel Before Dawn: Pentecostalism and Politics in Post-Colonial Zimbabwe', *Africa* 70.2 (2000), 249–77.

Mazambani, D., 'Peri-urban cultivation within Greater Harare', *The Zimbabwe Science News* 16.6 (June 1992).

Mazarire, Gerald, 'Reflections on Pre-Colonial Zimbabwe c850–1880s', in Brian Raftopoulos and A S Mlambo, eds, *Becoming Zimbabwe* (Harare: Weaver Press, 2009), 1–38.

———, 'ZANU-PF and the Government of National Unity', in Brian Raftopoulos, ed., *The Hard Road to Reform: The Politics of Zimbabwe's Global Political Agreement* (Harare: Weaver Press, 2013).

Mbara, T.C. and D.A.C. Maunder, 'The initial effects of introducing commuter omnibus services in Harare, Zimbabwe', Transport Research Library, working paper, 1996.

Mbiba, Beacon, 'Institutional responses to uncontrolled urban cultivation in Harare: prohibitive or accommodative?' *Environment and Urbanization*, 6.1 (1994), 188–202.

—*Urban Agriculture in Zimbabwe* (Aldershot: Avebury, 1995).

Mbire, Moreblessing, 'Seeking Reconciliation and National Healing in Zimbabwe: Case of the Organ on National Healing, Reconciliation and Integration (ONHRI)', (Master's dissertation, The Hague, 2011).

McCandless, Erin, *Polarization and Transformation in Zimbabwe: Social Movements, Strategy Dilemmas and Change* (Lanham, MD: Lexington Books, 2011).

McGregor, JoAnn, 'The Politics of Disruption: War Veterans and the Local State in Zimbabwe', *African Affairs* 101 (2002), 9–37.

———, 'Surveillance and the City: Patronage, Power-Sharing and the Politics of Urban Control in Zimbabwe', *Journal of Southern African Studies* 39.4 (2013), 783–805.

Mehler, Andreas, 'Peace and Power Sharing in Africa: a not so obvious relationship', *African Affairs* 108.432 (2009), 453–73.

Melber, Henning, *Limits to Liberation in Southern Africa* (Uppsala: NAI, 2003).

———, *Understanding Namibia* (London: Hurst & Co., 2014).

Meredith, Martin, *Mugabe: Power and Plunder in Zimbabwe* (Oxford: Public Affairs, 2002).

Mitchell, Timothy, 'Society, Economy and the State Effect', in George Steinmetz, ed., *State/Culture: state formation after the cultural turn* (Ithaca, NY: Cornell University Press, 1999).

Mkodzongi, Grasian, 'New People, New Land and New Livelihoods: A micro-study of Zimbabwe's Fast-Track Land Reform', *Agrarian South: Journal of Political Economy* 2.3 (2013), 345–66.

———, '"I am a paramount chief, this land belongs to my ancestors": the reconfiguration of rural authority after Zimbabwe's land reforms', *Review of African Political Economy* (2015), 1–16.

Mlambo, A. S., *The Economic Structural Adjustment Programme: The Case of Zimbabwe, 1990–1995* (Harare: University of Zimbabwe, 1997).

———, *White Immigration into Rhodesia: from occupation to federation* (Harare: University of Zimbabwe, 2002).

Moorcraft, Paul, *Mugabe's War Machine* (London: Pen and Sword, 2012).

Moore, David, 'The Zimbabwean "organic intellectuals" in Transition', *Journal of Southern African Studies* 15 (1988), 96–105

———, *The Contradictory Construction of Hegemony in Zimbabwe* (PhD thesis, York University, Toronto, 1990).

———, 'The Ideological Formation of the Zimbabwean Ruling Class', *Journal of Southern African Studies* 17.3 (1991), 488–95.

———, 'The Zimbabwe People's Army: Strategic Innovation or More of the Same?' in Ngwabi Bhebe and Terence Ranger, eds, *Soldiers in Zimbabwe's Liberation War* (Harare: University of Zimbabwe, 1995), 73–86.

BIBLIOGRAPHY

————, 'A Decade of Disquieting Diplomacy: South Africa, Zimbabwe and the Ideology of the National Democratic Revolution, 1999–2009', *History Compass* 8.8 (2010), 752–67.

Moore, Donald S., *Suffering for Territory: Race, Place and Power in Zimbabwe* (Harare: Weaver Press, 2005).

Moyo, Dumisani, 'Re-regulation or over-regulation: broadcasting regulations in Zimbabwe', africafilmtv.com, n.d.

Moyo, Jonathan, 'State Politics and Social Domination', *Journal of Modern African Studies* 30.2 (1992), 305–30.

————, *Voting for Democracy: Electoral Politics in Zimbabwe* (Harare: University of Zimbabwe, 1992).

————, *Politics of the National Purse* (Harare: SAPES, 1992).

Moyo, Sam, *NGO Advocacy in Zimbabwe: Systematising an Old Function or Inventing a New Role?* (Harare: ZERO, 1992).

————, 'Towards an Understanding of Zimbabwean NGOs', paper prepared for the NANGO/MWENGO Self-Understanding Workshop, November 1995.

————, *The Land Question in Zimbabwe* (Harare: SAPES, 1995).

Moyo, Sam, John Makumbe and Brian Raftopoulos, *NGOs, the State and Politics in Zimbabwe* (Harare: SAPES, 2000).

Mpofu, Busani, 'The struggles of an "undesirable" alien community in a white settler colony: the case of the Indian minority in Colonial Zimbabwe, with particular reference to the city of Bulawayo, c.1890–1963' (Master's thesis, University of Zimbabwe, 2005).

Msindo, Enocent, *Ethnicity in Zimbabwe* (Rochester: University of Rochester Press, 2012).

Muchadenyika, Davison, 'Land for Housing: A Political Resource–Reflections from Zimbabwe's Urban Areas', *Journal of Southern African Studies* 41.6 (2015), 1219–38.

Muchaparara, Musemwa, 'Perpetuating Colonial Legacies: The Post-Colonial State, Water Crises and the Outbreak of Disease in Harare, Zimbabwe, 1980–2009', in Sarah Helen Chiumbu and Muchapara Musemwa, eds, *Crisis! What Crisis?* (Cape Town: HSRC 2012), 3–41.

Mujere, Joseph, 'Land, Graves and Belonging: Land Reform and the Politics of Belonging in Newly Resettled Farms in Gutu, 2000–2009', *Journal of Peasant Studies* 38 (2011), 1123–44.

Mukasa, Stanford, 'Press and Politics in Zimbabwe', *African Studies Quarterly*, 7.1/2 (2003), 37–41

Mungure, Solomon, 'Informal Armed Formations and The State: The Case of Zimbabwe', *Journal of Peacebuilding and Development* 9.2 (2014), 71–6.

Munro, William, *The Moral Economy of the State: Conservation, Community Development and State-making in Zimbabwe* (Athens, OH: Ohio University Press, 1998).

BIBLIOGRAPHY

Murapa, Rukudzo, 'Race and the Public Service in Zimbabwe 1890–1983', in Michael G. Schatzberg, ed., *The Political Economy of Zimbabwe* (New York: Praeger, 1984).

Musarurwa, Albert, 'The labour movement and the one-party state', in Ibbo Mandaza and Lloyd Sachikonye, eds, *The One Party State and Democracy: the Zimbabwe Debate* (Harare: SAPES, 1991), 143–54.

Mutambara, Arthur, 'The One Party State, Socialism and Democratic Struggles in Zimbabwe: A Student Perspective', in Ibbo Mandaza and Lloyd Sachikonye, eds, *The One-Party State and Democracy* (Harare: SAPES, 1991), 139–42.

Mutizwa-Mangiza, Naison D., 'Urban Informal Transport Policy: the Case of Emergency Taxis in Harare', in Lovemore Zinyama, Daniel Tevera and Sioux Cumming, *Harare: the Growth and Problems of the City* (Harare: University of Zimbabwe, 1993), 97–108.

Muzondidya, James, *Sitting on the fence or walking a tightrope? A political history of the coloured community in Zimbabwe, 1945–1980* (PhD thesis, University of Cape Town, 2001).

———, 'The Opposition Dilemma in Zimbabwe: A Critical Review of the Politics of the MDC Parties under the GPA Transitional Framework 2009–2012', in Brian Raftopoulos, ed., *The Hard Road to Reform: The Politics of Zimbabwe's GPA* (Harare: Weaver Press, 2013).

Ncube, Cornelius, *Contesting Hegemony: Civil Society and the Struggle for Social Change in Zimbabwe, 2000–2008* (PhD thesis, University of Birmingham, 2010).

———, 'The 2013 Elections in Zimbabwe: End of an Era for Human Rights Discourse?', *Africa Spectrum* 48.3 (2013), 99–110.

Ncube, Welshman, 'The Post-unity Period: Development, Benefits and Problems', in Canaan Banana, ed., *Turmoil and Tenacity, Zimbabwe 1890–1990* (Harare: College Press, 1989).

———, 'Controlling Public Power: the role of the constitution and the legislature', *Legal Forum* 9.3 (1997), 12–22.

Ndlovu-Gatsheni, Sabelo, 'Mapping Cultural and Colonial Encounters, 1880s-1930s', Brian Raftopoulos and A S Mlambo, eds, *Becoming Zimbabwe* (Harare: Weaver Press, 2009), 39–74.

———, *Do 'Zimbabweans' Exist? Trajectories of Nationalism, National Identity Formation and Crisis in a Postcolonial State* (Bern: Peter Lang, 2009).

———, *The Zimbabwean Nation-State Project: A Historical Diagnosis of Identity and Power-Based Conflicts in a Postcolonial State* (Uppsala: Nordic African Institute 2011).

———, ed., *Mugabeism? History, Politics and Power in Zimbabwe* (New York: Palgrave Macmillan, 2015).

Nest, Michael, 'Ambitions, Profits and Loss: Zimbabwean Economic Involve-

BIBLIOGRAPHY

ment in the Democratic Republic of the Congo', *African Affairs* 100 (2001), 470–1.

Nhema, Alfred G., 'Post-settler state–society relations in Zimbabwe: the rise of civil society and the decline of authoritarianism', in Sandra J. MacLean, Fahimul Quadir and Timothy M. Shaw, eds, *Crises of Governance in Asia and Africa* (Aldershot: Ashgate, 2001).

————, *Democracy in Zimbabwe* (Harare: University of Zimbabwe, 2002).

Nhongo-Simbanegavi, Josephine, *For Better or Worse? Women and ZANLA in Zimbabwe's Liberation Struggle* (Harare: Weaver Press, 2000).

Nkiwane, Tandeka, 'Opposition Politics in Zimbabwe: the struggle within the struggle', in Adebayo Olukoshi, ed., *The Politics of Opposition in Africa* (Uppsala: Nordiska Afrikainstitutet, 1998).

Nolutshungu, Sam, 'Fragments of Democracy: Reflections on Class and Politics in Nigeria', *ThirdWorld Quarterly* 12.1 (1990).

Nordlund, Per, *Organising the Political Agora: Domination and Democratisation in Zambia and Zimbabwe* (PhD thesis, Uppsala University, 1996).

Nyambara, Pius S., 'The Politics Of Land Acquisition And Struggles Over Land In The "Communal" Areas Of Zimbabwe: The Gokwe Region in the 1980s and 1990s', *Africa* 22.3 (2001), 253–85.

Orgeret, Kristin Skare, *The drumbeat of the nation? A study of the Zimbabwe Broadcasting Corporation's News at Eight* (PhD dissertation, University of Oslo, 1998).

Palley, Claire, *The Rhodesian Election* (London: CIIR, 1979).

Palmer, Robin, 'Land Reform in Zimbabwe, 1980–1990', *African Affairs* 89.355 (1990), 169–71.

————, 'Mugabe's land grab in regional perspective', paper presented to the Conference on Land Reform in Zimbabwe–The Way Forward, SOAS, London, 11 March 1998.

Pape, John (*aka* James Kilgore), 'Chimurenga in the kia: domestic workers and the liberation struggle', in Brian Raftopoulos and Tsuneo Yoshikuni, *Sites of Struggle: Essays in Zimbabwe's Urban History* (Harare: Weaver Press, 1999), 257–71.

Parliamentary Human Rights Group, 'Free and Fair? The 1979 Rhodesian Election', Parliamentary Human Rights Group, May 1979.

Patel, Diana H., 'Government Policy and Squatter Settlements in Harare, Zimbabwe', in R.A. Obudho and Constance C. Mhlanga, eds, *Slum and Squatter Settlements in Sub-Saharan Africa* (New York: Praeger, 1988).

————, *Chirambahuyo* (Gweru: Mambo Press, 1983).

Phimister, Ian and Brian Raftopoulos, '"Kana sora ratswa ngaritswe": African Nationalists and Black Workers–The 1948 General Strike in Colonial Zimbabwe', *Journal of Historical Sociology* 13.3 (2000), 289–324.

Phimister, Ian, 'The combined and contradictory inheritance of the struggle against colonialism', in Colin Stoneman, ed., *Zimbabwe's prospects: issues of race, class, state and capital in Southern Africa* (London: Macmillan, 1988).

Potts, Deborah, 'City Life in Zimbabwe at a Time of Fear and Loathing: urban planning, urban poverty and Operation Murambatsvina', in Garth Myers and Martin Murray, eds, *Cities in Contemporary Africa* (London: Palgrave Macmillan, 2006), 265–88.

Potts, Deborah with CC Mutambirwa, 'High-density Housing in Harare: Commodification and Overcrowding', *Third World Planning Review* 13 (1991), 1–25.

Potts, Deborah with Chris Mutambirwa, '"Basics are not a luxury": perceptions of structural adjustment's impact on rural and urban areas in Zimbabwe', *Environment and Urbanization* 10.1 (1998), 55–75.

Raftopoulos, Brian, *Problems of Research in a Post-colonial State: The Case of Zimbabwe* (Harare: ZIDS, 1988).

————, 'Beyond the House of Hunger: Democratic Struggle in Zimbabwe', *Review of African Political Economy* 54 (1994), 59–74.

————, 'Nationalism and Labour in Salisbury', *Journal of Southern African Studies* 21.1 (1995), 79–93.

————, *Race and Nationalism in a Post-Colonial State* (Harare: SAPES Books, 1996).

————, 'The Labour movement in Zimbabwe 1945–65', in Brian Raftopoulos and Ian Phimister, eds, *Keep on Knocking: A History of the Labour Movement in Zimbabwe 1900–97* (Harare: Baobab, 1997), 55–90.

————, 'Nationalism, Violence and Politics: an outline of an overview of Zimbabwean politics', Britain–Zimbabwe Society Research Day, Oxford, 3 June 2000.

————, 'Briefing: Zimbabwe's 2002 Presidential Election', *African Affairs* 101 (2002), 413–36.

————, 'The Zimbabwean Crisis and the Challenges for the Left', *Journal of Southern African Studies* 32.2 (2006), 203–19.

————, 'Reflections on the Opposition in Zimbabwe: The Politics of the Movement for Democratic Change', in Stephen Chan and Ranka Primorac, eds, *Zimbabwe in Crisis: The International Responses and the Space of Silence* (London: Routledge, 2007), 125–47.

————, 'The 2013 Elections in Zimbabwe: The End of an Era', *Journal of Southern African Studies* 39.4 (2013), 971–88.

————, ed., *The Hard Road to Reform: The Politics of Zimbabwe's Global Political Agreement* (Harare: Weaver Press, 2013).

Raftopoulos, Brian and Jean-Paul Lacoste, 'From Savings Mobilisation to Micro-Finance: An Historical Perspective on the Zimbabwe Savings Development Movement', paper presented at the SARIPS Colloquium 2001, 'Social Policy and Development in Southern Africa', Harare, 23–26 September 2001.

BIBLIOGRAPHY

Raftopoulos Brian and Gerald Mazarire, 'Civil society and the Constitution making process in Zimbabwe: NCA 1997–2000', in Kayode Fayemi and Sam Moyo, eds, *Evaluating the Constitutional Process in Zimbabwe* (SAPES Books). MS dated September 2000.

Raftopolous Brian and Alois Mlambo, eds., *Becoming Zimbabwe* (Harare: Weaver Press, 2009).

Raftopoulos, Brian and Sam Moyo, 'The Politics of Indigenisation in Zimbabwe', *East African Social Science Review* XI.2 (1995), 17–32.

Raftopoulos, Brian and Sachikonye, Lloyd, *Striking Back: The Labour Movement and the Post-colonial State in Zimbabwe 1980–2000* (Harare: Weaver Press, 2001).

Rakodi, Carole, *Harare* (Chichester: John Wiley, 1995).

Rakodi, Carole with Penny Withers, 'Land, Housing and Urban Development in Zimbabwe: markets and policy in Harare and Gweru', Final Report on ESCOR Project R4468 (Cardiff: University of Wales, 1993).

Ranchod-Nilson, Sita, 'This too is a way of fighting: rural women's participation in Zimbabwe's Liberation War', in Mary Ann Tétrault, ed., *Women and Revolution in Africa, Asia, and the New World* (Columbia, SC: University of South Carolina Press, 1994).

———, 'Gender Politics and the Pendulum of Political and Social Transformation in Zimbabwe', *Journal of Southern African Studies*, 32.1 (2006), 49–67.

Randolph, R.H., *Dawn in Zimbabwe: The Catholic Church in the New Order. A report on the activities of the Catholic Church in the Zimbabwe for the five years, 1977–1981.* (Gweru: Mambo, 1985).

Ranger, Terence, *The African Voice in Southern Rhodesia 1898–1930* (London: Heinemann, 1970).

———, *Peasant Consciousness and Guerrilla War in Zimbabwe* (London: James Currey, 1985).

———, 'Missionaries, Migrants and the Manyika: The Invention of Ethnicity in Zimbabwe', in Leroy Vail, ed., *The Creation of Tribalism in Southern Africa* (James Currey, 1989), 118–51.

———, 'Legitimacy, Civil Society and the State in Africa', First Alexander Visiting Professor Lecture, presented at the University of Western Australia, 2 December 1992.

———, *Are we not also men? The Samkange Family and African Politics in Zimbabwe: 1920–64* (London: James Currey, 1995), 88–93.

———, 'The Zimbabwe Elections: A Personal Experience', unpublished MS, 19 March 2002.

———, 'Nationalist Historiography, Patriotic History and the History of the Nation: The Struggle over the Past in Zimbabwe', *Journal of Southern African Studies*, 30.2 (2004), 215–34.

BIBLIOGRAPHY

Rich, Tony, 'Legacies of the past? The results of the 1980 election in Midlands province, Zimbabwe', *Africa* 52 (1982), 42–55.

Rotberg, Robert, 'Africa's Mess, Mugabe's Mayhem', *Foreign Affairs* 79.5 (2000), 47–61.

Rowland, John Reid, 'Amendments to Zimbabwe's constitution: a summary', *Legal Forum*, 6.2 (June 1994), 38–42.

Rubert, Steven C., *A Most Promising Weed* (Athens, OH: Center for International Studies, 1998).

Rutherford, Blair, *Working on the Margins: Black Workers, White Farmers in Postcolonial Zimbabwe* (Harare: Weaver Press, 2001).

Sachikonye, Lloyd, 'The National-state project and conflict in Zimbabwe', in Liisa Laakso and Adebayo Olukoshi, eds, *Challenges to the nationstate in Africa* (Uppsala: Nordiska Afrikainstitutet, 1996).

———, *When a state turns on its citizens: 60 years of institutionalized violence in Zimbabwe* (Harare: Weaver Press, 2011).

———, 'Continuity or Reform in Zimbabwean Politics? An Overview of the 2013 Referendum', *Journal of African Elections* 12.1 (2013), 178–85.

Sadomba, Zvakanyorwa Wilbert, *War Veterans in Zimbabwe's Revolution: Challenging Neo-Colonialism & Settler & International Capital* (Woodbridge: Boydell & Brewer Ltd, 2011).

Saunders, Richard, *Information in the Interregnum: The Press, State and Civil Society in Struggles for Hegemony, Zimbabwe 1980–1990* (PhD thesis, Carleton University, 1992).

———, 'Life in Space–the new politics of Zimbabwe', *Southern Africa Review of Books*, January/February 1993, 19.

———, 'Associations and Civil Society in Zimbabwe', Conference on the Historical Dimensions of Democracy and Human Rights in Zimbabwe, 1996.

———, 'The Press, Civil Society and Democratic Struggles in Zimbabwe', paper presented to the Conference on National Identity and Democracy, Cape Town, March 1997.

———, *Never the Same Again: Zimbabwe's Growth towards Democracy, 1980–2000* (Harare: Strand, 2000).

— 'Trade Union Struggles for Autonomy and Democracy in Zimbabwe', n.d.

Scarnecchia, Tim, *The Urban Roots of Democracy and Political Violence in Zimbabwe* (Rochester, NY: University of Rochester Press, 2008).

———, 'The "Sellout Logic" in the Formation of Zimbabwean Nationalist Politics, 1961–1964', in Sarah Helen Chiumbu and Muchapara Musemwa, eds, *Crisis! What Crisis?* (Cape Town: HSRC, 2012), 225–40.

Schatzberg, Michael, 'Power, legitimacy and "democratisation" in Africa', *Africa* 63.4 (1993), 445–61.

Schiphorst, Freek, *Strength and Weakness: The Rise of the Zimbabwe Congress of*

Trade Unions and the Development of Labour Relations, 1980–1995 (PhD thesis, Leiden University, 2001).

Schlyter, Ann, *Multi-habitation: urban housing and everyday life in Chitungwiza, Zimbabwe* (Uppsala: Nordiska Afrikainstitutet, 2003).

Schmidt, Elizabeth, *Peasants, Traders and Wives: Shona Women in the History of Zimbabwe, 1870–1939* (Harare: Baobab Books, 1996).

Schou, Arild, 'The Adaptation of Quasi-Citizens to Political and Social Marginality: Farm Workers in Zimbabwe', *Forum for Development Studies* 1 (June 2000), 43–63.

Scoones, Ian, 'Zimbabwe's Land Reform: New Political Dynamics in the Countryside', *Review of African Political Economy* 42.144 (2015), 1–16.

Scoones, Ian et al., 'The New Politics of Zimbabwe's Lowveld: Struggles over Land at the Margins', *African Affairs* 111 (2012), 527–50.

Scott, James, *Weapons of the Weak* (New Haven, CT: Yale University Press, 1985).

———, *Seeing Like a State* (New Haven, CT: Yale University Press, 1998).

Scott, Peter, 'Migrant Labour in Southern Rhodesia', *Geographical Review* 44.1 (1954), 29–48.

Seirlis, J.K., 'Undoing the United Front? Coloured Soldiers in Rhodesia 1939–1980', *African Studies* 63.1 (2004), 73–94.

Selby, Angus, *Commercial Farmers and the State: Interest Group Politics and Land Reform in Zimbabwe* (PhD thesis, University of Oxford, 2006).

Shadur, Mark, *Labour relations in a developing country: a case study of Zimbabwe* (Aldershot: Avebury, 1994).

Shamuyarira, Nathan, 'An overview of the struggle for unity and independence', in Canaan Banana, ed., *Turmoil and Tenacity, Zimbabwe 1890–1990* (Harare: College Press, 1989), 13–24.

Sibanda, Maxwell, 'Complete control: music and propaganda in Zimbabwe', 20 September 2004, freemuse.org.

———, 'Music central tool in Zimbabwe election', 29 March 2005, freemuse.org.

Sims, Bryan M, *Conflict in Perpetuity? Examining Zimbabwe's Protracted Social Conflict through the Lens of Land Reform* (PhD thesis, Stellenbosch University, 2015).

Sinclair-Bright, Leila Tafara, 'Relationships between Farm Workers and Land Beneficiaries in a New Resettlement Area of Zimbabwe', paper presented at the African Studies Conference, University of Sussex, September 2014.

———, 'This Land: Land Reform, Authority, Morality and Politics in Zimbabwe' (PhD thesis, University of Edinburgh, 2016).

Sithole, Masipula, 'The General Elections 1979–1985', in Ibbo Mandaza, ed., *The Political Economy of Transition, 1980–1986* (Dakar: CODESRIA, 1986).

———, 'Zimbabwe's Eroding Authoritarianism', *Journal of Democracy* 8.1 (1997), 127–41.

BIBLIOGRAPHY

————, *Struggles within the Struggle*, 2nd edition (Harare: Rujeko, 1999).

————, 'Fighting Authoritarianism in Zimbabwe', *Journal of Democracy* 12.1 (2001), 160–9.

Skålnes, Tor, *The politics of economic reform in Zimbabwe: continuity and change in development* (Basingstoke: Macmillan, 1995).

Skelton, Kenneth, *Bishop in Smith's Rhodesia* (Gweru: Mambo, 1985).

Sklar Richard, 'Reds And Rights: Zimbabwe's Experiment', in Dov Ronen, ed., *Democracy and Pluralism in Africa* (Boulder, CO: Lynne Rienner, 1986).

Spiegel, Samuel J., 'Legacies of a Nationwide Crackdown in Zimbabwe: Operation Chikorokoza Chapera in Gold Mining Communities', *Journal of Modern African Studies*, 52.4 (2014), 541–70.

Spierenburg, Marja, *Strangers, Spirits and Land Reforms* (Leiden: Brill, 2004).

Stewart, Sheelagh, 'Working with a Radical Agenda: The Musasa Project Zimbabwe', *Gender and Development* 3.1 (1995), 30–5.

Stoneman, Colin, ed., *Zimbabwe's Prospects* (London: Macmillan, 1988).

Stoneman, Colin and Lionel Cliffe, *Zimbabwe: Politics, Economics and Society* (London: Pinter, 1989).

Stott, Leda, *Women and the Armed Struggle for Independence in Zimbabwe* (Edinburgh: Centre of African Studies, 1990).

Sylvester, Christine, 'Zimbabwe's 1985 Elections: A Search for National Mythology', *Journal of Modern African Studies*, 24.1 (1986), 229–55.

————, 'Simultaneous Revolutions: the Zimbabwe Case', *Journal of Southern African Studies*, 16.3 (1990), 452–75.

————, 'Unities and disunities in Zimbabwe's 1990 election', *Journal of Modern African Studies* 28.3 (1990), 375–400.

Taylor, Charles, 'Interpretation and the Sciences of Man', in Charles Taylor, ed., *Philosophy and the Human Sciences*, vol. 2 (Cambridge: Cambridge University Press, 1985).

Taylor, Scott, 'Race, Class and Neopatrimonialism in Zimbabwe', in Richard Joseph, ed., *State, Conflict and Democracy in Africa* (Boulder, CO: Lynne Rienner, 1999).

Tendi, Blessing-Miles, 'Patriotic History and Public Intellectuals Critical of Power', *Journal of Southern African Studies* 34.2 (June 2008), 379–96.

————, *Making History in Mugabe's Zimbabwe* (Bern: Peter Lang, 2010).

————, 'Ideology, Civilian Authority and the Zimbabwean Military', *Journal of Southern African Studies* 39.4 (2013), 829–43.

————, 'Robert Mugabe's 2013 Presidential Election Campaign', *Journal of Southern African Studies* 39.5 (2013), 963–70.

Tengende, Norbert, *Workers, Students and the Struggles for Democracy: State–Civil Society Relations in Zimbabwe* (PhD thesis, Roskilde University, 1994).

Towriss, David, 'Buying Loyalty: Zimbabwe's Marange Diamonds', *Journal of Southern African Studies* 39.1 (2013), 99–117.

Turino, Thomas, *Nationalists, Cosmopolitans, and Popular Music in Zimbabwe* (Chicago, IL: University of Chicago Press, 2000).

Ucko, Peter J., 'Museums and sites: cultures of the past within education–Zimbabwe, some ten years on', in Peter G. Stone and Brian L. Molyneux, eds, *The Presented Past: Heritage, Museums, and Education* (London: Routledge, in association with English Heritage, 1994), 237–82.

Vambe, Maurice Taonezvi, 'Popular songs and social realities in post-independent Zimbabwe', *African Studies Review*, 43.2 (2000), 73–86.

———, 'Thomas Mapfumo's "Toi Toi" in context: popular music as narrative discourse', *African Identities*, 2.1 (2004), 89–112.

Vekris, John, 'Chronicle of two strikes', *Social Change and Development* (February 1997), 3–7, 29.

Wallerstein, Immanuel, 'Voluntary Organisations', in J.S. Coleman and Carl Rosberg, eds, *Political Parties and National Integration in Tropical Africa* (Berkeley, CA: University of California Press, 1966), 318–38.

Wamba-dia-wamba, Ernest, 'Discourse on the National Question', in Shivji, Issa G., *State and Constitutionalism: An African Debate on Democracy* (Harare: SAPES, 1991), 57–69.

Watson, Peggy, *Determined to Act: the first 15 years of the Women's Action Group* (Harare: WAG, 1998).

Watyoka, C. D., *25 Years of Struggle* (Harare: ZCC, 1991).

Weiss, Ruth, *Zimbabwe and the New Elites* (London: BAP, 1994).

Weiss, Ruth with Jane Parpart, *Sir Garfield Todd and the Making of Zimbabwe* (London: BAP, 1999).

Weitzer Ronald, 'In Search of Regime Security: Zimbabwe since Independence', *The Journal of Modern African Studies* 22.4 (1984), 529–57.

———, 'Continuities in the Politics of State Security in Zimbabwe', in Michael Schatzberg, ed., *The Political Economy of Zimbabwe* (New York: Praeger, 1984), 81–118.

Wekwete K. H., 'Development of urban planning in Zimbabwe', *Cities* 5.1 (1988), 57–71.

Werbner, Richard, *Tears of the Dead: The Social Biography of an African Family* (Edinburgh: Edinburgh University Press, 1991).

———, 'Smoke from the Barrel of a Gun: Postwars of the dead, memory and reinscription in Zimbabwe', in Richard Werbner, ed., *Memory and the Postcolony* (London: Zed Books, 1998), 71–102.

West, Michael O., 'Nationalism, Race and Gender: The Politics of Family Planning in Zimbabwe, 1957–1990', *Social History of Medicine* (1994), 459–65.

———, 'Indians, India, and Race and Nationalism in British Central Africa', *South Asia Bulletin* XIV.2 (1994), 86–103.

———, *The Rise of an African Middle Class: Colonial Zimbabwe, 1898–1965* (Bloomington, IN: Indiana University Press, 2002).

BIBLIOGRAPHY

White, Luise, *The Assassination of Herbert Chitepo: Texts and Politics in Zimbabwe* (Bloomington, IN: Indiana University Press, 2003).

———, 'Civic virtue, young men and the family: conscription in Rhodesia 1974–1980', *International Journal of African Historical Studies* 37.1 (2004), 103–21.

———, 'Precarious Conditions: A Note on Counter-Insurgency in Africa after 1945', *Gender and History* 16.3 (2004), 603–25.

———, *Unpopular Sovereignty: Rhodesian Independence and African Decolonization* (Chicago, IL: University of Chicago Press, 2015).

Williams, Gavin, 'There Is No Theory of Petit-bourgeois Politics', *Review of African Political Economy* 3.6 (1976), 84–9.

———, *Fragments of Democracy: Nationalism, Development and the State in Africa* (Cape Town: HSRC Publishers, 2003).

Win, Everjoice, 'When Sharing Female Identity Is Not Enough: Coalition Building in the Midst of Political Polarisation in Zimbabwe', *Gender & Development* 12.1 (May 2004), 19–27.

Wood, Brian, 'Trade Union Organisation and the Working Class', in Colin Stoneman, ed., *Zimbabwe's Prospects* (London: Macmillan, 1988).

Worby, Eric, 'Tyranny, Parody and Ethnic Polarity: ritual engagements with the state in north western Zimbabwe" *Journal of Southern African Studies* 24.3 (1998), 561–78.

Yeros, Paris, 'Labour Struggles for Alternative Economics in Zimbabwe: Trade union nationalism and Internationalism in a Global Era', unpublished MS, 2000.

Young, Crawford, *The African Colonial State in Comparative Perspective* (New Haven, CT: Yale University Press, 1994).

Zamchiya, Phillan, 'The MDC-T's (Un)Seeing Eye in Zimbabwe's 2013 Harmonised Elections: A Technical Knockout', *Journal of Southern African Studies* 39 (2013), 955–62.

———, 'The Role of Politics and State Practices in Shaping Rural Differentiation: A Study of Resettled Small-Scale Farmers in South-Eastern Zimbabwe', *Journal of Southern African Studies* 39.4 (2013), 937–53.

ZimRights, *Choosing the Path to Peace and Development: Coming to Terms with Human Rights Violations of the 1982–1987 Conflict in Matabeleland and Midlands Provinces* (Harare: ZimRights, 1999).

Zinyama, Lovemore, 'The evolution of the spatial structure of Greater Harare', in Lovemore Zinyama, Daniel Tevera and Sioux Cumming, eds, *Harare: the Growth and Problems of the City* (Harare: University of Zimbabwe, 1993), 7–32.

Zolberg, Aristide, *Creating Political Order: The Party States of West Africa* (Chicago, IL: Rand McNally, 1966).

Zwana, Solomon, 'Church-related universities as a manifestation of new frontiers in mission: the Zimbabwean experience', *Missionalia* 35.2 (2007), 71–88.

————, 'Struggles and strides: religion and politics in the evolution of church-related universities in Zimbabwe', *Studia Historiae Ecclesiasticae* 34.1 (2008), 279–304.

————, 'Failure of ecumenism: the rise of Church-related universities in Zimbabwe', *Exchange* 38.3 (2009), 292–311.

INDEX

INDEX

Common Market for East and
Southern Africa (COMESA), 165
Commonwealth, 77, 157, 165, 206
communal areas, 47, 48, 54, 55,
170
Community Based Organizations
(CBOs), 53
Community Share Ownership
Trusts, 195
Compagnon, Daniel, 89
compensation, 136, 148
Confederation of Zimbabwe
Industries (CZI), 94
Congo War (1998–2003), 116,
117, 121–2, 123, 127, 130, 163
Congress of South Africa Trade
Unions (COSATU), 165
conscription, 26, 27
Conservative Alliance of Zimbabwe
(CAZ), 38, 67, 94
Constitution, 9, 35, 71, 91, 95,
107, 111–12, 115, 124–40, 141,
151, 152, 167, 168, 188, 190,
192, 196–7, 200, 207, 217
Constitutional Commission (CC),
116, 127–40, 141, 153, 163, 168
Constitutional Court, 197, 207
Constitutional Parliamentary
Committee (COPAC), 196, 197,
200, 203, 204
constitutional referendums
2000, 116, 132, 141–4, 154,
156, 175, 186
2013, 197
constructivism, 10
Consumer Council, 171
contraceptives, 51
Cooper, Fred, 219
corruption, 3, 46, 66, 71, 72,
75–6, 81, 91, 93, 100, 113, 121,
208
Crisis Group, 200

Cross, Eddie, 171
Crystal, Jill, 45
Culture House, Murehwa, 45; *see
also* museums
currency, 73, 171, 172, 185, 189

Dabengwa, Dumiso, 39, 82, 208–9
Daily Gazette, 97
Daily News, 123, 150, 151, 180
dance, 43
Danhiko, 49
Dashwood, Hevina, 7, 74
Davies, Angela, 27
de-industrialization, 74
death sentence, 128
deep state, 196
delegitimization, 3, 17, 20, 36, 93,
138, 141, 142, 155
Delimitation Commission, 88, 164
demobilization, 3, 5, 11, 16, 17,
31, 34, 35, 36, 41, 45, 49–50,
54–70, 143, 212, 214–18
Democratic Party, 94
Democratic Republic of the Congo
(DRC), 116, 117, 121–2, 123,
127, 130, 163, 186
democratization, 1, 6, 71, 92
Denmark, 124, 129, 166
Department of Cooperatives, 51,
52
Depo-Provera, 51
depoliticization, 5, 17, 34, 70, 143,
215, 216–17
deracialization, 34, 37, 45, 50, 56,
66
Destiny of Africa Network, 203
development, 14, 28, 33, 34, 35,
36–7, 40, 45–9, 50, 53, 59, 63,
65, 66, 70, 71, 72, 73, 74, 75,
80, 86, 108, 110, 112, 113, 147,
150, 216–17, 218
Devitte, James, 168

328

INDEX

INDEX

Mandaza, Ibbo, 59, 60, 123, 129, 132, 151–2, 132, 151–2

Mangwende, Helen, 106

Mangwende, Witness, 89

Manicaland, Zimbabwe, 41, 46, 52, 59, 68, 85, 90, 124, 156, 158, 163, 164, 178, 181, 182, 184, 189

Manyame River, 118

Manyame, Mashonaland West, 164

Manyika, 18

Maoism, 145

Mapfumo, Thomas, 97, 152–3

Maputo, Mozambique, 66

Marange, Manicaland, 185

markets, 58

Marondera, Mashonaland East, 145

Marxism, 6, 67

Maseko, Owen, 206–7

Mashonaland, Zimbabwe, 25, 45, 46, 52, 57, 59, 67–8, 96, 103, 117, 118, 145, 158, 161, 164, 177–8, 181–2, 205

Masiiwa, Medicine, 146

Masiyiwa, Strive, 124

Mass Media Trust, 66

Masuku, Lookout, 39

Masunungure, Eldred, 191, 192

Masvingo, Zimbabwe, 44, 94, 143–4, 149, 181, 205

Matabeleland, Zimbabwe, 19, 22, 31, 34–5, 40, 43–4, 46, 52, 56, 66–8, 70, 76, 80–2, 84–5, 94–5, 99, 102, 107, 117, 123, 133, 149, 156, 158, 164, 175–8, 181–2, 184, 194, 201, 206, 208–9, 211

Matabeleland Action Group, 107

Matabeleland Conflict (1981–7), 34, 35, 40–1, 44, 52, 66, 67, 70, 102, 123, 150

Matabeleland Zambezi Water Project (MZWP), 107, 150, 194

Matlose, Khabela, 164

Matombo, Lovemore, 214

Matyzak, Derek, 193, 198

Mavhaire, Dzikimai, 91

Mawowa, Showers, 185

Maxwell, David, 18, 22, 54, 102

Mazarire, Gerald, 18, 144, 168

Mazowe, Mashonaland Central, 205

Mbare, Harare, 57, 77, 96

Mbeki, Thabo, 192

McCandless, Erin, 9, 82, 136, 144, 148

McGregor, JoAnn, 10, 22, 168

McNally, Nicholas, 167, 168

Media Monitoring Project (MMPZ), 136–7, 151

media, 2, 5, 14, 34, 36, 41, 65–7, 76, 93, 96, 101, 115, 120, 121, 122–4, 131, 132, 136–7, 139, 149, 150–4, 180, 183, 191, 198, 220

mega-churches, 203–4

Mehler, Andreas, 193

Melber, Henning, 37

memorialization, 42–4, 149, 206–7, 216

Methodism, 20, 63, 101

Mgagao camp, Tanzania, 149

Mhanda, Wilfred, 148

Mhashu, Fidelis, 79, 89, 96, 103, 178

middle class, 26, 56, 84, 105, 112, 125, 142, 217, 219

Midlands, Zimbabwe, 19, 39, 42, 52, 56, 67, 68, 88, 93, 118

migrant labourers, 55

minimum wage, 38, 45, 62

mining, 18, 24, 28, 185–6, 193, 194, 195

and churches, 52, 63–4, 102, 103, 127, 177–8, 204
and Congo War, 122
and corruption scandals, 71, 75
and elections, 88, 94, 103, 117, 134, 157–8, 165, 173–4, 176–9, 192, 197–200, 204, 211
and farm invasions, 144
and GPA, 193, 197
and homosexuality, 102
and intellectuals, 60
and judiciary, 167
and land politics, 39, 144, 146
longevity, 3–4, 12, 71, 211
and one-party rule, 42, 71
and nationalism, 33, 141
presidentialism, 83
public perception of, 8, 69, 72, 83, 88, 117, 153, 177
and race politics, 60, 84, 87, 94, 145–6, 173
and socialism, 64, 71
and street names, 43
and unity, 33, 36, 41, 86
and war veterans, 82, 117
Mugabe, Sabina, 118
Mujere, Joseph, 205
Mujuru, Joyce, 153
Mukoko, Jestina, 199
Murehwa, Mashonaland East, 45
museums, 44–5; *see also* Culture House; monuments
Mushayakarara, Lupi, 131
Mushumbi Pools, Mashonaland Central, 59
music, 14, 43, 97, 152
Mutambara, Arthur, 156, 200, 201
Mutambirwa, Chris, 57
Mutare, Manicaland, 59, 90, 101, 124, 163, 181, 182, 185, 189, 192

Mutasah, Tawanda, 124
Mutoko, Mashonaland, 68
Mutsvairo, Solomon, 154
Mutume, Patrick, 102
Muzenda, Simon, 64, 88
Muzondidya, James, 26
Muzorewa, Abel, 20, 25–6, 29, 41, 59, 65, 95
Mvenge, Moses, 90

Namibia, 37, 69, 166, 217, 219
nation-building, 1–6, 33–70, 72, 73, 83, 87, 137, 145, 206
national anthem, 154
National Association for the Advancement of Coloured People (NAACP), 165
National Association of NGOs (NANGO), 50, 108–9, 111, 130, 181, 204
national consensus-building, 137
National Constitutional Assembly (NCA), 9, 71, 115, 124–7, 129, 130–40, 145, 155–6, 167, 175, 178, 180, 200, 201
National Council for Higher Education Act (1990), 101
National Dance Company, 43
National Debate Association (NDA), 180
National Democratic Institute (NDI), 165
National Democratic Party (NDP), 19, 22
national dress, 43
National Heroes' Acre, Harare, 44, 149
National ID, 160, 161
National Oil Company of Zimbabwe (NOCZIM), 121
National Organisation for the

INDEX

Agreement, 6, 28, 29, 38, 87, 125, 128, 133, 138, 197, 218
Southern Rhodesia African National Congress (SRANC), 19
Southern Rhodesian National Council of Social Services (NCSS), 50
Southern Rhodesian Native Congress, 18–19
Soviet Union (1922–91), 19
special interest councillors, 55
spirit mediums, 22, 25, 44–5
splinter unions, 98, 175
spoils politics, 5, 207, 219
Sports and Recreation Commission Act (1991), 90
squatter settlements, 24–5, 57, 59, 77, 89, 119, 184
Standard, 123
Stevenson, Trudy, 88
Stewart, John, 64
street children, people, 77, 104, 183
street names, 35, 42–3, 149
Streets Ahead, 104
strikes, 23, 62, 73, 80–1, 84, 97, 98, 99, 117, 124, 155, 218
structural adjustment, 34, 72, 73–4, 85, 86, 117, 120, 221
Students Representative Councils (SRCs), 100–1
students, 13, 59–62, 72, 75, 99–101, 113, 124, 131, 174, 202
Students' Representative Council (SRC), 61
subsidies, 73, 80
Sudan, 166
Sunday Gazette, 97
Sunday Mail, 38, 180
Sunday Times, 66
Sunningdale, Harare, 96

Supreme Court, 89, 92, 95, 96, 106–7, 111, 126, 151, 152, 163, 167, 168
Svovse, Mashonaland East, 119, 120
Sweden, 124, 129
Sylvester, Christine, 10, 30, 39, 67, 94

Tafara, Harare, 182
Tanzania, 50, 149, 166
taxation, 92, 117, 124, 155, 185, 219
taxis, 25, 58, 78
tear gas, 101
Tekere, Edgar, 93, 94
tele-evangelism, 203
television, 66, 82, 96, 97, 121, 122, 133, 134, 136–7, 138, 151, 154, 191
Tender Board, 91
Tendi, Blessing-Miles, 168, 198, 212
Tengende, Norbert, 36, 98
Tevera, Daniel, 79
think tanks, 60
Tibaijuka Report, 184
Times, 66
tobacco, 172, 173, 194
Todd, Garfield, 53, 109, 162–3
Todd, Judith, 53
Tonga, 18, 46
Tongogara, Josiah, 206
torture, 39, 40, 123, 145, 157, 167, 180, 199
tourism, 44–5, 171–2
town names, 42–3
trade unions, 9, 12, 13, 18, 22–3, 34, 36, 48, 62–3, 72, 80–1, 84, 87, 97, 98–9, 100, 101, 109, 113, 115, 117, 124–6, 130, 137, 154–5, 170, 174–5, 181, 218

341

election, 27, 33; minimum wage introduced, 38, 45, 62

1981 establishment of VOICE, 51; student demonstrations against dissidents, 61; bishops reassert control of CCJP, 64

1982 Nkomo and ZAPU ministers removed from cabinet, 39; former ZIPRA soldiers arrested for treason, 39; Banana announces unity of church with government, 63; University of Zimbabwe Act, 61; Paweni grain scandal, 46; licensing of 'Emergency Taxis', 58

1983 Nkomo flees into exile, 39; ZANU officials detained for supporting Kombayi, 39; Operation Clean-up, 59, 105; launch of ZIDS, 59; Muzorewa detained, 41

1984 remaining ZAPU ministers removed from cabinet, 39; creation of District Councils, 54; Godwin threatened with detention, 66; ZAPU and UANC offices ransacked, 68

1985 UANC murdered in Hwange, 68; creation of VIDCOs and WADCOs, 54; parliamentary elections, 56, 67

1986 arrest of CCJP leaders, 52; Presidential Powers (Temporary Measures) Act, 152; Non-Aligned Summit, 59; Labour Relations Act, 63; Raath deported, 66

1987 Unity Accord, 42, 43, 49, 52, 62, 68, 71, 83, 86, 87, 93,

103, 113; election of activist SRC, 100

1988 election of activist SRC, 100; Rural District Council Act, 55; Nkomo appointed vice president, 68; Tsvangirai elected Secretary General of ZCTU, 98; Willowgate scandal, 66, 73, 75, 93, 100

1990 official establishment of ZNLWVA, 49–50, 81; establishment of IBDC, 83, 84; May Day demonstrations, 98; general election, 53, 84, 87, 88, 93–4; University Amendment Act, 100; National Council for Higher Education Act, 101

1991 War Veterans Administration Bill, 81; Sports and Recreation Commission Act, 90; Commonwealth Heads of Government Meeting, 77

1992 War Veterans Act, 81; Land Acquisition Act, 86, 173; Political Parties (Finance) Act, 91, 95; Nkomo meets with chiefs, 92; Labour Relations Act amended, 98; foundation of ZimRights, 109

1993 War Victims Compensation Act, 81; Nkomo clashes with Bulawayo council over indigenization, 84–5; Churu Farm evictions, 77–8; food riots, 80

1994 new national anthem introduced, 154; establishment of AAG, 83, 84; LOMA ruled unconstitutional, 99; establishment of MZWPT, 107

1995 arrest and trial of Sithole, 94–5, 157; parliamentary elections, 79, 85–6, 88–9,

94–5, 112, 160, 164; Private
Voluntary Organizations Act,
91, 106, 109–12
1996 civil service strike, 80;
healthcare workers strike, 99;
Harare municipal elections,
89, 95
1997 CCJP/LRF publish report
on Matabeleland atrocities,
102, 123; formation of NCA,
124; PVO and Political Parties
Acts ruled unconstitutional,
91, 95, 107, 111–12; war
veteran protests, 81–2, 91,
117; general strike, 81, 97,
99, 117, 124
1998 food riots, 117; national
strike, 99, 117; creation of
Unity Day, 43, 86; Traditional
Leaders Act, 92, 169, 204–5;
troops sent into Congo,
116, 117, 121–2, 123; Land
Reform Donors' Conference,
87, 119, 173; protests over
fuel prices and Congo War,
117, 127, 130; stay-aways and
demonstrations banned, 155;
establishment of ZUD, 154
1999 Standard and *Mirror* journalists detained and tortured,
123; doctors' strike 119; death
of Nkomo, 149; foundation of
MDC, 138, 155; UN assesses
electoral roll, 160; World
Bank suspends loan, 122
2000 resignation of Hatendi,
159–60; constitutional referendum, 116, 132, 141–4,
154, 156, 175, 186; farm
invasions begin, 143–4; NCA
marches disrupted, 145; Post
and Telecommunications Act,

152; parliamentary elections,
12, 88, 145–6, 151, 156, 159,
160, 161, 174, 175–6, 177,
178; death of Sithole, 149
2001 Broadcasting Act, 152;
death of Hunzwi, 148; General Laws Amendment Bill,
165
Citizenship Act amended, 162;
establishment of ZANU labour
committee, 175
2002 Public Order and Security Act, 127, 157, 179, 194;
Apostolic Faith attack MDC offices, 178; Tsvangirai arrested, 157; presidential election,
149, 157, 159, 161, 163, 165,
169; Protection of Rural Land
Occupiers Bill, 173
2003 Daily News shut down,
151
2004 Electoral Act, 95, 161,
166; NGO Act, 181, 200;
clearances in Harare; Porta
Farm evictions, 183
2005 compensation granted
to ex-detainees, 148; establishment of ZEC, 160; 190;
parliamentary elections, 151,
156, 158, 160, 161–2, 164,
165, 166, 190; Operation
Murambatsvina, 162, 183–4,
189; Operation Garikai/
Hlalani, 185; resettlement
land nationalized, 173; partial
floating of ZWD, 172; Senate
elections, 156, 158, 161, 162,
165, 166, 190
2006 Operation Chikorokoza
Chapera begins, 185
2008 Indigenization Act, 195;
general election, 187, 190–2,

196; Global Political Agreement, 187–8, 189, 192–209;
Zimbabwe Peace Project leaders abducted and tortured,
199
2010 unveiling of Nkomo monument, 206; Maseko arrested,
207
2013 constitutional referendum,
197; general election, 188,
196, 197–9, 200, 205, 207,
211
Zimbabwe African National
Liberation Army (ZANLA), 19,
21, 41, 154
Zimbabwe African National Union
(ZANU)
anti-foreigner/Western rhetoric,
5, 85, 122, 138, 142, 145, 177
capitalism, 7, 112
clientelism, 2, 219
coercive force, 6, 8, 10, 11, 21,
22, 36, 40, 51, 67, 141, 142,
145, 156–9, 174, 186, 191,
193–4, 196, 198, 199, 212
corruption, 3, 46, 66, 71, 72,
73, 75–6, 81–3, 91, 93, 100,
113, 121
delegitimization of opponents,
3, 17, 20, 36, 93, 138, 141,
142, 155
demobilization, 3, 5, 11, 12,
16, 17, 31, 34, 35, 36, 41,
45, 49–50, 54–70, 143, 212,
214–18
developmentalism, 14, 33, 34,
35, 36–7, 45–9, 50, 53, 59,
63, 65, 66, 70, 71, 72, 73,
74, 75, 80, 86, 108, 110, 112,
113, 147, 150, 216–17, 218
election rigging, 67, 88–9,
159–66, 191–2

factionalism, 85, 92, 144, 207,
208
legalism, 3, 70
nation-building, 1–6, 33–70, 72,
73, 83, 87, 137, 145, 206
national unity, 3, 4, 16, 34, 35,
36, 39–45, 48–9, 63–4, 66,
71, 83, 85–6, 111, 214
party unity, 39, 85
socialism, 7, 64, 67, 71, 73, 83,
101, 113
Zimbabwe African National
Union–Ndonga (ZANU-N), 20,
24, 26, 41, 85, 94–5
Zimbabwe African People's Union
(ZAPU), 19, 22, 24, 26, 34, 35,
39, 41, 42, 44, 50, 52, 53, 65,
67, 68, 86, 208–9
Zimbabwe Broadcasting
Corporation (ZBC), 121, 124,
133, 134, 138, 151, 152
Zimbabwe Catholic Bishops
Conference (ZCBC), 64, 102,
131, 178
Zimbabwe Christian Alliance, 204
Zimbabwe Congress of Trade
Unions (ZCTU), 23, 48, 62–3,
80–1, 98–9, 100, 117, 124–6,
130, 154–6, 167, 174
Zimbabwe Council of Churches
(ZCC), 64–5, 102, 107–8, 109,
110, 124, 126, 127, 130–1,
155–6, 165, 166, 178, 204
Zimbabwe Defence Industries, 86
Zimbabwe Election Support
Network (ZESN), 163, 191
Zimbabwe Electoral Commission
(ZEC), 160, 164, 190, 197
Zimbabwe Farmers Union, 107
Zimbabwe Federation of Trade
Unions (ZFTU), 175
Zimbabwe Human Rights